KENTUCKY'S MOST HATED MAN

Other books by John Sparks:

The Roots of Appalachian Christianity: The Life and Legacy of Elder Shubal Stearns

Raccoon John Smith: Frontier Kentucky's Most Famous Preacher

The Last Dance of Gus Finley: A Tale of Eastern Kentucky Justice

Kentucky's Most Hated Man

Charles Chilton Moore and the *Blue Grass Blade*

John Sparks

WIND PUBLICATIONS

 For information address Wind Publications, 600 Overbrook Drive, Nicholasville, KY 40356

International Standard Book Number 978-1-893239-99-9
Library of Congress Control Number 2009932569

First Edition

Cover illustration: Charles C. Moore about 1886, courtesy Special Collections, Bosworth Library, Lexington Theological Seminary, Lexington, Kentucky.

In memory of two sailors:

Lieutenant Junior Grade Richard C. Wallace
1938-1968

Young historian from the University of Kentucky, whose early researches partially inspired this book, taken before his time from a world where ignorant armies clash by night, and

Fire Control Technician First Class D. H. Sparks
1916-2005

An unbowed head and an unconquerable soul if I ever knew one, and my mentor both in living and in dying; sailor now home from the sea, hunter home from the hill. I miss you, Big Sparks.

artwork by Sarah Sparks

My town, Lexington, Kentucky, is for its size the worst town in all the world and for its population...does more to demoralize than any place of its size in the world. This is because the chief productions of the Blue Grass Region of Kentucky are whiskey, tobacco and race horses.... The only remedy for this condition in Kentucky has been to build more Christian colleges and more fine churches and to hire more and finer priests and preachers.

In this state of Kentucky I have had the honor to be regarded by thousands of people, and especially by the clergy, as the worst man who has ever lived in the state.

— Charles Chilton Moore, 1903

Why, in any case, do we so readily accept the idea that the one thing you must do if you want to please God is believe in him? What's so special about believing? Isn't it just as likely that God would reward kindness, or generosity, or humility? Or sincerity? What if God is a scientist who regards honest seeking after truth as the supreme virtue? Indeed, wouldn't the designer of the universe have to be a scientist?

— Richard Dawkins, 2006

Contents

Charles C. Moore in 1903 aboard the *S.S. Moltke,*
a pencil sketch drawn by a fellow passenger.

Courtesy Bosworth Library,
Lexington Theological Seminary,
Lexington, Ky.

Introduction: The Battle of Evermore

Here lies an atheist—all dressed up and no place to go.
—*Epitaph in a Frederick County, Maryland, cemetery*

In its two-and-a-quarter-century existence, the historic city of Lexington, Kentucky, has seen more than its share of comedy and tragedy, laughter and tears, drama and sideshow, battle and three-ring circus. One wonders if a more bizarre conglomeration of all such elements ever came together in the city than on Easter weekend 1984.

One ingredient of the collective drama involved the large and prestigious Southland Christian Church on Harrodsburg Road near the outskirts of the city, which had invited an out-of-town guest minister, one William J. "Bill" Murray, to deliver its Easter Sunday sermon. Murray had achieved his first notoriety by association, as it were, a little more than twenty years beforehand; he was the son of the notorious atheist activist Madalyn Murray O'Hair, and years before, she had initiated her successful Federal suit to abolish prayer in United States public schools ostensibly for the teenaged Bill's benefit. Bill and his younger brother, Jon Garth Murray, had long been their mother's devoted helpers, but five or six years previously Bill had rebelled against both his mother's domineering nature and the hedonistic lifestyle he had chosen, and shortly thereafter had undergone a powerful religious conversion. Though he had been unable to coax a daughter by an early first marriage, Robin, away from the side of her grandmother and her uncle Jon, Bill Murray was now a passionate Baptist evangelist and his presence at Southland that Easter in and of itself could have been seen as remarkable. Baptists and Stone-Campbell Christian Churches such as Southland hadn't always gotten along all that well in Kentucky, more than any other reason because so many of the state's earliest Stone-Campbell churches had defected from the Baptists under extremely bitter circumstances. Although the sum total of Baptists in the United States had always led the entire three-faceted Stone-Campbell Movement in terms of numerical superiority, hard feelings still remained in some quarters of both groups. Easter 1984 was a tense season, though, and the logic might have been that it was high time that Baptists, "Campbellites," and other Christian denominations began to try to see eye to eye. After all, the Apostle Paul—or at least somebody writing under the name of the Apostle Paul—had told the Ephesians that as Christians they wrestled not against flesh and blood but against principalities, powers, the rulers of the darkness of this world, and spiritual wickedness in high places,[1] and this fair April weekend may have seemed to bring home Paul's warnings in a most unusual way.

The reason for the heightened state of tension was the fact that Bill's mother, brother, and oldest daughter were in town too, and not to hear him preach at Southland Christian either—though there was no doubt that they were the principal reason the big Bluegrass congregation had solicited Bill's labors that Easter. Madalyn Murray O'Hair called herself, Jon Garth, and Robin the "Founders" of her national activist group American Atheists, and they had selected Lexington as the site of the organization's tenth annual convention, a yearly meeting which, incidentally, they always managed to schedule for Easter weekend. One of the reasons they had chosen the central Kentucky city for the gathering was a point of historical interest. The year 1984 was supposed to be the centennial anniversary of the founding of an atheist newspaper in Lexington, the *Blue Grass Blade,* which had flourished briefly through the first decade of the twentieth century, despite its editor's being threatened, attacked, and imprisoned repeatedly. The trio's American Atheist Press had reprinted and planned to sell the three published books of this historic freethinking editor, Charles Chilton Moore, at the convention, hoping to inspire further interest both local and national, and for the new American Atheist editions of Moore's works someone, whether Madalyn or a subordinate, had meticulously—obsessively painstakingly, even—altered each and every one of his original capitalizations of religion-associated words and

[1] Ephesians 6:12.

names in the texts such as God, Jesus, Christianity, Jews, Mohammed, and so forth, to small-case lettering.

And so in that same spirit, as members of American Atheists poured into the city from all points of the compass and checked in to the enormous, luxurious Radisson Plaza Hotel at the corner of Broadway and West Vine Streets for the convention, Madalyn had begun proceedings on Friday, April 20, with a vengeance. A placard in the Radisson's lobby entitled "Pennies from Heaven" indicated that all coins tossed into the lobby fountain would be donated to charity, and one of the first remarks Madalyn made in opening the convention was to threaten to get the hotel manager to do something about that nonsensical sign with its absurd reference to a nonexistent place.[2] Of course, she adored the outrage she generated in the Lexington community when this remark hit the newspapers.

Still, according to her biographer Ann Rowe Seaman, Madalyn harbored a positive dread for this 1984 American Atheists Convention, and for more than one reason. To begin with, Bill Murray had hardly been the only one ever to defect from her cause. Break-off atheist groups of her former followers, most of whom she had either personally purged from her organization or who had quit of their own volition in response to her autocratic management style, had already begun to make noise on their own, and Madalyn could exhibit no more charity towards them—or they to her—than the Kentucky Baptists and early Stone-Campbell "Reformers" had allowed one another one hundred fifty-odd years before. Perhaps partially as a result of the defections or, equally likely, due to Madalyn's evangelistic, exhortatory tendency towards extremism, her American Atheists had developed the reputation within some media circles of being "the freest of the nation's freethinkers," well outside the mainstream of responsible American atheism, and—perhaps the most damning charge of all to a group of self-proclaimed damned souls who were proud of their damnation—as an attractor of mere vulgar sideshows.[3] Only a month or so before the 1984 convention Madalyn had been forced to give up a lucrative deal

[2] Mead, "Strong Feelings Accompany Opening of Atheists' Convention." *Lexington Herald-Leader,* April 21, 1984.

[3] Seaman, 216, quoting a reporter of the *Wall Street Journal* present at the 1984 Convention.

for the distribution of her *American Atheist* magazine by *Hustler* publisher Larry Flynt due to Flynt's fifteen-month imprisonment in a Federal penitentiary for contempt of court, but even while the arrangement had still seemed salvageable to both parties Flynt's flamboyant (and, well, for lack of a better-sounding term, wide-spread) advertising for American Atheists in *Hustler* had so shocked and repulsed the majority of the group's membership that, according to Seaman, donations to Madalyn had fallen off by 41%.[4] At this juncture in the existence of American Atheists the group's legitimacy and credibility were slipping visibly, and it badly needed a strong booster dose of both.

Unfortunately for the Murray O'Hairs, at the 1984 conference credibility and legitimacy were not all that easy to earn. As serious scholars attempted to lecture in the Radisson's numerous conference rooms on legitimate academic topics, such as the famous Dr. John Glover Jackson with his presentation of "The Black Atheists of the Harlem Renaissance,"[5] a few other exhibitors conducted what could be classified only as freak shows. In the running for the worst of these was a homemade video of an "atheist burial" conducted by a visiting leader of an American Atheists state chapter, taking charge of the last rites of a deceased convict whom the state leader had converted (or unconverted, perhaps?) through an atheist prison outreach program. Attendees to the presentation looked on in horror as the tape played, showing the presenter, shirtless and clad only in cutoff jeans, dragging the plastic-shrouded nude corpse out of the back of a pickup truck onto the ground, scooping out a shallow grave with a few dozen tosses of a shovel, unceremoniously shoving the body into the hole and finally throwing a new penny on top of it in case anyone dug it up in the future and needed to know the date of its interment. The atheist activist concluded the presentation with a selected reading of letters he had received in response to the video from critics in his home state, some of which had prompted him to start sleeping with a pistol under his pillow. Though Madalyn had thus far somehow been able to give a good missionary, evangelical-style spin to most of her misfortunes with both

---

[4] Ibid., 215.

[5] John G. Jackson, "The Black Atheists of the Harlem Renaissance." Presented at the American Atheists' Convention, 1984. http://www.africawithin.com/jgjackson/black_atheists.htm

Flynt and her defectors as persecutions for her own outspoken, brave stance in defense of the First Amendment, the atheist burial video very nearly left even her without words. She came to the podium and tried to make a joke of the whole thing, quipping that she certainly didn't want the star of the show (the live star, at any rate) burying *her*. And to top off the whole, picketers associated with Bill came from Southland Christian to the hotel lobby where Robin manned the American Atheist Press's display of the edited, de-capitalized if not decapitated literary works of the historic Kentucky infidel editor Moore, offering to "dialogue" with Madalyn's atheists.[6]

Time and chance, cause and effect; Bill Murray had been invited to Lexington in defense of the city because his terrifying termagant of a mother was going to be there, and in her turn, Madalyn Murray O'Hair was present to celebrate the memorial of an ancestor in unfaith, whose grave she planned to decorate as a conclusion to the convention on Easter Sunday morning. If, then, it could be argued logically that Bill's sermon at Southland Christian Church was a direct result of his mother's conjuring of the memory of the long-dead editor Moore, the moment carried a modicum of irony. Once upon a time, Charles Chilton Moore had been not only an ordained minister in Southland Christian's very same faith tradition, but he was also the grandson of the venerable pioneer evangelist Barton Warren Stone, the co-founder of the entire movement that had brought Southland Christian's faith tradition into being. Had events, in some bizarre way, thus come full circle with the presence of all the Murrays and O'Hairs in Lexington at Eastertide 1984? And if they had, what could the purpose be, or *was* there even a purpose to begin with?

Some people believe that there exists a divinely-ordered rationale for everything that happens. Others believe that, while dogma may chase karma, karma ultimately runs over dogma—God/god, Jesus/jesus help me, I can *not* resist lame puns even though they run both true-believer activists' and academic reviewers' blood pressures up and I should know better anyway—while atheists, and even some religious people as well, believe rather that we have to make our own meaning out of the world and the life in which we find ourselves. Purpose or purposes notwithstanding, though, as the years rolled by after Conven-

[6] Seaman, 215-217.

tion 1984 in Lexington, little ironies continued to augment in odd, sad ways. Madalyn had said, albeit jokingly, that she certainly didn't want the live star of the 1984 Convention's infamous film attraction burying her. He didn't even get the chance, but his version of a proper atheist burial was a great deal more respectful than the one that poor Madalyn, Jon Garth, and Robin were actually given, eleven years later in the fall of 1995. Cruelly murdered by an ex-convict in Madalyn's employ at the American Atheist Center in Austin, Texas, in a weird, unplanned twist of a kidnapping and extortion scheme, the three bodies were left in a storage unit until they had begun to decompose; they were then dismembered, set on fire, and finally buried in a shallow, unmarked grave on an isolated south Texas ranch. Their remains were not discovered until 2001 with the assistance of their killer as part of his plea bargain, and when they were all reburied, the sole family mourner at the gravesite was Madalyn's "traitor" Christian son Bill. Finally, though he himself was still deeply committed to his faith, Bill Murray attempted to give his mother, brother, and daughter only the burial rites that they would have wanted[7]—in fact, much like the respects that Madalyn herself had attempted to pay at the grave of Charles Chilton Moore in the old Lexington Cemetery on West Main Street, back on Easter Sunday 1984.

To return, then, to Kentucky and to the story: *Lexington Herald-Leader* reporter Andy Mead related that Madalyn Murray O'Hair, Jon Garth, Robin, and about sixty of their followers gathered in the cemetery that day, thanking "nature" for giving them a beautiful, sunny morning; only an hour before they began their sparse rites, the sky had been completely overcast and everyone had fully expected rain. Jon Garth Murray, Madalyn herself, and American Atheists member Gerald Tholen all spoke extolling Charles Moore's work and his infidel legacy, some of them throwing a few accusations, perhaps merited to an extent, against the city of Lexington for covering up the old editor's memory. Finally Madalyn laid a wreath[8] and, according to one independent source, planted a small "devil's hosta" lily at the base of Moore's head-

---

[7] Ibid., 11-13.

[8] Mead, "Atheists Laud Founder of 'Heathen' Paper, *Lexington Herald-Leader,* April 23, 1984.

stone,[9] and the memorial, the atheists' convention, and the 1984 Easter moment were over.

Perhaps there is, and was, always an element of the surreal in Easter. Though the four separate accounts of the Resurrection found in the Gospels are grossly contradictory when the fine points of each are compared with those of the other three, the general consensus among them all appears to have been that that first Easter day was one largely of confusion, bewilderment, and apprehension among male and female followers of Jesus alike. According to Luke's Gospel, until Cleopas and his unnamed companion brought word to the disciples that the Lord had appeared to them on the road to Emmaus late that night, all that the first followers of Jesus had to pin their hopes upon was an empty tomb. Even then, they didn't know exactly why the tomb was suddenly empty, and Cleopas himself was said not to have recognized Jesus until the Lord revealed his identity, as they sat down together over supper and Jesus broke bread.[10] In short, if the accounts in Scripture be true or at least legitimate, the principal characters in the drama of that first Easter could have enjoyed it only in retrospect and memory. Until the disciples heard and weighed the testimony of Cleopas and his companion, no one could even have begun to know *what* to believe. Hence the element and the sensation of the surreal, especially since we, like the early disciples on that first Easter, have to accept the Resurrection story on faith, either as literal truth or valid spiritual allegory, if indeed we accept it at all. Madalyn Murray O'Hair most emphatically did not accept it at all, but on Easter Sunday 1984 she perhaps caught and harnessed a bit of that same surreal quality in her own unique way: amid the tombstones of the historic Lexington Cemetery, the most hated woman in late twentieth-century America resurrected, as it were, the memory and the testimony of the most hated man in late nineteenth-century Kentucky.

Atheism has been defined in different ways at different times in history, and perhaps none of the definitions have ever been entirely satisfactory either to those framing them, or to those identifying

[9] Scott Harp, "Charles Chilton Moore."
http://www.therestorationmovement.com/cc_moore.htm

[10] Luke 24:13-34.

themselves as atheists. *The American Heritage Dictionary* lists the meanings of the word as the disbelief in or denial of the existence of God or gods, emphasizing the term's connotations of faith, or the lack thereof; as the *doctrine* that there is no God or gods, paradoxically making atheism a matter of religion or at least dogmatism; and finally as godlessness or immorality,[11] as if those two words were strictly synonymous with atheism and each other, and bringing into the debate over the existence or nonexistence of God the question of good versus evil. However, *The Oxford Dictionary of Current English,* considered by many to be *the* final arbiter of the meanings of English words, defines atheism strictly from a negative viewpoint—and much more vaguely—as "disbelief in the existence of God or gods," in essence merely as the belief that God, or a god, does not exist rather than the positive declaration that there is *no* God.[12]

British scientist and freethought activist Richard Dawkins and some of his allies often appear to many readers to be so zealous for materialistic Darwinism, and so vocal about their lack of belief in anything except the scientific method, as to make atheism a rationalist religion on its own terms, with propositional declarations of unfaith that must be defended with passion and vigor against attacks by theists in a wry mirror image of the Archangel Michael and Satan fighting over the body of Moses.[13]

Retired Episcopal bishop and popular liberal Christian author John Shelby Spong asserts that atheism is merely the rejection of the theistic definition of God rather than the entire concept of the Divine, and that it is entirely possible to reject classical formulations of theism without rejecting alternative concepts of God. Here he echoes Paul Tillich, who remarked once that the God that the atheists reject is rightly rejected.[14] Perhaps both views, and all points in between, come together in a sense under contemporary journalist and author Susan Jacoby's definition of the word *freethought* as the aspiration to be governed mentally and spiritually by reason alone, a broad ideology running the gamut from

---

[11] *American Heritage Dictionary,* 18.

[12] *Oxford English Dictionary of Current English,* 49.

[13] See Haught, "Amateur Atheists: Why the New Atheism Isn't Serious," *The Christian Century,* 125, 4, February 26, 2008; Scriptural reference is to Jude, verse 9.

[14] Spong, *Jesus for the Non-Religious,* 214.

the truly antireligious (those who regard all forms of religion as superstitious and wish to reduce its influence in every aspect of society), through the agnostic (the term having been coined by British scientist Thomas Huxley to represent the viewpoint that the question of the existence, or nonexistence, of God is unanswered and unanswerable), to those who adhere to a private, unconventional faith revering some form of God or Providence but at odds with orthodox religious authority.[15] But whether or not *The American Heritage Dictionary, The Oxford Dictionary,* or any of these writers', scientists', and thinkers' definitions of atheism, agnosticism or, if one prefers the term, freethought, are complete or entirely fair, many, perhaps a great many, Christians in the United States have always regarded self-proclaimed atheists (and/or freethinkers) with a certain morbid fascination, as if they equated the lack of belief in an external, transcendent deity and its consequent freedom of thought with the gleeful selling of one's soul to the devil himself. Americans always have been fond of suspense novels and movies, and to American conservative Christians, outspoken atheists and freethinkers are—to borrow a little of the imagery of Jonathan Edwards—genuine living, breathing suspense stories, courageously dancing over the Eternal Fiery Pit with a cocky grin and suspended by a tightrope no thicker than a spider's silk.

Of course, those of us who remember Madalyn Murray O'Hair in her heyday know that she did absolutely nothing to tone down this perception, or the image associated with it. Her atheism could appear dogmatic and even more religiously passionate than that of Richard Dawkins, and her son Bill, whether rightly or wrongly, always maintained it was more personal than intellectual or philosophical. She was always mad at God, Bill asserted.[16] For some years she actually traveled with a Louisiana evangelist on impassioned revival-style crusades, both she and the preacher working the crowds for their respective stances, fleecing the flock for every penny they could get, and splitting the take each evening after the benediction.[17] For all that, Murray O'Hair nonetheless had a deep intellectual side and an intense appreciation of the history of the movement she represented. In fact, had it not

---

[15] Jacoby, 4.
[16] Seaman, 46.
[17] Murray, 222-226.

been for her encouragement of the research of a few of her followers in the Bluegrass State, particularly John C. Crump, who helped her edit the three 1984 reprints of the Moore books and otherwise assisted in the preparation of microfilms of crumbling, dry-rotted old issues of the *Blue Grass Blade* for deposit in various Kentucky historical collections, the name of Charles Chilton Moore might have lain buried forever, virtually lost to the citizens of Kentucky, the members of his former Christian faith tradition, and modern freethinkers alike. Nearly the only modern historical interest shown his story up to the time of the 1984 American Atheists convention had been that of a young graduate student at the University of Kentucky in the early 1960s, Richard C. Wallace, who had been called up to duty in Vietnam and tragically killed before he could publish his research.[18] Thus we must wonder how that Madalyn Murray O'Hair and Charles Chilton Moore might have gotten along, if they had ever had the chance to meet one another. There was a great deal of difference between the two, but perhaps even more similarity.

In a manner of speaking, Madalyn Murray O'Hair came to prominence from the ground up. She entered onto the public stage from a background of relative poverty juxtaposed with a high level of intelligence, often a very volatile combination. Her atheism was fueled by a variety of influences including Depression-era working class politics, the pro-Socialist, anti-Nazi ethic prevalent among American liberals during and immediately after World War II, and her own rejection of conformist American "social religion." If Bill Murray was even partially correct, we might therefore safely speculate that Madalyn's atheism began with a passion and, from that basis, grew an intellectual side. Living almost a century before, Charles Chilton Moore came from a distinguished Kentucky family and had gold and silver under his hand from the day of his birth. His progression to atheism (or perhaps more accurately his own preferred term of *infidelity,* since the bulk of his writings reveal more of a rejection of the Christian Bible and other supposedly inspired texts, blind faith, revelation, and the classical theistic definitions of God and immortality than a complete and permanent spurning of all religious concepts) appears to have occurred over at least two years and was definitely an intellectual and philosophical

---

[18] See O'Hair's and Crump's introductory remarks to *The Rational View,* i-vi.

process that had begun, surprisingly enough, with a heritage and a background in an expression of Christianity that made the religion, in his own words, "an eminently rational and comprehensible thing"[19]—plus the absolute best "Christian" college education that his parents could afford and that his grandfather Stone's developing faith tradition could give him. He never categorically disavowed a belief in *any* form of god whatsoever, as opposed merely to the Christian God, until the last year of his life, and even then, the question of whether or not he ever intentionally retracted the statement is a matter of some controversy that merits further discussion later. Thus Moore's infidelity began with his intellectual bent, later developing into a passion as he became inspired to articulate it in his newspaper and his books.

Madalyn could exhibit considerable personal charm when the need arose, but her entire personality was fueled by a deep-seated rage only barely concealed at the best of times and which she often let explode vehemently against opponents both real and imagined. Though she was an author, an editor, and a public speaker alike, her primary weapon was the Federal lawsuit, by which she attempted, and often succeeded in, imposing upon the United States at large her particular view of how the First Constitutional Amendment's provisions for the separation of Church and State should be interpreted and enforced.

Moore, on the other hand, was the consummate Southern gentleman in person, by both birth and breeding. This is not to say that he didn't harbor any latent rage or that he couldn't be coarse, outspoken, and guilty of some extremely vituperative rhetoric outrageous even by modern standards, but like the editors of the periodicals and journals of his family's faith tradition (he got at least a portion of his editorial style from his *religious* background, of all things) he generally reserved both coarseness and vitriol for the printed page, and most of his infidel activities were strictly contained within that time-honored medium. He was more like H. L. Mencken, caustic but maintaining a healthy respect for personal honesty wherever and in whomever he found it. If he did perceive a fallacy or an inconsistency between a public figure's profession of faith and his or her personal, public, or business conduct—and in the day of the retribution-demanding Southern code of honor or Fool's Code, he could always find such inconsistencies with ease—

[19] Moore, *The Rational View,* 14.

Moore could and often did gleefully lay on sarcasm with a number-four coal shovel. With her trademark in-your-face expression of her atheism, Madalyn Murray O'Hair was forever looking for, and exploiting, some means or other to challenge conventional piety and morality, evermore-provocative ways to bring rhetorical and dramatic two-by-fours smashing down on the collective skulls of her targeted audiences. There is no question that Charles Moore likewise wrote some extremely harsh articles and essays virtually guaranteed to overwhelm and outrage any conservative Christian who perused them—as well as, surprisingly, a book containing at least one argument with which many nineteenth-century Christians complacently agreed but which would horrify not only modern Christians but even many contemporary atheists and agnostics.

All his professional life Moore waged war against the idea that good and workable moral and ethical systems required a theistic foundation, but he always strictly (yet not quite consistently logically) maintained that "we owe an inestimable debt of gratitude [to Jesus of Nazareth] for the impress of his ideas that stands stamped upon all of our highest institutions."[20] And yet, Moore's most lengthiest term—five months, certainly a longer period than Madalyn or any of her family ever spent incarcerated for anything including their time as hostages at the hands of their killer—was the result of an accusation that he had violated the nineteenth and early twentieth century's repressive Federal Comstock Laws in printing alleged "free love" articles in the *Blue Grass Blade.*

At the time of this writing a multitude of Christian conservative activist groups, including one led by Bill Murray, labor doggedly and tirelessly to undo what they believe to be the damage caused by Madalyn Murray O'Hair's lawsuits to the American public. No doubt this process will continue for many years to come, and no one can now say with any certainty what the end result will be or forecast posterity's final judgment upon the work of Madalyn Murray O'Hair and her American Atheists. As for Charles Chilton Moore, his labors have long since been forgotten by the larger world and even by most Kentuckians, and although I recognize the irony of a believer who presumes to render an objective presentation of a nonbeliever's biography (albeit a

---

[20] Ibid., 8.

believer that has admittedly felt compelled to spend an enormous amount of time trying to winnow wheat from chaff in his own theological thought), I see this obscurity as rather a shame. With one glaring exception Moore came to his conclusions honestly and with a good deal of intense personal reflection and concern, and if he maintained a flippant, even insolent, demeanor in the writing of his books, essays, and newspaper articles he was no more defiant in manner than a good many of his contemporaries writing for religious periodicals.

Even today I anticipate that the majority of this book's readers will be believers in God, and I hope to present Moore's story here in a manner such that even those who would have disagreed or disputed with his declarations of unfaith might still understand how he came to be the sort of individual that he was. In that spirit, while we bat around the questions of both faith and belief and the idea of whether to define atheism according to the terms of Richard Dawkins or of John Shelby Spong, we might do well to keep in mind the paradox implicit within at least a few of the lesser-known words attributed to Jesus of Nazareth: his fiery, impassioned condemnation, written in the twenty-third chapter of Matthew's Gospel, of those who gilded the tombs of the prophets whom their ancestors had injured and slain, those who piously asserted that if they themselves had lived in the days of their forefathers they never would have persecuted and murdered the visionaries of their nation.[21] The likelihood is, of course, that during most of its existence the Temple priesthood in Jerusalem would have denigrated any proclaimed prophet who happened to be antagonistic to the Temple priests or their agenda, just as the Temple leadership likely snubbed both John the Baptist and Jesus himself. Likewise, the descendants of those same priests as well as those of their followers would have been equally ready to praise those selfsame prophets' brave outspokenness—when it was politically advisable, and of course safe, to do so.

"Controversial" was, is, and shall remain a gross understatement for Madalyn Murray O'Hair's articulation of her principles. We have already intimated that at least to our modern sensibilities, be they theistic or atheistic, one of her predecessor Moore's own ideas matched, even outmatched, anything that she ever tried to hurl at the public for sheer gall and outrageousness. But it might surprise and even shock

---

[21] Matthew 23:1-39.

some readers to learn just how many "radical" ideas that Moore and his *Blue Grass Blade* once advocated, have by now become mainstream American, and in some instances even conservative Christian, thought. Among others, Moore's contentions included the ideas that women should be given the rights to own property, to be responsible for their own earnings, and to vote, propositions all forbidden by Kentucky law until near the dawn of the twentieth century and one of which was not passed into law until after World War I; that husbands and wives alike had the solemn duty to exercise commonsense family planning and thus owned the fundamental right to use artificial birth control, a belief which in Moore's day was condemned not only by the Roman Catholic Church but virtually all Protestant denominations as well, to say nothing of being classified by Federal law as obscene; that other matters dealing with sexuality needed to be discussed between adults in a frank, open manner rather than "polite society's" attempts to pretend such things didn't exist, a lesson with which more than one generation has struggled; that the governments of the world needed an international "congress of nations" for mutual cooperation, which of course had to wait for the horrors of two world wars and the threat of worldwide nuclear annihilation to establish itself permanently; that gambling at horse racing was a dissipated habit and a dangerous addiction, a controversial point even now in some parts of Kentucky; and that the use of tobacco was hazardous to the health, which the tobacco industry vigorously contested until only fairly recently and which did not really become part of the public consciousness until at least the 1960s. And to top it all off, Moore's aggressive activism in behalf of the cause of Prohibition outstripped any similar efforts of Kentucky Christian preachers and periodicals of the same era, and whether for good or ill his anti-liquor pronouncements actually served as a comfort and an inspiration to conservative Kentucky Christians in the late 1880s and 1890s who categorically rejected almost everything else he ever said or wrote. Considering that Paul—or again, someone writing as Paul—once advised his protégé Timothy not to drink water any more but rather take a little wine for his stomach's sake[22], in his own day Moore couldn't have used what was then viewed as a "strict" interpretation of the Bible to defend any of these ideas even if he had been so inclined,

[22] I Timothy 5:23.

except perhaps his condemnation of gambling. In many ways the Bluegrass editor was thus a living, breathing exemplar of Bertrand Russell's pithy observation that it was amusing to him to hear his Christian contemporaries hold forth on how mild and rationalistic Christianity really is, completely ignoring the fact that whatever mildness and rationalism the religion possessed was largely due to the teaching of men who in their own day were persecuted by all orthodox Christians. To Russell, the "gradual emasculation" of Christian doctrine was effected in spite of the most vigorous resistance, and solely as the result of the onslaughts of freethinkers[23]—just like Kentucky's own Charles Chilton Moore.

Strangely enough, though, it has never been all that difficult for evangelical Christian and other conservative communities and movements to assimilate the changes to their attitudes and mores that are suggested above, since changes of this type are usually completed before very many, if anyone, within the conservative or evangelical tradition admits that they are needed and the fact of change is most often concealed until *after* it has taken place. The process by which this occurs is arguably the bedrock of the very vice upon which Jesus was supposed to have heaped such scorn, but in terms of sociology and anthropology it very well may also be a cultural adaptation absolutely necessary for conservative groups to survive. It allows at least quasi-sensible changes and adaptations over time, without necessitating the alteration of any of the actual maxims and formulae traditional to order conservative culture.[24] Because the process more often than not makes martyrs out of prophets and visionaries, it can also embody all the appearances of blatant hypocrisy, yet if sociologists be correct it is as natural as peristalsis even if close study makes it no more attractive—or fragrant—than peristalsis' end product. Under such circumstances it is small wonder that a conservative culture can maintain the myth that the values it upholds at any given moment in time are the values it has always upheld, "time out of mind."

There can be no doubt that Bill Murray and all others who are working so hard to reverse the legacy of Madalyn Murray O'Hair

---

[23] Russell, 36-37.

[24] Ault, 204-217, referring to the work of sociologists James Barr and Susan Friend Harding. See also Jacoby, 186-187.

would agree vehemently with Shakespeare that the evil that men—and women—do lives after them. But lest we should inter the good anyone has done along with his or her bones, we should likewise remember the man on whose shoulders Madalyn confessed to standing, as it were, by the honors she gave him at his burial site at Easter 1984—and compare his outlook with that which was considered good, conservative old-time religious writing in his own Antebellum youth and Civil War- and Gilded Age-era adulthood. It is within this context that I hope we can remember and appreciate the life and work of Charles Chilton Moore, because if we cannot hear him speaking in his own day—arguing for such reforms, both religious *and* secular, as even the most religiously conservative modern men and women now enjoy and some of whom firmly believe have existed for their benefit "time out of mind, exactly according to Scripture"—we can never hope to hear him speak to us in ours. The memory of a prophet always seems just a little more agreeable than the actual appearance of the prophet, himself or herself.

Lest we forget, then: regardless of whether one believes that the deeds of Madalyn Murray O'Hair were good and beneficial, evil and harmful, or any combination of the two, it might pay us to take another look at the memory and the legacy of the controversial Kentucky ex-Christian she resurrected for us at Easter 1984, Charles Chilton Moore, and the aptly named *Blue Grass Blade* that he wielded as his editorial scythe at the clove of the nineteenth and twentieth centuries.

In my writing and preparation of this book I would like to thank the following individuals for their kind assistance and friendship: Kenneth H. Williams, Lynne Hollingsworth, Sally Bown, Diane Shelton, Bill Morris and Brenda Smith of the Kentucky Historical Society, Frankfort, Kentucky, for research assistance and to the Society itself for the Basic Research Fellowship that enabled me to polish and complete this project; Carrie May, Walter Bowman, and James M. Prichard of the Kentucky Department of Libraries and Archives, also of Frankfort, both for assistance in researching Charles Moore's commonwealth criminal cases and for access to extremely rare original copies of his newspaper; Charles Heaberlin of the Special Collections Department, Bosworth Library, Lexington Theological Seminary, Lexington, Kentucky; the staff of the Young Library and the Margaret I. King Library at the University of Kentucky, Lexington, Kentucky (especially Kellie

Bowman, Casey Ferrell, Brooke Stutler, and Rebecca Clark of the Young Library's Periodicals Section); Charlie G. Hughes of Wind Publications, Nicholasville, Kentucky, for several rare supplementary articles about Moore in the *Lexington Morning Herald* and other newspapers; B. J. Gooch of the Special Collections Department, Transylvania University, Lexington, Kentucky; Jeanne Cobb, College Archivist, and Heather Ricciuti, Coordinator of Library Public Services, at the T. W. Phillips Memorial Library of Bethany College, Bethany, West Virginia for rare data that was absolutely vital in filling out Charles Chilton Moore's youth, young manhood, and college career; my good friend and research colleague Deborah P. Barrett of Darien, Illinois, for help in tracing the lives and activities of Moore's friend George Owen Barnes and his nemesis John Alexander Dowie, as well as assistance in running down the surviving records of Charles Moore's 1899 Federal trial in the United States Court, Division of Southern Ohio, in the Great Lakes (Chicago) Division of the National Archives; Scott Forsythe, archivist at the National Archives' Great Lakes Division; Arlene Royer, archivist of the Southeastern (Atlanta) Division of the National Archives, for records of Moore's 1895 and 1900 Federal trials in the United States Court, District of Western Kentucky; Bob Treadway, Lexington attorney and my friend, for assistance in developing an understanding of the concept of blasphemy as it related to English common law and the development of its counterpart in nineteenth-century rural America; "Buckeye" local historian and taphophile Beth Santore of Columbus, Ohio, for her generous donation of photographs of "Bankers' Row" in the old Ohio State Penitentiary; Michael Adcock, fellow Moore researcher and writer, and Emmitt F. Fields, owner and webmaster of the online "Bank of Wisdom," both of Louisville, Kentucky; Leslie Nash Huber of Lagrange, Kentucky, historian of the Old Union Christian Church on Russell Cave Road, Lexington, Kentucky, where the Moore family once worshiped; Danna Estridge, curator of the Woodford County Historical Society and Ivy Hughes, Administrative Associate at Charles Moore's former pastorate, the First Christian Church of Versailles, Kentucky; Scott County local historian Ann Bolton Bevins of Georgetown, Kentucky; Karen Daniels, Esther Titlow, Mary Anne Runyon, Lee Pack, Ryan Skaggs, Jean Christian, Sandra Brown, and the rest of the staff of the Johnson County Public Library, Paintsville, Kentucky; my occasional volunteer research assistants (and co-clutterers of my daughter Amie's room) Sandi Carpenter, Shumyla Azeem, and Lisa Blair; and Joyce Harrison, formerly of the University Press of Kentucky and now of Kent State University Press in Ohio.

And finally, a sincere thanks once again to my wife Sheila and my daughters Sarah, now of St. Louis, Missouri and Amie still at home (briefly anyway; I expect she'll be an undergrad at UK by the time this goes to press), for putting up with yet another book from the lone man in the house.

Chapter 1

Faith of the Forefathers

Sir, allow me two or three assumptions,
and I don't know what I could not prove.
—Alexander Campbell

In 1805 Kentucky minister and religious leader Barton Warren Stone had to have experienced one of the most tumultuous years of his life. Two signal events, milestones even, occurred for him during that twelvemonth; he wrote and spoke copiously about one of them, but the other he barely acknowledged in his published works, if indeed he ever commented about it at all. Both will be noted and discussed in due course.

To begin, Stone's budding frontier religious movement, known first as the Springfield Presbytery and subsequently as the Christian Church, was very nearly destroyed in 1805 by a rival group that had come to Kentucky originally purporting overtures of friendship. The thirty-two year-old Stone had worked tirelessly to earn legitimacy for his Christian Church ever since its inception during the heady aftermath of the so-called Great Revival all across the American South. The Great Awakening, a similar religious phenomenon of a generation before, had given the American colonies their first real taste of what might now be classified as evangelical "born-again" Christianity with the ministries of the Puritan Jonathan Edwards, the Anglicans and Anglicans-turned-Methodists George Whitefield, John and Charles Wesley, Devereux Jarratt, and Archibald McRoberts, the Dutch Reformed pastor Theodorus Frelinghuysen, the Presbyterian Samuel Davies, and the Baptists Daniel Marshall and Shubal Stearns, among others. However, the rationalistic temper of Revolutionary and post-Revolutionary times had made many American citizens lackadaisical about religious matters, if not actively influenced towards skepticism against all claims of revealed religion by the then-popular writings of the Deists Voltaire, Thomas Paine, Ethan Allen, the Baron d'Holbach, and the Comte de Volney. Thanks to Barton Stone and his cohorts, the Great Revival would, remarkably enough, metamorphose the South back into the entity now known as the Bible Belt. Voltaire and his fellow Deists had set "belief of the head," as it were, on a pedestal superior to the "belief of the heart" idealized in Great Awakening-style Christianity, but with the new Revival "belief of the heart" had actually come to redefine "belief of the head" in light of the dramatic so-called spiritual manifestations that had come to be associated with Barton Stone's and other Revival ministers' preaching and exhorting.

In fact, these spiritual manifestations—the "barks," the "jerks," the dancing, running, rolling, and singing "exercises," all the ways in which the hundreds of penitents and converts at Stone's central Kentucky camp meetings made spectacles of themselves—had caused Stone to take his own exposition of Christian doctrine a step further than had been previously known among even among enthusiastic American evangelicals. Up to and including Stone during his early ministry, rural American evangelical Christians influenced by the pre-Revolutionary Great Awakening had never worried much, if at all, about proofs of the existence of God or questions of the possibility that the entire scheme of faith upon which they had built their lives might be nothing more than a delusion. They rather depended on God to manifest himself, as it were, by means of "spiritual witness"—what they perceived as influences of the Holy Ghost associated with the preaching of the Gospel, both to themselves and to those around them. In other words, so long as they personally could feel this inner "witness" of the Holy Ghost in their lives and actions, and could see sinners weep, sink down to the ground, cry for mercy, what have you, in response to a well-articulated (or in the case of rural southeastern Separate Baptists, at least a well-sung) sermon, they believed that God himself was faithfully providing all the testimony anyone needed, both of his own divine presence in the universe and involvement in human affairs, and of the literal truth of the Holy Scriptures from which truly divinely-inspired ministers took, or were given, their sermon texts. Just let any Paine- and Volney-reading skeptics come to Separate Baptist, Methodist, or "New Side" Presbyterian religious services to scoff and make fun. If—and only if—the Lord got hold of them, they'd lose their skepticism and sense of humor quickly enough. God would see to that himself. Paul Tillich once made the comment that mysticism was the mother of rationalism, and at least in this instance he was completely correct. The mysticism in which these children of the Great Awakening and the Great Revival framed their experiences of God and conversion became the basis of their entire mindset.

A Maryland native who had spent most of his childhood and youth on the frontier of Pittsylvania County, Virginia, Barton Stone came from a conventional Anglican family but was much more deeply influenced in his early days by the early Methodists and Separate Baptists who provided most of Pittsylvania County's backwoods farmers with divine services. In later years he voiced not-unpleasant recollections of the Pittsylvania County Separate Baptist leaders Dutton Lane, Samuel Harris, and their junior preaching colleagues' "art of affecting their hearers by a tuneful or singing voice in preaching" and the early Methodist preachers' "often electric [effect] on the congregation,"[25] and he had imbibed, almost with his mother's milk, their Great Awakening-style paradigm of thinking about God. Stone's mother became a Methodist in her later years, and Stone himself embraced Presbyterianism over the Methodist and Baptist influences of his childhood more than any other reason because it was the fashion in the upcountry school in which he studied law as a young man. Even so, the Presbyterianism he found at Rev. David Caldwell's Academy, thirty-odd miles from Pittsylvania County in Guilford County, North Carolina, was of the New Side, Great Awakening style and consequently little different in terms of evangelistic fervor from the Separate Baptists who had planted themselves in that same North Carolina upcountry in the 1750s and from thence spread into the Southern mountains. In fact Stone first met his colleague in the leadership of the Great Revival, James McGready, not in Kentucky but rather in North Carolina when McGready was a visiting speaker at the Caldwell Academy. Little did either man then

[25] Williams, 13-14, quoting Barton Stone's *Autobiography.*

anticipate the notoriety that awaited them after they relocated to Kentucky, McGready to the south in Logan County and Stone to Cane Ridge in Bourbon County, near the turn of the nineteenth century.

What, then, were Barton Stone's additions and contributions to Christian theology in light of the Great Revival? For starters, he somehow squeaked by his 1796 ordination as a Presbyterian minister in spite of a marked tendency towards Arminianism, the belief that salvation was offered to all humankind rather than just an elect few as per Calvinistic Presbyterian orthodoxy, and consequently voicing only a partial, qualified acceptance of the Presbyterians' formal statement of faith, the Westminster Confession. As he put it, he agreed to receive and adopt the Confession only "as far as I see it consistent with the Word of God."[26] Though a bit brash, it was a characteristic response from a young American evangelical who had imbibed the idea, developed from the time of the self-taught New England farmer-preachers of the Great Awakening through Thomas Paine's publication of *Common Sense* before Paine had fully revealed himself as a Deist, to depend on good old American common horse sense in the interpretation of Scripture along with all other matters—so long as the experience of conversion, the born-again experience, had allowed one to establish the proposition that Scripture was inspired and infallible. Frontier American Baptists, Methodists, and even some Presbyterians had come to a point of view that the self-taught student of Scripture deserved respect equal to, and at least with the Separate Baptists and Methodists greater than, those who had undergone formal, conventional theological training.

Thus having established his own measure of independence within the Presbyterian framework, Stone began to admit to others as well as to himself that he couldn't really make sense of any of the common interpretations of the doctrine of the Trinity, from that of St. Athanasius to that of Isaac Watts. Over time, Stone retooled the ideas and concepts of the relationship between Father, Son, and Holy Ghost in terms of what *did* make sense to him in light of what he found in Scripture. To him, the "incomprehensible mystery" of One God in Three Persons was made simpler by the propositions that God the Father was a single eternal being, his Son was the "Instrumental Cause" of creation but yet

---

[26] Ibid., 45.

himself a created being, and that the Holy Ghost was the divine power or energy through which God revealed himself to and communicated with humankind.[27] Stone's grandson, however, stated the case in a more blunt, direct way that might make even the apologists of Stone's own faith tradition wince: that "the great distinguishing feature of the [Christian] creed that my grandfather originated and inculcated was the change from the recognition of three persons in the Godhead to only one God, the Father, and Jesus Christ as a demigod, while the third person in the Trinity was reduced to a mere impersonal religious influence."[28] (Throughout this work, in all cases where American Atheist Press reprints have been quoted, capitalizations from the original editions of the works have been restored.)

Stone had some original thoughts on the doctrine of the atonement as well, again in light of what made sense to him in the context of his background. The idea that God's son was some sort of a blood sacrifice to satisfy the divine vengeance against a fallen humanity was both nonsensical and repulsive to him, so in Stone's theology the death, burial and resurrection of Jesus became the means God had chosen to lead men and women to consider more closely the testimony given in the Bible and from thence to faith in God and repentance of their sins. The blood of Christ led humankind to a relationship with God, but it did not purchase salvation.[29] Though this in and of itself was a significant departure from what was then commonly accepted Protestant doctrine, it is by no means certain that all of Stone's followers accepted it implicitly. However, they did very much accept the framework around which Stone put his theological scheme together: the idea that the manifestations attributed to the Holy Ghost as seen in the Great Revival were not only God's signs to sinners that they could put their trust in the truth and reliability of Scripture, they were the *Bible's* signs of its *own* power. To put it another way, the preached word of the Bible itself was the very repository of the Holy Ghost from whence the signs originated; the Scriptures themselves caused people to repent, and the very word of the Gospel, as much or even more than the intangible Spirit that was supposed to have moved the biblical authors to write

---

[27] Garrett, 85.

[28] Moore, *The Rational View,* 2.

[29] Boles, 153-154.

down that same Gospel, therefore brought pardon. According to one source, albeit arguably prejudiced, Stone and his closest ministerial colleagues—Matthew Houston, Robert Marshall, Richard McNemar, John Dunlavy, and John Thompson—made the claim that they were preaching the "new true Gospel possessed only by them."[30] As such, they were often referred to in these early days as New Lights, but again, Stone, Houston and the rest believed they were exercising simple common sense, plain Christian doctrine that anyone who had experienced the New Birth in Christ could see if he or she only examined the Scriptures honestly and without prejudice and let the Lord remove the blinders from his or her eyes.

Still, harboring such deviations from accepted Presbyterian orthodoxy, Stone, Marshall, Thompson, Dunlavy, Houston, and McNemar knew they could not long expect to remain immune from the wrath and retaliation of their Kentucky Synod in spite of the dramatic increase in converts they had brought to the Presbyterian denomination. And so in 1803, some two to three years after the Great Revival reached its peak of intensity and questions of their orthodoxy had begun to be voiced formally within the Synod, they, their congregations, and a number of other individuals and whole churches voluntarily withdrew from the body to form the independent Springfield Presbytery. They subsequently renamed their organization, such as it was, the Christian Church after the form of a Virginia Methodist breakaway group with which they had established some contacts through immigrant minister Rice Haggard, and which had also developed a set of beliefs heterodox to Methodism and roughly equivalent to those presently classified as "Jesus-only" or "Oneness" theology.[31] Despite the fact that the heterodoxy of Stone and his companions was not quite the *same* heterodoxy as that of the Virginia group, they got along, and for the time being the future looked full of promise for the new Christian Church in Kentucky.

Then came 1805 and the addition of the United Society of Believers in Christ's Second Appearing, more commonly known as the Shakers, to the mix. This group, which had originated in Manchester, England and had moved its headquarters to New Lebanon near Albany,

---

[30] Ibid., 149, quoting a statement made by Presbyterian minister John Lyle.
[31] Ibid., 145.

New York, was a sort of communistic cult that believed that Jesus Christ—or at least his spirit—had returned to the earth in the person of its founder, "Mother" Ann Lee. Celibate, extremely spiritualistic, and claiming to possess all the "gifts of the Spirit" enjoyed by the earliest Christians of the New Testament, the Shakers forsook the world, as it were, to live and labor on communal farms. They were rabidly evangelistic as well, though, and the formation of a Kentucky religious group that everyone called "New Lights" and which itself preferred the name of the Christian Church or the Church of Christ, seemed to them to be a field white unto the harvest. The Shaker leadership at New Lebanon dispatched three missionaries on New Year's Day 1805 to travel to Kentucky, and they arrived among Stone's people some time in March.

Accepted by Stone initially as fellow New Lights with a message complementary to his own, the Shaker missionaries quickly brought complete chaos to Stone's flock. Speaking in tongues both known and unknown—the Shakers were the very first American religious group to employ *glossolalia* as an act of worship and exploit it aggressively as a proof of their favor in God's eyes, and the Mormons in their early days were the second—and dancing and displaying every other "spiritual gift" of which anyone who had ever picked up the Bible could possibly conceive (short of handling snakes, drinking poison, and sticking their heads and limbs into the fire), the missionaries decimated Stone's congregations, split up families, and even succeeded in converting John Dunlavy, Matthew Houston, and Richard McNemar. All this took some time to accomplish, but by the time the dust settled, the Shakers had pooled their New Light converts' money and real estate, purchased farmland, and organized two large communes in Kentucky, one at South Union in Logan County and the other on Shawnee Run in Mercer County. Of Barton Stone's five most important early ministering partners in the Springfield Presbytery, Dunlavy, Houston, and McNemar were counted among Kentucky's leading Shakers, and the two others, Marshall and Thompson, returned to the Kentucky Presbyterian Synod in disgust at the whole imbroglio and apologized to the body for ever getting mixed up with Stone's movement in the first place.[32]

For all this, the Stone Christian Church survived, but from the spring of 1805 to the year's end the prospect of the flock's complete

---

[32] Ibid., 156-158.

dissolution must have appeared to be a very near thing to its one remaining leader. Stone himself later wrote that he never exerted himself more, or harder, "than at this time to save the people from this vortex of ruin."[33] He preached and wrote against the Shakers incessantly, fighting like a pit bull to convince his hearers—and very likely himself, as well—that the Shakers were "worldly-minded, cunning deceivers, whose religion is earthly, sensual and devilish," and that "of the twelve who followed Christ, one proved to be a devil, and another denied him, and all the rest forsook him; but all repented, except Judas."[34] Barton Stone is generally remembered, with great justification, as a kind, gentle, spiritual man and leader. We can see very little either of kindness or gentleness, though, in the warrior persona he felt compelled to adopt through much of his troubles with the Shakers. As an apology for his conduct, in the long run he can be viewed as the victor in terms of perseverance in the mighty Shaker war over the souls of his Kentuckians: his movement recovered to prosper, and although the Shakers have not yet died out completely, today they exist only in one tiny commune and that in rural Maine rather than Kentucky. Their two fine properties in Mercer and Logan Counties are now well-run, extremely appealing museums, attracting tourists from all over the United States—but no converts.

One historical tidbit regarding Barton Stone has seemingly escaped the attentions of most of the scholars who have studied his life and work: the memory, supposedly handed down among his children and grandchildren, that he once actually admitted a strong inclination to infidelity after being ordained as a minister. By the word "infidelity" he is supposed to have meant the repudiation of the supernatural claims of Christianity.[35] Though infidelity was a charge that other preachers, most particularly Presbyterians, were prone to fling at Stone,[36] the source of this particular anecdote can hardly be counted either as completely unprejudiced or always entirely accurate: he also related the claimed family story that Barton Stone was "one of twenty children of

---

[33] Stone, 185.
[34] Williams, 126, quoting Stone.
[35] Moore, *The Rational View,* 2.
[36] E.g. Wrather, II, 148, quoting Presbyterian minister John Poage Campbell.

the son of the Earl of Surrey." [37] The Stone family connection to English nobility was not quite a lie, but yet in this case it was exaggerated to proportions one rarely finds anywhere apart from the asseverations of Southern—and perhaps particularly Kentucky—genealogy buffs.[38] In the good old days, every man in Kentucky possessed at least the rank of colonel.

At any rate, Stone's own surviving writings reveal no evidence of any such inner crisis of faith. Neither does anything else in his character indicate, before nor after the Shaker disaster, that he ever allowed a place in his mind for religious doubt. But if the alleged family memory does happen to be true, we must suspect that Stone's moment of doubt and pain likely occurred during his fiercest battles of words against the Shakers. They claimed the same "spiritual witness" as did his own people in their barking, jerking, dancing and singing exercises, though their interpretation of Scripture was as different from Stone's, and for that matter those of all other denominations involved in the Great Revival, as different could be. The "common sense" attitude of the day towards religious doctrine and belief allowed no answer to the conundrum of who was right and who was wrong, for all involved in the dispute invoked identical spiritual "witnesses" of faith right along with that same common sense. At this point in time the Baptists in Kentucky were experiencing eerily similar disasters: the Regular and Separate components of the denomination had joined one another to form the United Baptists at the zenith of the Great Revival in 1801, yet by 1805 the United Baptists were ready to fragment half a dozen different ways from internal and inter-associational dissensions.[39]

It is not inconceivable that, at this time, Stone could have come to that realization so unsettling to anyone who has somehow become convinced and assured that he or she possesses pure biblical truth: that no one's system of belief can truly be a straight exegesis from Scripture

---

[37] Moore, *Behind the Bars,* 1.

[38] Interestingly, Barton Stone actually was a great-great grandson of Maryland's first Protestant colonial governor, William Stone, but the family came from London's merchant class. Barton Stone's actual possible family relationship to the Earl of Surrey is outlined more accurately, clearly, and concisely in Wrather, II, 143-144.

[39] For further information see Sparks, *The Roots of Appalachian Christianity,* Chapter 8, and *Raccoon John Smith,* Chapters 2 and 5.

so much as it is, and ultimately always proves itself to be, instead more of an eisegesis, that is, an attempt to reconcile one's own varied passions and prejudices with one's perception of the Bible. It is a frightening thought to the dogmatically faithful heart, and yet one that necessarily presents itself from time to time to anyone involved in such a doctrinal war as Stone was, or the Kentucky Baptists were, at that juncture. Nonetheless, if Stone ever harbored any such heretical musings, he got over them in time, and if they had any consequences at all they have not been recorded.

The second 1805 milestone for the leader of the Christian Church in Kentucky might appear to be prosaic in light of all the other events swirling through his life, and certainly Stone himself felt little or no impulse to record his impressions of it. But Barton Stone left legacies in Kentucky in more than one way, and it so happened that on September 21 of that year, the first day of autumn, his wife Elizabeth was brought to bed to be delivered of her third child in four years of marriage, a girl named Mary Anne. Elizabeth Stone would go on to have a total of five children in eight years of wedlock, before the law of averages of the times caught up with her and she herself went the way of all the earth—or "suffered the curse of Eve," as folk were wont to put it in those days—before her twenty-seventh birthday. She is supposed to have fallen sick in May 1809, two months or so before her youngest child, Barton Warren Stone Jr., was born, and both she and the little boy survived for about ten months after the birth. The chief written testimony to the fact that Elizabeth ever existed at all was her husband's praise of her as "pious, intelligent, and cheerful," "truly a helpmeet to me in all my troubles and difficulties," who had affectionately encouraged him during the development of his atonement doctrine and had "praised God most fervently for the truth."[40]

Tragically cut short though her existence was, perhaps no one can expect to leave life with a better memorial. Still, much of Elizabeth Stone's story is lost forever to obscurity, as in fact is her husband's in terms of being a family man as opposed to a public figure and Gospel preacher. Though Stone left an autobiography and the story of his ministry has been competently retold by more than one Christian histo-

[40] Williams, 128-132.

rian, we know next to nothing about his private family life. The most we can speculate or hope for in that regard is the probability that, all in all, Stone tried to be kind to his children and to discipline them only with mild, encouraging methods. He spoke harshly of a tyrannical teacher under whom he had suffered in his childhood, and in his autobiography and his own sporadic stints as schoolmaster and headmaster he advocated the moderate approach, recommending the use of corporal punishment only "rarely" and advising that if teachers would gain the "respect and love" of their pupils they would "delight in obedience, and rarely fail to learn the lessons given to them."[41] Though we all have our private and our public faces, the likelihood is that Stone would have given as much thoughtful consideration to his children as he allowed for his students.

The great problem with this was that mistreatment can be passive as well as active, completely unintentional as well as deliberate. For all too long a portion of his little girls' early childhood years, Barton Stone rarely even saw them, let alone had enough time with them to abuse them physically. Of course, emotional abuse was and is another matter, but the possibility of its existence was not even acknowledged at this period. Throughout the span of the girls' mother's short life with him, Stone had been inundated with responsibilities for the upkeep of his Christian Church. He traveled regularly and often, and even when he was at home he was occupied not only with writing and with preaching to his nearest congregations, but with managing his own farm as well. A consistent and committed emancipationist, he had freed the only two slaves he had ever owned, given to him by his mother, before he had ever married Elizabeth. And after her death matters only became more unsettled for the four little ones: Stone and his colleague Reuben Dooley, who had just then lost his wife as well, got it into their heads that the Lord wanted them to sublimate their grief by becoming traveling evangelists. Both men boarded, or perhaps more accurately bound out, their children with church members, and they hit the sawdust trail.[42]

We do not know the names or characters of the family, or families, with whom Barton Stone placed his daughters for his stint as a traveling preacher. Neither do we know exactly how long little Mary Anne

---

[41] Ibid., 11-12.
[42] Stone, 65-75; Williams, 131.

and her sisters had to lodge after this fashion. Stone and Dooley traveled, preached, and gathered new churches throughout the settled areas of central Kentucky, southern Ohio, and central and western Tennessee, but late in the next year Stone changed careers once again. He visited an aunt of the deceased Elizabeth's near Nashville and wound up marrying her daughter Celia, Elizabeth's first cousin and twenty years younger than he was, on the last day of October 1811.

Stone sold his Bourbon County, Kentucky, farm the spring following, evidently intending to settle permanently in Tennessee, but we do not know if he took his children southward to live with him and their stepmother or not. Apparently he and Celia stayed briefly in Kentucky before he sold his Cane Ridge property, either with or without his daughters by his first marriage, but the couple quickly set to work on their own houseful of children on Celia's mother's land. In 1814, however, after Stone came to the realization that his new mother-in-law did not intend to deed him any of her real estate in spite of the fact that he had built a house for himself, Celia, and their children on the property, he resolved to leave Tennessee and make another fresh start in Kentucky. According to his recollections his new wife approved of the action,[43] though it must be admitted that, in terms of the law and custom of that era, she had little other choice.

Stone received a hero's welcome once again from his Kentucky brethren, apparently about the time that the War of 1812 ended. However, the circumstances of that conflict, coupled by both the increase in construction of turnpikes in the state and the beginnings of steamboat traffic on the Ohio and Mississippi Rivers, had wreaked havoc on Kentucky land prices. Property that had gone for $12 per acre at the time Stone had sold his Cane Ridge farm was now worth $30 or more per acre, so he wasn't able even to buy back either his own farm or one equivalent to it. His followers promised to rent him a house in Lexington and to supply his and his family's every need, but they never quite followed through with their good intentions. Stone settled back into Kentucky life by establishing and operating schools in Lexington and Georgetown to finance his family and his ministry, and he finally saved enough capital to buy land and establish a home just outside the latter city in Scott County.

---

[43] Stone, 68; Williams, 139-140, 149.

The years 1815 through 1820, between Mary Anne's tenth and fifteenth birthdays and the beginning of that prosperous period of American history that has come to be called the Era of Good Feeling, were thus probably the most stable that she ever knew while growing up. Modern psychologists would probably have much to say about the effects of her topsy-turvy early life on her personality and its ramifications for her relationships, but her son described her as "a woman of strong common sense [who] inherited her father's strong religious convictions"[44] and from all appearances she herself simply took the events of her life in stride and attempted to make the best of them. Too, we have considerable cumulative evidence that she regarded her father, despite his preoccupations with both his ministry and his younger children by his second wife, with near-complete adoration.

For all her resilience and optimism, though, neither can we expect that the chaos of her formative years had no effect upon her whatsoever. Some time during her fourteenth or fifteenth years her father permitted her to "accept calls," as the saying went, from a bachelor sixteen years her senior, one Charles Chilton Moore. Chilton, as he was familiarly known, was a Virginia native who had been brought to Kentucky as an infant by his parents, William and Hannah, and according to family lore he had been named for his father's Revolutionary War commanding officer. Something of a self-made man in spite of his father's acquisition of considerable Bluegrass land, Chilton Moore had served as a private in the War of 1812 along with his brother Thomas, surviving capture by the British and Indians after the disastrous Battle of the Maumee of the Lakes in Canada (also known as Dudley's Defeat after William Dudley, Chilton's luckless commanding officer) to be spared by the Indian leader Tecumseh himself.[45]

Though he had been a lowly private, Chilton's neighbors and acquaintances stayed true to Kentucky etiquette and entitled him Captain Moore.[46] Following Jackson's victory at New Orleans, Chilton had

---

[44] Moore, *Behind the Bars,* 2.

[45] In Kentucky Adjutant General Sam E. Hill's 1891 Report on Kentucky soldiers serving in the War of 1812, Thomas and Charles C. Moore are listed as privates in Captain James Dyametto's Company of Col. William Dudley's Regiment, Kentucky Militia, "Detached." It is noted that they were "Paroled by the enemy" on May 5, 1813. Hill, 192-193.

[46] Moore, *Behind the Bars*, 7.

taken a thousand-dollar patrimony and set himself up as a merchant in Winchester, but by the time he began to pay court to Mary Anne Stone his business acumen had enabled him to augment his inheritance and he was a comfortably-fixed planter and slaveowner with 850 acres near the properties of his parents and brothers John and Thomas on Elkhorn Creek near Russell's Cave in what is now northern Fayette County. This section, and the entire surrounding area from the Lexington city limits to the county line between the present Paris and Newtown Pikes, came to be known in the nineteenth century as the Dog Fennel Precinct or simply Dog Fennel, after one of the area's—and in fact the entire South's—most common weeds.

That Chilton Moore owned slaves might have been a stumblingblock to his friendship with young Mary Anne, considering that her father was so dead-set against slavery, but in a border state like Kentucky pro-slavery and antislavery advocates had to come to some sort of agreement to disagree or else maintain a continual feud with one another. If the recollections of his children are to be trusted, Chilton himself was a kindly man whose sole defense of the "peculiar institution" was that he thought Kentucky blacks would be worse off as freemen than as slaves.[47] However, independent evidence exists that at least for one period in his life Chilton was an aggressive pro-slavery politician who campaigned for a seat in the Kentucky legislature against Robert Todd, the father-in-law of Abraham Lincoln, on a platform favoring laws that would allow the importation of more slaves into the state.[48]

If one should wonder how Chilton Moore could have left behind such contradictory and perhaps even hypocritical evidence of his slavery ideology, no less an observer than Harriet Beecher Stowe is said to have admitted that Kentuckians generally exercised a consummate skill in portraying their state as a "Camelot" sort of place where the relationship between masters and slaves was about as ideal as the system would allow.[49] Whatever his actual stance on slavery, Chilton's only other vices appear to have been the playing of backgammon and the chewing of tobacco; he dressed well, was literate, articulate, and unfail-

---

[47] Ibid., 27.
[48] Richardson, 48-49.
[49] Ward, 26, quoting Stowe.

ingly polite after the "old school dignity" of antebellum Southern mores and eighteenth-century pronunciation, bowing low to Mary Anne and other ladies and greeting them with, "Sarvant, Madam." And besides all this, although Chilton and his family were not yet members of the Stone Christian Church,[50] they were all extremely friendly to its objectives.[51]

Thus, one thing was allowed to lead to another and on September 5, 1821, three months before Chilton's thirty-second birthday and two weeks or so before Mary Anne's sixteenth, the couple were wed and set up housekeeping at Forest Retreat, Chilton's elegant plantation house on Elkhorn Creek. With her marriage Mary Anne thus became mistress of a mansion boasting thirteen rooms, seven "halls," a two-story front porch and a one-story porch in back, "very commodious," as her son remembered it, "and splendidly adapted to the hospitality for which it was famous."[52]

Although the Russell's Cave community was more or less dominated at that time by the Presbyterian Church and its most influential local adherents, the Breckinridge family of "Cabell's Dale" plantation, within two years Mary Anne's father and his preaching colleague Francis Palmer were able to gather a few families into a little Stoneite Christian congregation a few miles from Forest Retreat, which they called Union (now, of course, known better as the *Old* Union) Church. In its first half-dozen or so years of existence the congregation was pastored by Michael and John Rice and Thomas Allen in succession,[53] and in time the larger Moore family and a respectable contingent of their neighbors (slaves too, because they were generally required to attend services with their owners in whatever denomination the owners espoused) adopted Mary Anne's faith tradition and her church community as their own. Not to be outdone, the Breckinridges, who had been accustomed to worship at the Lexington's Second (formerly Associate Reformed, or "Seceder") Presbyterian Church on Market Street, in 1827 themselves founded a small Presbyterian house of worship a few

---

[50] Dates that various members of the Moore family joined Union Church are listed in the church's Record Book 1823-1890, Bosworth Library, LTS.

[51] Moore, *Behind the Bars,* 12, 67.

[52] Ibid., 14.

[53] Huber, 10.

miles from Old Union, which they proudly named Mt. Horeb after the peak of the same name listed in the Old Testament.[54]

Mary Anne herself is listed as the forty-fourth member on Old Union Christian Church's earliest register roll, evidently having transferred her membership from her father's congregation in Georgetown or perhaps from Cane Ridge.[55] She seems to have made this move somewhere around the time that Old Union got its first long-term pastor, John Allen Gano. The grandson and namesake of a hard-bitten pioneer Kentucky Regular Baptist preacher who had believed and contended for every article of Calvinistic Christianity from non-elected infant damnation to the final, eternal perseverance of the elected saints,[56] and whom some Baptists have mythologized as the Revolutionary chaplain who (they allege) immersed the Deistic George Washington and made a good evangelical Calvinist Baptist out of him, John Allen Gano abandoned his grandfather's stern faith after hearing and embracing the kinder, gentler preaching of Barton Stone, and he remained as member and senior pastor of Old Union Church for as long as Mary Anne was connected with it.[57]

Truly, Mary Anne Stone Moore revered her father. But her tumultuous early childhood just might have forced her into a make-or-break mentality in which she learned early to depend on her own wits in order to survive with any peace of mind at all, and with her marriage to the thirty-one year-old landed gentleman Chilton Moore the adolescent Mary Anne shrewdly managed to capture a stable, dependable home life, that very domestic security which circumstances had so often denied her as a child. As her son averred, she was a woman of strong common sense indeed.

---

[54] Breckinridge, *Cabell's Dale,* 37-39.

[55] Old Union Christian Church Record Book, 1823-1892, courtesy Bosworth Library, LTS.

[56] Ibid.; Wolever, 44; Huber, 10. For further information on the elder John Gano's effect on late eighteenth-century and early nineteenth-century Kentucky Baptists, see Wolever, and also Sparks, *Raccoon John Smith,* Chapter 5.

[57] Old Union Christian Church Record Book, 1823-1892, courtesy Bosworth Library, LTS; Huber, 10.

Perhaps needless to say, early nineteenth-century America's Era of Good Feeling was a time of unbridled optimism—however much based on a fallacy the optimism may have been. Virtually everyone, even the politicians and military men who knew better, took it for granted that Andrew Jackson's victory at the Battle of New Orleans in January 1815 had definitively won the War of 1812 for the United States, but in truth the only reason that Jackson and his British opponent, General Sir Edward Pakenham, had ever matched their armies was the inability of their respective governments to communicate efficiently with them. The War had been formally concluded as more or less a draw at Christmastime 1814 with a treaty executed between British and American diplomats at Ghent in Belgium, but in this pre-telegraph, pre-telephone era no one on this side of the Atlantic could even learn about the Treaty of Ghent until after the Battle of New Orleans had been fought. It would be too much to expect that Chilton and Mary Anne Moore themselves did not share in this general misunderstanding. For right or wrong, though, the belief that Jackson had in effect won the War only gave that much more impetus to an already-burgeoning sense of nationalism in the United States, as well as the notion among revival-encouraged white American Christians that America was the veritable city set on a hill that could not be hidden, the special recipient of the blessings of the Lord for being a righteous, pious nation in the center of God's will. If everything hadn't exactly made sense before, events had vindicated the nation and things certainly made perfect sense now.

It was within this worldview that Chilton and Mary Anne Moore reared their children at Forest Retreat. From the record of the tombstones in the small plantation cemetery it would appear that three, Charles S., Mary J. W., and an unnamed, possibly stillborn male, died young,[58] but the first four to survive babyhood were named for their Moore and Stone grandparents: daughters Elizabeth and Hannah, sons William Henley and Barton Warren Stone. Comparatively little is known about these older offspring. It is recorded that Barton Warren Stone Moore died on July 20, 1849 at twenty years of age, and some time in the late fall of 1850 William left Forest Retreat to live in Louis-

[58] Bevins, "Monuments Falling in Cemetery…," *Lexington Herald-Leader,* 7/5/64, 18. Bethany College collection.

ville, where he also died as a young man.[59] Elizabeth married one Robert Clark and is said likewise to have died at a fairly young age after emigrating with her husband, first to California and then to Cuba. Interestingly, though, a seemingly general consensus among genealogists holds that Hannah and her husband, Dr. John de Lafayette Grissom of Georgetown, were the great-grandparents of the twentieth-century billionaire Howard Hughes.[60] Like Adam and Eve, as their son later wryly noted, Chilton and Mary Anne Moore were among the so-called "first families" of their region, and the opportunities given their children reflected the general respect in which the Moores were held.

As Chilton and Mary Anne's family grew and matured, so did Mary Anne's father's religious movement. Beginning in the summer of 1823 the attention of a great many of Barton Stone's younger ministers was captured by an up-and-coming Baptist preacher and writer from the northeast, a Presbyterian proselyte of Irish birth and Scottish Presbyterian and French Huguenot ancestry named Alexander Campbell. Campbell's brand-new, radical *Christian Baptist* newspaper advocated the exact same ideal of simple, non-denominational Christian unity as did Stone's Christian Church, but with a fresh, newly-articulated system of logic—and an enthusiastic, post-War of 1812, Era of Good Feeling-style vengeance. Over time, the baptismal ritual in Stone's churches had evolved from Presbyterian-style sprinkling to the Baptist custom of total immersion; although Stone did not put an extreme doctrinaire stress on the question, he had submitted to the rite himself and now believed and preached that immersion was the correct, Scriptural mode of administering the ordinance. By far the great majority of his followers accepted his position on baptism, although as of yet none had made Baptist-style immersion an all-or-nothing test of their fellowship. All this, plus the traditional way of looking at salvation as per the Great Awakening and the Great Revival, would change once Alexander Campbell's influence began to be felt within Stone's movement.

---

[59] Old Union Christian Church Record Book, 1823-1892, courtesy Bosworth Library, LTS; Huber, 10.

[60] In researching the Moore and Stone family trees on the website *Ancestry.com* I ran across at least four pedigree charts constructed by different genealogists who make this claim, and I see no reason to doubt its veracity.

As a child of the remarkable combination of the Enlightenment, the "Scottish Common Sense Realism" school of philosophy, and an evangelical Presbyterian pastor father who was forever in trouble with his synod because of his ecumenism, Alexander Campbell believed that the Bible, specifically the New Testament beginning most especially with the Acts of the Apostles, ought to be viewed as a virtual scientific blueprint for salvation. The operative word here was *scientific* so long as one accepted a certain type of selective Scriptural literalism as a given, without the need of further proofs other than those that could be found in the natural-theology apologetic tomes of the C. S. Lewis and Josh McDowell, respectively, of their day, the Anglican bishops William Paley and Joseph Butler. The works of these two divines, especially in light of Campbell's as well as Charles Chilton Moore's relation to their thought, must be discussed more fully in succeeding chapters. But to return: Campbell's newspaper advocated a sort of Scottish Common Sense logical system, as it were, imposed on the text of Scripture, a combination of so-called direct commandments, implied propositions, and necessary inferences that he majestically labeled "the Ancient Order" and on which he believed and preached that literally *every* Christian could, and should, agree—even Paley and Butler with whom, in spite of Campbell's dependence on their theological works, he disagreed completely in matters of baptism and church government, among a good many other things.

Considering that Campbell held in extreme, bitter contempt the emotion-based religiosity that had fueled both the Great Awakening and the Great Revival and consequently Barton Stone's religious movement as well, it might be seen as surprising that Stone's younger preachers should have become so captivated with *The Christian Baptist.* By this time, though, Great Revival religiosity had all but trumped every other mode of religious thought in the South, and we must reiterate that the idea of the plenary inspiration of the Bible was once again practically a given that could be stated without further proofs—even those of Paley and Butler. It was quite sufficient for most people to assert that God existed because the Bible said he did, and the Bible couldn't be wrong. Barton Stone himself had played his own part in preaching that the words of Scripture themselves were the vehicle by which the Holy Ghost worked, and thus that the Bible itself, in a sense, brought pardon to sinners. Alexander Campbell, in his newspaper, merely gave this already well-established belief a rationalistic, almost legalistic, tone, and solidified it by two distinctive doctrines: true faith, he argued, was simply no more and no less than the willing reception of Scripture's testimony of the facts of the Gospel, and the rite of baptism by immersion was God's chosen means to convey the results of Christ's death, burial, and resurrection, the remission of sins, to repentant sinners.

Until Campbell, most if not all of the denominations most passionately involved in the Great Awakening and the Great Revival, including Barton Stone both before and after his Christian Church adopted immersion, preached salvation using more or less as a paradigm the biblical story of Cornelius the centurion found in the tenth chapter of the Book of Acts: lost Cornelius receiving divine inspiration to seek the Apostle Peter to hear Gospel preaching, Peter in his turn being given a vision directing him to preach before Cornelius, the Holy Ghost "falling" on Cornelius and his family as Peter spoke, and finally the family submitting to baptism as a testimony that they had received the Holy Ghost during Peter's preaching. In Campbell's mode of logic, this had to have been a miracle that happened only in apostolic times, with no application to modern Gospel preaching, and the doctrine of "justification by faith" that had developed from it was "absurd in theory and false in fact, full of misery, darkness, and doubt."[61] Rather, Campbell viewed Peter's Pentecost speech in the second chapter of Acts, verse 38, exhorting the multitude in Jerusalem to "repent and be baptized every one of you in the name of Jesus Christ for the remission of sins, and ye shall receive the gift of the Holy Ghost," as a far more logical paradigm for the mechanics of salvation. Although his emphasis on immersion for remission of sins waxed and waned back and forth over the years, a great many of his followers, including those within Barton Stone's Christian Church, passionately and permanently committed themselves to this idea.[62]

The early lives of little Elizabeth, Hannah, William, and Barton Moore thus passed largely in a time of further religious controversy among their elders, certainly not as tense a time for their grandfather Stone as the year of their mother's birth had been but yet an era in

---

[61] Hughes, 28.

[62] Ibid.; see also Sparks, *Raccoon John Smith,* Chapter 6.

which Barton Stone and Alexander Campbell and their respective followers nonetheless traded a great many words, sometimes friendly and sometimes not, through the news media. In 1826 Stone started his own church periodical in Georgetown, *The Christian Messenger,* either as a complement to Campbell's *Christian Baptist,* an answer to those questions on which Stone disagreed with Campbell or, equally likely, something of a mixture of both. Stone could not reconcile himself either to Campbell's seeming extreme legalism, the notion that the rite of immersion in and of itself was the complete vehicle for divine pardon, or for that matter, Campbell's overall optimism: in brief, to Campbell, Jesus was coming again because the world was going to get better and better, while to Stone, the Lord was returning because it was getting worse and worse.[63] And for his own part, Campbell never managed to get completely comfortable either with Stone's Christology or his take on the atonement.

But for all this, Stone was more receptive to Campbell's thought than might have been expected for an old-style Great Revival evangelist, certainly more so than he had even been to the preaching of the Shakers—and one reason very well may have been because Campbell never tried to establish the validity of his message by any "spiritual witness" such as both Stoneite Christians and Shakers had attempted to claim for themselves back in 1805, but on a system of seemingly cold, hard, objective logic based on Campbell's view of Scripture truths as "first principles"[64] that Stone could readily accept even if he could not completely appreciate. The Shakers had made him painfully aware that "spiritual witness" was an extremely risky double-edged sword, one that could cut both wielder and opponent, and although Stone always looked back fondly on the good old days of the first blush of the Great Revival he very much agreed with Campbell that the Bible and the Gospel, to be legitimate, had to be settled on a firmer foundation than the mere sensation of emotional intensity. It had even become conceivable to him that the beloved paradigm of salvation found in Acts 10 could be discarded, as long as the paradigm change was beneficial to the advancement of the Kingdom of God on earth.

---

[63] Ibid., 92-116.

[64] Wrather, II, 252, quoting an open letter from Alexander Campbell to Barton Stone.

So may have thought Stone, but as we have indicated in this work's Introduction, the Baptists, whom Campbell still counted technically as his church brethren, were on the whole a lot less yielding to his ideas. At that point in time neither Campbell's Baptist followers nor their traditionalist counterparts possessed the theological language necessary to reconcile the two differing paradigms of salvation that they preached, from Acts 10 as opposed to Acts 2; sadly, many on both sides of the question *still* lack it. Add to that impasse Campbell's bellicose, peppery, sarcastic editorial style in *The Christian Baptist* and its post-War of 1812, Era of Good Feeling-style military imagery, and one had the perfect recipe for an instant, extremely dirty fight. Both Campbell followers and traditionalist Baptists demonized each other, and their conflict escalated until *The Christian Baptist* became the veritable flaming paper bag on the Kentucky Baptists' front porch, the Baptists just getting themselves further and further into messy difficulties as they tried to stamp out the fire while the "Campbellites" looked on from the bushes with appropriate Southern-style coprophagic grins. As late as 1975 one Kentucky Baptist historian felt the need to write that his ancestors in the faith had dealt properly with Alexander Campbell by training all the guns in their arsenal on him and blowing him out of the saddle,[65] and to this day one can still find Baptists, especially in Kentucky, who will gnash their teeth at the mere mention of the name "Campbell" or the titles "Church of Christ" or "Campbellite." On the other side of the coin, though, a good many generations of traditionalist Campbell-influenced preachers and "editor bishops" (the power structure of Campbell's religious movement was such that it was once remarked that his followers didn't have any bishops; they had editors instead[66]) were every bit as prone to misrepresent and disparage the Baptists, other denominations, and even rival Stone-Campbell editors and preachers with whom they differed.[67]

Truth be told, though, Alexander Campbell never was literally blown out of the saddle any more than the Kentucky Baptists ever were

---

[65] Sparks, *Raccoon John Smith,* xvii, quoting Harold G. Sanders. For further information on Alexander Campbell's conflicts with the Kentucky Baptists, see chapters 6-8.

[66] Garrett, 273.

[67] Sparks, *Raccoon John Smith,* 278-281.

the actual victims of a pesky Halloween trick—however much that either side would have liked such fates to befall their respective opponents. Campbell replaced his first newspaper with a second, larger one, which he titled *The Millennial Harbinger* in reference to his firm belief that his "Ancient Gospel" and "Ancient Order" would triumph throughout the world and thus initiate the Millennium, and so long as this vision lasted among his followers his influence continued to grow. Roughly through the years 1829-1831 traditionalist Baptists and "Campbellites" separated themselves from one another all across the settled territories of the eastern United States, with predictable extreme acrimony. That left Campbell's followers, most of whom at first preferred the name of Disciples of Christ, cast adrift from the larger Protestant denominational world, independent congregations with their only formal connection being their mutual presence on Alexander Campbell's mailing list.

It so happened, though, that in Georgetown Barton Stone chanced to make friends with one of Campbell's most popular and capable young preachers, one John Telemachus Johnson, and when Johnson agreed to take the associate editorship of Stone's *Christian Messenger* newspaper the ground was made ready for union between Stone and Campbell groups. Another of Johnson's closest associates was the senior minister of Campbell's Disciples in Kentucky, "Raccoon John" Smith of Mt. Sterling, and thus by New Year's Day 1832 Johnson was able to broker a deal wherein Smith and Stone ceremonially shook hands over the beginnings of a formal union between the Disciples and a majority of Stone's Christians. The Stone-Campbell union took place, and the Stone-Campbell Movement was thus born, before Alexander Campbell, who published his periodicals from his home in Bethany in what is now the northern panhandle of West Virginia, was ever aware that it had occurred. And though the Movement itself has since split at least three ways, into Disciples of Christ, Independent Christian Churches/Churches of Christ, and *a cappella* Churches of Christ, all three of the divisions pay historical homage to Barton Stone and Alexander Campbell alike.[68]

It is not quite certain, however, that in 1832 all of Barton Stone's numerous family members viewed his union with Alexander Campbell

---

[68] See Ibid., *Raccoon John Smith,* Chapters 8-9.

as being altogether productive. The only interpretive recollection of the union that any of Stone's grandchildren left on paper certainly sounds less than completely enthusiastic: "Alexander Campbell came . . . to America and, accepting the distinguishing religious tenets of my grandfather, added to them the doctrine known as 'baptism for the remission of sins' and urged that doctrine with such special force that it, being quite unpopular, attracted much attention, and resulted in the religious body being called 'Campbellites' and in Mr. Campbell taking precedence over my grandfather as the leader in the religious denomination. Stone and Campbell were respectively like Melancthon and Luther in 'The Reformation,' as the new sect was called; my grandfather being mild, gentle, retiring, and unobtrusive, and Mr. Campbell being very ambitious [ellipse added]."[69] In another place, the same grandchild was perhaps even more acerbic: "Born of religious parents, I am the grandson of Barton W. Stone. He has been deeply loved by as many people, perhaps, as any man that has ever lived in [Kentucky]. My understanding is that he was the founder of the 'Christian' or 'Disciples' Church, prominent in [Kentucky] and some surrounding states, and that this distinction was given to Alexander Campbell, because of a quite subsidiary doctrine regarding baptism, the argument concerning which was more appreciable by the masses of the people."[70]

As near as can be ascertained, Barton Moore was a toddler at the time that his grandfather shook hands with Raccoon John Smith over the prospect of a Stone-Campbell union.[71] Only two years later, Barton Stone, his second wife Celia, and all of his children from both marriages with the exception of Mary Anne pulled up stakes permanently from Kentucky and departed to settle in Illinois, primarily because of Stone's strong anti-slavery convictions.[72] The slave-owning Chilton and Mary Anne elected to remain where they were at Forest Retreat in the good old Dog Fennel Precinct, probably with much gladness on Mary Anne's part; now that she enjoyed the security and stable

---

[69] Moore, *Behind the Bars,* 1.
[70] Moore, *The Rational View,* 2.
[71] Ibid., *Behind the Bars,* 138, on the evidence that Barton Moore was seven years older than Charles.
[72] Williams, 202.

home life that she had been denied for so much of her childhood, it is doubtful that even her father could have persuaded her, much less her husband, to give it up for a risky migration. And so finally, with Barton Stone settled northward in Illinois and others of Mary Anne's full sisters and half-brothers and -sisters settled in both that state and westward in Missouri, she and Chilton had four more children: Charles Chilton Jr., born December 20, 1837; Mary Anne, born perhaps a little more than two years afterward; Jane or Jennie, following little Mary Anne by two to four years; and finally, about the year 1850 when her mother was approximately forty-four and her father sixty, the "baby" of the family, Alicia Warren Moore.[73]

Sadly, this last birth occurred a few months to a year after the death of Barton Moore at age twenty. William evidently passed away in Louisville not too many years after this as well, and thus by his early teenage years Charles Jr.—named for a deceased older brother as well as for his father, even as his younger sister Mary Anne had been named for another deceased sibling and her mother—was left as his parents' sole male heir. In the mores of the time, that meant that young Charles could expect to become the squire of Forest Retreat when he reached adulthood. Add to that his relationship with the religious pioneer Barton Stone and his parents'—or at least his mother's—possible consequent spiritual hopes for him as well, and it can be seen that must have known from the earliest that he was expected to fill a rather large pair of shoes.

When his life is examined critically, it can be seen that Charles Chilton Moore Jr. did indeed fill the shoes made ready for him. The direction he took them when he began walking, though, ultimately drove his fellow Kentuckians up the wall backwards.

---

[73] Moore, *Behind the Bars,* 25, 128.

Chapter 2

Back When It All Made Sense

> Ethiopians imagine their gods as black and snub-nosed; Thracians blue-eyed and red-haired. But if horses...had hands, or could draw and fashion works as men do, horses would draw the gods shaped like horses.
>
> —*Xenophanes*

In the heart of the Dog Fennel Precinct of Fayette County, not far from where the property line between Chilton Moore's old Forest Retreat farm and that of the Breckinridges' Cabell's Dale plantation once lay, one lone grave is overshadowed by a massive yet elegant tombstone that somehow captures the essence of the precinct's entire personality. It is inscribed as follows:

Here lies the fleetest runner the American Turf has ever known,
And one of the gamest and most generous of horses
DOMINO

The sleek, spirited, star-crossed stallion named Domino—who in his tragically brief life gained the all-time world record for Thoroughbred race earnings, and maintained it twenty to thirty-odd years until the more famous Man O' War out-earned him—was buried at the edge of the old Breckinridge place in the last days of July 1897, at this writing more than a century ago. And even more than a century before that, this section of present northern Fayette County, Kentucky, was horse country, perhaps the best in the county—which means, many

Fayette Countians would argue, it was, and still is, the best horse country in the world. As such, it has an odd, perhaps unique juxtaposition of influences: rural Kentucky heartland, prime farm and field only a few miles and yet an entire world removed from the contradictory bustle and rush of Lexington, with the whole overlaid by an inescapable aura of flamboyance—the heraldry and pageantry of the horse race. Domino's headstone, which is a far finer monument than can be found in many of the community's cemeteries of human deceased, says it all, and in fact silently declares more. Game and generous the horse was, and had to be. Run so hard that he bowed his tendons early in his career and afterward always had to compete with his hocks and fetlocks in bandages, "terrific tattoos" hammered on his hindquarters in all but one of his races by a brutal jockey whom he consequently hated and tried to attack every time he had the opportunity, Domino lived only six years before succumbing to meningitis.[74] Had he been broken to the lowly plow or even to the sulky harness he might have enjoyed an existence three or four times as long. Such was not the case, though, and his monument sits majestically on Huffman Mill Pike as mute testimony of one tendency Kentuckians seem to share, alas, with the rest of humanity: they often lavish tokens of tender affection and respect upon the dead that they deny to the living.

So here at Forest Retreat and next door to the Breckinridges' Cabell's Dale farm was born Charles Chilton Moore Jr., five days before Christmas 1837. Not only was he heir to the community pageantry of horse racing, the traditions of which sport were well established in the British Isles before America was even settled, but to another sort of pomp and circumstance, the passing of which has become a well-deserved banal cliché: to read Moore's recollections of his childhood is to wonder if Margaret Mitchell used his autobiography and newspaper editorials as source materials for *Gone With the Wind,* even as she is reputed to have used a Lexington whorehouse operator, Belle Brezing, as the real-life basis for her character Madam Belle Watling. In the fall of 1890 Moore offered readers a tongue-in-cheek

---

[74] Jones, "Domino." http://www.thoroughbredchampions.com/biographies/domino.htm; Moore, *Behind the Bars,* 16.

view of the circumstances of his youth, and it carries the side benefit of providing an apt introduction to his writing style, such as it had become:

> In [my young] days when the aristocracy went "calling," they took along their great big leather trunks and spent three or four days. They went in great big carriages, the stomachs of which hung down with a storage capacity that beat anything since the days of the Trojan horse. They were ostensibly intended for only four inside passengers, but they were always jollier when there were two girls and a boy on each seat and the boy was sandwiched between the girls. Sometimes the boy was troubled to know what to do with his arms, so as to keep his elbows from bothering the girls. Sometimes he wasn't. The most intimate male acquaintance I ever had was one of the latter kind.
>
> The motor that propelled one of those big carriages was… two big mules. A big Negro man on the "box" outside held the reins and beside him sat a colored woman to wait on the girls. These carriages left home after an elaborate injunction from the *paterfamilias*… of which the core is, "Don't use the whip, they're ticklish things/ But whatever you do, hold onto the strings." The injunction was always observed until the driver got out of sight of "Ole Marster."
>
> The house and grounds… was, like Washington [D.C.], a place of "magnificent distances." The farm and the yard and the house were all on a big scale. The dominant idea in architecture in those days had as its model a goods box, with a porch as high as the house and about half as big, that was ingeniously constructed with reference to keeping neither sun nor rain off anybody or anything…
>
> In such [houses] as…we have described, large and spacious, and filled with elegant furniture, books, music, family portraits, &c., with Negro slaves, male and female, old and young, *ad libitum,* we were entertained. Every meal, set in the most elegant of china, was a *chef d'oeuvre* of the *cuisine,* and nuts and raisins, and fruits domestic and tropical, set around in the most inviting *neglige,* in silver services to be sampled between meals. But this merely material feature was the smallest part of the entertainment. The host and hostess were most elegant people, and dressed elegantly—"neat and not gaudy," as the monkey said when he painted the cat [all emphases (and spelling puns) in original; ellipses added].[75]

---

[75] Moore, "A Homemade Sunday School Story." *The Blue Grass Blade,* I, 28, October 25, 1890. UK.

In short, though Charles Moore often lampooned his antebellum relatives and neighbors as mere dilettantes in terms of true wealth and culture, all his ridicule could not quite erase the fact that he was of the same Bluegrass planter aristocracy, literally the leisure class. With slaves to wait hand and foot upon his every whim, he never learned nor even had the occasion to acquire the manual skills to do the most basic household, yard, and farm chores until the circumstances of the post-Civil War era forced him to do so.[76] His youth was a far cry from that of his grandfather Stone and even that of his parents, both of whom had had ample opportunities before they ever met to learn to live by their wits. Both then as now, though, fathers and mothers tried to do "the best that they could by their children," and whether in the long run these efforts always turn out entirely beneficial for the children thus favored is a matter of some debate. Long after he had grown to maturity Charles was known even among those he counted as his most trustworthy acquaintances as a man who was not practical in any sense of the word, who gave no thought to prudence, protocol, or policy in anything that he did, and who was so frank and open in his manners that he was a "mere child" where some of the more down-to-earth, prosaic aspects of existence were concerned.[77] In addition, as is obvious from the above example of his writing, he had the habit of making himself sound flippant, as if he took everything lightly and with a peppery dose of contempt. Much of his prose requires a certain degree of thoughtful rereading to ascertain any serious intentions he may have harbored,[78] and his surviving poetry reads as if he were attempting to compete with William Topaz McGonagall for the title of world's worst

---

[76] Ibid., *Behind the Bars,* 128-129.

[77] Ibid., *Behind the Bars,* 176, quoting a newspaper article by Dr. J. B. Wilson of Cincinnati. Moore adds the comment that "it is so evident that [Wilson] is not prejudiced in my favor that it seems to me he says things that are unnecessarily hard on me, and almost unjust to me."

[78] In a previous work *(Raccoon John Smith: Frontier Kentucky's Most Famous Preacher)* I accused Moore of taking his Christianity and his atheism equally lightly. I admit that this was not an entirely fair accusation on my part, but as I have said, much of Moore's writing appears at first glace simply to be flippant.

versifier.[79] Whether these were the particular faults of his upbringing as a rich antebellum Bluegrass planter's sole surviving son is anybody's guess; certainly not all of his childhood playmates grew up to be either as unrealistic or as acerbic as he proved to be, and as we shall see, at least part of Moore's blatant impracticality lay in the irony that, at heart and in his own way, he always insisted on being every bit as much a strict, inflexible moralist as was his grandfather Stone. At least it can be said of Moore that he tried to prepare his own three sons and his surviving daughter for a more rational, no-nonsense world than he had known in his own younger days.

Charles Chilton Moore's childhood thus may be characterized within a too-well-known stereotype, or perhaps even two separate stereotypes, but nonetheless we may be able to fill his story out just a little with a few vignettes demonstrating the particular Kentucky-gentry culture in which he grew up. He recalled a boyhood memory of hearing the family's slaves sing the old spiritual "As I Went Down in the Valley to Pray,"[80] since popularized by the Coen Brothers' movie *O Brother, Where Art Thou,* and another of having seen his father let his

---

[79] Moore includes a few samples of his poetry in *Behind the Bars.* Much of it was written as advertising copy for a coffee company for whom he worked as a traveling salesman in between stints of journalism and farming, under the sophomoric pen name of Perry P. Tetik. Perhaps a verse each from two of his poems (the first from *Behind the Bars,* 163, and the second from his college's literary magazine) will suffice for us to let him stand as a challenge to McGonagall's supremacy, such as it is, without including any more of his poems in the main body of this work:

> Then Jones, like a Christian, gentleman, scholar,
> Put his hand in his pocket and pulled out a dollar,
> Which bought him five pounds [of coffee], that's the lowest figger,
> And had it sent round to his house by a nigger.
>
> Mysterious things had long foretold some dire, calamitous event,
> And Superstition, child of mountain home, had bound with mystic hands in one consent
> The minds of those upon whose hearth she familiar sat—a welcome guest.
> And all agreed that many portent signs some evil, yet unseen to man, expressed.
> The eerie bairntime o'dearies, glow'ring to the anxious mither, come;
> While the father tightens the horse-shoe o'er the door of his mountain home.

[80] Moore, *Dog Fennel,* 177.

little sister Mary "ride horsie" on the father's shin while the old gentleman recited the ancient but well-known Banbury Cross nursery rhyme to her.[81] Moore's earliest male playmates, though, were the grandsons and great-grandsons of daunting, redoubtable old Mary "Polly" Cabell Breckinridge, family matriarch and mother and grandmother to two Presbyterian ministers and an entire gaggle of Kentucky politicians. Her home, the famous Cabell's Dale, had been named in her honor by her late husband, the first John Breckinridge, and it was bordered not only by the Moore farm but by the homes of several of her sons and daughters. Among the grandchildren about the same age as young Charles and Mary were William Campbell Preston Breckinridge, whom Charles always called Billy, and his brother Robert; one about the ages of Charles' brothers Barton and William was John Cabell Breckinridge, later Vice President under James Buchanan and candidate for the Presidency against Abraham Lincoln. Polly's great-grandchildren included John J. and Fannie Castleman, grandchildren of David and Mary Ann (Breckinridge) Castleman who had been given a handsome portion of Cabell's Dale as a wedding present; they had bestowed the name of Castleton upon this part of the plantation, and under this title it became, and still remains, one of the most famous of all Bluegrass horse farms. It was here that Domino spent his final months at stud, after retiring from racing.

The old lady Breckinridge was often called "Grandma Black Cap" (behind her back, of course) by her grandchildren, because of her habit of wearing a mourning headdress, and she maintained her position in both family and community with an iron fist in a lace glove.[82] For all the Breckinridge clan's accumulated land and wealth, though, the old woman insisted on keeping hers and her long-deceased husband's first log home standing in Cabell's Dale's front yard, and although in Charles' youth it was used merely as a slave dwelling Mrs. Breckinridge would still enthrall her grandchildren and great-grandchildren and their friends with tales of the days of a very young United States of America, when the senior John Breckinridge was Thomas Jefferson's Attorney General and she had entertained Vice President Aaron Burr and Chief Justice John Marshall in that simple old house.

---

[81] Ibid., *Behind the Bars,* 106.
[82] Heck, 2-5.

Anyway, as next-door neighbors Mary Anne Moore and Polly Breckinridge observed a time-honored custom still extant among Kentucky families in some rural areas: they gave one another small presents from time to time such as fresh fruit or produce from their respective gardens in the summer, a helping of "cracklins" after a hog killing, and what not, and once in a while each came up with a special present for any young ones in the other's family. Charles remembered that, when he was very small, the old lady Breckinridge gave him and his sister Mary little tin plates engraved around their outside edges with the alphabet, and that it was by this gift that he first learned his letters. Unlike most Kentuckians both then and now, however, Polly and Mary Anne for the most part did not exchange these gifts personally, but rather sent them to one another by their respective servants.

It came to trouble Mary Anne that on occasion Polly Breckinridge's presents to her and her family seemed to go past customary generosity to the point of being prodigal. On some days a Breckinridge slave would show up at the house two or three different times with treats for the Moores to eat, once even with a sizable helping of oysters which, at that time, were extremely hard to procure in Kentucky and were consequently frightfully expensive. By the time Charles was born Mrs. Breckinridge was nearly seventy and blind, so Mary Anne simply thought that the older woman was becoming absentminded and careless of how much she gave away. She went to see Mrs. Breckinridge and delicately attempted to introduce her concern, but at Mary Anne's barest, most diplomatically-phrased hint that she might be growing just a tad forgetful the old lady drew herself up imperiously, every inch the proud Kentucky pioneer mother she had been in her youth, and retorted, "I am blind, Madam, but thank God, I am not a fool, and if you will just attend to your own business, I will try to attend to mine!"

Her cheeks burning with humiliation and the sting of the rebuke, Mary Anne fled home undoubtedly thinking that she had committed an unpardonable social breach. She soon found out that this was not the case, however: treats and presents kept coming to Forest Retreat from the bounty of Polly Breckinridge's table as if no exchange of insults whatsoever had taken place, and the proud old lady continued the practice right up until her death at age 89 in 1858.[83]

---

[83] Moore, *Behind the Bars,* 14-19.

Another story of Charles Moore's childhood involves his father's brother John, and John's slaves. Let me apologize in advance for its appearance here. There is no way to relate an antebellum slavery story as it would have been perceived by a young boy raised from birth in the Southern planter class and in the common natives' perception of Kentucky-as-Camelot as noted in the previous chapter, without the tale's sounding unbelievably crass and condescending to modern ears. At any rate, in a day and time when some Kentucky planters took pride in being strict with their slaves while others preferred the reputation of being kind masters, John Moore fell squarely within the latter category while another neighbor was in the former. It so happened that, one fall day, John's slaves were all engaged in cutting and shocking fodder, and they had happened to bring the plantation's pack of hounds to the fields with them. Suddenly one of the hounds jumped a rabbit and began to run it; the entire work force in turn dropped their corn knives and followed the hounds, just at the time that the neighbor came riding by. Bristling with indignation, the neighbor stopped off at John's house to inform him that his field hands had all dropped their work to run a rabbit, but John laughed the matter off, retorting, "If they hadn't done it, I would have whipped every rascal of them!"

Many years later, Charles Chilton Moore would accuse the noted Kentucky author James Lane Allen of plagiarizing this anecdote from him in a short story. Apparently Allen, a Fayette County native a decade or so younger than Charles and who knew the Moore family well, had come by the farm, fallen into conversation about his beginning career in writing, and wound up collecting several of Moore's memories about "the best sides and the worst sides" of slavery.[84] Later on, Moore claimed that he found his uncle John's rabbit tale in *Harper's Magazine* as one of the first of Allen's published pieces, and thereafter he had very little that was good to say about his fellow Kentucky writer. He saved especial, Puritanical (and therefore extremely ironic) vitriol for Allen's famous novel *The Choir Invisible,* the story of unfulfilled romantic love between a young single schoolmaster and an older, married woman in pioneer-era Kentucky, as being "the most demoralizing book in America" because it "romanticized illicit relation[s] between the sexes," leaving its readers "in no sense advanced, morally or

---

[84] Ibid., 21-22.

intellectually."[85] Adding to the irony of the whole story of his relationship with Allen are the fact that he gave *The Choir Invisible* this scathing assessment only after falling foul of the law for writing an essay that gave at least the appearance of being sympathetic to such an unconsummated romantic relationship as the book described,[86] and the distinct possibility that Allen, in his own turn, developed the character of David, the earnest young preacher-turned-freethinker in his later novel *The Reign of Law,* in no small degree from Moore's own real-life example.

A third sketch from Charles Moore's childhood involves both his uncle John and his father, the War of 1812 and its aftermath, the concepts of Southern honor, chivalry, and hospitality—and a complete stranger by the name of Parker Craig Nicholson. Nicholson was one more permanent fixture of Charles' childhood. According to the story as Moore had heard it from his father and uncles, one day about the year 1816 Nicholson simply showed up at John Moore's doorstep with a horse or two and a grip of clothing, seeking a meal and a bed. He said that he hailed originally from "Jersey" (New Jersey, Moore assumed) and had been battle companions in Ontario during the War of 1812 with John's brothers Thomas and Chilton. Naturally John, who himself had not gone away to the Canadian campaigns, took Nicholson at his word and invited him to "light and be easy," as the saying went in those days. Nicholson was an interesting conversationalist and he and John talked the evening away, resumed their discussions over the breakfast table the next morning, talked again until lunchtime and returned to the dining room without breaking their conversation—and so it went for the better part of a week, until John invited Nicholson to come with him to a public sale that was being held somewhere in the Dog Fennel Precinct. Here John introduced Nicholson to his parents and brothers and got a couple of sudden, rude shocks. For one thing, though the Moore brothers were too well-bred to make a scene about it, neither Chilton nor Thomas Moore could remember anything whatsoever about Nicholson from their days of military service; then, as if that revelation were not unsettling enough, when another neighbor asked Nicholson

---

[85] Ibid., 118-119.

[86] See the *Blue Grass Blade,* VI, 52, October 3, 1897.

where he lived, he replied, as if it had been established as a matter of general consensus, "At Captain John Moore's, sir."

"Major" Nicholson (like the character of the Judge in William Saroyan's *The Oyster and the Pearl,* he said he was one and evidently nobody ever checked his story out; after all, it *was* Kentucky, where colonels, if not majors, were and are thicker than average in other states) stayed with John Moore for the next forty years, until his death on March 7, 1856.[87] After Chilton and Mary Anne married and set up housekeeping at Forest Retreat, the Major would come to spend a few days with them every two or three weeks, and he arranged to keep his fine, blooded saddle mares in Chilton's barn. The sale of these mares' colts provided him with a little spending money, though so far as Charles could ever ascertain, the Major never paid one red cent for his board at John Moore's nor for stabling his horses at Chilton's. Though he spoke so often of returning to "Jersey" that it became a running joke among Charles and his siblings and cousins, Major Nicholson made only one actual attempt to do, and even then he seems to have changed his plans and fled back to the collective bosom of northern Fayette County and the Moores after only one or two months. Nicholson even joined the Moores' church at Old Union and he was buried in the churchyard, and at his death and in the disposition of his personal estate the family learned that he had managed to sell enough colts over the years to save up $800 in a Lexington bank.[88]

Who, indeed, *was* "Major" Parker Craig Nicholson, why did he think he had the right to impose on the Moores' hospitality to the point that they virtually adopted him—and more significantly, why did the Moores all accept such an imposition without question, at least any that they dared utter out loud? The only actual, verifiable record of Nicholson's military service in the War of 1812 places him as a private soldier, not an officer, in the company of Captain George Trotter in Colonel James Simrall's Regiment of Kentucky Light Dragoons (an archaic term for mounted infantry) between August 27 and October 31, 1812—a two-month enlistment. Thomas Parke Dudley, brother of Charles and Thomas Moore's Colonel William Dudley, was in this

---

[87] Moore, *Behind the Bars*, 11-12; Old Union Christian Church Record Book, 1823-1892, LTS.

[88] Moore, *Behind the Bars*, 12.

same company with Nicholson, as was a Riding Master named John Moore and another private named Thomas P. Moore,[89] but neither of these Moores had any known connection with Charles's father or uncles. One possibility is that Nicholson came to Dog Fennel looking for either or both of the Moores he had known in his company of mounted infantry, and was too proud to admit his mistake once he settled in with Charles's uncle John. In turn, under the rules of Southern hospitality the Russell's Cave Moores might not have dared to voice the possibility to Nicholson that he had made such a misstep. We will never know all the answers. To young Charles and his siblings and cousins the Major was simply *there,* perhaps like Penelope's suitors in *The Odyssey* or, to indulge in a couple of anachronisms, Jimbob Buel in Richard Bradford's *Red Sky At Morning* or Richard Brautigan's Kool-Aid Wino who was able to create his own reality and illuminate himself by it—and that was that. Regardless either of Nicholson's integrity or the lack thereof, chivalry demanded that the Moores take "the Major's" word at face value and that they continue to extend their generosity to him so long as he deigned to accept it. Though the days of Southern gentility may be (to squeeze one last drop of juice out of our banal cliché) gone with the wind, the mysteries surrounding some of the particulars of old-style Southern etiquette remain like sore thumbs sticking out of our history—every bit as enigmatic as the mores of Homer's Greeks.

Charles Chilton Moore noted that his father loved the works of Charles Dickens,[90] and in fact the older man seems to have built a stone guest house on the Forest Retreat plantation that the family even called, in the fashion of good Dickens fans, Bleak House.[91] In truth Moore's own writing style reveals this same influence to a certain extent. In Charles' stories of Polly Breckinridge, John Moore, and Major Nicholson one can fairly see the Dickensian small boy gazing up in gentle bemusement at the ostensibly benign eccentricities of his elders, much like David Copperfield with Mr. Dick and Miss Trotwood or Pip with Miss Havisham and her retinue of patronage. Of course, there was the unavoidable darker side to life in the antebellum Bluegrass: "the worst," as Moore himself used the term in speaking with James Lane

---

[89] Hill, 34-35.
[90] Moore, *Behind the Bars,* 2.
[91] Ibid., 144.

Allen, of slavery, the political arguments that had so many Kentucky planters forever challenging one another to fights and duels, and church scandals which, alas, appear to have changed little in character not only from the time of either Martin Luther's or Alexander Campbell's Reformations but all the way back to the days of the ancient pagan Celsus. Moreover, a scrap of evidence indicates that Charles himself may not have been raised with the kind of consistent, thoughtful discipline of which his grandfather Stone would have approved: he once observed that, whereas in his youth the saying had been "spare the rod and spoil the child," in his old age the maxim seemed to have been reversed to "spare the child and spoil the rod."[92] Too, he recalled a bitter memory of being taught the doctrine of hell as a child and weeping in utter terror at its prospect.[93] Notwithstanding either the temporary damnation of the woodshed or the eternal damnation of a burning hell, though, to his boyish eyes the 1840s and 1850s and the Dog Fennel Precinct were by and large still snugly tucked within the warm, womblike folds of the Era of Good Feeling, with God in his heaven; all, free and slave alike, in their proper stations on earth; the plan of salvation articulated by his grandfather and Alexander Campbell and which described the appropriate, reasonable relations and interactions between the heavenly and earthly realities, as plain as the nose on one's face; and where everything, all of it, made perfect sense.

Barton Stone visited Kentucky for the last time in the summer of 1843. He had returned to the state briefly in May 1840 to attend the first scheduled statewide meeting of Kentucky Disciples in Harrodsburg,[94] but he was back this time to try to provide a mediating force, and perhaps an example, to several entities that he perceived were rending his beloved Stone-Campbell Movement with discord. In his newspaper, Stone only spoke of these tempests in generalities. It seemed to him that more attention was being given to making converts than to teaching them how to live holy lives once they had been immersed, and that evangelists were being glorified over pastors though the work of both was equally important. He alleged that many of the

---

[92] Ibid., 22-23.
[93] Moore, *The Rational View,* 8.
[94] Fortune, 206.

male Disciples he observed were so worldly-minded that, just as soon as church services were over—sometimes, exactly like the Baptists from whom Alexander Campbell's contingent of the Disciples had split, after not only one long, tiring sermon but several—they made a beeline for their hats and clapped them on their heads right in the house of God, a practice Stone found to be inexcusably disrespectful if not sacrilegious. Worst of all, during the rite of the Lord's Supper he observed all too many church members sitting and gossiping idly with one another even while the elements of Holy Communion were being passed around by the deacons. All things considered, it seemed to him that Kentucky Disciples—or Christians, to use his own preferred term—were getting too worldly, comfortable and extravagant, and in the young people especially he noticed an alarming lack of "sobriety."[95]

But there may have been other, more serious matters that Stone had to consider, for which such generalized complaints could have served at least partially as a cover. Some years before, a ferocious quarrel had erupted among Montgomery County, Kentucky, Disciples over a Congressional election. The brother-in-law of prominent Mt. Sterling Disciple Kenaz Farrow, a judge and attorney named Richard French, ran for the House of Representatives on the Democratic ticket unsuccessfully against a political novice of the Whig party named Richard Hickman Menefee. Young Menefee, likewise an attorney and who subsequently gained the reputation of being one of the greatest orators that Kentucky ever produced, was the preferred candidate of Kentucky Disciple pioneer Raccoon John Smith, the very man whose hand Stone had shaken at the beginning of the Stone-Campbell union on New Year's Day 1832—and also, unfortunately, the Farrow family's pastor.

A pre-election fight of either a secular or religious nature was bad enough on its own, but even after the victorious Menefee went away to Washington the ill feeling between the Farrows and Smith had festered, ultimately causing a split in the Mt. Sterling Christian Church. Not long after the division, another minister came forward to lead the disaffected Farrow faction of Mt. Sterling's Disciples, a younger preacher with a background in the churches of Stone's side of the union and whose name was James McVay. The stage was thus set for a good old-fashioned

---

[95] Williams, 246-247, quoting several of Stone's articles in issues of *The Christian Messenger* during the fall of 1843.

prophets' war between Smith and McVay, and it had continued, with increasing bitterness, right up to and including most of the year 1843—ironically, two years past the tragic death from tuberculosis of young Richard Menefee, the ostensible causative agent of the entire mess.

In detailing this particular fight we must keep in mind that, though Barton Stone and his Christians had in times past utilized certain basic organizational structures such as presbytery boards and local conference assemblies for simple administrative convenience, Alexander Campbell had convinced most of Stone's flock as well as all his own, who were by and large ex-Baptists fed up with the political machinations of their former denomination's own local associations, that such entities were without Scriptural precept and therefore unwarranted. Thus it had turned out that in the new, united Stone-Campbell denomination, the only forum in which an erring or controversial preacher could be cited and censured was the local church itself. However, in cases such as the Smith-McVay war where churches had split into factions over a preacher or neighboring congregations disagreed with each other in ways beyond the capability of individual local church government to control, the denomination's principal periodicals, Campbell's *Millennial Harbinger* and Stone's *Christian Messenger,* had by necessity been forced into the void once occupied by Stone's and the Baptists' presbytery boards, associations, and conferences for the maintenance of denominational discipline. Once the Smith and McVay factions of Mt. Sterling's Disciples of Christ had gone to battle with one another, *The Millennial Harbinger* had been the first forum by which the Stone-Campbell Movement at large had become aware of the conflict, via an angry letter from Raccoon John Smith five long years after the fracas had begun.

In his missive Smith accused McVay of a myriad of charges including sanctimonious, affected hypocrisy, horse swindling, sexual immorality, and even of having had his nose nearly bitten off in a fight (which, considering frontier and antebellum Kentucky manners, was probably quite true). Campbell printed the entire thing along with a request for the movement's other "Editor Bishops" including Barton Stone, Arthur Crihfield, John R. Howard, and Walter Scott to republish the charges in their own periodicals.[96] Stone refused to take the

---

[96] Letter of John Smith to Alexander Campbell in *The Millennial Harbinger,*

bait, however. Rather than joining in wholeheartedly with Smith and Campbell's condemnations, he merely announced briefly in *The Christian Messenger* that Smith and Campbell had *accused* McVay of being a bad man and referred interested readers to the *Harbinger's* past issues for further information.[97] We cannot say whether Stone was attempting a subtle defense of one of his ministers against the political power of Campbell and Smith here, or whether he had simply gotten tired of being pushed around by the more aggressive Campbell and his likewise combative minions. Nonetheless, in those days as later, unless all the journals and periodicals of the Stone-Campbell Movement (or any branch thereof) pronounced a unified, identical anathema against an individual, group, or church perceived as errant, disagreement about the alleged heretic or heretics would continue and, as often as not, exacerbate. And with the publication of Stone's neutral, bare recitation of Smith and Campbell's accusation against McVay in the *Messenger,* so it went with the Smith-McVay war until Stone arrived in Kentucky for that last visit—and unfortunately, beyond.

After the first newspaper article and notice were published Raccoon John tried to bring charges against McVay at the historic Cane Ridge meetinghouse, the site of the beginning of the Great Revival in the Bluegrass. Though he spent two whole days reciting his accusations to the Cane Ridge congregation with all the dogged vigor of an old mossbacked backcountry Baptist associational clerk, most of the charges rolled right off McVay and the accused preacher left the house making genial announcements for his subsequent speaking appointments. At the "Editor/Bishop" end of the difficulty Alexander Campbell then tried to calm the tumult with a recitation of the errors of both Smith and McVay, but when that didn't work he came out once again as a furious Smith partisan in two more articles in *The Millennial Harbinger;* without Stone's endorsement, though, all he managed to accomplish was to split Smith's flock further and alienate some of his own erstwhile partisans.

The whole sordid affair reached its climax, if it could be called that, in November 1843 just as Raccoon John readied himself to assist

---

11, No. 11 (November 1841); 536, DCHS. See Sparks, *Raccoon John Smith,* 355-356.

[97] *The Christian Messenger,* 12, No. 2, December 1841; see Sparks, *Raccoon John Smith,* 357-358.

Campbell in a major doctrinal debate against Presbyterian minister Nathan L. Rice in Lexington. As was usual for him, Smith put his church affairs over even the most pressing domestic concerns, and he had arranged for his wife, some hired laborers, and perhaps one of his older sons to butcher some hogs in his absence. In a freak accident his youngest son, seven year-old Richard Menefee Smith, slipped and fell into a wash pot of boiling-hot water to be used for "scalding" the hair off the hogs, and was burned to death. The little boy suffered absolutely unimaginable agonies during the last eight hours of his life, but surprisingly, this unspeakably cruel tragedy wouldn't have been seen by most of Raccoon John's acquaintances as any sort of circumstance to cast doubt on either God's existence or his benevolence. Rather, it would have been viewed by all but the most courageous objective thinkers as a judgment by God against Smith; in other words, for God to "take a child" in such a brutal way as he had obviously taken the little boy Richard, Raccoon John had to have been wrong and James McVay must have been right. The horrible irony in all of this was the fact that, long years before, Raccoon John had already created a theodicy for himself in which he viewed the deaths of at least two, and possibly as many as four or five, of his children as messages from God that he had better get himself away from the Baptists and join up with Alexander Campbell's movement as the veritable restored New Testament Church of Christ. With the sordid climax of the McVay controversy, Raccoon John's children's deaths became the breaking, as well as the making, of his Bluegrass ministry. After half a dozen years or so Smith was able to pick up a few of the pieces of his shattered vocation, but other than serving as the figurehead Grand Old Man of the Kentucky Disciples he was never quite the same again.[98]

To return to our story, though, at the time of Barton Stone's return to Kentucky in the summer of 1843 this dirty little church war would have been in its brightest, and most malodorous, bloom. As we have outlined, Campbell's *Millennial Harbinger* featured articles detailing its warp and woof in no less than three issues between November 1842 and September 1843. The first piece tried to be neutral and balanced; the second and third were vigorously and even rabidly pro-Smith, but the paper and its editor were decidedly silent about the affair after the

---

[98] See Sparks, *Raccoon John Smith,* 348-371.

horrible hog-killing accident. There can be no doubt that news of the fracas was all over the Bluegrass at the very time Stone was attempting to enjoy a little peace and joy of the Holy Spirit among his old Kentucky neighbors. Six year-old Charles Chilton Moore was, of course, unaware that anything remiss was going on; thankfully, church scandals are mostly lost on children. The only memories he retained of Stone from this, the only period he was ever in his grandfather's company, was an occasion when he observed the aged Stone smoking a corncob pipe on the front porch of Forest Retreat, and one more in which he watched his father count out a quantity of silver dollars into the old man's hand as a gift.[99] The venerable old pioneer preacher was gathered to his reward a year later while visiting another daughter, Amanda, in Hannibal, Missouri.

The Dog Fennel Precinct had its secular scandals as well, some of which could not be hidden away quite in the manner of the Smith/McVay controversy but a great many of which involved the bizarre, schizophrenic union of evangelical Christianity and the Southern code of honor that represented Kentucky culture of the day—God and country, as it were. As an example we may speak here of the famous fight between the noted abolitionist newspaper editor Cassius Marcellus Clay and Samuel M. Brown, a partisan of Clay's political opponent Robert Wickliffe Jr. and who may have been a paid thug of Wickliffe's. This battle took place during a public debate at Russell's Cave Spring between the Democrat Wickliffe and Whig politician Garrett Davis, on the first of August of the very same year of Barton Stone's last visit to the Moores. Brown apparently became furious at Clay for standing up and voicing an uninvited, impromptu rebuttal to one of Wickliffe's statements, and he called Clay a liar, pulled a pistol, and shot him in the chest. Luckily for Clay, who was a Baptist at least in name,[100] the bullet hit a silver knife case in his coat pocket and he suffered only a bruise, but once he had a legitimate excuse to defend himself he took no time to ponder either the inscrutable will of Providence or the vagaries of time and chance—or to wait for Brown to shoot again. He pulled his Bowie knife and before he was done with Brown, his now thoroughly repentant assailant was missing an eye, an

---

[99] Moore, *Behind the Bars,* 1.
[100] Richardson, 22.

ear, a portion of his scalp right down to the bone and perhaps even a little past, and his nose had been slit almost in two. Finally Brown fainted from loss of blood, and the stalwart Clay picked up his attacker's limp body, carried it to the edge of the field, and tossed it down the bank of Elkhorn Creek before he himself even became aware that his own pocket knife case had saved him from a mortal wound.

Whether Clay's survival of the brawl could have been called a miracle from heaven or Old Scratch looking after his own, Brown's recovery was certainly no less astonishing—but it actually happened, though of course Brown had an extremely long convalescence and even then could never look in a mirror again without thinking of Cassius Clay. He subsequently died in a steamboat explosion. As for Cassius, the heavily Democratic Fayette County grand jury indicted him for mayhem even though Brown had attacked him first. He called on the services of his more famous cousin Henry as his defense attorney, who adroitly argued that Cassius was only acting in self-defense against stacked odds—and that had he not done so, he "would not have been worthy of the name he [bore]." Cassius Clay was a Baptist, Henry subsequently an Episcopalian, and both were Whigs politically, but in the courtroom that day defendant, lawyer, judge, and jurymen all embraced and rejoiced in the Kentuckian religion and the Kentuckian party, as it were, instead. Thus whether on the basis of the legitimacy of the defense, his skill with the knife, or Henry Clay's crowd-pleasing and eloquent closing argument, Cassius was acquitted.[101]

One wonders how a boy not quite six years old would have viewed the Clay-Brown knife and pistol fight. This, if not the more discreet and elegant backstabbing of the Smith-McVay war, could hardly have escaped his notice. Adults—males at least—in the Russell's Cave community all admired Cassius Clay for standing up for his positions even if they didn't agree with his abolitionist philosophy. Perhaps his Bowie knife itself simply inspired their respect, philosophy or not. Thus to little Charles Chilton Moore, the Russell's Cave Spring knife fight may have been just one more Dickensian scenario in which the zany antics of the adults in his life were simply the norm for him. Still, even then Charles was not too young to begin to become aware of one fact: in both the religious and secular aspects of his world, editors of

---

[101] Ibid., 35-39; Smiley, 61-63; Moore, *Behind the Bars,* 18.

periodicals were crusaders, prophets, agents of positive change, even heroes. His grandfather was a periodical editor; so was the old man's swashbuckling junior partner Alexander Campbell, and so was Cassius Clay, who wielded pen and knife with equal skill. Even if one didn't agree with all the convictions espoused by an editor, one could still admire the courage of those convictions and the intellect that articulated them. One of Charles Chilton Moore's first memorable impressions had to have been that the position of editor was among the noblest to which he could aspire.

Charles' first formal schooling began perhaps two years after these events, in a log building known as Valley School House and about a mile and a half from Forest Retreat. He was not sent to school until he was eight years of age, but he had already learned his letters in part due to old Mrs. Breckinridge's gift and it's likely that his parents had given him at least some informal tutoring beforehand. Surprisingly enough, at this school, students from families both rich and poor mingled as equals, and Charles recalled one incident in which he took a young classmate named Ed Grimes all the way home for lunch because the boy was from a poor family and couldn't bring a lunch to school. The three-mile round trip to and from the Forest Retreat kitchen made them extremely late for afternoon "books," but as Charles remembered it, the schoolmaster punished neither him nor young Grimes: Kentucky hospitality was, after all, an institution all on its own, and it is highly likely that the teacher understood Charles's motive.[102]

A few years later, the Breckinridge family founded a school on the Cabell's Dale lands, mostly for the benefit of their own kinfolk and connections and which they called the Fort Hill Academy. "Fort Hill" was, apparently, the site of a prehistoric Indian mound with a moat-like ditch all the way around it, and the schoolhouse sat right in the middle of the circle inscribed by the ditch. Charles transferred from Valley School House to this new location, and his teacher was a young man named Samuel Barton, naturally under the patronage of the Breckinridges and teaching school to earn his bread while he studied for the Presbyterian ministry. Fort Hill Academy may have been a bit more exclusive, if not more exacting, than the community school, although

---

[102] Moore, *Behind the Bars,* 23-24.

Charles remembered at least one poor boy, Samuel Sloan, attending there as well. He was, or at least could claim to be, a cousin of the late President William Henry Harrison, however, so his lineage may have been a factor in his admittance to the Breckinridge's academy. Charles himself was more of an idiosyncrasy in this setting: he was the only student from a Stone-Campbell Disciple family in a houseful of little Presbyterians and under a Presbyterian schoolmaster. Charles's playmates would often call him "Campbellite," sometimes in harmless jest and at other occasions with the common schoolyard cruelty one always finds in children when enough of them are thrown together long and closely enough to establish a pecking order. In years to come he wrote tongue-in-cheek of his Fort Hill Academy days as his first experience as a religious martyr.[103]

One reason that Charles' young Breckinridge schoolfellows may have taunted him during these years was that the Moore family became, if it were possible, even more involved in worship at Old Union Church than they had before. We have noted that Charles' mother, Mary Anne, was one of the congregation's earlier members, and beginning in 1841, roughly coinciding with the births of two more daughters Mary Anne and Jane, her husband and older children started to follow enthusiastic suit. The oldest surviving daughter, Hannah, was immersed and joined the church in May 1841; she was followed on July 14, 1842 by her brother Barton, and a month after that, on August 13, the Moore patriarch Chilton finally submitted to immersion. Sadly, old Barton Stone had no occasion to immerse any of his family members during his last visit to Kentucky in 1843, but Elizabeth Moore was baptized on February 9, 1845, then William on November 14, 1846, and finally Hannah's suitor and later husband, John deLafayette Grissom, on October 14, 1847. In between the baptisms of William Moore and John Grissom, at the Old Union Church's December 1846 business meeting, Chilton Moore was appointed along with Jacob Sidener as an elder in the church[104]; among Bluegrass Disciple congregations this meant that he assumed the obligation to oversee the congregation's temporal affairs, as well as to deliver short discourses and Scripture readings for mid-

---

[103] Ibid., 25.

[104] Old Union Christian Church Record Book, 1823-1892, courtesy Bosworth Library, LTS.

week prayer services[105] and perhaps in emergencies when Pastor John Allen Gano had to be absent. Thus at age nine, Charles found himself not only the grandson of a preacher, but the son of one as well—at least in a minor way.

But of course, there were griefs too. We have noted that Barton Moore died at about the age of twenty on July 20, 1849. Considering that Chilton and Mary Anne Moore's three lost children most likely had been born and died before Charles's birth and that his grandfather Stone had died far away in Missouri, Barton's sudden and unexpected demise—we do not know its cause—may have been eleven year-old Charles's, as well as little Mary and Jane's, first real experience with losing a loved one. Apparently Barton and Charles had been extremely close despite the difference in their ages. Charles recalled stealing away to the guest room at Forest Retreat normally reserved for Major Nicholson on his regular visits, and weeping there the entire afternoon after Barton breathed his last. A deathwatch beetle hidden in the windowsill kept mournful cadence the while.[106] Naturally, though, the entire family tried to take comfort where they could, in the fact that young Barton had lived and died a Christian.

The autumn of the following year, October 27, 1850 to be exact, William Moore "took his church letter" away from Old Union in preparation for his move to Louisville[107]—and all too soon returned home again in a coffin, to be buried near his brother Barton and his smaller siblings in the family cemetery. In this case, Chilton and Mary Anne's grief might have been eased just a fraction with the birth of their youngest child Alicia, occurring in the very same year of William's departure from home. As far as can be ascertained, Charles never wrote anything about William, his life, or his death, and we are left to wonder if some scandal might have precluded Charles's and the family's mention of his memory. It's hard to say either way. Nonetheless, it is fairly certain that by the mid-1850s young Charles had become the heir apparent of Forest Retreat, with all the dignities and privileges appointed thereto, and for better or worse, he began to be treated accordingly.

---

[105] Moore, *Behind the Bars,* 108-109. Moore spoke of "the average elder's prayer-meeting talk in Kentucky."
[106] Ibid., 138.
[107] Old Union Christian Church Record Book, 1823-1892, courtesy Bosworth Library, LTS.

In the summer of 1852 Chilton and Mary Anne imported a governess and tutor for their fourteen year-old son and two pre-teen daughters, a New York native named Arlotta Maria Bass. Harriet Beecher Stowe's *Uncle Tom's Cabin* had just been published that March, and Charles recalled that Miss Bass brought a copy of it with her to read on her journey south. By the time she reached Forest Retreat she had become something of an abolitionist herself, but at least in Charles's memory the kindness with which his father and his uncle John treated their slaves tempered her anti-slavery zeal considerably. She may have simply succumbed to the already-noted Kentucky-as-Camelot perception which the Moores and other Kentucky slave-owners worked so hard to give to out-of-state visitors. Miss Bass not only gave the Moore children their lessons, but Chilton and Mary Anne allowed her to accept two more students from the community, Sarah Smith and Elizabeth Herndon, whom they let room and board with their own daughters.

In this setting, Charles received most of what we would now call his secondary education, and passed from childhood through adolescence into young manhood. Under Miss Bass's tutelage he studied history, Latin, French, English literature, and a bit of Greek, learned to play the flute and the piano, and the meanwhile seems to have flirted more than a little with both his fellow students and his teacher.[108] Most boys of his social class in Fayette County tended to be stylish and even gaudy dressers, and from Charles' own description of his clothes we might wonder if he made a habit of wearing horse racing silks for leisure dress: his favored garments included a black cap made of silk and velvet[109] and a bright red flannel suit with matching cap and shoes that, by his own admission, made him look almost like Faust's Mephistopheles.[110] And although we cannot say whether or not he had the usual introduction to sex for a rich planter's son, as if to top off this ironic mix of influences, at the age of sixteen Charles Chilton Moore professed faith in Jesus Christ as his Lord and personal savior and requested baptism at Old Union Church on June 18, 1854. His sister

---

[108] Moore, *Behind the Bars,* 25-29.
[109] Ibid., 47.
[110] Ibid., 55.

Mary Anne was baptized the same day.[111] To his credit, young Charles would appear to have imbibed alcohol only sparingly at this period of his life (the Temperance Movement had not yet caught on in Kentucky except among the Methodists, and in fact would not come into vogue for at least a decade more) and at least about his studies and his grades he could be serious. In many other aspects of his life, though, ironically, he was still the very picture of the "worldly-minded," self-satisfied, giddy, flippant young Kentucky professors of Christianity that his grandfather Stone had so roundly condemned in his final editorials for *The Christian Messenger.*

Charles seems to have gotten his first genuine setback to his sense of self—and perhaps consequently, his first actual experience of growing up—at Lexington's historic Transylvania College (now Transylvania University), where he matriculated after Miss Bass returned to New York to marry and start a family, and he and his father took a brief excursion down the Ohio and up the Mississippi to visit Mary Anne's sister Amanda in Hannibal. One wonders if he might have chanced on this vacation to see a young Samuel L. Clemens, one of his strongest literary influences in later years and who had been the childhood playmate of some of Charles's cousins. At any rate, at least in the first few weeks after Charles got back to Kentucky and enrolled at Transylvania, and his sisters Mary and Jane in their turn became students at the respected Daughters' College of Harrodsburg,[112] all seemed to be going well. His mother noted in a September 1855 letter to her daughter Mary at Harrodsburg that "Charley is much pleased with his school. Studies my how [*sic*]. Sister said he studied all the time he was at Han[nibal] except when he went to church. He has to keep up in Greek."[113] Years later, however, Charles himself could recall no such idyll of learning; in his autobiography he blustered—well, actually more or less ranted—that

---

[111] Old Union Christian Church Record Book, 1823-1892, courtesy Bosworth Library, LTS.

[112] Moore, *Behind the Bars,* 75.

[113] Letter from Mary Anne Moore to her daughter Mary dated September 27, 1855; Moore Family Papers, UK Special Collections.

> [My year at Transylvania] was to me a most unhappy year, caused by the fact that I could not learn mathematics easily, and had as a professor in that department one of these mathematical fanatics who think that the ability to learn mathematics is the only standard of intellectuality, and who have no sympathy for any boy who cannot easily learn mathematics and is devoted to it. His influence on me was very bad, because he so discouraged me that I hardly had the heart to learn anything. I am sorry that I did not abandon mathematics when I knew only elementary arithmetic and the rudiments of geometry. Mathematics is the only one of all the sciences of which a man may know absolutely nothing and yet be a valuable, educated and accomplished gentleman. It is indispensable that *somebody* [emphasis added] should know mathematics, but there are always more people who can learn it with ease and pleasure than there is any demand for the practical application of mathematics, and these people should learn it, and people who cannot learn it easily should never waste their time upon it. Nothing can be well learned, the learning of which is not a pleasure to the learner, and that is especially true in mathematics. The greatest of all the mistakes in all our public schools is the grading of every student by his advancement in mathematics. I have known smart men who could not learn mathematics, and smart men who could learn it and very inferior men who could learn it. The time, labor and money put upon the study of mathematics by anyone who does not learn it easily and pleasurably would be worth more to him on any science other than mathematics.[114]

Considering the fact that, in this one paragraph of his autobiography, Charles had more to say in complaint about mathematics and its unnamed teacher at Transylvania than he did about either the life or the death of his brother Barton, we might pause for a moment to speculate on what exactly could have provoked such a violently negative reaction—all the more ironic since in years to come, before he settled permanently on an occupation, Charles had to spend various short periods working for banks and finance companies in Lexington, and thus in these instances owed his very livelihood to his arithmetical skills. It could have been nothing more than a personality clash with his professor, who is believed to have been James B. Dodd, Transylvania's acting

---

[114] Moore, *Behind the Bars,* 30.

president between 1850 and 1856 and also Professor of Mathematics and Natural Philosophy (Physical Sciences).[115] Dodd's enthusiasm for higher mathematics simply could have rubbed Moore the wrong way, or for that matter, Moore's gaudy silken and velvet leisure outfits and his social standing in the Lexington/Fayette County area could have had, with excellent reason, a similar effect on Dodd. Either way, it's fairly certain that teacher and student never really understood what made each other tick—perhaps most especially if Dodd was wont to make frequent repetition of the old Newtonian saw that mathematics was the language of God, when Moore's entire faith tradition assured him that the complete scientific blueprint of God's plan for the human race lay within the pages of Scripture and could be unlocked by anybody who chose to employ Alexander Campbell's key of Scottish Common Sense Realism.

Finally, it must be admitted that we cannot rule out that one factor so integral to most, if not all, relations between middle- and upper-class Kentucky males in this antebellum era: the Code of Honor or Fool's Code, the same set of values that had gotten Cassius Clay shot and had caused Samuel Brown to lose an eye and some hair and to gain an extra nostril. It is tempting to read into Moore's bluster a similar tale to that of another of Margaret Mitchell's, the Tarleton twins expelled from university and their older brother leaving as well because Southern honor demanded that he quit any school at which the twins were not welcome. Perhaps Dr. Dodd could count himself lucky that neither Chilton nor Charles challenged him to a duel, but we can never know for sure.

Considering Chilton and Mary Anne's financial position as well as their social standing, however, Charles's sorry showing at Transylvania proved to be only a minor setback. After all, Transylvania was not the only college in the world: though the Kentucky Disciples' own Bacon College had had to close its doors a few years before, the state boasted several other worthy institutions of higher learning, and this was not even to mention the older and more established colleges in the northeast. More prestigious than any of them either within Kentucky or

---

[115] Letter to the author from B. J. Gooch, Special Collections Librarian and University Archivist for Transylvania University, Lexington, Ky., July 13, 2006.

outside it, though, at least as far as the Moore family and their coreligionists were concerned, was the veritable flagship school of Barton Stone and Alexander Campbell's entire religious movement: Bethany College, established in 1840 by Campbell himself near his home on Buffalo Creek in the northern panhandle of what is now West Virginia. Here, it was certain, the talents of a young man with the very blood of *the* pioneer Reformer Stone coursing through his veins would be appreciated, upheld, and even honored. So approximately three months short of his nineteenth birthday—we can date the event by the fact that he had his church membership transferred away from Old Union to the Christian Church on the Bethany campus on September 2, 1856[116]—young Charles Chilton Moore, rich as Croesus, gaudily dressed as Beau Brummell, and yet disarmingly innocent and gourd-green in the way only a young man of the antebellum Kentucky planter class could have been, stepped out into the wider world, steamboating upriver from Louisville to Wheeling, Virginia and thence to Bethany, to be educated and polished by his grandfather Stone's partner in religious reform.

---

[116] Old Union Christian Church Record Book, 1823-1892, courtesy Bosworth Library, LTS.

Chapter 3

Paley Ontology: Life at Bethany College in the Good Old Days

A person may be intellectual and believe in miracles, but the miracles must be very old.
—Clarence Darrow

About a year before Charles Chilton Moore began his studies at Bethany College there occurred an incident at the institution of the type that, a century or so later, would become something of a by-word and even a joke for American colleges and universities: in 1855, Bethany fell prey to one of the very first student demonstrations in American academic history. Though at that time there was not one single slave in Brooke County, Virginia, where Bethany was located, and none of the undergraduates regardless of regional origin were allowed to keep either "a servant, horse, or dog,"[117] only 30 of the college's 130 students were from Free states.

In spite of the school's stated policy that "strictly scientific, literary, and moral" subjects should be pursued and "sectional" controversies should be avoided, there was a pronounced pro-Southern bias among faculty and scholars alike.[118] The few Northern students often

[117] Goodnight and Stephenson, 103.
[118] Garrett, 340.

felt that they were imposed upon by the Southern majority, and so one Sunday evening a Canadian ministerial student attempted to restore the balance, as it were, by preaching a vigorous anti-slavery sermon at the church on Bethany's campus. Not long into the discourse many young Southern men in the congregation began to hiss and stamp their feet in anger, and when the young preacher bravely ignored them and continued, about 20 or 30 of them got up and left with "lots of noise, both with their feet and canes." Alexander Campbell, who himself was present at the service, condemned the "unjustifiable and rude" behavior he saw at the gathering—not of those who had hissed, stamped their feet, and departed the meetinghouse, but of the student who had dared to deliver the controversial sermon. The "much-vexed question of slavery"[119] was simply not to be aired in the Bethany pulpit.

In furious response to Campbell's anathema, Bethany's Northern and Canadian students all went on strike, refusing to attend classes until Campbell and the college allowed the slavery issue to be debated and the Southerners were rebuked for their behavior at the church service. Matters worsened as the faculty, as a group, condemned the Northern students for insubordination and ruled that they must return to classes immediately or be expelled from the college. Finally, five of the offending Northerners were kicked out, and five others left Bethany in sympathy with them—a third of the institution's entire Northern student body. The dissenting students fled to Indianapolis, Indiana where North-Western Christian College (later known as the Christian Theological Seminary) admitted them, further insulting Campbell and the Bethany faculty for North-Western's flouting of the then-common practice of colleges to honor the disciplinary actions of one another. Ultimately, the fight escalated into a battle not only between Bethany and North-Western Colleges but, predictably, between the various Stone-Campbell journals and periodicals that supported either one college or the other.

As with the Raccoon John Smith-James McVay controversy more than a decade earlier, and a dozen or so other conflicts tragically similar to it, everybody in the brotherhood got a taste of the war through the headlines of whatever Reform periodical they happened to receive. And the college fight didn't even take into account the additional battle

[119] Ibid. 341.

pitched right afterward between Bethany faculty member and *Millennial Harbinger* writer Robert Richardson and Nashville editor and preacher Tolbert Fanning over the fine points of Alexander Campbell's much-touted Ancient Gospel and Ancient Order, with Campbell himself right in the middle of the two men, sometimes favoring one and sometimes the other, trying to make peace and wishing that their conflict would simply go away. Though Campbell and Richardson were ultimately reconciled, for a period Richardson actually left Bethany to teach at Kentucky University, a successor to Bacon College in that state. It is not likely that Fanning ever completely made up with either Campbell or Richardson. [120]

As luck or chance would have it, then, in the fall of 1856, when the Bethany vs. North-Western periodical battle would have been heating up to its very warmest temperature but the seeds of the Fanning-Richardson fight had not yet quite started to sprout, a stylish and agreeable but naïve and green young Kentuckian named Charles Chilton Moore arrived at Bethany fresh from Fayette County's Dog Fennel Precinct and plunged merrily into the swirling mix of campus life and campus ideas. Nearly nineteen years old, his frame barely hinting at the heavy yet muscular build he would maintain all his life (around five feet, eleven inches and weighing approximately 185 pounds, according to one observer), dark-haired and only that year beginning to grow the black curly beard that would likewise remain a permanent fixture,[121] and his pockets full of his father's spending money,[122] he came not only with his trunks of clothing and supplies but with the baggage of his and his family's entire past experiences with slavery. Full of the idealistic rhetoric of his planter father that slavery, though evil, was a more humane and merciful existence for blacks than an impoverished freedom, and of his crusading maternal grandfather who had manumitted his own slaves, consistently preached against slaveowning, and had even left Kentucky to get himself and most of his family away from the "peculiar institution," Charles was willing to tolerate the kind of slavery he

---

[120] Hughes, Richard T., 70-75; Goodnight and Stephenson, 168-200.

[121] Moore, *Behind the Bars,* 27. Moore's physical description and vital statistics are also listed in a newspaper article, author and publisher unknown but dated November 18, 1899, preserved in the Moore Vertical File, Special Collections, Transylvania University.

[122] Ibid., 30.

had known and observed on his father's and uncle John's farms but he could not endorse the practice as he had heard many native Southern Disciple preachers do. When he made this statement publicly—that he could never teach or endorse slavery like most of his grandfather and Alexander Campbell's Restoration Movement's Southern preachers—Dr. J. D. Pickett, Professor of Modern Languages at Bethany, himself a Kentucky native and one of the Southern ministers in question,[123] quickly and quite warmly read Charles the Riot Act, as it were, on the basis of the first five verses of the sixth chapter of the New Testament's First Epistle to Timothy:[124]

> Let as many servants as are under the yoke count their own masters worthy of all honor, that the name of God and his doctrine be not blasphemed. And they that have believing masters, let them not despise *them,* because they are brethren; but rather do *them* service, because they are faithful and beloved, partakers of the benefit. These things teach and exhort. If any man teach otherwise, and consent not to wholesome words, *even* the words of our Lord Jesus Christ, and to the doctrine which is according to godliness: He is proud, knowing nothing, but doting about questions and strifes of words, whereof cometh envy, strife, railings, evil surmisings, perverse disputings of men of corrupt minds, and destitute of the truth, supposing that gain is godliness; from such withdraw thyself [emphases, indicating editorial interpolations, in original].[125]

In a strictly political sense it was understandable that Pickett acted as he did to try to alter Charles' mode of thinking. No one on the faculty and indeed few within the student body wanted a repeat of the 1855 demonstration, and any high-spirited undergraduate youngblood who started feeling his oats and giving the appearance that he might attempt to agitate the slavery issue once more would have been quickly and deftly hushed, no matter how illustrious his Restoration Movement pedigree or, for that matter, whatever Scripture did or did not have to say about the issue. There can hardly be any doubt that Pickett counseled Charles with the knowledge of Alexander Campbell himself, most likely with his approval and perhaps even at his tacit urging. Charles's keenest memory of Pickett's rebuke was his teacher's perfect,

---

[123] Goodnight and Stephenson, 184-185.

[124] Moore, *The Rational View,* 5; *Behind the Bars,* 26.

[125] I Timothy 6:1-5, King James Version.

Campbell-style, Scottish Common Sense Realism-founded argument that, based on the very Word of God as found in this passage of Scripture, the institution of slavery as practiced in the antebellum American South was completely Scriptural; and, being Scriptural, American-style slavery was therefore not only good, but *very* good, no matter *what* Barton Stone or any pesky Northern abolitionist had to say about it. Anyone who was so foolish as to argue with such a plain text of Scripture should in fact be shunned.[126] But ere a decade had passed and the Civil War had forever altered the context of the dispute, one of Campbell's lunatic-fringe conservative followers in Nashville followed Pickett's exact same logic out to an unexpected tangent. Using what he believed was the same Scottish Common Sense Realism as his editorial master in *The Christian Baptist* and *The Millennial Harbinger*, Buckner Harrison Payne, a former preaching colleague of Raccoon John Smith back in Kentucky and at one time even named as a trustee of Bethany College itself, wrote a pamphlet purporting to prove by the plain text of Scripture that blacks were not only inferior to whites, they weren't even human, and the only way that God would ever bless the United States again was for the nation either to re-enslave its blacks or send them all to Africa.[127] For his own part, Charles later credited Pickett, and the I Timothy passage too, with something that neither the good professor, the ancient New Testament writer, nor even the demented Buckner Harrison Payne ever intended to effect within a million years: from both an intellectual and a moral standpoint, they sowed within Charles's heart and brain the first seeds of doubt as to the consistency and the literal accuracy of the Bible, and consequently, he claimed, the very first vague and incoherent inklings of his later infidelity.[128]

In fact, during Charles's tenure at Bethany a rumor made its rounds through the halls and dormitories that the school actually did have one lone infidel student, the proverbial campus atheist one supposes, and, perhaps true to the legend's type, purported to be the son of a

---

[126] Moore, *The Rational View,* 5; *Behind the Bars,* 26.

[127] Payne's pamphlet, which he wrote under the pen name of "Ariel," was entitled *The Negro: What Is His Ethnological Status?* See Sparks, *Raccoon John Smith,* 391-395, 434 nn 29-33.

[128] Moore, *Behind the Bars,* 26.

minister.[129] Moore's own de-conversion, as it were, though, was no split-second all-or-nothing matter, and for as long as he was at college he remained an essentially orthodox, if not an always quite well-behaved, believer and student. He came to Bethany quite as full of idealism as Alexander Campbell had been when the great Reformer had founded the institution in 1840, and was still every bit as willing to study "my how," in his mother's words, as he had been when he started at Transylvania. For Campbell's part, Bethany was *the* college, even the *only* college of his Movement if need be, supposedly impartially serving all sections of the brotherhood and the United States, not any contemptible man-made or denomination-led theological school but rather "a literary and scientific institution built upon the Bible" and serving "the greatest cause pled by man."[130] Bethany graduates, he was convinced, would be no mere foot soldiers but captains and generals in his Reformation as it matured and conquered the world.

The basics of Campbell's outlook on Christianity and proper worship have been sketched in an earlier chapter. We should note, though, that although he had mellowed sufficiently by the time he founded the college to be willing to invite "respectable ministers of various denominations" to preach at Bethany's chapel services to further the cause simply of "that common Christianity" in which "all good men of all denominations are agreed,"[131] he and his closest followers still regarded his own system as the most reasonable, ecumenical, and altogether complete expression of the Christian religion that had ever been, or ever would be, articulated. The Bible, most especially the New Testament from the Acts of the Apostles through the General and Pastoral Epistles, was flatly a book of facts, containing essentially a scientific blueprint for salvation and thus an expertly-drawn map for all humans en route from God's Footstool to the Glory World. Although God no longer revealed himself to the world through the kinds of miracles to which the Bible testified, he was still in his heaven and all was nonetheless well because Scripture itself contained all the revelation and witness of the Holy Spirit that modern humankind needed. It was this belief, more than any other, that caused Campbell and his followers to

---

[129] Ibid., 66.

[130] Garrett, 340, quoting Campbell.

[131] Hughes, 40.

ridicule the doctrines and practices of Baptists, Methodists, and other evangelical denominations as regarded the witness of the Holy Spirit to individual sinners, and the personal experience of conversion. Faith in response to the preached word, that is, the acceptance of the testimony of the facts of the Gospel of the death, burial, and resurrection of Jesus Christ, and repentance, followed and attested by total-body immersion, absolutely guaranteed the grace of God, salvation, and the gift of the Holy Spirit to the believer.

But when all was said and done, if, as both Barton Stone and Alexander Campbell averred in slightly different ways, the Holy Spirit manifested itself in the modern era solely through the words of Scripture and not through the bizarre, irrational, subjective individual impressions to sinners that they criticized the Baptists and Methodists for preaching, then Scripture had to have the dependable support of a strong and trustworthy natural theology: that is, a sure knowledge of God and, in logical turn, Christian doctrine, achieved through reason alone. For this, likewise as we have noted earlier, Campbell and his entire religious movement depended more than anything else upon the theological writings of two eighteenth-century Anglican divines: Joseph Butler with his 1736 *Analogy of Religion, Natural and Revealed, to the Constitution and Course of Nature,* and William Paley and his 1790 *Horus Paulinae, or the Truth of the Scripture History of St. Paul,* his 1794 *View of the Evidences of Christianity,* and his magnum opus, the 1802 *Natural Theology; or, Evidence of the Existence and Attributes of the Deity, Collected From the Appearances of Nature.* In fact at this post-Great Revival but antebellum period in American history nearly all Protestant colleges in the United States, Bethany of course included and even some with no formal denominational connection, maintained an undergraduate course entitled "Evidences of Christianity" or something similar, more often than not as a prerequisite for graduation, with the works of Butler and Paley as major components of the course's required reading—and little, if any, study of the thought of any scholar who might disagree with them.

The most famous of these three books, Paley's *Natural Theology,* began its thread of reasoning with the author's famous Watchmaker Analogy:

> In crossing a heath, suppose I pitched my foot against a *stone*, and were asked how the stone came to be there; I might possibly answer, that, for any thing I knew to the contrary, it had lain there for ever: nor would it perhaps be very easy to show the absurdity of this answer. But suppose I had found a *watch* upon the ground, and it should be inquired how the watch happened to be in that place; I should hardly think of the answer which I had before given, that, for any thing I knew, the watch might have always been there. Yet why should not this answer serve for the watch as well as for the stone? Why is it not as admissible in the second case, as in the first? For this reason, and for no other, viz.: that, when we come to inspect the watch, we perceive (what we could not discover in the stone) that its several parts are framed and put together for a purpose, *e. g.* that they are so formed and adjusted as to produce motion, and that motion so regulated as to point out the hour of the day; that, if the different parts had been differently shaped from what they are, of a different size from what they are, or placed after any other manner, or in any other order, than that in which they are placed, either no motion at all would have been carried on in the machine, or none which would have answered the use that is now served by it … the inference we think is inevitable, that the watch must have had a maker—that there must have existed, and at some time or place or other, *an artificer or artificers* who formed it for the purpose which we find it actually to answer, who comprehended its construction and designed its use. [132]

And so on. Design, using the hypothetical watch as an example, implied a designer; the accuracy of function, predicate upon the intricacy of construction, implied that the designer was intelligent and, by a slightly longer stretch of logic and reason, kindly disposed to that which he had designed and created; and finally identifying the Abrahamic Creator God as the Divine Benevolent Watchmaker of the Universe, in a complex and convoluted trail of reasoning all the way up through the *Natural Theology* and then in, out, and through the *Evidences* and the *Horus Paulinae,* ultimately Paley's logical construct purported to prove that the miracles and the resurrection of Christ, the testimony of the Apostles, and by definition the Old and New Testaments themselves, were all completely accurate and trustworthy. On this basis, over and above what any church's creed had to say about it,

[132] Paley, *Natural Theology,* 7-9.

the Bible had to be recognized as a simple book of facts and Christianity and the Gospel must be realized as pure and eternal truth. No matter that miracles and divine healings no longer occurred in the world, or that God did not deign to manifest himself with fire from heaven as he did to both the sinful priests Nadab and Abihu[133] and the righteous prophet Elijah[134]; Paley's logic was good enough to reaffirm the convictions of a great many nineteenth-century Christians that such events had happened in the past and that their Divine Instigator could, and indeed must, therefore be trusted in the present.

Protestant denominations by and large loved Paley's books and his Watchmaker Analogy, because they could serve as a workable foundation for virtually any Christian creed or confession of faith; hence the widespread use of his works throughout the academic world of that day and time. Alexander Campbell's own personal contribution to Paley's construct, though, was to have introduced, to his rural American readership at least, the scientific philosophies of Francis Bacon and John Locke and how they could further complement the Watchmaker Analogy and the so-called argument from design that sprung from it. Citing Locke, Campbell reasoned that the human mind was a *tabula rasa,* or blank tablet, at birth and had no innate conception of God. Therefore, he continued, since humankind does possess the idea of God, then the Creator must have manifested himself to humans in some primal Divine revelation, and as human nature was spiritual, humans in turn readily accepted the revelation and acknowledged the existence and interested benevolence of God.[135] To put it in the words that Charles Moore himself heard often from Campbell's lips while at college, one of the highest evidences that there existed a God who had communicated with humankind was the fact that humans could talk; according to Campbell, the human race never could have invented language, and could only have known of such a thing by hearing God himself speak.[136]

Perhaps needless to say, this reverence for the spoken and written word colored Campbell's whole outlook on religion, and framed his

---

[133] Leviticus 10:1-2.
[134] II Kings 2:9-15.
[135] Garrett, 166.
[136] Moore, *The Rational View,* 27.

entire concept of faith. Within such an ostensibly clear and simple system atheists, Deists, and skeptics of any stamp were at best misguided or at worst flatly foolish, and any believers who still depended on so-called "experimental" religion and subjective personal and emotional experience were just not letting the simple logic of the Gospel speak to them. Thus the particular rational system that Campbell followed and imposed upon the text of Scripture to articulate his so-called Ancient Gospel and Ancient Order fit quite as comfortably on top of Paley's natural theology foundation as any revelation- and spirituality-based Anglican, Baptist, Methodist, or evangelical Presbyterian belief, though Campbell seems never to have seen the need to follow Paley's train of thought quite all the way back through sacred Scripture to the Watchmaker himself: as he once opined to Charles's grandfather Stone, "The truths of the bible [*sic*] are to be received as first principles, not to be tried by reason, one by one, but to be received as *new principles* [emphasis added], from which we are to reason as from intuitive principles in any human science."[137] On the basis of this logical construct, even before Charles Moore's time, extremists among Campbell's newspaper subscribers had begun to take his peppery, sarcastic rhetoric so seriously that they proclaimed Campbell's religious movement to be not only *a* church, but *the* church—even as Campbell himself retreated from such an aggressive position.

Despite the modern resurrection of the name and fame of William Paley by Seattle's Discovery Institute as a sort of alleged elder statesman and first prophet of the modern Intelligent Design movement, neither science, nor theology, nor philosophy has been very kind to the ideas that the old priest left behind. The theological argument from design came under heavy criticism from such differing philosophers as Immanuel Kant and David Hume before Paley ever articulated it to the British and American Christian masses, and subsequently various thinkers have used Paley's same train of logic to demonstrate that the Watchmaker Analogy can be used with equal facility to prove the existence of not only the Abrahamic/Christian Creator God, but virtually any other conceivable type of creator deity or deities from the pantheon of the ancient Greeks and Romans to the austere, impersonal First Cause and Unmoved Mover of Aristotle and of the eighteenth-

[137] Wrather, II, 252, quoting Campbell in an open editorial letter to Barton Stone.

century Deists. Others have made sport of the irony that Paley never considered that the technical skill of watchmaking itself had had to evolve over time and through several different inventors and developers rather than springing into existence *ex nihilo* by the hand of one single omniscient and omnipotent proto-artisan,[138] and Richard Dawkins' 1986 work *The Blind Watchmaker* subjects the entire theory to a stinging critique in light of evolutionary biology. Moreover, even if Paley's system could withstand the most rigorous modern scientific challenges, it would still be unable to reveal anything objective as to the character of its theorized Divine Designer, or Designers. As John Polkinghorne, a modern particle physicist and, like Paley himself, an Anglican priest as well, admits, "Even at its most persuasive, natural theology can only lead to a limited concept of God as the Great Architect of the Universe, the One whose mind and will are behind cosmic order and fruitfulness, but no more than that."[139]

Likewise Paley's *Horus Paulinae* and *Evidences,* though the arguments he employed within the works have largely been borrowed and rehashed by later writers and preachers from C. S. Lewis and F. F. Bruce to Josh McDowell and W. Gene Scott and are therefore still extremely popular in many evangelical circles, have also come under the scrutiny of scholars employing the tools of historical and form biblical criticism. Many, if not most, of Paley's key apologetic contentions and propositions have been called into question from both logical and historical standpoints, and one has difficulty avoiding the thought that the Paley system and the entire argument from design might be, in even the best light, merely an evangelistic tool to confirm or reinforce an already-extant faith, and in the most jaundiced view as an ideological crutch to be leaned on by any individual to uphold a set of fundamentalist or evangelical religious propositions he or she is determined to assert anyway, with or without Paley's support.

This is certainly how Charles Moore came to view Paley and his ideas in later life. Not many years before his death he grumbled about having to listen to a missionary preacher from the Holy Land, whom he had hoped might be capable of expounding at least a few new and innovative theological ideas, instead preach "the same old rot about old

---

[138] E.g. McDougall, "William Paley's Wonderful Watch."
http://www.butterfliesandwheels.com/articleprint.php?num=232

[139] Polkinghorne, 84.

Paley and his old turnip of a watch that a theological college had loaded me to the muzzle with" years before.[140] Even as a young man he could discern, in spite of himself, that the link between Paley's watch on the heath and Professor Pickett's Timothy-based defense of slavery in the South was a long, complicated, convoluted, and actually very fragile absurdity. In fact it couldn't have been the only supposedly Paley-based intellectual farce that he ever observed in his tenure at the college, only the most egregious for the time. James Lane Allen, who taught literature at Bethany fifteen to twenty years after Charles graduated,[141] related a tale in *The Reign of Law* that he could have gathered directly from some of his Bethany students debating in traditional Stone-Campbell scholarly style—or perhaps, even, like the antebellum fox-hunt story noted in the previous chapter, taken directly from the lips of Charles Chilton Moore himself:

> [Doctrinal] controversies overflowed from the congregation to the Bible College. The lad in his room at the dormitory one Sunday afternoon heard a debate on whether [the use of] a tuning fork [as an aid to congregational singing] is a violation of the word of God. The debaters turned to him, excited and angry:
>
> "What do you think?" they asked.
>
> "I don't think it is worth talking about," he replied quietly.
>
> They soon became reconciled to each other; they never forgave him.[142]

Yet, for all the inconsistencies that Charles could, if he would, already see, in the middle to late 1850s, and the alleged presence of Bethany's lone and unknown campus atheist, Paley and Paley's watch were by and large good enough for him and most of his professors and fellow students. And as he stated outright, Bethany College absolutely loaded him to the muzzle with both.

It should not be construed, however, that natural theology, the argument from design, biblical studies, and *a cappella* singing without the aid of tuning forks were all that Alexander Campbell and his faculty attempted to teach the young men under their care (like most colleges of this period, in its antebellum and early postwar years Bethany admit-

---

[140] Moore, *Dog Fennel,* 314-315.
[141] Ward, 40.
[142] Allen, *The Reign of Law,* 87.

ted only males as students; it did not become coeducational until the middle 1880s, though one of Campbell's cousins operated a "Young Ladies' Seminary," that day's approximate equivalent of a middle or high school, nearby). To Campbell, *all* good education was moral and worthwhile[143]; Bethany was, and is, an eminently-qualified liberal arts institution, and although in the 1850s the concepts of specialization and major and minor areas of undergraduate study were not yet fully formed throughout American academia, even in Charles's time a Bethany student had every opportunity to acquire a good education in the humanities, the sciences, or both. Though at this period both Charles and his parents viewed his college years not as career preparation but, along with a European grand tour, simply the necessary polish that a young man of his social and financial class needed to be recognized as a gentleman,[144] Charles himself concentrated especially on the biological and physical sciences and developed a keen appreciation for both. In years to come he recalled an especial fondness for the geological studies and writings of Hugh Miller (this was, of course, the pre-Darwin era)[145], and in years to come Moore would encourage his sons, and perhaps his surviving daughter as well, to prepare themselves for careers in the scientific disciplines.

Even so, Charles's fellow students recognized his aptitude for the humanities, particularly journalism, early on as well. There were two student literary organizations at Bethany, the Neotrophian Literary Society and the American Literary Institute, and together they published a small campus magazine known first as *The Stylus* and after December 1857 as *The Neotrophian.* In the June 1857 issue of *The Stylus* Charles was listed as having made a speech entitled "Do We Progress?" for the American Literary Institute's sixteenth annual Exhibition, and during March, April, and May 1858 he served as corresponding editor for *The Neotrophian.* Among the articles he contributed were one simply entitled "Government," and a satirical piece called "Bethany on the Stage," evidently spoofing a troupe of musicians who had once performed at Bethany's commencement exercises.[146] During a summer vacation at home and perhaps with the help

---

[143] Garrett, 234-235; Wrather, II, 72.
[144] Moore, *Behind the Bars,* 147.
[145] Ibid., 63.
[146] Cobb, letter to the author, May 24, 2007.

of his father's influence in Lexington, he managed to get another piece entitled "On the Edibility of Crows"—which he later solemnly averred was a serious essay that explored the question quite literally, though nearly everyone who read it thought it was intended to be a cutting Jonathan Swift-style political satire—printed in the *Lexington Observer and Reporter.*[147] Perhaps we shouldn't read too much into the fact that Charles seems never even to have tried his luck getting published in *The Millennial Harbinger* or any other of the Stone-Campbell Movement's numerous and continually-multiplying periodicals, or perhaps we should. Either way, it appears that by the time he wrote the "Crows" essay he was already recognized as being entirely capable of the kind of sarcastic lampooning that Alexander Campbell himself had practiced in his early days as the editor of the old *Christian Baptist.*

Too, and despite the endless inconsequential arguments between students and ministerial cubs over proper church practice, he had about as much fun as a young man in his circumstances could be expected to experience at a church-based college—and perhaps, sometimes even a little more. Tuition plus room, board, clean sheets and weekly laundering at Steward's Inn, the college's principal residence hall, came to $150 per year with an additional $10 entry fee for freshmen. Charles was of course able to pay all his expenses in advance, and the school took pride in the fact that the Inn's table fare was comparable to that of the University of Virginia itself.[148] Bethany's vice-president, William Kimbrough Pendleton, who had been married to and widowed in succession by two of Alexander Campbell's daughters and was now lately wed a third time to a very attractive young lady fifteen years his junior and only five years older than Charles, kept a keg of good beer on tap in the front hall of his residence for the refreshment of fellow faculty members and students alike. During the last academic term of his senior year Charles was allowed to keep a tapped keg in his room as well, but he claimed that he did not avail himself of any of his home state's specialty, whiskey, until his graduation day.[149] Despite the marked unpleasantness of the student demonstration in 1855 and its aftermath,

---

[147] Moore, *Behind the Bars,* 147-148.
[148] Goodnight and Stephenson, 100-101.
[149] Moore, *Dog Fennel,* 12.

we might thus reasonably conclude that life at Steward's Inn could be, for the most part, quite convivial.

Then again, not only was beer tolerated, but in spite of the school's stated policy against the possession of guns and gunpowder some of the young gentlemen managed to smuggle firearms onto campus as well.[150] The concepts of honor that a great many of the Southern students brought with them thus might have resulted in considerable tragedy if the beer, the weapons, the Northerners' anti-slavery pronouncements, or any other Northern-Southern cultural differences were ever allowed to mix and mingle too much. At least twice, once in a private quarrel at Bethany and again in a very public imbroglio with the peace officers and citizenry of the nearby Pittsburgh suburb of Allegheny City, Pennsylvania, Charles found himself in situations that could have gotten him, and in one of the cases three or four of his fellow students as well, killed in so-called affairs of honor. Both events involved his classmate Alexander William Doniphan Jr., son of the Missouri lawyer and militia general who had been one of that state's first residents to befriend the Mormons after they split Campbell's Disciples of Christ in Kirtland, Ohio and migrated west[151], and so we shall note and discuss both in due course.

It so happened that young Doniphan brought with him to Bethany a fine dueling pistol and explicit instructions from his proud father as to what should be done with it: "Shoot the first damned rascal who insults you!"[152] In the initial, private incident, it would appear that Charles himself came within a hairsbreadth of being that very damned rascal. Not long after Moore got acquainted with the Missouri youth, Doniphan became extremely angry at him for some supposed offense of which Moore was in fact entirely innocent. Luckily young Doniphan was either informed of his error or discovered it on his own, and once he found out that he had very nearly wronged Charles he tried to atone for his hostile behavior in every way he felt proper—usually in the form of various small courtesies, pretty much any favor within reason yet short of an actual admission of guilt. Even-tempered and genial Charles was entirely satisfied with Doniphan's oblique, offhand mode

---

[150] Goodnight and Stephenson, 103.
[151] Brodie, 136-137, 227-229, 237, 241.
[152] Moore, *Behind the Bars,* 38.

of apology, and was probably quite relieved that he had avoided Doniphan's outright challenge before the boy had realized his mistake. Doniphan was noted for a markedly melancholy disposition, and Charles later commented that he was glad of an opportunity to be friends with a boy who seemed to be so sad all the time.[153]

The second and more notorious incident—documented, interestingly, by Charles himself in a series of articles and editorial-page letters he submitted to the northern Virginia panhandle's local newspaper, *The Wheeling Intelligencer,* and of all things, a poem in *The Neotrophian* that ranked right up there with McGonagall's finest[154]—got its start on December 10-11, 1857. with an early-morning fire that completely destroyed Bethany College's main classroom building. In the various biographies of Alexander Campbell and Bethany's other early faculty members the source of this blaze is generally downplayed or at least deemphasized, but all testify to the character of both faculty and students that neither group were willing to let the building's destruction impede the institution's academic work. Classrooms were simply make-shifted in other buildings, and Campbell and his teachers and scholars all committed themselves to raising money to rebuild the fallen structure.[155] So far, so good, but within hours of the building's burning the rumor got about among the students, particularly the Southern ones, that the fire had been a case of arson. The prime suspect was one Owen McNally, an Irish coal miner and sometimes unlicensed and illegal whiskey "retailer" (the term "bootlegger" hadn't been coined yet) from Castleman's Run near Bethany and whose family was said to have harbored a long-standing grudge against that of Alexander Campbell.

Whether or not he was guilty of setting the blaze, McNally, who had had the ill luck to have hosted a drunken party a few nights before at which another Irishman had been killed and who was probably scared to death that he'd wind up being lynched at Bethany for either the manslaughter, the fire, his illegal "retailing" of whiskey, or all

---

[153] Ibid., 38-39.

[154] Moore, "Night of December 10, 1857," *The Neotrophian Magazine,* III, 5, April 1861; see n 79, chapter 2 of this work.

[155] E. g., Goodnight and Stevenson, 185-187; Richardson, II, 631-639; Moore writing as "Chalybs," articles in the *Wheeling Intelligencer* dated December 10, 11, 12, and 18, 1857.

three, immediately fled the northern Virginia panhandle for his mother's house in Allegheny City. Sure enough, as if to confirm the luckless Irishman's worst nightmares, five students, all of them Southerners—Moore himself, gloomy Doniphan, another Kentuckian named James Rogers, and two other boys named Smith and Burke—got together with one local non-student, James Casner, and formed up a good old-fashioned Southern-style "Regulator" posse with the determination to journey to Pennsylvania and bring the miscreant back to face law, order and the Christian American way directly at the scene of his crime, their beloved alma mater. Rogers and/or Doniphan may have been the leaders of the gang, but the boys' enthusiasm was equal, and needless to say, as extremely volatile and dangerous as they were all young and headstrong. It is not known whether Alexander Campbell or any other faculty member attempted to urge restraint upon them, or at least to reason with them; as with so many other little incidents of his life in which he found himself left looking less than calm, collected, poised, and verbally victorious, Campbell remained curiously but perhaps naturally reticent about the entire affair and its aftermath.

We cannot be sure where the youthful vigilantes acquired all their armaments, but Charles's own newspaper accounts admit that they brought along a good deal more weaponry from the hills of Bethany than Doniphan's lone pistol. At any rate, after persuading a Brooke County, Virginia magistrate to issue a warrant for McNally's arrest and then to deputize Rogers (probably the oldest of the students) as a constable to serve it, the hotheaded, wild-eyed young Southern boys proceeded, apparently by steamboat and adrenaline-pumped boot leather rather than on horseback, to the Allegheny City Hall and laid the writ on the desk of Mayor Herman Jeremiah DeHaven. DeHaven felt compelled, grudgingly, to honor the legality of the Virginia magistrate's warrant, but he sent two of his police officers along to assist the boys—probably, in the hope of keeping them out of even more trouble than that into which they'd already stepped.

Though we do not know exactly how the Bethany boys obtained their information, they learned that McNally's mother's house was located in the Fourth Ward of the city, on Water Street near Pitt Alley and in one of the toughest sections of what could sometimes be a very tough mill and factory town. They recklessly proceeded to the suspected hideout with the bemused city policemen in tow. As the frightened and intimidated Mrs. McNally admitted them by the front door one of them glimpsed Owen slipping out the back, and the posse threw all restraint to the winds, drew their pistols, and rushed through the house into the rear alley after him, yelling bloody murder as if they were a pack of blooded Southern Walker hounds baying the trail of a terrified immigrant-rabble fox.

As they should have anticipated, though, their commotion attracted every hard-bitten neighbor and passerby within a one- or two-block radius, and as if to add frosting to the cake of all the confusion the teachers of the Fourth Ward schoolhouse chose that moment to dismiss their pupils into the street as well. Adults and children alike now joined in a free-for-all in behalf of their compatriot McNally, and in spite of their loaded guns the young Southern gentlemen suddenly found themselves in immediate danger of getting thrashed within an inch of their lives, if not killed outright, by the rough-cut factory workers living along Water Street and Pitt Alley. Now scared completely back to their senses, they quickly pocketed their weapons for their own safety and quietly began looking for some face-saving way out of both the street and the riot they had initiated. For their part, the schoolchildren singled out one of the college boys, "a queer-looking customer" wearing a rough woolen coat and who may actually have been Doniphan or even curly-bearded Charles himself, dubbed him with the title of "Wooly Horse," and shouted the epithet at him over and over as their elders closed in on the pack of young Southerners for a good afternoon's rough sport.

Somehow—it may have been partially through the efforts of the two official policemen, but it still almost seems miraculous—cooler heads prevailed. One of the older and more articulate neighbors stepped forward on his own and began to upbraid the boys for their recklessness. He warned them to get out of the Fourth Ward immediately, or else he and the other local men would take summary measures to punish, as he worded it, "people who are so cantankerous." And so finally the two professional officers restored a modicum of order on Water Street and got their feisty charges back to Mayor DeHaven—who, as a proper *denouement* to the entire adventure, informed them that the good Mother McNally had already hastened to see him and had offered to produce ironclad testimony from no less than twenty witnesses that Owen was at her house on the night of the fire. DeHaven concluded the drama by giving the cowed college boys yet another reprimand, laced with the sternest invective for their heedless behavior, and he sent them back to the steamboat docks with their collective tail tucked between their collective legs. A gaggle of city children, including perhaps even a few tagalongs from the Fourth Ward School still yelling at old "Wooly Horse," escorted them out of town with jeers and maybe some rocks, sticks, and mud clods as well, and it is unlikely that any prophets, or sons of prophets, in history ever prayed harder for the timely appearance of a pair of good hungry orthodox Old Testament-style she-bears.[156] Owen McNally was never apprehended; he seems to have been acquitted of any wrongdoing in the matter of the killing at his house and his illegal selling of liquor, perhaps by affidavits from him and his mother, and Alexander Campbell declined to press any charges of arson against his fellow countryman.[157]

In years to come, Charles tried to recount this incident as tersely and as vaguely as possible. He was very probably extremely ashamed of it, for more than any other reason because it showed him, as no subsequent incident in his life ever would, falling headlong and unthinking into all the foolish romance and mystique of the Southern code of honor. He claimed that he had never done anything in college that he would have hesitated to admit to his parents or other relatives,[158] but at least in this case he probably knew that they would applaud him for his brief career as a vigilante; such feckless heroics were, in fact, so eminently a *Kentucky* thing. The only mention whatsoever he made of the story in his later autobiographical writings consisted of two brief sentences, that "The next piece [after the "Edibility of Crows" article that] I ever wrote for any newspaper was two or three columns for the Wheeling (VA.; now W. VA.) *Intelligencer* [*sic*]. It was written when I was at college and was a report of a somewhat dramatic episode in

---

[156] The Scriptural reference is to II Kings 2:23-24.

[157] Letter to the author from Jeanne Cobb, Bethany College Archivist, dated May 30, 2007; Moore writing as "Chalybs," articles and letters to the editor in the *Wheeling Intelligencer,* dated December 6, 12, 18, 20, and 21, 1857. I owe an inestimable debt to Ms. Cobb's disinterested—or more likely, very interested—benevolence in visiting the Wheeling, West Virginia public library and copying these newspaper features for me from microfilm, without charge. Allegheny City, by the way, was subsumed into metropolitan Pittsburgh in 1907.

[158] Moore, *Behind the Bars,* 30, 43.

which I had participated as a member of a sheriff's posse in Pittsburgh, Pa. [*sic*]"[159] In fact, in the autobiography he didn't even see fit to bring up the occurrence of the college fire.

Perhaps the one silver lining in the cloud, though, was this practical sharpening of his journalistic skills—he employed the pen name "Chalybs" in preparing the accounts for the *Intelligencer,*[160] although perhaps he should have thought twice about signing his real name to his McGonagall-style poem about the conflagration—and at least in his last semester at Bethany he could be good-humored enough about his Allegheny City experience to joke about it. After all, he included the details about the schoolchildren and the "Wooly Horse" moniker in his newspaper reports even though his companions probably would have preferred that he hadn't, and in writing subsequently to his friend Richard H. Prewitt, a recent Bethany graduate, on January 28, 1858, he remarked that "I have become something of a public character since my return to B[ethany]—You've seen my name in the papers—haven't you[?] Really, I am beginning to feel my importance. Well, we had a royal time of it anyhow, & I'll make you laugh till your sides ache over it though I'll not attempt it now, however, as I never could do the subject justice in a letter…." [161]

We are left with one melancholy footnote to the posse incident. On the eleventh day of either April or May 1858 (the surviving records are slightly ambiguous as to the month) Alexander Doniphan, James Rogers, and a student from Mississippi named Yates all decided to go for a swim in nearby Buffalo Creek. Charles had planned on going swimming with them but a class prevented his doing so. The season had been unusually rainy, and a freshet earlier that day had caused a rapid headwater flood in the already-swollen creek. Nonetheless, Doniphan was known to be an excellent swimmer and was apparently unafraid of the current. After the boys disrobed on a sandstone bank above the watercourse, he regaled his companions with a declamation of Shakespeare's version of Caesar's challenge to Cassius to swim the Tiber, and immediately jumped in. He swam to the middle of

---

[159] Ibid., *Behind the Bars,* 148.

[160] Cobb to the author, May 30, 2007.

[161] Letter from Charles C. Moore Jr. to Richard H. Prewitt, dated January 28, 1858; Bethany College Collection.

the stream where the current was at its swiftest, looked back at Rogers, and suddenly and unexpectedly but very calmly and earnestly called out, "If you can help me, now is the time to do it!"

Those were the last words his friends ever heard him utter. The current swept him down Buffalo Creek too rapidly for the other two boys to save him, and he drowned. In spite of the fact that Rogers and Yates rushed to alert the entire Bethany community to Doniphan's sad fate, the body was not recovered for nearly a month. It was floating almost seventeen miles downstream, in the Ohio River. On its shipment back to Bethany, Charles and others of the dead boy's schoolmates were given the task of preparing it for the coffin. The corpse was so decomposed and its flesh so friable, though, that Charles's fingers actually sank into its waterlogged skin and tissues as he helped lift it, and the memory of that and Doniphan's sightless, clouded eyes—the lids already either rotted away, or perhaps eaten by Ohio River catfish and carp—haunted him for the remainder of his life.[162]

Almost, if not every bit, as disturbing as the sight of the decayed, waterlogged body was Charles's suspicion, shared by Rogers and Yates, that Doniphan had intentionally taken his own life. Rogers and Yates were certain that, despite his reputation as a skilled swimmer, Doniphan had made no visible attempts to save himself,[163] and in fact when Charles had apologized to him for not being able to go swimming with him that fateful afternoon Doniphan had made it a point to shake Charles's hand and tell him goodbye.[164] Though perhaps no "damned rascal" had ever deliberately and publicly insulted him at Bethany, both Mayor DeHaven's rebuke to him and his compatriots and the ridicule of the Water Street and Pitt Alley children during his Pennsylvania expedition in December had to have been a bitter pill for proud Doniphan to have to swallow. Moreover, the boy must have heard a good deal of rhetoric in Bible and religion classes at Bethany itself that, over time, could have hurt his feelings equally deeply. Although neither he nor his parents had ever joined the Mormons, we noted earlier that his father had been among their first defenders in Missouri, and given the

---

162 Moore, *Behind the Bars*, 38-42; Campbell, "Obituary," Millennial Harbinger, June 1858, 359.
163 Moore, *Behind the Bars,* 40-41.
164 Ibid., 39, 122.

fact that Alexander Campbell had maintained a vigorous anti-Mormon polemic both in the pulpit and in print ever since the group had first split his Disciples of Christ in Ohio[165] it was entirely possible that young Doniphan could have imbibed the rhetoric and inferred that Campbell was tacitly accusing his father of being foolish, if not outright sinful, for his pro-Mormon stance.

Had automatic assault weapons been available in that long-ago era, would young Alexander Doniphan have let his rage over DeHaven's scolding, the Allegheny City children's taunting, and such a presumed insult as Campbell's anti-Mormonism turn outward, rather than in upon himself, and then set the precedent for the unspeakable tragedies at the Virginia Polytechnic Institute and State University and Northern Illinois University a century and a half later? If Doniphan did in fact twist some such unnamed and unmentionable angry confusion inward and finally let it lead him to self-loathing and suicide, it would not be the only time Charles Moore would be faced with the tragedy of a friend's self-destruction over his disappointments with the ultimate hollowness of the Southern honor code and, consequently, of a world in which it somehow no longer made sense to a Southern gentleman to go on living. But that is another story, and there is no way we can ever know its truth for sure, any more than Charles could have accurately read Doniphan's mind on the day he drowned.

What we can say with certainty is that Doniphan's coffin remained unburied for at least four, and possibly five, more months. Whether an undertaker ever tried to work with the body or not, we do not know, but by the time the corpse was recovered it was so decomposed that even a creosote, arsenic, or zinc chloride embalming, if it were possible to perform such procedures at that stage of decay, wouldn't have been able to preserve it to any great degree further. So, embalmed or not, Doniphan's lifeless body and its coffin were stored, of all places, on two trestles under the rear part of the campus church where the floor was about four feet off the ground, in plain sight of anyone who ventured back there. Charles thought that some of Doniphan's other friends might have taken the body back to Missouri with them after the college's commencement exercises in July, at which he himself graduated, but he was mistaken: Alexander Campbell noted in the November 1858

---

165 Brodie, 69-70, 102-103; Garrett, 258-262.

issue of *The Millennial Harbinger* that the boy's remains, after a memorial service, were finally shipped to his parents by rail on October 15.[166] For all we know, Campbell might have insisted on holding it through the humid summer months into the fall out of consideration for the trainmen that would have to handle it on its journey west, or perhaps out of a sense of delicacy and courtesy to the boy's parents.

Thus, finally, the most unsettling aspect of the entire sordid story of Doniphan's death is that of the atmosphere of the worship services conducted in the Bethany Church house during the course of that hot summer of 1858. Within a few short years, the setting would become an entire metaphor of late nineteenth-century Christianity to Charles Chilton Moore: a houseful of believers, claiming the promise of the Holy Spirit, resurrection, and eternal life through God's own Book, Christ's own blood and their own immersion in water, all trying their best to ignore the faint but ever-increasing odor of a waterlogged, decomposing, dead body—carefully hidden away, but not entirely invisible if the believers dared to explore too closely under the foundations of their edifice.

According to Charles, the social structure of the community of faculty and students at Bethany pretty much mirrored that of the state of Virginia itself in the nineteenth century. Despite college and commonwealth's mutual upholding of the Declaration of Independence ideal that all are created equal, both had three fairly rigid castes, which he described, in the good academic Greek of which his mother was so proud, as *hoi aristoi* (of course, the few, or the aristocrats), *hoi barbaroi* (again needless to say, the barbarians or the uncultured), and a third which he may have made a play on the words *hoi polloi* in calling "hoi phizeroi" (one assumes the lowest class; possibly he meant to include free and enslaved blacks here, or perhaps other supposed inferiors like European or Irish immigrants such as Owen McNally).[167] Sad to say, this wasn't just Charles's own opinion either. His claims about the Bethany caste structure are backed up by at least one other contemporary source, the letters of the wife of his classmate Virgil Wilson. In

[166] Moore, *Behind the Bars,* 42; Campbell, "Tribute of Respect," *Millennial Harbinger,* November 1858, 655.
[167] Moore, *Behind the Bars,* 47.

correspondence with her relatives back in the North Carolina piedmont from whence she and Virgil hailed, young and outspoken Martha Wilson noted that, although the professors were "all very sociable and friendly," there were "rather more grades and circles in society than I think ought to be in a christian [*sic*] community," and that she frankly did not like to pay or receive social calls on campus; "the people visit too fashionably." Even so, Virgil, a ministerial student, was very pleased with his prospects, since "owing to the reputation of Bethany for its instruction, [graduates] command[ed] enormous prices [for their preaching]."[168] Still, we must wonder if the inevitable bitterness that *hoi barbaroi* students would have felt towards both those known to be *hoi aristoi* and the faculty members who upheld and maintained the caste system, might have played its own part in the subsequent liberal-conservative divisions in the Stone-Campbell Movement. There have been bigger religious fights with less impetus.

As both Barton Stone's grandson and a rich Kentucky planter's scion Charles was, of course, an undisputed member of *hoi aristoi,* and according to his own recollections the most popular boy at college during his tenure there.[169] It's doubtful that he could even have gotten away with his Pennsylvania posse trip and all its ensuing woes if it had been otherwise. We have already noted that he claimed never to have engaged in any behavior as a student that he would have been ashamed to confess to his parents. Besides this, he once observed that he consistently maintained his religious demeanor at college, citing as proof his gift of a bound set of the works of Charles Dickens to a profane roommate, if only the boy would promise to quit swearing until the end of one fall term.[170] But as might be expected, *hoi aristoi* could still get away with a good many things that *hoi barbaroi* hardly dared dream of, and young Moore wound up indulging himself in a few other activities besides his vigilante experience that, even if he wouldn't have minded relating them to his father and mother, would have left his pietistic grandfather Stone turning in his grave. Some of these were the eternal pranks and practical jokes played by college students throughout the

[168] Hughes, 109, quoting July and September 1858 letters from Martha and Virgil Wilson.
[169] Moore, *Behind the Bars,* 47.
[170] Ibid., 48.

world and the recorded history thereof: taking naïve freshmen "snipe hunting" and leaving them in the hills to discover they'd been duped, "borrowing," if not stealing, foodstuffs from the kitchens for midnight feasts in the dormitory, and what not. Others simply defy explanation, at least in modern terms, and of these certainly the most remarkable involved Charles's relationship with Bethany Vice President W. K. Pendleton's young and pretty third wife, Katherine—or, as Charles called her in spite of the fact that he was only five years her junior, Aunt Kate.

Kate Pendleton had borne her first child the same year in which Moore matriculated at Bethany, and she had a stepdaughter (Alexandrina Campbellina Pendleton, known to her friends as Cammie) who was more of an age to socialize with young college men than she herself was. Nonetheless, if Charles's memories are to be trusted, Kate seems to have adopted him as her companion in merriment and mischief—and just perhaps, in the subtle indulgence of a small fantasy. On one occasion when her husband was absent, she invited Charles and several of his friends to her home for an all-night frolic at which a couple of so-called *barbaroi* girls, perhaps cooks or housemaids she had hired for the occasion, were also present. For some unknown and unknowable reason, about midnight Kate told Charles to lock all the doors and hide the keys without letting anyone catch him doing so. Soon after, when the two young lower-caste girls insisted that they must go home, they found all the doors locked and neither Kate, Charles, nor any of the other partiers would let them out. They were forced to climb through a window about ten feet off the ground in order to get out of the house.

Was the locking of the doors simply Kate Pendleton's idea of an *aristoi* joke at the expense of two frightened country girls who, for all we know, might have been all the more panicked because even Christian boys would still be boys and they had cause to fear for their honor and their well-being? We will never know. It's a fair bet, though, that if some tough-bitten old frontier preacher like Barton Stone, Rice Haggard, John Mulkey or Raccoon John Smith had had the pastoral charge of the Bethany Church at this time, the entire pack of partygoers, Kate included, would have been soundly rebuked and then excommunicated for the sin of "walking disorderly before the world." (And then, like as not, the church would have kicked the pastor out just as had happened in New England a century earlier with Jonathan Edwards.) As it was, Kate and her young revelers continued their party until sunrise, when she treated them to an enormous gourmet breakfast.[171]

In another instance, Kate and Charles sat together at an academic convocation at the campus church listening to a guest lecturer. In his lap, Charles held his fancy black silk and velvet cap—and within the cap, a whalebone bean shooter and a generous quantity of beans. And so it came to pass when the pair got bored with the visiting professor's exposition of the life and times of Napoleon, Charles began shooting beans at him with a deftness and subtlety that a sleight-of-hand artist might have admired, and so thoroughly pelted the globes of the lamps in the pulpit, and the speaker himself, that he single-handedly almost broke up the lecture. Naturally, the faculty called him up on the carpet for his misbehavior—but then acquitted him entirely, on the basis of Kate Pendleton's pious and matronly testimony that she had sat beside him throughout the entire lecture and had never seen him shoot a single bean. One of the professors even apologized to Charles for having suspected him of the crime.[172]

The most curious of all Charles's recollections of Kate Pendleton, however, involved the extended absence of her husband and Alexander Campbell from Bethany after the December 1857 fire, touring Kentucky and Ohio soliciting funds from prominent Disciple congregations to rebuild the college's destroyed classroom building. It was perhaps only natural that Campbell and W. K. Pendleton should board at the homes of the parents of their Kentucky students while visiting the state, and in fact Chilton and Mary Anne Moore hosted the pair at Forest Retreat for several days while they made the rounds of Lexington and central Bluegrass churches. Charles's sister Mary was home from Harrodsburg as well and by this time she had grown into a tall, beautiful young woman, perhaps even then having begun to accept the calls of the dashing Bourbon County visitor, Thomas Young Brent, who would soon become her husband. For all that, though, W. K. Pendleton was a long way from the hills of Bethany and, though he was at least twenty-two years older than Mary, he was by no means immune to the charms of a fair face, a well-turned ankle and a sparkling personality. In fact,

---

[171] Ibid., 47-48.
[172] Ibid., 47.

he came to admire Mary so much that he wrote to his wife about her, and Mary in turn wrote to Charles with an amused account of Pendleton's crush-like attentions towards her.

On reading Mary's letter Charles had a good laugh, then visited the Pendleton house and jokingly told Kate that her husband had fallen in love with his sister. Completely unperturbed, Kate shot back, "I know all about it; that's all right; you and I will get even with him!" This they proceeded to do on a few late-evening sleigh rides that winter,[173] and although Kate and Charles's "revenge" probably involved nothing more salacious than a bit of hand holding, some conventional words of Sir Walter Scott-style courtly and chivalric romance murmured in each other's ears, and maybe a peck or two on each other's hands and cheeks, it's hard to read Moore's later account of the friendship without wondering how he could later condemn James Lane Allen's *The Choir Invisible* so roundly. It was all too easy for a twenty-year-old college boy to get caught up ever so slightly and briefly in the chivalric ideal of a platonic yet romantic attachment with an older woman. And it was just as plausible—and equally human—for a twenty-five year-old mother, the beaux of her single days an ever-fading memory now that she was married to an older man who was far away from home and doing some looking about on his own, to gaze with fond thoughts upon a handsome *aristoi* Southern firebrand who, just barely out of his teens, had proven his mettle in the foreign wilds of Pennsylvania, battling city rabble in a chivalrous attempt to bring a vicious criminal to the bar; a boy, as Don Henley and Glenn Frey put it more than a hundred years later, with fiery eyes, and dreams no one could steal.

Pendleton returned to hearth and home, wife and child, in tow with Alexander Campbell, but in his last semester at Bethany Charles went right on sledding—not with Kate, of course, but with a bevy of young unattached beauties, some romantic interests and some not, so many in fact that the sequence of his courtships and friendships is a little hard to follow. In later years Charles recalled Ellen Campbell, daughter of a cousin of Alexander's family and who lived nearby, as the first young woman with whom he made friends after arriving at

---

[173] Ibid.

Bethany, but not as a serious romantic interest. He also recounted that Ellen's sister Jane, or Jennie, was the fiancée of his classmate Thomas Allen,[174] and yet he wrote to his friend Richard Prewitt in February 1857 that he had become "desperately smitten" by Jane Campbell's "attractions" himself.[175] As late as January 1858, at the same time Pendleton was gone to Kentucky and he was sledding with Kate, he was writing to Prewitt that he hoped to marry that same summer,[176] one assumes to Jane. College boys being college boys, it's difficult to ascertain exactly what happened here; it's even possible that Jane could have quietly broken up with Charles over his propensity to go sleighing with Kate Pendleton.

Whatever his attachments with Alexander Campbell's cousins, though, Charles's interactions with Campbell's own daughters were close, informal, and very warm. He recalled spending a lot of time in 1856 and 1857 in the company of Virginia Campbell, the family's second-youngest daughter and who herself later married the Versailles, Kentucky, native William Thompson and served as postmistress of Louisville. Charles and Virginia often traipsed the Bethany hills with a shotgun, sport shooting and exchanging pleasantries; in his memory, the two of them interacted and talked as if they were of the same sex, sometimes as two boys and others as two girls, and he was even a frequent guest at the Campbells' dinner table.[177] Interestingly, Charles and Virginia could also share a laugh over her father's preaching. For all the glowing accounts left behind by various hearers of Alexander Campbell's clear, incisive, spellbinding oratory,[178] both Virginia and Charles considered the sermons of his older years to be long, dry, and boring.[179] Even so, Campbell's pulpit efforts seem not to have been insipid enough for Charles to try his luck once again with his bean shooter, and it is probably very fortunate that he never took the chance.

Apparently, up until the early part of 1858 Charles had never met Campbell's youngest daughter, Decima. She had been away at a girls'

---

[174] Ibid., 31, 35-37, 44-45.
[175] Moore to Richard Prewitt, February 15, 1857; Bethany College Collection.
[176] Moore to Prewitt, January 20, 1858; Bethany College Collection.
[177] Moore, *Behind the Bars,* 49.
[178] E.g., Wrather, II, 43-45; Garrett, 170.
[179] Moore, *Behind the Bars,* 49.

school in Washington D. C. through most of his tenure at Bethany. However, he recalled that in 1856 or 1857 Virginia Campbell had shown him a miniature portrait of Dessie, as her family and friends all called her, and had warned him that when he did meet her he was sure to fall "dead in love with her" no sooner than he should lay eyes on her.[180] In his own memory this is exactly what happened, and both the meeting and the birth of his romantic attraction to her occurred in the late spring or early summer of 1858;[181] yet, his letters to Richard Prewitt in January and February of that same year tell a slightly different story. Dessie was home with her mother by the end of January—the same time Charles was courting Jane Campbell and talking of marriage with her, *and* sledding with Kate Pendleton in her own tempting interpretation of the word revenge—and Charles commented to Prewitt in his January 28 letter that Dessie "is as beautiful a specimen of humanity as I ever beheld. She is turning the heads and stealing the hearts of all who venture inside the charmed circle of her influence. I'm telling the truth. Come see for yourself!" But even so, it would appear that he entertained no designs to strike up a special relationship with Dessie, even though Prewitt seems to have jokingly asked Charles to "court her for him."[182]

Within a month, everything had changed. Gone were his love for, and apparently even his thoughts of, Jane Campbell, as well as any temptations he might have entertained towards Kate Pendleton. The winter of 1858 must have been a cold one in the northern Virginia panhandle, though, because at the end of February he was still sledding—now, with Dessie Campbell instead:

> Well, Dick, the funniest thing that has been taking place here for some time is the *sleigh riding* we have been having for some time [*sic*], and I ain't known when I have had so familiar an opportunity to "court Dessie" for you—as I have had lately. I have been sleigh riding every day since the sun fell—I believe—Thomson [*sic*] says you have not sleighing in Kentucky—but we have had the finest kind here—and you may be sure that I have enjoyed it. My last big *bust*

---

[180] Ibid., 50.
[181] Ibid., 50-51.
[182] Moore to Prewitt, January 28, 1858; Bethany College Collection.

> was down to Wheeling—and coming back you may guess that I gave Dessie some *Moonlight Soft Solace* for you. But I find it a dangerous business for myself... [Ellipse added; all emphases, spelling, and punctuation in original][183]

Thus much for the pure and unsullied romance of it all, but then again boys of the age as Charles was at this time generally prefer moonlight soft solace, as he termed it, to the genuine article of true love even if the administration of the moonlight soft solace is in fact a dangerous business. And yet strangely enough, a blossoming of intense romance seems to have been exactly the way the relationship developed by the late spring. We might wonder at what qualities Charles perceived in Dessie that he didn't see in her less glamorous cousin Jane, but whatever they were, his feelings toward Dessie were real and very powerful. In his fourth semester at Bethany Charles finally earned enough credit hours, when added up with his courses at Transylvania, to entitle him to apply for his bachelor's degree; and so by the time of the Doniphan tragedy in April or May and the beginning of the reconstruction of the destroyed classroom building, he had fallen absolutely head over heels for Dessie Campbell, and she seems to have given him every indication that his love, or at least his infatuation, was entirely requited. We should be thankful, though, that he seems never to have penned a poem about Dessie for publication in *The Neotrophian*—or as one of the editors of the magazine, if he did dare write such verses, some lowly *barbaroi* college printer's devil wisely and discreetly "lost" them.

For all his Scottish and French heritage and Irish birth, or perhaps because of it, Alexander Campbell entertained a respect for the symbolism of the independence of the United States, and the holiday set aside to celebrate it, that few native-born Americans have shared in intensity. Though he remained a controversial writer and preacher until the end of his days, he dedicated his life to trying to prove the proposition that Christian unity could best be achieved and reach its highest expression in a democratic republic, and he made full use of Independence Day imagery in both his periodicals and in his leadership of his religious movement at large. In the heady, early days of America's Era

[183] Moore to Prewitt, February 26, 1858; Bethany College Collection.

of Good Feeling, he had purposely chosen July 4, 1823 as the publication date for the pilot issue of his very first newspaper, the old *Christian Baptist,*[184] and as long as he was the president of Bethany College he and his trustees made sure that the school regularly held its yearly commencement exercises on Independence Day as well.[185] It was thus both ironic and tragic that, whereas Bethany was known primarily as a Southern college in 1858, less than a decade would pass before it would be known as the very opposite of a Southern school—and that the interim would see the democratic republic that Alexander Campbell had adopted as his home and loved so much, divide itself and the halves go to war with one another over a question both sides believed was answered in a book that Campbell himself upheld as a clear, concise, scientific blueprint of salvation and Christian living direct from the hand of the Almighty. Under the circumstances, for all we know it could have been a mercy that Campbell became senile before his death in 1866.[186] He simply may not have been constitutionally able to face life with a clear head in the brand-new Northern state of West Virginia, the citizen of a newly-reunified nation wherein the incisive theological pronouncements made by the Reverend Doctors Ulysses Simpson Grant and William Tecumseh Sherman during their itinerant ministries, as it were, through Tennessee, Virginia, and Georgia, had carried more actual weight than his own thoughtful essays and exhortations ever had or ever could.

Charles Chilton Moore was to live many years after his graduation from Bethany, and although in later life he often spoke critically and dismissively of the ideas of Alexander Campbell he seems always to have held his grandfather's pioneer co-Reformer in the warmest personal regard. And on his graduation day of July 4, 1858 he had especial reason to look kindly on Campbell as he accepted his diploma from the old preacher and editor's hand: apparently Campbell had approved, if not actually blessed, Charles's courtship of his youngest daughter, and though Charles thus may have left behind him one, and possibly even two, broken hearts at Bethany, life could not possibly have seemed better to him than at that moment. True, Charles and his beloved Dessie

---

[184] Wrather, II, 14.
[185] Goodnight and Stephenson, 103.
[186] Hughes, 44; Moore, *Behind the Bars,* 38.

must spend several months apart, he in Kentucky and she in Washington D. C. as well as the northern Virginia panhandle, but he could and would write to her continually, and with the benevolence of Divine Providence, one day, as soon as such a proposal was proper, he would ask for her hand in marriage...

The dead body of Alexander Doniphan still moldered under the Bethany church house floor. Among the living in both faculty and student spheres, pro- versus anti-slavery tensions continued to ferment quietly but inevitably, and Charles had never yet quite reconciled that nagging little matter of the good Dr. Pickett's interpretation of I Timothy either to William Paley's Watchmaker Analogy or to his own inner principles of charity, rationality, and common sense. But for all that, on July 4, 1858 God was yet in his heaven, Dessie Campbell was on earth, and all was right with the world.

Chapter 4

Romance, Rejection, Religion, and Reflection

Believe me, I can quote the Koran too;
The unbeliever knows his Koran best.
—attributed to Omar Khayyam

Within three weeks of his graduation at Bethany, Charles had returned to Dog Fennel and had "laid in his church letter" once again at Old Union.[187] He remained in a veritable amorous trance over Dessie Campbell, though, and from all appearances he continued therein for at least fifteen months or so. Not that he had much of anything else besides romance and churchgoing to occupy either his mind or his time. He came back to Forest Retreat with a college education but otherwise essentially as he had left it, as a plantation owner-to-be and gentleman of leisure, perhaps waiting on his obligatory European grand tour only until his marriage to Dessie so she could accompany him. His parents' house servants attended to his every mundane need and his mother still managed the house and his father the farm. The one possible exception to his status of perpetual relaxation may have been in the political arena. After Henry Clay's death in 1852 his Whig Party had faded out of existence, and although the majority of Northern Whigs

[187] Old Union Christian Church Record Book, 1823-1892. Lexington Theological Seminary. Charles Chilton Moore Jr. rejoined the church by letter on July 25, 1858.

readily joined the new Republican Party, many Southern Whigs as well as the members of the short-lived American or "Know-Nothing" Party were left more or less politically adrift in the late 1850s. In 1859, however, a sizable number of these Southern ex-Whigs under the leadership of John J. Crittenden of Kentucky organized the Constitutional Union Party, and it appears that the elder Chilton Moore became a Fayette County leader of this latter group. In December 1858 young Charles attained his majority and became eligible to vote, and both his father's influence and the reputation for journalistic wit his "Edibility of Crows" essay had established for him guaranteed him a solid footing in Fayette County Constitutional Union Party circles.[188]

Of course, though, if there was one thing the Bluegrass gentry utterly adored, it was playing host to visitors and throwing parties, barbecues, and balls, and in this connection Charles got to see Dessie again in the autumn of 1858. She and her sister Virginia traveled to Kentucky in company with other Bethany friends to visit several acquaintances in the Bluegrass, in Virginia's case probably to see William Thompson at Versailles, and the party of travelers tarried long enough at Forest Retreat for Charles to arrange a three- or four-day chaperoned excursion southwest to Mammoth Cave for himself, Dessie, the entire group of Virginia visitors, his sisters Mary and Jane, and several more Kentuckians thrown in for good measure. By this time he had worked up enough courage to ask Dessie to marry him, and as he recalled it, he proposed to her on the return leg of this trip at the plantation of the Moore family's friend Richard White about six miles south of Richmond, Kentucky. She accepted, and the overjoyed Charles ordered a fine diamond engagement ring for her from a Lexington jeweler, with the date of her consent to his proposal—which, unfortunately, Moore never noted in his later autobiographical writings—engraved on the inside.[189]

After that, nothing would do but that he should journey back up the Ohio to Bethany to spend Christmas, or at least a portion of the holiday season, with Dessie and her parents. The young couple spent a good deal of time simply talking in front of the Campbells' hearth, and frequently Dessie's mother had to upbraid them for keeping late hours.

---

[188] Moore, *Behind the Bars,* 148.
[189] Ibid., 52-57.

Often as not, though, as soon as the older Campbells retired for the night, Charles and Dessie would get back up, meet again in the parlor, and whisper together until dawn. Even so, Dessie never would commit herself to an actual wedding date, but Charles's love seems to have taught him a degree of patience; they were both young yet, he told her, and he was willing to wait for her as long as she chose.[190]

Thus after his return to Forest Retreat that winter he pined for Dessie once more, though the two still wrote to one another almost daily. And so when Bethany College's commencement time rolled around again on July 4, 1859, he used the occasion as another excuse to pay her a visit. Both he and his sister Mary journeyed to the northern Virginia panhandle to attend the festivities. Not too long afterward, Dessie and her sister Virginia again traveled downriver by steamboat, this time to visit friends in St. Louis, and from here Charles received news, probably from some of his cousins who had moved there from Hannibal, that seemed to shake his world absolutely down to its foundations. Dessie was flirting, dancing, and altogether receiving a great deal of moonlight soft solace (though in this instance the slang expression would have hurt Charles too badly ever to use it in connection with her) from a blush of young male St. Louis admirers and giving no indication whatsoever that she was affianced to Charles. Wild with alarm, he wrote to her asking her about the veracity of the rumors, with a few pointed remarks of rebuke if they happened to be true; she replied with what he later recalled was a "sweet and affectionate letter," but she denied none of the accusations and, moreover, asked him to release her from her promise of marriage.[191]

In that time and place, such behavior on the part of any young woman would have immediately earned her the reputation of being a bad girl, almost on our modern par with certain youthful female celebrities and heiresses who had perhaps best remain nameless (and who would, in an ideal world, be completely ignored and shunned by the media). Even now we might criticize Dessie Campbell for being spoiled, immature, flighty, and perhaps even a bit callous. For all that, though, alas, broken hearts were and are a dime a dozen among the young, and in modern-day hindsight we can look at both Charles and Dessie with some understanding and perhaps even a little compassion.

---

[190] Ibid., 57-58.
[191] Ibid., 58.

Though her suitor was a young gentleman of wealth, leisure, and impeccable religious pedigree, Dessie had been brought up not only to those same inheritances of faith and economic independence but to intense and continual intellectual and social stimulation as well. The daughter of one of antebellum America's most celebrated religious figures, she had grown to young adulthood in a house forever filled with important and exciting guests talking and sometimes arguing with her father; her fellow students at her girls' school in Washington D. C. were the crème of the national capital's society, and their fathers were likewise celebrated personalities in the America of that day; and on her return trips home to Bethany she had continually been admired and feted by the highest aristocracy among both young college men and the sons and daughters of visiting dignitaries. Charles might simply have been the Bethany catch of the day for her in the spring and early summer of 1858.

Thus, although Dessie could have arrived in Kentucky still with stars in her eyes over her Bluegrass suitor, and accompanied him to Mammoth Cave and then to Richmond with what she thought was true love in her heart, after she accepted his marriage proposal it's not unlikely that she did a good deal of quiet thinking and reassessing of her life on the return journey. If, en route back to Dog Fennel, Charles had tried to make her laugh with such rough jests and jibes about his parents' house and its surrounding community as he later penned in newspaper editorials like the example quoted in the second chapter of this work, we can fairly imagine her consternation at seeing the place again. Dessie may have been seized with the sudden fear that, after the honeymoon and the grand tour were all over, she would literally be out to pasture at Forest Retreat, with only Charles's mother and sisters and the household servants to keep her company except when they happened to host summer and Christmas balls and barbecues with other rural gentry guests every bit as bucolic and provincial as the Moores themselves. For all his Bethany education, when at home Charles still called an ear of corn a "year"![192] And in the modern era too, more than halfway through the nineteenth century! How gauche! And so, despite the area planters' and turfmen's well-deserved reputation in the breeding, raising, and training of Thoroughbreds, settling down in the friendly but

[192] Moore, *Dog Fennel,* 35.

ever-so-rustic bosom of northeastern Fayette County may have appeared to be just too daunting a prospect for this nineteen-year-old celebrity daughter to handle.

As it was, Dessie landed on her feet and, presumably, lived a very happy life. She remained single at Bethany for a few years more, then married John Judson Barclay, son of James Turner Barclay, her father's first Disciples of Christ missionary to the Holy Land.[193] Young Barclay had received an excellent education at various mission schools in Europe and the Near East, and at the time of his visit to Bethany and subsequent whirlwind courtship and marriage he held an important and lucrative position with the American diplomatic corps on the island of Cyprus. He took Dessie to honeymoon in Paris and then back with him to Cyprus, where their first child was born and where they remained some years.[194] In later life, however, the widowed Dessie returned to Bethany once more, where she lived out her last decade, poignantly, in the house in which she was born as the *de facto* curator of her father's religious, educational, and editorial memorabilia.[195]

taken in Paris, France
Mr & Mrs J. J. Barclay -

Back in Kentucky in the fall and winter of 1859, and despite his own earlier flippancy towards his relationship with Dessie's cousin Jane, Charles was inconsolable. To the end of his days he bitterly recalled picking up Dessie's dear-john letter to him from the

---

[193] Brown, 440-441.

[194] Moore, *Behind the Bars,* 58-59.

[195] Holloway, "Archives Receives Campbell Communion Chalice." From *The Envoy,* V, 4, November 1999, Emmanuel School of Religion, Johnson City, Tenn.

Lexington post office. After he steeled himself to read it and mustered enough dignity and courage to scrawl out an answer and give it back to the postmaster, he chanced to wander by the historic Kentucky Eastern Lunatic Asylum, now known as the Eastern State Hospital, and located, both then and now, on Fourth Street in the city. In a daze of sorrow he looked across the grounds and up at the barred windows and wondered how long it would be before he wound up being committed as a patient in the institution himself.[196] Actually, this thought may not have been merely the idle hyperbole of a heartbroken youth. At that date the Asylum housed at least one well-known inmate, Henry Clay's eldest son Theodore, who had been committed several years before for exhibiting abnormally obsessive behavior toward a young Lexington lady and making terroristic threats to her parents. Of course many Bluegrass citizens, perhaps Charles's mother and father too, had categorized and oversimplified the case as being only that of a young man somehow gone mad for love. Charles had to have known at least something about the younger Clay's circumstances, which would have been all the more terrifying to him since by this time Theodore had begun to believe he was George Washington and was fond of making appearances to the Asylum's visitors "in the traditional attitude of the Father of his Country." [197]

Yet, fortunately, Charles's mind was made of sterner stuff. He later claimed that it took him six full years to get over Dessie, but by hook or crook, get over her he finally did. The first year may have been the hardest: his father turned seventy that winter, and might already have been showing some signs of failing health; his sisters Mary and Jane had completed their studies at Daughters' College, had become engaged to Thomas Young Brent and James E. Cantrill, respectively, and were making wedding plans of their own; and so while he could hardly have immersed his sorrows in any hard work, there wasn't quite time

---

[196] Moore, *Behind the Bars*, 58. The Eastern State Hospital has had several name changes in its long history; the title listed here was the one used just before the Civil War.

[197] Obituary of Theodore Clay dated May 19, 1870 and published in *The Cincinnati Enquirer;* reprinted in *The Farmer's Cabinet,* Amherst, N. H., May 26, 1870; found in "Eastern State Hospital, Lexington, Kentucky: Deaths Reported in Newspapers, 1826-1890." http://www.rootsweb.com/~kyfayett/esh_newspapers.htm

for him to retreat to some secluded spot and be a hermit, either. Thus he saw both Mary and Jane happily married even if he couldn't entirely share in their joy, and in one bright spot in this dark twelvemonth he accompanied Mary and Thomas Brent on their honeymoon as far as Niagara Falls. When the newlyweds entered the Cataract House Lodge there, he wrote, they were such a strikingly handsome couple they attracted the attention and admiration of more people than he had ever seen.[198] Within a year, too, Thomas and Mary became the proud parents of a baby daughter, whom they named Mary Chilton Brent as if there were not already enough Marys and Chiltons in the family to confuse any outsider, and Charles adored his new niece as well.

Perhaps for the sake of his father's pride in him, he allowed himself another adventure of sorts that spring and summer as the Constitutional Union Party began to organize for the purpose of fielding a presidential and vice-presidential candidate in the 1860 election. His "Edibility of Crows" essay still qualified him as an astute political satirist in the minds of his father's Lexington friends and acquaintances, and so the Lexington Constitutional Unionists sent him as one of their representatives to the Party's convention meeting at Louisville. The convention nominated John Bell for President and the famous orator Edward Everett for Vice-President, and while Charles confessed to knowing absolutely nothing practical about politics and caring less, to the point in fact that he didn't have any idea who John Bell was, he seems to have behaved himself in Louisville and perhaps he thus gave his good old father another bit of boasting material. He later speculated that if he had only possessed the inclination, the savvy, and the presence of mind to manage the political boost that his "Crows" essay had given him, he might even have made a successful run for Congress that year.[199] Interestingly, John Bell, who was the one 1860 presidential candidate who absolutely refused to discuss the issue of slavery in any form or fashion whatsoever, carried the state of Kentucky, and the four-way vote split brought about by his presence on the ballot along with candidates from two different factions of the Democratic Party, one of them Charles's

---

[198] Moore, *Behind the Bars,* 52.
[199] Ibid., 147-148.

old Dog Fennel neighbor John C. Breckinridge, pretty much guaranteed Lincoln's victory.[200]

Along with a good many of his neighbors, Chilton Moore had predicted that civil war would result if the Republican candidate were elected to the Presidency.[201] Perhaps fortunately for him, though, he never lived to see his prophecy come true. According to the Old Union Church's records he died on the third day of August 1860[202], leaving the care of his wife and daughters and the responsibility of settling his estate to his only surviving son. Charles estimated the estate's total net worth at about $100,000 in land, personal estate, and cash, probably the equivalent of around 2.5 million dollars at modern exchange rates; his father had left outstanding debts totaling approximately $6000, half of which Charles paid off immediately by selling some household items and perhaps farm equipment. He said later that he would have had to sell some slaves in order to get ready cash enough to make good on the other $3,000, but being unwilling to split up Forest Retreat's black families he borrowed the money on his own credit to finish paying his father's old debts.

After Lincoln was elected that November Charles figured Forest Retreat's blacks would be emancipated in the coming war anyway, and being opposed to slavery to start with, he wanted them all to go free from the old home.[203] Thus the idealistic and ever-impractical Charles put himself into an extremely curious position for the time; he was vocally pro-South, yet for all of Professor Pickett's Scriptural counsel he was still determinedly anti-slavery just like his sainted grandfather Stone—both at the same time.[204] He later observed that his political views thus left him pretty much completely without representation in the contest between North and South after the 1860 Presidential election,[205] but he does seem to have made one ardent convert to the Confederate cause quite by accident. Before and during Thomas Brent and

---

[200] Thanks to Civil War historian Edward R. Hazelett of Paintsville, Kentucky, for this information.

[201] Moore, *Behind the Bars,* 27.

[202] Old Union Christian Church Record Book, 1823-1892. Lexington Theological Seminary.

[203] Moore, *Behind the Bars,* 61.

[204] Ibid., 76.

[205] Ibid., *The Rational View,* 5.

Mary Moore's first months of marriage, Brent had leaned towards support of the Federal Government if war was to be declared, but when Charles once rather casually happened to recount to him Dr. Pickett's Bethany exposition of the sixth chapter of 1 Timothy, Brent completely changed his mind. Charles's tale convinced him that the Bible passage was, in Brent's own words, "God's ordinance of secession."[206] In days to come, Moore would have much cause to brood about the effect of the Scripture text he had thus nonchalantly dropped in family conversation.

For now, though, he still lamented his own personal woes, first his lost Dessie and secondly his father's death. Gone was his desire for the cheer of a tapped keg of beer in the hallway, and for the nip of a stronger beverage on holidays and special occasions; gone with his father's passing too, apparently, was his inclination to keep up his Fayette County Constitutional Unionist political connections, and he even sublimated his wishes to spend time with other young men and women in the Dog Fennel and Lexington communities. Little by little the year 1860 saw Charles's sorrows turn him into quite as intense a pietist as old Barton Stone had ever been, and so at some point during this twelvemonth, perhaps even before the Louisville convention and his father's death, he resolved to vanquish his grief in his faith tradition and his religious heritage: like his grandfather Stone he would spend his life preaching the Gospel and bringing the good news of salvation through Jesus Christ to a lost and dying world.

He must have communicated his desire to his pastor Gano and to Old Union Church soon after his resolution, perhaps as early as January or February before his father's death in August. Though no record of his preaching at Old Union exists from that time, he later recalled that, about the summer of 1862, he had been involved in the ministry approximately two and a half years.[207] If his memory was correct in this particular he thus might even have gotten his ministerial start under his ailing father's eldership on prayer meeting nights that winter and early spring, but it's certain that he was established as a ministerial candidate at the least very shortly after his father's passing. That fall, Gano and the congregation determined that he needed just a few extra academic

---

[206] Ibid., 5.
[207] Ibid., *Behind the Bars,* 71.

Bible courses to ready himself for the ministry, and so he returned northeast to Bethany for one last semester to acquire them. Old Union's records indicate that he transferred his membership back to the college church on December 22, 1860[208], and he later recalled finishing up his Bible training and being ordained to the ministry at Bethany by Alexander Campbell, W. K. Pendleton, and J. D. Pickett in the late spring of 1861 "when the war was almost upon us and military companies were organizing."[209]

Anyone who had known Charles in his undergraduate years was undoubtedly surprised—and some were perhaps even chilled—by the changes in his deportment and his personality, but it did fall his chance to see Dessie Campbell one last time at the very end of his extra semester, after he was already packed to go back home. He gathered up his courage and paid a call at the Campbells', and he and Dessie walked together into the hills and cried in one another's arms as if Dessie were every bit as heartbroken as Charles. As he recalled it, "goodbye" was almost the only word that they exchanged together, and he never spoke to her again—although a few years later she did write him a proud, joyful letter from Cyprus announcing the birth of her oldest daughter.[210]

And so Charles returned to Kentucky, left Forest Retreat in the care of his mother and the family's slaves, and served perhaps sixteen months, more or less, as a missionary preacher in the mountains southeast of Richmond. It's probable that John Allen Gano helped him secure this position, for which, as he was still an independently wealthy young Bluegrass aristocrat, he served without salary, his mother regularly sending him money from home for necessities. His area of itinerary seems to have encompassed a range from southern Madison County through Jackson and Clay Counties and ending somewhere around the Knox County seat of Barbourville, and his partners in the Gospel work were four rural preachers, all sons of a backcountry Madison County Disciple couple named William and Alah Asbell (or Azbill). Charles did a great deal of preaching and performed a good many baptisms at

---

[208] Old Union Christian Church Record Book, 1823-1892. Lexington Theological Seminary.

[209] Moore, *Behind the Bars,* 58; *The Rational View,* 5.

[210] Moore, *Behind the Bars,* 58-59.

the little mountain Disciple churches under the Asbell brothers' care—most of them that survived later forsaking the Disciple title for the name of Church of Christ—and he helped to ordain the youngest Asbell exhorter, Overton, to the ministry. After the state of Kentucky finally declared itself formally for the Union side Charles's new brothers-in-law Brent and Cantrill joined an independent but pro-Confederate unit, known initially as the Lexington Rifles and headed up by a brash Mexican War veteran named John Hunt Morgan. The Moore girls moved back in with their mother for the war's duration. In Charles's own role as a minister, though—and perhaps also because the Asbells and a good many of his other contacts in the hills were all as strongly pro-Union as he himself was pro-Confederate—he now downplayed his political views, preferring instead to call himself "a private soldier under a flag with a cross on it."[211]

If he ever entertained any particularly high opinions of his own preaching, Charles's later writings didn't indicate it. Perhaps they wouldn't have under any consideration, although, as we shall see, at least at one brief period did allow himself a few aspirations to glory and good works through scholarship. As might be expected, though, the southeastern Kentucky mountains were something of a rude awakening to him. From the bear-gnawed pines and the "witch charm," carved into a tree and shot with a silver bullet, that Overton Asbell showed him on his first day in the backcountry, to the occasional congregational shouting of the kind his grandfather Stone had known and joined even though Charles himself preached only in Alexander Campbell's customary conversational style, he was in brand-new territory both socially and intellectually. He recalled basing some of his texts on Butler's *Analogy* and Paley's *Evidences*,[212] but he might as well not even have bothered because he was definitely preaching to the choir, as it were, about such subjects in the hill country. Among believers here and regardless of sect or denomination, the existence of God didn't need to be proven; it could be stated categorically as a fact for no other reason than that the Bible said it was true. The shouts of the sisters (and often as not, the brothers) only went to confirm it, and besides, everyone knew that God was jealous and liable to strike down anyone who was

[211] Ibid., 61-64.
[212] Ibid., 72.

fool enough to express any doubt of his presence, by lightning, earthquake, or even worse.

On the other hand, three nonconformist individuals he met while on his mountain missionary junkets, and whom he then regarded as freethinkers or infidels, wouldn't listen to him reason about Butler and Paley either—or perhaps some of them did pay attention to his arguments and simply weighed and rejected them. The oldest of these, the respected gentleman farmer and salt maker Daniel Garrard of Goose Creek near Manchester in Clay County, would sit near Charles's pulpit placidly as he expounded upon biblical and theological themes, apparently fully enjoying the young Gospel battler's discourses for no other cause than, as he himself put it to Charles, "I always enjoy hearing any man reason on any important subject."[213] But then again, Garrard was no ordinary case. He was the son of Kentucky's second governor, James Garrard, who himself had once been a Baptist preacher before he came under the religious influence of his secretary of state, the English Unitarian minister and Transylvania College president Harry Toulmin. The senior Garrard was actually kicked out of the United Baptist Church in the Bluegrass for so-called Unitarian heresy at about the end of his second term as Governor.[214] Daniel Garrard had married Harry Toulmin's daughter Lucinda as his first wife, and over the years he had seen and heard so much doctrinal disputation between the Baptists, the Unitarians, and every other denomination represented either in the Bluegrass or the mountains, that he didn't find it personally worthwhile to embrace any religious position at all. By the time Charles met Garrard his first wife had died, and Charles actually succeeded in converting and immersing his much-younger second spouse, Mary, while visiting Manchester with the Asbells to hold preaching services. But the venerable Daniel remained unmoved, placidly waiting on whatever might, or might not, follow his final breath; and until that fateful moment should fall upon him he was entirely content to spend his time as a vigorous Confederate sympathizer.[215]

---

213 Ibid., 67.

214 See Sparks, *The Roots of Appalachian Christianity,* 200-201; *Raccoon John Smith,* 149-150.

215 Moore, *Behind the Bars,* 66-68.

Another freethinker Charles met in Clay County was an old, pipe-smoking mountain mother named Mary Links, the wife of the Belgian-born manager of the Garrard Salt Works, Frederick Links. "Old sister Lynx," as Moore wrote of her, could be placid in her state of unbelief too, but only up to a certain point past which she adamantly refused to be pushed without pushing back. Frederick Links and his daughters were enthusiastic Disciples, and although the couple's sons were not Christians they listened to Charles's sermons respectfully. For her part, Mrs. Links was the perfect hostess to Charles and other visitors, and she would cheerfully help both her husband and her children ready themselves to attend church of a Sunday morning. However, when Charles conducted worship at the Links house itself—home services having been a common practice in eastern Kentucky since its first settlement, and often still seen in modern times as well—the old lady would turn her rocking chair around towards the fire, light her pipe, and ignore the singing and preaching completely. As to the possibility of confronting her personally about the welfare of her soul, her husband warned Charles, in a thick Flemish accent that the young preacher understandably mistook for German, that if he tried it he would receive a tongue lashing that he would never forget. Thus he never made the attempt, and he stayed on her good side.[216]

The third freethinker Charles met in the mountains was a young farmer and cooper that had somehow gotten himself a good education for his time and place, and actually boasted a small collection of high-quality books in his cabin. By the time Charles penned his autobiography he had forgotten the man's name, but he did remember that he hadn't really made any ambitious attempts to convert him; so impressed was Charles with the young cooper's library, and perhaps so lonesome for a good college-style intellectual discussion as well, that he rather fell into conversation with him about his various books.[217]

Actually, he recalled that not only the cooper but most of the mountain people to whom he preached were just as ready, and amenable, to listen to him talk about science, history, or any other of his college subjects, as they were to hear a sermon. They were literally starved not only for education but for news of the wider world, and if

---

[216] Ibid., 64-66; Clay County, Kentucky, 1860 Federal Census.
[217] Moore, *Behind the Bars,* 70.

Charles had for some reason elected to remain in the hills and teach school he might have accomplished an enormous amount of positive good among them. But teaching, at least below the collegiate level, seems not to have been considered a proper profession for his class in the Bluegrass, and despite his possible natural knack as a schoolmaster he never formally attempted a teaching career. However, this experience of speaking with his mountain listeners about the concepts of both science and religion did inspire him to what might have been, at least in the abstract, his noblest ambition as a young Christian minister: in spite of that inchoate but still-gnawing little doubt over Dr. Pickett and I Timothy that remained in his mind, he firmly believed that if he could somehow collate all the evidences of the truth of Christianity he then believed could be found *outside* the Bible, to that *within* the sacred text itself—in essence, to become Kentucky's own modern-era combination of William Paley, Joseph Butler, Alexander Campbell, and his grandfather Stone all—he could usher in an entirely new interest in Christianity in the mountains, and perhaps all over the now war-torn state.[218] In this glorious light he may have seen even his three hill-country infidel acquaintances as all part of God's personal plan for his ministry, working, as Providence always did, in a mysterious way its wonders to perform. Besides, they'd surely all be converted—just as soon as he could make a visit back home, reread a few of his Paley and Butler textbooks, get all his scientific and biblical data lined up, and come back and preach to them once again.

This first trip back to the Bluegrass could have occurred for Charles quite involuntarily and as early as the third week of September 1861, when the forces of Confederate general Felix Zollicoffer attacked the Federal recruiting station of Camp Andy Johnson near Barbourville.[219] Moore wrote later of holding services one day at a little meetinghouse on the north side of the road leading to Barbourville from the Cumberland Gap, and that he and his congregants could hear the boom of cannon and the report of rifle and musket fire throughout the service. After his arrival back in Barbourville he was placed under arrest by Union officers on suspicion of being a Confederate spy, but

---

[218] Ibid., 72; *The Rational View,* 3-4.
[219] Charles Reed Mitchell, "Barbourville." *The Kentucky Encyclopedia,* 51.

rather than subjecting him to a court-martial the Federals merely sent him out of the mountains under the guard of a cavalry officer.[220] One wonders if, on this occasion, he might have met his two proud brothers-in-law on his journey back north; on the day after Zollicoffer's Barbourville skirmish John Hunt Morgan and his Lexington Rifles, with Thomas Brent and James Cantrill in tow, began to ride southward from the Bluegrass to Tennessee waging Morgan's own style of aggressive guerrilla warfare as they went. Morgan's Lexington Rifles formally joined the Confederate Army in Tennessee on October 27. Their leader himself was officially commissioned first as a captain, then as a colonel and finally as a brigadier general,[221] and Charles's brothers-in-law ultimately became Major Brent and Captain Cantrill respectively.

For Charles's part, though, the Federal authorities had never told him he couldn't come back to preach in the southeastern Kentucky mountains, and so after a brief rest and a skim through his books he did just that. Despite his best intentions, though, his first attempt at carrying out his grand ambition to articulate the scientific basis of the Bible and its writings to his mountain hearers—a sermon wherein he tried to prove the existence of the ruins of the Book of Genesis' fabled Tower of Babel—was a complete failure and both he and his congregants recognized it as such.[222]

Eventually, escalating Union-Confederate hostilities in the mountains pretty much ended Charles's career as a missionary. After another term of hill-country preaching (with sermons probably mostly less ambitious than his abortive Tower of Babel discourse) he remembered following Confederate Major General Edmund Kirby Smith's army northward as it marched and fought its way up from the Cumberland Gap through Richmond to Lexington, and this hectic and bloody journey had to have occurred during the last week of August 1862. If our timeline for his activities is correct he probably hadn't yet entirely given up his plans of combining internal and external biblical and theological proofs to forge a brand-new interest in Christianity in the mountains, and perhaps the intensity of his vision of the project blunted the scenes of devastation that he passed by on his way. Some of the most intense fighting between Kirby Smith's Confederates and Major

---

220 Ibid., *Behind the Bars,* 71.

221 James A. Ramage, "John Hunt Morgan." *Kentucky Encyclopedia*, 650-651.

222 Moore, *The Rational View,* 4; *Behind the Bars,* 72.

General William Nelson's Federals occurred right at the same house and farm where he had proposed marriage to Dessie Campbell back in the fall of 1858.[223]

When he arrived in Lexington he recalled listening while General Smith, who was an Episcopalian, personally conducted a service of thanksgiving at the city's historic Christ Church; the Federals had fallen back to Nicholasville, the town was literally swarming with Smith's soldiers, and grateful Southern sympathizers were bringing them all the hot food and coffee they could eat and drink. From this heady atmosphere he made the final leg of his hike back to Dog Fennel and Forest Retreat, and his mother was so overjoyed to see him and so grateful that he hadn't been hurt or killed he decided that, in spite of his grandiose hopes to kindle a new mountain interest in Christianity, perhaps he should give up his hill-country ministry at least temporarily and remain home for a while.[224]

Charles still didn't know how to chop wood for himself or to plow his own straight furrow, but at least it could be said of him that after Kirby Smith's 1862 Kentucky campaign he no longer lived a rich planter's idle life. Though the Confederates had gained the advantage briefly, his mother was still mightily opposed to his joining the Rebel Army because of his positions both as ordained minister and as her only surviving son. However, with the Battle of Perryville southward in Boyle County a few weeks later, the Rebels pretty much lost all the advantage they had gained in August, and the returning Federals converted two large buildings belonging to Transylvania University, on the corners of Second and Third Streets and Broadway in Lexington, into military hospitals for both injured Union enlisted men and Confederate prisoners of war. If Charles accurately recounted the sequence of his memories he worked as a volunteer male nurse and part-time chaplain at one or both of these facilities. Before the War he undoubtedly would have considered such drudgery beneath his dignity, but by now the noblest of the Bluegrass gentry were willing to bend their backs for the sake of their soldiers. It wouldn't be the last time Charles would ever offer himself for this difficult and extremely disagreeable job, serving Union and Confederate wounded with equal care and concern, and he

---

[223] D. Warren Lambert, "Battle of Richmond." Ibid., 772-773.
[224] Moore, *Behind the Bars,* 71-72.

witnessed a good many unholy things and collected some horrifying tales: amputations all the way up to the hip joint under operating conditions any modern surgeon would find utterly intolerable, one unforgettable spore-contaminated leg wound that sprouted a huge and extremely nauseating quantity of mushrooms overnight, a teenage boy shot through the chest, arm, and knee who told Charles he didn't mind the first two wounds but that he feared his ruined knee would kill him with pain—which in fact it did, after days of indescribable suffering.

Alexander Doniphan's dead and rotten body would no longer be his most disturbing memory, but Charles could tell humorous and heart-warming stories of his hospital career too, mostly of the numerous young city belles who would come in to visit the sick Confederate boys and often wind up adopting one, as it were, as a personal patient. Such "adoptions" sometimes led to courtship and even marriage. Of course, when the Federal surgeons made their daily rounds they were always on the lookout for Confederates well enough to discharge and send to the Union's nearest soldiers' prison, Camp Chase near Columbus in Ohio, and the ever-rebellious Charles later admitted conspiring with his Confederate patients to make them look as sick as possible in order to put off their fates a little longer.[225]

Here, amid the blood and effluvia of the Civil War's wounded, Charles Chilton Moore finally began to mature to adulthood—and to feel his growing pains.

Thomas Young Brent took at least one furlough back to see his bride and baby daughter, probably in October 1862 during the last leg of John Hunt Morgan's second campaign through Kentucky. By the time he returned to his unit, now known throughout both the Bluegrass and the Confederacy as Morgan's Raiders, Mary was "in the family way" once again. In the spring of the next year Forest Retreat received

---

[225] Ibid, 71-72, 83-85. Charles's recollections appear to have been a little blurred here. He remembered working as a nurse in a military hospital before July 1863, but at the time he penned his autobiography he seems to have thought all his experiences in this regard occurred at Cynthiana. This wasn't possible, since the battle he recalled at Cynthiana, that of Kellar's Bridge, was not fought until the middle of June 1864. I suspect that in his older years his memories of the two Lexington hospitals and the Cynthiana hospital became garbled.

one more military guest as well: a young man named William Hatch, a distant cousin of the Moores and the scion of an old and respected Scott County Stoneite Christian family. Having moved with his parents to Missouri where his father had taken a position as the president of a college, Hatch had joined the Confederate Army there and had served with distinction as an officer up until the disastrous Battle of Pea Ridge in Arkansas. After that engagement, which had effectively ended the Confederate cause in Missouri, Hatch had quit the Army, but now he had come over to see his pro-Southern Bluegrass kinfolk to lay low for a while, regroup, and quietly search for another Confederate unit to join.

The war had temporarily gone elsewhere, and Charles, enjoying a much-needed respite from running bedpans and urinals and grasping limbs and steeling his nerves to listen to screams of pain during surgical operations and dressing changes, was delighted with Hatch's company. He later remarked that Hatch was, by far, the most scholarly young man he had ever met, counting even his former fellow students at Bethany College. When he began to inquire about his cousin's religious beliefs, he found Hatch unwilling to quarrel over dogma but mildly skeptical as to the claims of Christianity. Eager to try out his new missionary techniques once more, Charles thus decided to make Hatch his next test subject for an intellectually-based missionary effort, and so he talked the Missouri visitor into taking up a joint challenge with him during their spell of leisure: they would supply themselves with all the good books they could find both for, and against, the claims of Christianity, study them together carefully, and let the objective evidence lead both of them where it would.

As luck would have it, that very year the New York publisher D. Appleton and Company had begun to reprint and market a reasonably-priced series of British scientific and theological tomes that Moore and Hatch considered ideal for their purpose. These included a handsome duodecimo version of Charles Darwin's 1859 *Origin of Species;* a two-volume compilation of shorter Christian apologetic and polemical works entitled, respectively, *Replies to Essays and Reviews* and *Aids to Faith,* cannily marketed by the publisher as "The Two Great Answers to the Recent Attack on the Bible" and thus pretty much Darwin's diametric opposite; and last but not least, *The Pentateuch and Book of Joshua Critically Examined* by the Rt. Rev. John William Colenso,

Anglican bishop of the South African province of Natal, which made the argument, novel for its time, that the first six books of the Old Testament contained several glaring and unholy contradictions and were thus more likely themselves compilations from old oral legends than the fruits of any direct, inerrant, and untainted Divine inspiration.[226] And so Charles and Hatch purchased the books and eagerly set to studying, as Moore later remembered it, for a month and a half, often as long as twelve hours a day both in the house and on Forest Retreat's front lawn.[227]

Though Bishop Colenso actually barely scratched the surface of his subject matter in terms of the hypotheses later biblical critics would suggest, this one volume made the most significant—and ultimately unsettling—impression on Charles, more so at first examination even than Darwin's *Origin of Species.* As a missionary bishop on the east coast of South Africa, John William Colenso cared deeply about the native Zulu tribes under his spiritual guidance, and he stood up for their civil rights to the British colonial government so often that he was later hailed as one of the founding fathers of the so-called liberation theology movement. Proficient in Hebrew, Latin and Greek all, he had learned his parishioners' native tongue as well, translated the New Testament and significant portions of the Old into the Zulu language, and had even compiled a basic Zulu grammar and dictionary. For relaxation from these evangelistic and scholarly tasks he had become an enthusiastic hiker and amateur naturalist and geologist. Colenso had thus built his ministry in the province of Natal from the ground up and his native hearers accorded him the highest respect in return, but he had noticed that over the years a surprising number of his Zulu, themselves certainly no halfhearted fighters and most of whom, ironically, lived under much the same primitive conditions that the ancient Israelites had to have known, had frankly expressed doubts to him that either the

---

[226] I am greatly indebted to the Johnson County Public Library of Paintsville, Kentucky's Interlibrary Loan Program, and the University of Louisville Library for access to an original 1863 Appleton reprint of Colenso's work, which listed advertisements at the end for the other books cited. These jibe almost perfectly with Charles Moore's own description of the works he and Hatch studied, listed in Moore, *Behind the Bars,* 72-73.

[227] Ibid., 72-73; *The Rational View,* 5-6.

stories of the Fall and the Flood in Genesis or the Old Testament God's barbarous, casual cruelty could be literal truth.[228]

Though he himself had been raised and taught to believe—pretty much just like Charles Moore had—that every single word, even every letter of every syllable of every word, in the Bible was the direct utterance of the Most High[229], Colenso was impressed by the Zulus' forthright, honest, and benignly objective skepticism. So when he began to ponder this issue of biblical integrity on his own, he forced himself to study the Bible as he would approach any other allegedly nonfiction work, with a critical eye and no *a priori* assumptions or prejudices—and lo and behold, the Pentateuch suddenly crawled with an unsettling spate of numbers, time sequences, ages, and military and population counts that didn't tally, genealogies that contradicted themselves and one another, and geological and astronomical claims predicated on a flat earth with a small sun and moon and even tinier stars revolving around it and which simply could not be made to work under any known scientific conditions whatsoever. The bulk of *The Pentateuch and Book of Joshua Critically Examined* was comprised of Colenso's detailed itemization of the first errors and inconsistencies he had discovered.

We should make clear here that Colenso by no means intended to cast any doubt either on the Gospel, the miracles of Jesus, the Church, or even the later prophets of the Old Testament. The case was quite the opposite, but after his researches he concluded that the best way to study the Pentateuch was not as literal and infallible truth but as spiritual allegory, still to be held as inspired but with its message obviously filtered through the very earthy minds of the scribes and chroniclers who had penned and compiled it over the centuries. And for all Colenso's altruistic intentions of making the Bible easier for both his Zulu and English readers to comprehend, within two decades of this work's first publication it would inspire no less than three hundred extremely angry and sarcastic British and American retorts—including, apparently, even five or so essays in another of Charles and Hatch's new Appleton books—and its author at one point would come within a

---

[228] Colenso, 5-6, 46-48.

[229] Ibid., 46, quoting one of Colenso's seminary textbooks.

hairsbreadth of losing his standing in the Church of England and be dubbed finally as "The Wicked Bishop."[230]

Like Alexander Campbell in the old *Christian Baptist* newspaper forty years before, Colenso backed up his arguments with generous chapter-and-verse references to Scripture, and so over his six-week study period Charles was able to go through the book, the essays attempting to refute it, and the Scriptural references it cited, slowly and with a fine-toothed comb. As he read Colenso and compared his contentions with the responses of the bishop's detractors, as well as the Bible passages both Colenso and his opposing Scriptural-inerrancy essayists had referenced, he found himself quite unable to escape the conclusion that—horror of horrors—Colenso's arguments about the Pentateuch appeared to be reasonable and entirely correct. Still hoping to convert Hatch to Christianity and perhaps fearing for his own soul at the time if he couldn't redeem himself by managing the feat, Charles never confessed his growing, terrifying uncertainties about Old Testament infallibility either to his reading partner or to anyone else either at home or in the community.

There can be little doubt that Hatch would have surmised *something* had to be wrong, however: after finishing the project Charles immediately took to his bed with an affliction his worried mother's two physicians diagnosed as some sort of brain "fever", but which he himself described later as "nervous prostration superinduced [*sic*] by long and close study."[231] He couldn't sleep at all, and in early mornings spent after horrible long nights of tossing and turning amid twisted blankets within a twisting worldview, he found himself too weak even to get up and try to walk about the house and grounds. In short, what Alexander Doniphan's rotted body, Dessie Campbell's youthful perfidy, Kirby Smith's Bluegrass campaign, and the stinking wards of Lexington's military hospitals had never been able to do to his mind, his realization that the Pentateuch, if not the whole Bible, was chock-full of mistakes and contradictions actually accomplished: Charles now exhibited all the classic symptoms of a nervous breakdown.

Since he later prided himself on being able to face up to unpleasant truths bravely and forthrightly, Moore seems to have downplayed this

---

[230] Friedman, 27.
[231] Moore, *Behind the Bars,* 72.

uncertain period of his life in his autobiography not unlike the treatment he gave his Allegheny City posse experience; so much so in this case, in fact, that a cursory glance through this portion of his writings leaves the impression that he took both his faith, and the loss thereof, equally lightly. I admit with some chagrin that this represented my own too-brief analysis, in a previous work, of Moore's commitment to both his earlier Christianity and his later freethought.[232] But for all Charles's own efforts to deemphasize his predicament in the spring of 1863, no one who has not come out of some deeply conservative Protestant faith tradition claiming to emphasize *sola scriptura* can even begin to comprehend his terrors of mind when he allowed himself the possibility that the faith of his forefathers might be flawed. His spell of neurotic insomnia and muscular weakness after finishing reading Colenso was entirely understandable. At this stage of his thought processes he probably didn't even have any idea yet whether his spiritual props were completely gone and God even existed or not, or if that same possibly nonexistent but just, righteous, and now furious God had abandoned him to believe a lie and be damned because of the hardness of his own heart[233] and his sin in daring to read "The Wicked Bishop's" book in the first place. Though the dichotomy between these completely contradictory thoughts might seem to be simply too great for any individual to maintain them simultaneously, I suggest that both fundamentalists and evangelicals could, and ex-fundamentalist nonbelievers would, attest to both their frequency and the anguish they can cause among believers exposed to data they do not wish to face. Perhaps worst of all was Charles's likely perception that he couldn't even reveal his new but honest doubts to anyone, lest they think him altogether depraved, completely insane, or both. Hence his silence in the presence of Hatch, his mother, and her physicians.

Why, it may be asked, couldn't he just have accepted Colenso's conclusions with equanimity and simply let himself grow to be the kind of liberal Christian and Scripture expositor that Colenso himself had become? The sheer quantity of indignant replies to *The Pentateuch and Book of Joshua Critically Examined* that were published over the years,

---

[232] See Sparks, *Raccoon John Smith,* 388.

[233] Scriptural reference from II Thessalonians 2:11-12, a popular text in evangelical circles.

devoted specifically to the task of disproving Colenso's arguments, amply demonstrates how many even of the bishop's contemporary fellow Christian authors had difficulties with such an idea, let alone the number of believers in the general population. For Charles himself the thought couldn't have been any more easily digestible, at least at first, and his own personal unease of mind was only exacerbated by the distinctive view of Scripture that his Stone-Campbell faith tradition embraced. We have already discussed the conversion, or born-again, experience upheld as a tenet of the scheme of salvation by Baptists, Methodists, evangelical Presbyterians and other groups from which the budding Stone-Campbell Movement had gained its first following; and although plenty of converts still in Baptist, Methodist, and Presbyterian churches would have admitted to a full intellectual belief in the accuracy and consistency of Scripture even before their repentance and conversions, the phenomenon of the born-again experience itself veritably set a permanent seal on the question in virtually every convert's mind. In other words, being born again made everything *real,* as it were, not only the presence and benevolence of the Creator, Savior, and Sustainer God but the supposed consistency and inerrancy of the Holy Bible from which God's message was preached. And although Protestants were, and sometimes still are, quick to denounce Catholics for a lack of dependence on *sola Scriptura,* the Catholic convert and Kentucky Trappist monk Thomas Merton would describe in his young manhood exactly the same sort of personal experience-based, circuitous rationalizing in *The Seven Storey Mountain,* the kind of intellectual catch-22 fallback on which, actually, it seems that both Catholic and Protestant believers depended and yet depend. The testimony of Scripture provided sure validation for faith in Divine grace, and yet for some reason an act of Divine grace was necessary before an individual could even appreciate the testimony of Scripture, much less establish a faith in it:

> And how did we know? Because it was revealed to us in the Scriptures and confirmed by the teaching of the Church and of the powerful unanimity of Catholic tradition from the First Apostles, from the first Popes and the Early Fathers, on down through the Doctors of the Church and the great scholastics, to our own day. *De Fide Divina. If you believed it, you would receive light to grasp it, to understand it*

> *in some measure. If you did not believe it, you would never understand; it would never be anything but scandal or folly.*
>
> *And no one can believe these things merely by wanting to, of his own volition. Unless he receive grace, an actual light and impulsion of the mind and will from God he cannot even make an act of living faith. It is God who gives us faith, and no one cometh to Christ unless the Father draweth him* [emphasis added].[234]

Thus, even when Scriptural inconsistencies were pointed out to such true believers, of either Catholic or Protestant persuasion but especially the rural American inheritors of the eighteenth-century Great Awakening and the nineteenth-century Great Revival that comprised virtually all of Charles Moore's neighbors in other churches, they would often as not fall back on the position that they didn't understand such complexities but were content with the promise that one day in Glory they would. They could feel the Holy Spirit bearing witness to their own spirits that they had indeed become the children of God; they could likewise still experience the power and demonstration of that same Holy Spirit when they attended church, sang, listened to the preaching, and spoke to God in prayer; and so this perceived witness of the Spirit let them know that their souls were safe and their worldview was still intact, even if something in Scripture *appeared* to be contradictory.

For such a believer to doubt the existence of God he or she first had to doubt the validity, and the reality, of his or her conversion experience and the subjective witness of the Holy Spirit that he or she perceived in his or her conscience, and more often than not when this happened, the doubter experienced a lack of faith not in God or in the inerrancy of the Bible but rather in his or her own personal integrity. No less a religious personage than Billy Graham once admitted to such a circumstance befalling him, after his friend and onetime preaching partner Charles Templeton began to point out inconsistencies in Scripture to him. In grief and terror he fled to a desert retreat where he made the frightened promise to the Deity in prayer always to accept the Bible as God's Word strictly by faith over and above all his intellectual ques-

[234] Merton, 209-210.

tions and doubts, and he came back to his preaching in renewed joy and never let himself be bothered by such nagging trifles ever again.[235]

However comforting such a mindset might prove to be to an individual believer, though, even if the believer happened to be Thomas Merton or Billy Graham, we have seen that Charles's own grandfather Stone's bitter experience with the Shakers had taught him just how volatile that believers' trust in this sort of subjective "spiritual witness" could be. The Shakers had come among Barton Stone's churches preaching Mother Ann Lee as the female reincarnation of Jesus Christ, a heresy in terms of standard Christian doctrine if ever there was one. We have noted that Stone himself viewed both Christ and Christ's atonement slightly differently and in ways more liberally and than did his former fellow Presbyterians, but regardless, the celibate Shaker missionaries made a frightening number of converts from Stone's church, not because of any reasonableness in the doctrines that the Shakers preached but, seemingly, because they could shout and sing and claim the spiritual gift of tongues and make Stone's congregations feel like rejoicing and dancing and gibbering along with them. This was enough in the minds of many believers to constitute the very power and demonstration of the Holy Spirit. If anyone had asked the new Shaker converts why they had become proselytes as they did, as no doubt Barton Stone himself had queried many of his departing ex-New Lights, the reply invariably would have been that the Shakers had made the Holy Spirit bear witness with their own personal spirits to the truth of Mother Ann Lee's interpretation of the Bible.

Though Barton Stone's all-out preaching war against the disciples of Mother Ann is an extreme example, a good many doctrinal differences and disputes exist even between modern evangelical denominations over little or nothing more than this same supposedly spiritual principle, with a bit of the perfume of tradition sprayed onto either or both sides of it. And, we might add as a footnote to our recounting of Billy Graham's terrifying moment of doubt, journalist Perry Deane Young, himself once overwhelmed and converted as a Southern teenager in a Graham crusade, wryly notes that Graham's blind acceptance of Scripture on faith over and above all intellectual questions additionally appears to have enabled him to view, and promote, Richard Nixon

[235] Graham, 135-139; Young, 13-14.

as a great President and a good and decent man even as more and more responsible American thinkers found reason to question both Nixon's actions and his motives. After Graham's retreat experience he could see anything he wanted to, observes Young, because with his renewed commitment to blind faith he had chosen not to see at all.[236]

All things considered, then, back in the two decades before Charles's birth Barton Stone had been only too glad to accept Alexander Campbell's rationalistic and almost legalistic proclamation that true Christian faith didn't have anything to do with such foolish, emotion-based "spiritual witness" but was rather a penitent believer's acceptance of Scriptural truths followed and confirmed by the public witness of baptism by immersion for the remission of sins. So the Stone-Campbell union had taken place, and to such preaching Charles Chilton Moore had listened from John Allen Gano and other Disciple exhorters all his life. After 1860 he had added his own voice to the proclamation of the Gospel message, and so steeped was he in Alexander Campbell's Scottish Common Sense Realism and rationalism that, until he arrived in the eastern Kentucky mountains, he had never even seen or heard congregational shouting such as his grandfather had known in the days of the Great Revival. What to do, then, if, as Bishop Colenso argued and from all appearances plainly and correctly, the very entity that was supposed to *produce* saving faith according to the Stone-Campbell tradition—the purportedly plain testimony of Scripture itself—was flawed and inconsistent? It was simply no good to fall back on the notion that the wisdom of the world was mere foolishness with God and that it required Divine grace for a sinner even to be able to see the truth either of Scripture or of one or the other particular faith traditions of Christianity. That brought the argument right back to the differences of opinion over various points of Scripture that all sects and denominations maintained with each other. And as we have noted, the quarrel Barton Stone had had so long before with the Shakers was merely one extreme example, a glaring set of points comprising a small segment of a very vicious circle.

In the spring of 1863 this whole idea was simply too much for Charles either to grasp or to bear. He couldn't respond to his doubts

---

[236] Young, 14.

after Billy Graham's later fashion because his intellect was too resilient for him to ignore data he could plainly see, and though he had withstood being jilted by Dessie Campbell, his emotions were not as strong as his intellect and he could not yet face up to another jilting, this one from the faith of his childhood. And so finally he talked himself into a mental dodge that enabled him to go on believing and preaching at least a year to eighteen months more: Bishop Colenso had made no particular arguments against the New Testament for any inconsistencies, and since even his grandfather Stone and Alexander Campbell had emphasized profession of Christian faith on the New Testament rather than the Old, Charles resolved that in the future he would preach strictly from the New Testament and leave the troublesome Pentateuch and Book of Joshua entirely alone.[237]

The great irony of this entire episode is that Charles did, in fact, succeed in converting William Hatch to Christianity. Though Hatch studied the very same Appleton books that Charles had, from Colenso to Darwin to the varied upholders of Scriptural inerrancy who condemned both Colenso and Darwin, after his reading he was actually friendlier to religion than he had been before. Charles, true to his heritage and as of yet unwilling to voice any of his own doubts, simply advised Hatch to be immersed and become a Christian, and that is exactly what Hatch did. It is not certain that Hatch ever rejoined the Confederate Army after Charles baptized him, but once the Civil War ended he appears to have made his peace with the Union Government as well as with God, and he enjoyed a successful career as an engineer and inspector of levees on the Mississippi River.[238] And in the end, we know that if Charles's self-centered period of depression and neurosis hadn't run their course by Independence Day 1863, he at least had to bestir himself and think about others once again soon afterward: the Scripture text he had casually dropped to Thomas Young Brent at Forest Retreat in late 1860 finally came home to roost, and he was forced to sublimate his own concerns for the sake of his beloved sister Mary.

Morgan's Raiders had returned to southern Kentucky from their camp in Overton County, Tennessee in June, and on July 4 they clashed

---

[237] Moore, *Behind the Bars,* 73; *The Rational View,* 6.
[238] Ibid., *Behind the Bars,* 75; *The Rational View,* 6.

with a Michigan regiment at Tebbs' Bend on the Green River near Campbellsville. Though General Morgan offered the vastly-outnumbered Union force the chivalrous opportunity to surrender without bloodshed, its commanding officer refused to lay down the Union flag on Independence Day. He ordered his men to dig in and fight, and his small but well-trained infantry wound up defeating Morgan's proud brigade thoroughly. Among the targets easiest for the Michigan sharpshooters to pick off were the brave, young, headstrong cavalry officers leading the Confederate charges, of whom Morgan lost twenty-four in that one battle—including Thomas Brent, who caught a well-aimed minie ball in the chest while trying to guide his troops through fallen trees and brush, fell from his horse, and had time only to beg his soldiers to turn him on his side before he drowned in the blood pouring into his lungs.

News of the battle and its casualties appears to have reached the central Bluegrass within four days; the chilling record survives of the death of Brent's mother, Margaret, in Bourbon County on July 8,[239] and we must wonder if this second tragedy was a direct result of the elder Mrs. Brent's learning of her son's demise. For her part, his grief-stricken young wife, holding the hand of one small daughter and almost ready to bring another into the world, begged Charles to take a wagon to Tebbs' Bend, collect the body and bring it home for burial in the plantation cemetery near their father. He took along some of the family's slaves and obliged—the Emancipation Proclamation that President Lincoln had signed into law that year, incidentally, claimed authority only in those territories where it was impossible to enforce and thus did not affect the status of blacks in states like Kentucky that formally remained loyal to the Union—and while he visited with James Cantrill, waited for the construction of a coffin for Brent, and pondered over causes, effects, and the terrible text by which his proud young brother-in-law had become a Confederate, he served once more as a military nurse, this time in the Confederate field hospital set up for Morgan's wounded.[240]

---

[239] E.g., Mary Kerr, *Family Tree,* http://worldconnect.rootsweb.com , quoting the 1899 genealogical work *The Bowies and Their Kindred: A Genealogical and Biographical History* by Walter Worthington Bowie.

[240] Moore, *Behind the Bars*, 85-86.

Life had to go on even in the midst of death. Mary Brent's husband was gone, but she still had babies to raise and since Kentucky law at that time allowed her a only a third of her deceased husband's estate with the rest going to Thomas Brent's nearest surviving male relative, her mother, sisters, and brother pitched in to offer her all the loving support they could. When young Mary's second daughter was born she named the infant Margaret Thomas Brent, after both the father and the paternal grandmother who had, each in their own way, given up their lives in the Civil War.

At the same time Charles's youngest sister, Alicia, had grown to a teenager and was ready to further her education even though the war's prospects, as far as the Moore family was concerned, looked ever gloomier. It so happened that the Christian Church in Versailles, in neighboring Woodford County, had opened a small girls' school known as Woodford College, with a Missouri Disciple preacher's daughter named Elizabeth Jameson serving as principal and a petite Versailles damsel from up the street at St. John's Episcopal Church and known as Josephine Williamson, as a teacher. As luck would have it as well, the Versailles First Christian Church had come in need of a settled minister, and since Mary Anne Moore still feared for Charles to return to his former hill-country ministry both he and Alicia went to Versailles, she as scholar and he as pastor.[241] The last notation of him we find in Old Union Church's record book is his final request for a membership transfer by letter on February 13, 1864[242], although he could have accepted the Versailles pastorate even before that date, perhaps as early as December 1863.[243]

During his tenure with the Versailles congregation Charles roomed at the home of member John M. Wasson with one Richard Reid, a

---

[241] Ibid., 73-75; see also Klotter, *Kentucky Justice,* 14-15, 23.

[242] Old Union Church Record Book 1823-1892, Lexington Theological Seminary.

[243] Though the First Christian Church of Versailles, Kentucky, has no extant records for this period besides a brief history penned in 1930, we can date Charles's arrival there as pastor after November 1863 because by the time he met his roommate, Richard Reid, Reid's fiancée, Sarah Jameson, had died. The death occurred on November 11,1863. See Klotter, *Kentucky Justice,* 16.

young lawyer who hailed originally from Mount Sterling in Montgomery County. Reid had attended college at Georgetown with the Moore brother-in-law James Cantrill, and Charles in his turn had known one of Reid's brothers at Bethany; moreover, up until that very fall, Reid had been engaged to Sarah Jameson, the younger sister of Woodford College's principal, but two weeks before what would have been their wedding day Sarah had fallen ill and died. Charles thus left one house of sorrow simply to move into another with Dick Reid, as he affectionately called his new roommate, but the two young men rapidly became the best of friends. Reid told Charles that he really wanted to join the Confederate Army but was held back by his deep belief in Christian pacifism,[244] but this wasn't quite the entire truth. Reid had actually tried to enlist, but he had suffered since young childhood with severe bilateral abdominal or ventral hernias and this caused him to fail his medical examination. Profoundly ashamed of the demeaning condition, Reid had sworn his examining surgeon to secrecy, and most of the time he kept his handicap so well hidden by the use of trusses and thick clothing that no one outside his family knew about it, not even his closest friends.[245] Charles Moore appears to have remained completely in the dark about the young lawyer's disability even though he roomed with Reid at least four to six months.

Richard Reid (1838-1884)

Photo courtesy Bosworth Library, Lexington Theological Seminary, Lexington, Ky.

Despite Reid's possible white lie to Moore about his military intentions, though, he was an enthusiastic Christian and church member, having been the last recorded young convert immersed by Raccoon John Smith in Mt. Sterling before the aged pioneer departed Montgom-

[244] Moore, *Behind the Bars,* 76.
[245] Klotter, *Kentucky Justice,* 4, 97.

ery County to live closer to relatives in Georgetown. At the baptismal service the old Reform warrior, worn out not only by his quarrel with James McVay and the numerous tragedies within his family but by a fresh catfight at the Mt. Sterling Christian Church with a younger preacher named William P. Clark, had laid hands on Reid's head and uttered in what the family recalled as a "peculiarly affecting" tone: "Here is to be a man who will do great good in the world, who will stand up for Christ and if need be, lay down his life for him."[246] Whatever else may be said of Richard Reid, he did try to live up to old Raccoon John's expectations, and as long as he and Charles Moore boarded together at Versailles the two young men had a nightly Bible reading and prayer in their room. Charles remembered, with a touch of humor, that Reid would accept any speaking assignment Charles gave him at worship services, but that it was Reid's particular quirk to prepare himself by writing out what he wanted to say, memorizing it word-for-word after rereading it only once, throwing his notes away, and then in church repeating his speech exactly as he had written it—all the while with great drops of sweat from nerves and embarrassment standing on his face, although what he said was marvelous to hear. Thus, if Reid might have needed the nightly Bible study and prayer service with Charles to bolster his spirits in the wake of his bitter grief over the loss of his beloved fiancée, he also managed, in a very real way, to serve as pastor to Charles; and whatever his own mental peregrinations between faith and doubt, Charles remained convinced that if there existed one Christian who truly lived up to his profession of faith, that person was Richard Reid.[247]

Even as he became more involved with pastoral care both to Reid and the Versailles Church as a whole, though, the spring and summer of 1864 saw Charles's faith slip further and further away from him. We must repeat here that Moore was never so articulate about the actual process by which he lost his religious worldview as he was about the modes of thought he espoused once his childhood faith had become a thing of the past. Still, we can safely theorize that at least three factors continued to contribute to his religious doubts. One, most probably, was his manner of study once he finished with Colenso's *Pentateuch*

---

[246] Reid, 14; see also Sparks, *Raccoon John Smith,* 373-374.
[247] Moore, *Behind the Bars,* 75-76.

and Book of Joshua Critically Examined; after he had gotten used to reading the Pentateuch with the Anglican missionary bishop's sharp, critical eye, he likely discovered that he couldn't make himself stop there. Even though he had already promised himself to leave the Pentateuch strictly alone in his preaching, he would have found himself examining the Psalms, Proverbs, Prophets, Gospels, Acts, Epistles, and Revelation with the same observant and discriminating technique he had adopted to study the Mosaic Law.

Though Colenso himself had briefly explored the conundrum of why Jesus Christ, if indeed the Savior was supposed to be omniscient, would have fully endorsed the truth of the Pentateuch in such Gospel verses as Luke 16:29-31 and 20:37 and John 6:46-47, even a Kentucky boy like Charles could discern that the good bishop had to employ only slightly less spectacular apologetic acrobatics than his critics used, simply to maintain the doctrine of the divine wisdom of Christ and still answer his own questions.[248] Hence a great number of fresh Prophetic and New Testament problems that Charles had never heard explained by William Paley, Joseph Butler, or other Christian apologists (or just as likely, answered by them with twists and spirals of logic that would have tempted William of Occam to slit his own throat with his own razor if William himself hadn't been a monk) must have grown very real and important to him as he prepared his sermons for the Versailles pulpit.

For example, why did the same God that told Moses he would visit the sins of parents on the third and fourth generations of their descendants[249] turn around and rebuke his prophet Ezekiel for preaching essentially that exact message, claiming that he would never hold a son responsible for his father's sin or a father for his son's?[250] Conversely, why should God tell Ezekiel that he had no pleasure in the death of the wicked[251] when the Proverbs of Solomon, who was supposed to have

---

[248] Colenso, 30-32.

[249] Exodus 20:5, 34:7. Moore dealt with a great many such Scriptural contradictions in his 1890 book *The Rational View.* Chapter 6 of this work will examine *The Rational View* in somewhat greater detail, although to list any more such contradictions might well constitute overkill.

[250] Ezekiel 18:1-22.

[251] Ibid., 18:23.

been given Divine wisdom surpassing that of all other mortals, stated that the Lord had made all things for himself, yea, even the wicked for the day of evil?[252]

To follow the purportedly divine trail down through the Prophets into the New Testament itself, why were there two separate genealogical tables for Jesus' earthly family in the Gospels, one in Matthew and one in Luke and each listing markedly different sets of ancestors for Jesus? Or if, as many defenders of the faith claimed, one family tree was Joseph's and the other was Mary's, why were the Babylonian Captivity-era princes Salathiel and his son Zerubbabel listed in both genealogies—with a completely different set of ancestors for Salathiel in each, though both sets led back to King David through divergent paths, as well as completely differing sets of descendants from Zerubbabel all the way to the name of Joseph?[253] Did Luke choose a different set of ancestors for Salathiel than Matthew did because the king whom Matthew picked as Salathiel's father, Jeconiah, had been cursed throughout all his generations by the prophet Jeremiah[254]—or could either Matthew *or* Luke even be depended upon to know what they were talking about? Why did Matthew claim Isaiah 7:14 as a prophecy of Jesus' virgin birth[255] when the child that Isaiah foretold to King Ahaz was to be a toddler, able to eat butter and honey but not yet even able to discern between good and evil, by the time Ahaz should see his enemies defeated and scattered—centuries before the birth of Jesus ever took place?[256] Why, too, were those same enemies of Ahaz never brought to naught in actual history? Why did the Epistle to the Hebrews insist that remission of sins could not occur without the shedding of

---

[252] Proverbs 16:4.

[253] Matthew 1:1-16; Luke 3:23-38.

[254] Jeremiah 22:24-30.

[255] Matthew 1:22-23.

[256] Isaiah 7:1-16. I do not take into consideration the difficulty of Isaiah's Hebrew word *almah* (young woman) being translated in the Greek Septuagint to *parthenos* (virgin), it appearing that Moore was not conversant enough either in the Hebrew language or the Masoretic text to have known about, or articulated, this problem himself. His take on this passage of Scripture is, however, like the others noted above and below, noted in *The Rational View.*

blood[257] when the fifty-first Psalm indicated that true repentance was better than sacrifice,[258] and Jesus himself simply went around forgiving people as if his very words made the remission of their sins stand as fact, with no bloodshed involved?[259]

Why didn't a single one either of the lists of the Twelve Apostles or of the witnesses of the Crucifixion in the Four Gospels agree with any other list either of Apostles or Crucifixion witnesses? Why were there four different accounts of the Resurrection and as many of the Ascension (which wasn't mentioned in John's Gospel, though it was retold in the Book of Acts), none of which agreed with any other account completely and one of which, Matthew, had Jesus' ascension occurring in Galilee while Luke, Acts, and the King James Version of Mark all claimed it happened right outside Jerusalem?[260] Why did the Book of Acts claim, in one passage, that the Apostle Paul's companions on the Damascus Road heard a voice speaking but saw nothing,[261] yet in another passage describing the same event declared that they had *seen* a light but had *heard* nothing?[262] Why did the Acts likewise claim that Jewish persecution had forced St. Paul to escape Damascus by having his friends lower him down the outside of the city wall in a basket[263] when Paul himself blamed the persecution not on the Jews, but on an officer of the Nabataean King Aretas instead?[264] Why did the author of the Book of Revelation claim to see Jesus as King of Kings and Lord of Lords, the Lamb reigning alongside God the Father in Heaven at the end of time[265] while Paul preached that, after Doomsday, the Son would become subject unto God the Father so that God would

---

[257] Hebrews 9:22.
[258] Psalm 51:16-17.
[259] Mark 2: 1-12.
[260] Matthew 28:7-17; Mark 16:9-20, King James Version; Luke 24:50-53; Acts 1:1-9. Actually, the original book of Mark had nothing in it about any ascension, but again, it is unlikely that Charles Moore would have known about this circumstance.
[261] Acts 9:7.
[262] Acts 22:9.
[263] Acts 9:22-25.
[264] II Corinthians 11:32-33.
[265] Revelation 19:11-16; 21:22; 22:3.

be "all in all"?[266] And again, still reverberating throughout the hollow halls of Charles' doubt over and above all his other concerns remained the very question that Bishop Colenso himself had tried so hard to explain away: if Jesus was supposed to be all-knowing, or at least so sharp that he could outwit the doctors of the Law in the Temple at twelve years of age,[267] why did this wisest-of-all God-man give a blanket endorsement to a Pentateuch[268] that even Bishop Colenso had proven to be full of technical errors?

The questions would have multiplied for Charles every time he opened his Bible, and there must have come a point when he simply grew weary of twisting reason and logic around and around just so he could create the illusion for himself and his Versailles listeners that the writings of the New Testament were any more consistent and inerrant than those of the Old. Though the Bible might—or might not—represent sixty-six books' worth of the noblest efforts of the human race to transcend itself in a search for God, to Charles Moore it would forevermore remain just that: perhaps in some of its parts one of the best of all possible human creations, but still inescapably human, and flawed, rather than divine.

Still, though there were contradictions and inconsistencies in both the Old Testament and the New, did this mean to Charles that he must necessarily give up believing and preaching the essence of the Christian message altogether? There can be little doubt that he gave this question a great deal of thought, and all his life he consistently advocated the ethical teachings of Jesus found in Scripture even when he could no longer defend Scripture itself as a unified and inerrant whole. We might wonder here if a second factor thus eventually came into focus for him, that being the one final book from his 1863 study period with William Hatch: Darwin's *Origin of Species.* Since the ninetieth Psalm held that, to God, a thousand years was only a watch in the night[269] and the third chapter of II Peter stated with equal authority that a thousand years was but a day in the Lord's sight,[270] even a Scriptural literalist might still be

[266] I Corinthians 15:24-28.
[267] Luke 2:46-47.
[268] Luke 16:29-31 and 20:37 and John 6:46-47.
[269] Psalm 90:4.
[270] II Peter 3:8.

able to accept the idea that the seven days in which the heavens and the earth were supposed to have been created could have been seven very lengthy eons rather than seven actual twenty-four-hour time cycles.

However, it was still a fundamental article of Christianity that Jesus came to earth to restore the human race to an abundant life and a fellowship with God that had been broken by the disobedience of Adam and Eve, the parents of all humanity, in the Garden of Eden. The eating of the forbidden fruit was held to be the very cause of death itself in the world both for humans and lower animals.[271] But of course, if Darwin was to be believed, both primates and lower creatures had been dying and killing one another millions of years before any Garden of Eden ever could have existed. Even Barton Stone, whose take on the atonement was slightly different than that of most Protestants, would have blinked at this idea. Thus, even allowing for disagreement about the actual length of the seven days in which God was claimed to have created the world, Darwin's *Origin of Species* still managed to set the entire Christian concept of death, as solely the effect and the wages of human sin, completely on its head. Strange as it might seem, Charles could still actually be moved to tears by the thought and the picture of the brave young Galilean prophet who had charged his followers to love their enemies and render good for evil and then suffered death in the cruelest way imaginable for the sake of his message.[272] But with Darwin stacked on top of Colenso in his mind, the whole idea of sin, guilt and redemption through Christ's vicarious atonement that Charles had imbibed virtually with his mother's milk ultimately had to go by the board for him as well.

And for all this, the Christian Church was such a fundamental part of Charles's life and culture that he might have given it the benefit of all his manifold and multiplying doubts and remained with it through everything—if only he could discover and cling to one piece of objective, credible evidence that Christians were led by *something* if not some One, however nebulous, irrational, or contradictory the entity or entities might be, that actually influenced them to transcend their own humanity in some positive and loving way. Even as confirmed a secularist and humanist as Friedrich Nietzsche, himself the son of a German

[271] Romans 5:12-19.

[272] Moore, *Dog Fennel,* 291.

Lutheran pastor, once remarked that he would have found the redemption promised by Christianity more credible if only the Christians looked more redeemed.[273] And here, fatefully, lay the third factor in Charles's final change of mind and heart: of all times for an idealist to go searching for tangible evidences of divine, or at least transcendent, leadership among humans, the years of the American Civil War had to rank right among the worst possible eras in which to look.

In 2006 American Christian scholar Mark A. Noll published a concise little monograph, entitled *The Civil War as a Theological Crisis,* that fully examined the quandary into which the United States had gotten itself in the years leading up to the War: a nation convinced, at least ever since the Great Revival of 1800, that it could determine God's will by the plain interpretation of Scripture seasoned with good old American common horse sense, yet utterly unable to reach a consensus on God's will for the slavery issue because both abolitionists and slavery advocates could back up their positions equally by Scripture. And in the end, if God manifested himself at all it was not so much through one Scriptural position or the other as by seemingly casting in his lot for the stronger army and making Generals Grant and Sherman his holiest and most effective prophets. Even Abraham Lincoln, though he spoke much after his election and inauguration of the Union's anti-slavery Scriptural positions and the War as punishment for the United States for the sin of slavery, still remained a skeptic at heart; as Susan Jacoby observes, if Lincoln was a theologian, his was a theology filled with inconsistencies, hesitations, and unanswerable questions.[274] And perhaps the most honest and profound religious utterance he ever made in relation to the War, after seeing the full scope of the carnage it created on both sides, was that "I don't know what the soul is, but whatever it is, I know that it can humble itself."[275]

Lincoln and Charles Chilton Moore had this in common: they didn't merely study and brood over this theological crisis but lived it day by day, Lincoln in a capital city perched right at the Union-Confederate border of the Potomac River and Moore in the heartland of one of the most ideologically torn states in the entire Union. And by the

---

[273] Berger, 65, quoting Nietzsche.
[274] Jacoby, 121.
[275] Hofstadter, 172.

middle of 1864 Charles was not only completely convinced of the fallacy of believing the Bible to be either unified, consistent, or divinely inspired, he was thoroughly sickened, as he himself once phrased it, by the fact that "through a whole war in which the followers of a religion of peace were fighting one another, there prevailed an unusual religious sentiment[. It was] induced by the fact that the clergy had availed themselves of the opportunity to appeal to the political prejudices of the people, in order to affect them religiously, and the partisans of the two great political divisions were, respectively, praying to the same God to help them against the other."[276]

Though Charles was always a Southern sympathizer, during his eastern Kentucky mountain ministry he had tried to rise above the divisive war mentality to live under the ideal of, again in his own words, serving as a private soldier under a flag with a cross on it. No doubt, though, as he had watched and heard of Union and Confederate regiments clashing back and forth over the old Wilderness Road that led from the Cumberland Gap to the Bluegrass, and then through Richmond and Perryville to the terrible Independence Day 1863 tragedy at Tebbs' Bend, his thoughts had returned time and again to St. Paul's advice in the fourteenth chapter of I Corinthians: God is not the author of confusion, but of peace, as in all churches of the saints.[277] Where, then, was any hope for the long sought-after peace of God when his fellow ministers both of his own faith tradition and all others in the Bluegrass insisted on adding to the confusion by taking partisan positions in their own right and whipping up the feelings of their respective congregants to the point where each side accused the other of being under the leadership of Satan? Where *were* they all getting their orders, really, from a divine, almighty, and transcendent power that they had met through Holy Scripture and Holy Spirit—or merely from their mental projections of their own best and worst qualities, tacked lightly onto the traditions of their culture and ultimately objectified by them into something that they all called "God"? Charles had begun to believe that only his power of reasoning could supply him with the answers to such questions—and by now he was starting to face the answers calmly and resolutely.

---

[276] Moore, *The Rational View,* 6.
[277] I Corinthians 14:33.

Moreover, on July 4, 1863—one day after the ending of the event often called the turning point of the war, the Battle of Gettysburg, ironically—this issue of the application, or misapplication, of Scriptural texts for supposedly divine, but actually human, causes had come home to him in a most personal way. Though Charles never intended to hurt anyone, especially in his own household, we must remember, as he was compelled to, that he had in fact altered the course of his family's history by a few careless words of his own. It was Moore's idle recounting, around the Forest Retreat hearth, of J. D. Pickett's exegesis of I Timothy chapter 6 that influenced Thomas Young Brent to abandon his Union sympathies and declare for the Confederacy, the Scriptural passage being, in Brent's own interpretation, "God's ordinance for secession." And so with I Timothy as his oracle, Pickett as his prophet, and Charles as the prophet's unintended and certainly unwilling mouthpiece, Brent had gone on to enlist in Morgan's Raiders and die chivalrously, gloriously, and foolishly at the Battle of Tebbs' Bend, leaving a young and beautiful wife a bereft widow and two daughters, one not even born at the time of his fatal cavalry advance, fatherless.

How much did Charles actually blame himself for ever attempting the fateful discussion of the Timothy passage with his brother-in-law? He never really said in so many words. But he always had a soft spot in his heart both for his widowed sister and his orphaned nieces, and he did what he could to help fill the empty spot in their lives that Thomas Brent's death had created. And by the time Union and Confederate forces began to clash once again in the Bluegrass in the summer of 1864, he seems to have been fully ready to admit, at least to himself, that his own handling of Scripture both in the pulpit and out of it hadn't brought any true peace or joy either to him, his family, or to any of his present or former congregations in the mountains or Versailles. He had been responsible only for more confusion just like that which all the other supposedly divinely-inspired preachers he knew had managed to create. He wasn't following God; he couldn't even tell who or what God was anymore and to the best of his guesses neither could anybody else, and he was heartily ready to abandon it all.

The real hurdle now, of course, was admitting the change in his beliefs to anybody else, either at Versailles or at his home. Charles had to have known in the most personal way that his congregation at large would be scandalized. Richard Reid, still grieving over his dead sweetheart, would only have his sorrow renewed in the knowledge that his beloved pastor and roommate had become an infidel in spite of all the sweet prayers and Bible studies that the two had shared, and there was no doubt that Alicia, as a student in the church's girls' school, would be subjected to a load of gossip about her apostate big brother that would drive a hardened adult, let alone a sensitive, self-conscious teenager, to distraction. And this wasn't even counting what that tough, resolute, commonsense daughter of Barton Stone, Mary Anne Moore, might do or say when she got the news that the heir to the Stone religious legacy had sold his birthright for a mess of infidel pottage. If only there was some way he could bow out of the ministry and save face at the same time, some means that would be acceptable to his mother and simultaneously bring honor to the family in the eyes of his sisters…

Family meant, and still means, a lot to many Kentuckians. And in this vein of thinking, more than likely combined with a bit of inward guilt over Thomas Young Brent's death, it would seem that Charles managed to place himself in one of the most harebrained, impractical schemes of his young life thus far: in the summer of 1864 he tried to get himself captured and impressed into service by Morgan's Raiders.

In late May and early June 1864 General John Hunt Morgan, himself by now an escaped Federal prisoner of war, brought James Cantrill, his other cavalry officers, and his brave, headstrong Raiders back to central Kentucky. Among other skirmishes in which they engaged was a battle at Kellar's Bridge near Cynthiana in Harrison County northeast of Georgetown. After beating the forces of Union General Edward Hobson on June 11 and taking almost a thousand of Hobson's soldiers as prisoners, Morgan's Raiders were in turn thoroughly trounced the next day by Federal reinforcements led by General Stephen Gano Burbridge, himself possibly the most hated military official in the Kentucky of that day. A great many of Morgan's soldiers were themselves wounded or captured after fleeing to Cynthiana, and Morgan and the remnant of his forces had to abandon their prisoners and make a hasty retreat south. The Battle of Kellar's Bridge pretty much represented the lowest wane of Morgan's star, and although he managed to lead his Raiders at least once more through Lexington and

Georgetown in July he met his death after a battle—and a betrayal—in Greenville, Tennessee that fall.[278]

One wonders if either General Morgan or Captain Cantrill, while on their advance northward through the Bluegrass to Cynthiana in June and possibly once or twice on their July campaign in the country outside Lexington and Georgetown as well, noticed a forlorn, sneaky-looking figure hanging to their brigade's flanks like a botfly buzzing a horse's rump. Of course, it was Charles. Eager to get himself extricated from his increasingly untenable situation at Versailles yet insistent upon honoring his mother's wishes not to *volunteer* for the army, in a supreme irony and absurdity of a tale already chock-full of ironies and absurdities he now actually sought escape through capture—though if his ruse had succeeded he couldn't even have revealed his true motives to James Cantrill. According to his own memories, he tried at least three times to venture close enough to the moving unit to be seen and accosted, once even attempting to rent a good horse from the Versailles livery stable and leaving money for its purchase in his room after he should be captured. Unfortunately for him, though, the owner of the stable had already taken all his horses out of town and hidden them because he suspected that some of Morgan's men might venture close enough to Versailles to steal his entire stock.

Charles was thus reduced to attempting his scheme on foot, and it never worked out for him. After the rout at Kellar's Bridge, though, he did manage to blunder close enough to Cynthiana either to be drafted, or volunteer, as a nurse at the temporary hospital the Confederates had set up inside a large church building in the town and which the Federals commandeered once they gained the field.[279] This occasion seems to have been the final episode of Charles's career as a military nurse. And in the end, everything may have turned out for the best for him, but he was still stuck with the unnerving task of making a public confession of his lack of belief.

As 1864 drew to its close, Richard Reid moved out of the rooms he had shared with Moore and returned to his hometown of Mt. Sterling to practice law.[280] After Charles came back to Versailles from Cynthiana

---

[278] Ramage, "John Hunt Morgan," *Kentucky Encyclopedia,* 651.
[279] Moore, *Behind the Bars,* 76-77, 83-.
[280] Reid, 45.

and his subsequent attempts to get himself shanghaied, chagrined but still having performed an honorable work at the military hospital, he remained in charge of the Versailles pulpit—no doubt feeling damned if he did and damned if he didn't. Still, he appears to have clung to one final hope to bow out of the ministry by a means that would enable his family to save face. Like most congregational-based sects and denominations such as the Disciples of Christ and the Baptists in that day and age, the First Christian Church at Versailles elected its pastors on a yearly basis. According to the old saying, politics always was the damnedest in Kentucky, and this applied not only to the secular political arena but in the evangelical religious sphere as well; stories of church election frauds were legion, especially in the state's early Baptist associations from whence Alexander Campbell had derived a great portion of his *Christian Baptist's* first readership,[281] and anyone who could weather such hot contests even as a mere voter or spectator had to have both a strong faith and a strong stomach. Thus it happened that the Versailles Church's election was scheduled for some time probably between December 1864 and February 1865, and as luck would have it another young Disciple exhorter, John Samuel Shouse, offered his name as a candidate for the pastorate.

Charles didn't even enter his name into the lists, nor would he allow any of his friends to nominate him, but in the final and crowning farce of his preaching career he received every single vote cast in the election with the exception of one lone Union sympathizer who thought Charles was too much of a Rebel. Shouse accepted a pastorate outside Versailles at Midway, and now Moore was left with two choices: either to live a lie for another year, perhaps somehow preaching sermons on morals without touching any other aspect of Scripture, or face up to that ticklish entity known as the truth and tell his congregation, his family, and his community exactly how he felt.

---

[281] If the reader is interested in any examples, a short list of sources include John Taylor's *History of Ten Baptist Churches of Which the Author was Alternately a Member* (1828; reprinted by Mercer University Press as *Baptists on the American Frontier*); J. H. Spencer's two-volume *History of Kentucky Baptists,* 1769-1885 (1886; reprinted 1976 by Church Research & Archives); and Sparks, *The Roots of Appalachian Christianity,* and *Raccoon John Smith: Frontier Kentucky's Most Famous Preacher.*

And so, shortly after his successful re-election to the Versailles pastorate in early 1865, Charles Chilton Moore preached one final Sunday sermon, closed the Bible on the rostrum, picked up his hat, and walked down the pulpit steps via a side aisle and through the front door, never to return. That same evening he called together the elders and deacons of the church at his lodging and made the terse announcement to them that he felt compelled to quit preaching because he could no longer believe the truth of the Bible. He recalled that, at least to his face, they all treated him with great kindness and seemed not to doubt his sincerity; while they regretted his shocking announcement, they acknowledged that they didn't see how he could do anything else under the circumstances.[282] Charles didn't have as much luck with anyone else, though. He remembered one friend actually expressing the irrational fear to him that, since he had abandoned his belief in the Bible, Moore would now surely do something horrible such as murdering one or more of his family members. Infidels did those kinds of things.[283]

But in the end, Versailles, Kentucky, as a whole analyzed the problem and pronounced the precise judgment on Charles that could be expected from a genteel pro-Southern nineteenth-century Bluegrass town. Of course he wasn't a murderer, or even a potential murderer. Still, only an idiot or a lunatic could doubt the truth of the Bible, it was reasoned, and Charles's unlucky love affair with Dessie Campbell six years before had never been kept secret. The town's armchair philosophers of both genders (the vocations of armchair psychology and armchair basketball coaching not yet having been conceived in Kentucky, let alone become popular) thus simply joined the two propositions together, concluded that Moore was just a younger version of Theodore Clay, and levied a benediction on his ministry that he would never forget. As Charles himself heard a street loafer say behind his back not long before he departed the town for good: "There goes a preacher who went crazy about a woman."[284]

---

[282] Moore, *Behind the Bars,* 80.
[283] Ibid., *The Rational View,* 8.
[284] Ibid., *Behind the Bars,* 80.

Chapter 5

Dog Fennel in the Golden Age

Religion has not civilized man—man has civilized religion. God improves as man advances.
—Robert Green Ingersoll

If the good citizens of Versailles had dismissed Charles casually and with shallow complacency as a lunatic after his announcement of his change of beliefs, the response of Mary Anne Moore and her daughters at Forest Retreat more than made up for the lack of both depth and intensity. The only direct comment Moore ever made about this period was that "The world all seemed very dark to me, and especially as my leaving the pulpit, under the circumstances, was almost breaking the heart of my mother. She seemed to suffer great agony, and I tried to explain to her that there were reasons for my doing as I did, but she had never heard anything but one side of the argument about religion and I could not comfort her."[285] Even as evocative as this image may be, it can hardly tell the entire story. John and Hannah Grissom and Jane Cantrill's in-laws all lived in Georgetown, Alicia was still at school in Versailles under Elizabeth Jameson and Josephine Williamson, and Mary Brent remained at Forest Retreat mourning over the fresh grave of her husband; and, Bluegrass society gossip being what it was, and occasionally still is, every one of the sisters had to have felt that the

---

[285] Moore, *Behind the Bars,* 80.

entire world had the Moore family under a magnifying glass. It was no wonder that life looked so dark to Charles. Between his mother's tears and his sisters' alternating stony silences and icy retorts to any attempts at conversation he might have made with them, he undoubtedly felt as if he hadn't a friend left either in the world or out of it. And after a sufficiently lengthy period of this kind of emotional and mental pressure he might even have wondered if his former Versailles listeners were right, after all; maybe he *was* going crazy.

So, in the Confederacy's twilight days of early 1865 Charles Chilton Moore did something that in retrospect seems, at best, to have been impractical and quixotic, at worst incomprehensibly self-centered, but in truth quite necessary for both his physical and mental health: Forest Retreat was still making enough money from hemp and other crops for him to go on his old-fashioned Southern gentleman's European grand tour, and so, by the anthropomorphic God in whom he longer believed, he took it. Considering the tension between him and his mother and sisters he would have had to separate himself from them at least for a time in any case simply to regain his perspective on life, and Great Britain and Europe may have been a more appealing prospect than his other alternative, going to the western United States. And so he traveled by rail to New York and from there took a steamer to Liverpool, intending to journey southward to London, then Paris, then across the Alps to Italy and finally to the Holy Land, aiming, as he put it, "to try to relieve my mind and at the same time gain information upon the great subject of religion."[286]

There is even a shred of evidence that he may have told his mother that his primary purpose was to try to regain his faith while traveling, thus obtaining her blessing for the venture. One of his known stops in England was at Oxford University to pay a call on a clergyman who had written and published a rebuke to Bishop Colenso, and after hearing the individual in question conduct a service and preach a sermon at a university chapel Charles spent several hours with him in his lodging, discussing questions about theology and the inspiration of the Bible.[287] We cannot be certain who this minister was, since by the time Charles wrote about the experience he had either forgotten the man's name or

---

[286] Ibid., 93.
[287] Ibid., 108-109; *The Rational View,* 6.

did not deign to mention it. The most likely candidate, though, would appear to have been Rev. Henry Longueville Mansel, the one identifiable Oxford don who had contributed an essay, "On Miracles as Evidences of Christianity," to the 1863 Appleton edition of *Aids to Faith.*[288]

Whomever Charles's partner in discussion was, whether Mansel or another, Charles recalled this meeting as the one occasion that he came the closest to reclaiming his Christian orthodoxy. The minister actually brought up more logical objections to some of the texts Moore threw at him than even Colenso had articulated, and for the briefest of periods Charles was captivated by the clergyman's system of reasoning out the difficulties that the contradictions presented. Unfortunately for his mother's feelings, though, on later reflection Moore came to conclude that, although the minister was undoubtedly an ingenious logician, some of his arguments had been misleading and some ideas that he had propounded as facts could not be sustained.[289] And if his disputant did happen to be Henry Longueville Mansel, there was little wonder that Charles was at first impressed, but soon afterward disenchanted, with his arguments.

It is not our purpose to question Mansel's faith or his sincerity, only his apologetics and his method of biblical exegesis. But it was one thing to maintain a belief in God despite contradictions in Scripture and quite another to proclaim that Scripture was consistent and inerrant in spite of clear and tangible evidence to the contrary, and it would appear that Mansel fell prey to the latter fallacy. In a sort of reverse mirror image of the thought of Alexander Campbell, Henry Mansel's God was outside and above the finite, external world while human knowledge was bounded strictly within that limited world. In other words, humankind's ability to acquire knowledge had fixed restrictions, and God was simply beyond the confines of human reasoning. Thus in Mansel's economy, somewhat like that of Karl Barth, Scripture was pure divine revelation from this higher plane of existence and faith was superior to knowledge no matter what contradictions Scripture appeared to con-

---

[288] An advertisement for *Aids to Faith,* listing the essays contained therein and their authors, is in the back matter of the 1863 Appleton edition of Colenso's *Pentateuch and Book of Joshua Critically Examined.*

[289] Moore, *Behind the Bars,* 108-109; *The Rational View,* 6.

tain.[290] While his outlook enabled him to remain a good conservative Tory High Churchman and be hailed in some circles as the very defender of the faith against higher biblical criticism,[291] even some Christian reviewers in his own time recognized and noted that, though eloquent, Mansel still clung to his traditional faith by force of will, in defiance of all logical reasoning and at times even in contradiction of his own hypotheses.[292] Thus he appears ultimately to have been a theological thinker only on par with Billy Graham rather than Barth, and not even to have been as good an apologist as C. S. Lewis, but if he happened to be the one to impress the youthful Charles Chilton Moore at Oxford he must have had a real way with his words.

Besides his Oxford visit, Charles mostly tried to have fun and take some needed time for further reflection on the world and his place in it. Most of his adventures he was proud to relate, such as his rescue of a man drowning in the Seine at Paris;[293] others, though, like his story of one of the two mistresses of a wealthy young Frenchman with whom he fell in, and who happened to take a fancy to Charles and once entered his room unannounced and sat down and leaned on his bed so she "could hear him play his flute,"[294] he was content to keep under wraps for a few more decades. Regardless, though, he loved all the experiences of travel, and of all the varied types of writing he attempted over the years travel commentary was perhaps his favorite—and certainly his *forte.* The last of his works published during his lifetime was just such a travelogue, and even in his autobiography he almost gave more space to his 1865 English-European tour than he did to his career as a preacher. And since his travels obviously meant so much to him we likewise wish we could spend more time discussing them, but hopefully it will suffice to say that he was often able to relate his tales of the road with much the same humorous twist as Mark Twain in *The Innocents Abroad* and *Roughing It.*

---

[290] See Mansel, *The Limits of Religious Thought Examined in Eight Lectures Delivered Before the University of Oxford,* American reprint 1860.

[291] Baum, "Philosophy and the Knowledge of God," *The American Quarterly Church Review,* XIII, I, 1860, 1-48.

[292] See Gerhart, "Mansel's Limits of Religious Thought," *The Mercersburg Review,* XII, II, 1860, 294-319.

[293] Moore, *Behind the Bars,* 122-123.

[294] Ibid., 120-121.

As events transpired, though, Charles felt compelled to forego both Italy and the Holy Land to return to America after visiting France. Though he was no longer a believer in the supernatural he recalled falling prey in Paris to an uneasy feeling, perhaps even a premonition of sorts, that something was wrong back in Kentucky, and he was unwilling to continue his trip with the cloud of dread it produced hanging over him.[295] And so he retraced his steps back to England and then across the Atlantic, but on the return trip to Kentucky from the northeast he decided to stop off at Bethany College one more time to see how his old bishop and pedagogue, Alexander Campbell, was doing. He found Campbell as well in body as a seventy-seven year-old could be expected to fare, but the great Reformer's mind was far gone by this point. He told Charles a harrowing tale of once leaving a deceased travel companion unburied in the Syrian desert in order to escape a gang of marauding Bedouins, but soon afterwards Mrs. Campbell quietly informed Moore that Dessie had actually sent her father that story in a letter from Cyprus and he had gotten it confused with his own life experiences.[296] Charles bid goodbye to the Campbells and to Bethany, never to see his old teacher again but over the years thinking of him frequently and with a surprising degree of respect.

When Charles arrived back in Lexington he got news that chilled him to the marrow: his baby sister Alicia had sickened at Versailles and died in his absence, seemingly completely validating the feeling of unease, or premonition, he had sensed at the furthest point of his journeying from home. He rushed back to Forest Retreat to his mother and sisters, and as if to add another irony to the entire sad tale of his loss of faith, however much Charles had ever wrestled with the traditional theological concept of Jesus dying to reconcile lost humanity to God he discovered that the event of poor Alicia's demise now possessed the power to reconcile him with his family.

Mary Anne Moore met him at the gate of his old home with, as he termed it, "a mixture of sadness and gladness,"[297] and soon somehow found it in her heart to accept Charles's new opinions of Christianity as, if not entirely agreeable to her, at least honestly acquired by her own

---

[295] Ibid., 127-128.
[296] Ibid., 38.
[297] Ibid., 128-129.

flesh and blood. Whether empathy for Charles had anything to do with the circumstance is difficult to say, but in fact she herself "took her letter" from the Old Union Church on March 10, 1867[298] and it is not certain that she ever joined another congregation. Likewise Moore's sisters, though themselves retaining their church memberships, once again discovered that he was fit to live and converse with, and after Jane moved to Scott County with James Cantrill and his family and near the Grissoms, Charles and Mary Brent themselves pooled their resources to buy a house in Georgetown to complement the family's holdings in the Dog Fennel Precinct.[299]

Finally, Charles went to work and learned, little by little and in fits and starts, how to run a farm. The end of the war had brought emancipation to Kentucky; some of the Moore family's former slaves still lived on the land of Forest Retreat as sharecroppers while others managed to rent or purchase small holdings of their own at a new freedmen's settlement nearby and known as Maddoxtown, and so in essence he let his former servants become his teachers. For all his advocacy of emancipation it is not certain that he ever came to accept African Americans completely as his social equals. Few white Kentuckians did in that day and time, but it can be truthfully stated that Charles recognized and appreciated skill wherever and in whomever he found it and he was entirely candid and consistent in his condemnation of the way his class had exploited the labors of blacks for generations.[300] Would that he had been as tolerant of all minority ethnic groups as he became of African Americans, but that is another story.

And so the Moore family, along with the rest of the Dog Fennel Precinct as well as the entire Bluegrass, gradually healed from the scourges of war. Like Voltaire's Pangloss, Cunegonde, and Candide, Mary Anne Moore and her children ultimately found a measure of peace between themselves and with the world around them in the cultivation of their garden.

---

[298] Old Union Church Record Book, 1823-1892, Bosworth Library, Lexington Theological Seminary.

[299] Moore, *Behind the Bars,* 140.

[300] Ibid., *Dog Fennel,* 202.

At Christmastime 1865 Charles celebrated his twenty-eighth birthday, at long last having recovered from his heartbreak with Dessie Campbell but apparently never yet having met anyone who could take her place for him. Even a professed infidel, though, provided he happened to be young, of decent looks, from a good family, and with a healthy inheritance, could still be regarded as a catch among the young ladies of the Bluegrass gentry; after all, the old saying was that every good man was backed by a great woman, and one just couldn't tell what a moral reformer true love could be. In this spirit, Charles's sister Hannah and her daughter Lida seem to have made it a point to invite him along with the rest of the family to various public functions once he became a semi-regular resident in his and Mary Brent's new Georgetown house.

And so it happened that during such an event, a ball at Junius Ward's famous country estate of Ward Hall some time in the summer or fall of 1866, Charles met a young lady from the rural Scott County community of Stamping Ground named Lucinda George Peak who completely captured his fancy. The youngest daughter of the Scott County planter Leland Wilhoit Peak and his wife Eliza Ann, Lucinda—or "Miss Lucy," as Charles soon started calling her—was "formal sufficiently to be perfectly dignified and yet was not prudish … gracefully reserved, and not yet cold [ellipse added]," and after he engaged her in a stroll around Ward Hall and a bit of accompanying conversation it seemed to him that "the whole world had changed again, and I was exceedingly happy."[301] He saw her a second time a short while later with her father at a public horse fair somewhere near Stamping Ground, at that time obtained permission to come and visit her, and in a shorter time than had seemed possible he was head over heels in love once more. His mother and sisters were probably pleased with his new heart interest just as much because that she was almost, if not entirely, as wealthy in her own right as Charles was himself—and under Kentucky law at that time, all her money would come directly under Charles's control when he wed her. Charles himself was so smitten with Lucy that he didn't even care.[302]

---

[301] Ibid., *Behind the Bars,* 134.
[302] Ibid., 146.

And so there were more balls and picnics and barbecues that fall, one thing led to another, and around the middle of November 1866 Charles finally asked Lucy to marry him and she accepted his proposal. Though she wanted a June wedding, that season was just a little too far in the future to suit her happy groom and so the couple compromised by setting the date for Valentine's Day 1867. Despite Charles's departure from orthodox Christianity he was entirely amenable to a traditional church wedding, in full formal dress with "gentlemen attendants" to boot, and after a honeymoon trip to New York and Washington, D.C. he and Lucy settled down to begin their married life at the family's Georgetown house.[303]

Ironically, perhaps less can be found to comment about Charles's relationship with Lucy Peak than his engagement to Dessie Campbell because his and "Miss Lucy's" (he called her that all his life)[304] marriage was so stable and happy. Charles even recalled the Dickensian-style imagery in which he framed his childhood to refer to Dessie as his Dora Spenlow and Lucy as his Agnes Wickfield.[305] The couple gave one another their hearts, and for all Charles's later condemnation of James Lane Allen's *The Choir Invisible* for its alleged glorification of sexual impropriety he and Lucy would appear to have felt, and exercised, a healthy physical passion toward one another, with little indication that either of them gave much heed to the advice of the common Puritanical "marriage manuals"[306] of the Victorian Era. Charles all but described his wedding night in his autobiography; although he carefully omitted the most intimate details his account reads all the more intriguingly for their absence.[307] And though we can't really say exactly what Lucinda George Peak Moore's own personal religious beliefs were, or weren't,[308] at least her personal loyalty to her husband and her support

---

[303] Ibid., 139-141.
[304] Ibid., 141.
[305] Ibid., 146.
[306] See Thompson, 80-81.
[307] Moore, *Behind the Bars,* 141.
[308] In a January 1892 newspaper editorial, Moore made a little fun of a correspondent that suggested that he ask his wife some basic Bible questions since it was obvious he knew nothing about the book whatsoever. Moore retorted that perhaps the *correspondent* should ask Miss Lucy some basic Bible questions—if he dared. It seems safe to speculate that, though

of his right to express the honest impressions of his conscience were constant and unquestioned.

Over the next fourteen years and with the couple moving back and forth from Georgetown and alternating residences between a Lexington town house and the old family holdings in Dog Fennel, Charles and Lucy had five children, three boys and two girls: Eliza, named after Lucy's mother and born in 1868; Charles Chilton III, born in 1870; Leland, named after Lucy's father and born about 1874; Thomas Brent, named for his tragic uncle by marriage and born in 1877; and finally Lucille, namesake of sorts to her mother and born in 1880. They all lived to maturity except Eliza, who died of what was then called organic heart disease on October 25, 1879 and whose death, as Charles sorrowfully noted twenty years later, "put the first gray hairs in my head."[309] Grieved as he truly was at the loss of his beloved "curly-headed little girl," though—in an 1886 essay he recalled feeling as if the sun would never shine for him again after Eliza's death, and several years after that he confessed to a friend he could hardly even bear to visit her grave at the Lexington Cemetery since her burial always stayed every bit as fresh in his mind as the horrible day he had had to leave her there[310]—he stoically refused to fall back on the mental comforts that a return to his old religion and its confidence in an afterlife might have given him.

On a happier note, however, the Moore sons and surviving daughter Lucille appear all to have attended college, the boys at Georgetown in Kentucky[311] and Lucille in Washington, D.C.,[312] and each pursued successful careers. Charles III became a chemist, Leland an agriculturist, Brent a soldier and scholar, and Lucille a music teacher. The inscription on Brent Moore's tombstone[313] would indicate that he was, to

---

Lucy Moore might not have been a strict atheist, she wasn't exactly religiously orthodox either.

[309] Moore, *Behind the Bars,* 8, compared with "In Memoriam," 20, and the burial records of the Lexington Cemetery, West Main Street, Lexington, Kentucky.

[310] Moore, *Blue Grass Blade,* I, 5, February 13,1886.; XIV, 45, February 14, 1906. The anecdote was given in a letter by Dr. J. B. Wilson, Moore's constant critic and fast friend.

[311] Moore, *Behind the Bars,* 177.

[312] Ibid., 8.

[313] "Of all sad words of tongue or pen, the saddest are these: It might have been!"

say the least, ultimately somewhat less successful than his siblings, but like his father, Charles III ultimately seems—perhaps with a little quiet parental help—to have become a philosophical author, exploring not only the concepts of life, death, and religion, but afterlife versus eternal oblivion as well.

Leo Tolstoy may have been correct in his claim that all happy families are alike and that each unhappy family is unhappy in its own way. But as we have noted, from all available evidences Charles and Lucy Moore had a happy family, yet Moore's avowed lack of religious faith put them outside the norm no matter where they settled in the Bluegrass. We must remember that professed infidels, and indeed freethinkers of any stripe, were widely believed, especially in the South, to be profligate and egregiously immoral if not completely amoral, so perhaps Lexington local historian Elmer "Buddy" Thompson was correct in his opinion that Charles felt that he had to prove that he could be as moral as the next person by out-Christianing the Christians.[314] Either that, or he retained an amazing degree of his grandfather Stone's strict pietism, which he would have exercised now not from any traditional hope of heaven or dread of hell but most likely because he believed that life was just too short to live any other way than thoughtfully, philosophically, and stone-cold sober.

Kentucky's Thoroughbred industry was among the state's first business concerns to bounce back after the end of the Civil War, and as a large landowner in the Dog Fennel Precinct Charles had every opportunity to invest in some horseflesh and become a successful turfman like most of his neighbors. Yet he wouldn't raise Thoroughbreds or involve himself with horse racing in any form or fashion because he believed that gambling was immoral. Neither did he sell grain to any of central Kentucky's numerous distillery companies, because as a freethinker he was now a stricter Temperance advocate than he had ever been as a Christian and he refused to risk the appearance of hypocrisy.[315]

In the latter years of his life he graduated from Temperance advocacy to the promotion of complete Prohibition; this cause became a

---

[314] Thompson, 57.
[315] Moore, *Behind the Bars*, 186; see also 167-168.

crusade, for a few years even a mania, for him, and strangely enough his personal activities in behalf of the complete elimination of the liquor trade in America more closely mirror the professed beliefs of modern conservative Baptists, Pentecostals, and Stone-Campbell Churches of Christ than they did the beliefs or attitudes of either infidels or Christians (except perhaps rural Methodists of the "shouting" type whose descendants became Pentecostals) during his own lifetime. In that day and age, Prohibition was considered more of a progressive than a conservative cause, and Moore himself subsequently rationalized his outlook by reasoning thusly: he didn't oppose the Bible and Christianity simply because they were not true but because they were also destructive to happiness, and to him liquor was every bit as destructive to happiness as Christianity was—in his mind, one principal reason being that the Bible advocated liquor's use. After all, Jesus was attributed with turning water to wine and Paul was supposed to have advised Timothy not to drink water but rather a little wine for his stomach's sake.[316] But regardless, the one thing that could be guaranteed to put Moore into a foaming, barely coherent fury was to learn that some big, wealthy Bluegrass congregation either admitted bar owners and distillers as church members in good standing, or accepted financial contributions from them. To him such tolerance was a sign that the liquor industry exerted a financial control over the church and was thus the absolute lowest-of-the-low Christian hypocrisy.

Though until at least 1878 Moore both chewed tobacco and smoked cigars, he likewise seems not to have been willing to take profits from the raising and selling of tobacco because he wanted to discourage, rather than encourage, anyone to assume such a nasty and expensive habit,[317] and if he had been able to foresee the use for a certain type of hemp that young people would develop a century later he probably

---

[316] Moore, editorial in the *Blue Grass Blade,* XIII, 44, January 1, 1905. The Scriptural references are from John 2:1-11 and I Timothy 5:23. Susan Jacoby suggests an additional reason for Moore's strict Prohibitionist stance: in that day many freethinkers regarded alcoholism as one of the main causes of marital violence against women, and they wished to make drunkenness legal grounds for divorce so a woman might leave a violent, abusive, alcoholic husband without incurring social stigma. See Jacoby, 210.

[317] Ibid., *Behind the Bars,* 156-158.

wouldn't ever have raised any species of that either. In years to come he actually headed up a petition to the Lexington police force, signed mostly by Christians, demanding that the city close down the three most notorious brothels on the city's North Upper Street, those of the madams Lettie Powell, Molly Parker, and Belle Brezing,[318] and this though his own writings and especially his subsequent actions as an editor and literary agent aptly reveal quite a commonsense, even pleasantly earthy, attitude toward the fulfillment of physical desire within the bounds of wedlock.

During the term his brother-in-law, James Cantrill, served as Kentucky's Lieutenant Governor under Governor Luke P. Blackburn, the chief executive of Kentucky even issued a pardon to Belle Brezing for her offenses,[319] and it may simply have outraged Charles that his upright, churchgoing, married brother-in-law, other state politicians like Blackburn, and Lexington's city officials could look the other way for the benefit of the town's flesh trade while perhaps simultaneously discreetly sampling the wares that the Upper Street houses had to offer. In addition to his absolute intolerance for hypocrisy and his annoyance that houses of prostitution were "kept by unintelligent and immoral women and principally patronized by men of that kind,"[320] it would appear that Moore always nursed a naïve, idealistic hope that a progressive, rational, freethinking outlook on sexual relations between husbands and wives would someday render the profession of prostitution obsolete in America. At any rate, Charles's petition did drive at least Madam Brezing from Upper Street—right over to Megowan Street and a bigger and fancier house.[321] Perhaps Moore could at least take comfort, though, in the knowledge that he and his brother infidels were too few in number in and around Lexington to keep Belle and her girls in business. According to one popular but apocryphal tale, for some reason she once found herself able to pay off an enormous mortgage in its entirety right after a convention meeting of Baptists left the city.[322]

---

[318] Thompson, 57-58.
[319] Ibid., 50.
[320] Moore to Judge Farris Robert Feland of Lawrenceburg, Kentucky, the *Blue Grass Blade,* VI, 52, October 3, 1897.
[321] Thompson, 59-62.
[322] Ibid., 181.

And so to return to our story, whether in the church or out of it, Mary Anne Moore died apparently in the summer of 1872[323] and the old Forest Retreat plantation was split into two separate properties. As security for Mary Brent and her children Charles seems to have arranged for his widowed sister and her daughters to get the lion's share of the property, approximately 500 acres and their parents' home, while he kept the dwelling known as Bleak House and 347 acres for his own which he dubbed, of all things, "Quakeracre"—according to Charles because of his farm's "simplicity,"[324] but one wonders if he might also have been inspired by the fact that some of the more progressive members of the Society of Friends, at least in the north, were so religiously liberal that they were practically freethinkers themselves. In addition, he freed Lucy from the near-medieval Kentucky property laws by deeding the "Quakeracre" farm in its entirety to her and his children.[325] Unfortunately, though, in accidents at different times both Bleak House and the old Moore homestead caught fire and burned, Mary Brent's dwelling perhaps when she was absent at the family's Georgetown residence, but Bleak House by the hand of a feeble-minded indigent whom Charles and Lucy had befriended. Both Mary Brent and Charles rebuilt on their respective properties, though neither of their newer houses was as opulent as the old Forest Retreat mansion.[326]

As the market for Kentucky hemp slowly but inexorably dwindled after the Civil War due to the end of the slavery-based economy as well as competition from stronger and cheaper foreign imports, Charles's decreased landholdings combined with his self-imposed code of ethics to make it virtually impossible for him to maintain his father's degree of prosperity without seeking additional work away from the farm. Though he would have had plenty of garden produce and grain from year to year by the efforts of his sharecroppers and hired laborers as well as the sweat of his own brow, his refusal to sell corn to distilleries cost him a good deal of return, and his autobiographical writings appear to indicate that the raising of sheep and selling of wool was one of his

323 Some genealogists give the date of Mary Anne's death as August 31, 1872, but since she had left Old Union Church in 1867 there is no record in the congregation's books of her decease.

324 Moore, *Behind the Bars,* 8.

325 Ibid., 145-146.

326 Ibid., 144-145.

few profitable agricultural ventures.[327] Thus at various times, seemingly short and sporadic, he worked as a bank teller and insurance adjustor both in Georgetown and Lexington, co-owner and operator of a flour mill, Federal census enumerator for Fayette County, agent for a claimed railroad financier whom he later had to expose as a fraud,[328] candidate for Congress (he was elected by the people to remain at home, he wryly noted),[329] traveling salesman for a coffee company (which he resigned because he couldn't stand to spend that much time away from Lucy and the children)[330]—and early in his marriage, actually a fireman in Georgetown, which career he seemingly shelved fairly quickly after the June 1869 fire there that destroyed most of the old part of the city. Apparently while he and his cohorts were frantically trying to pump water from Elkhorn Creek into the tank of the town's horse-drawn fire engine to extinguish the blaze, a big catfish nosed into the end of the water hose and got itself stuck tight, and in essence, Moore guddled while Georgetown burned. He later made the tongue-in-cheek proposal that Georgetown should raise a monument with a bronze heroic statue of him on it, fire helmet on his head, fireman's trumpet in one hand and a fire insurance policy in the other, and inscribed at the base with the words *"Omnia ex igne."*[331]

Of all his varied professions, though, that of journalist seemed to satisfy him the most. As we have already indicated, it is probably extremely fortunate that he did not hold the poetry that he began writing at Bethany College and continued later as part of the advertising copy for his coffee firm, in the same serious regard as he did his prose. But in any case, Kentuckians sometimes have long memories, and it would seem that Moore's pre-War "Edibility of Crows" essay had never quite been entirely forgotten in Lexington. Thus after Mark Twain gained a national reputation as both a public lecturer and a writer of humor, Moore took a leaf from Twain's notebook, as it were, and began to churn out a series of comic essays probably classifiable in modern parlance as creative nonfiction and which set him, Lucy, and their

---

[327] See Ibid., 205 and *Dog Fennel,* 137.
[328] Ibid, *Behind the Bars,* 142-144.
[329] Ibid., *Dog Fennel,* 302.
[330] Ibid., *Behind the Bars,* 153.
[331] Ibid., 142. Thanks to Georgetown historian Ann Bevins for assistance in dating the city's post-Civil War fire.

children more or less in the role of Twain's fictional McWilliams family. He found a ready market for these in the Lexington newspapers, and two, entitled "Looking for the Pantry Key" and "The Lightning Rod Man" respectively, appear to have been especially popular and both enjoyed a number of reprints.[332] Moore recalled that a third essay he entitled "A Lay Sermon to Preachers" and apparently with similar thematic content to the first nine verses of the second chapter of his avowed favorite book of the Bible, the Epistle of James,[333] was printed in the *Lexington Daily Press* and was also a popular and much-requested item. This too was nonfiction, based on one of Moore's own experiences in attending an Episcopalian worship service.

And so finally, with the enthusiastic acceptance of Moore's "Lay Sermon" by the Lexington and Fayette County populace at large, Henry T. Duncan, editor and proprietor of the *Lexington Daily Press,* offered him a job as a staff reporter and commentator at what was then the munificent sum of $75 per month.[334] Moore seems to have been well established in the profession at least by the time of the American Centennial, for he wrote of attending a fair in Lexington that year in company with many of the city's other reporters and editors.[335] Even as a professional writer, though, he remained something of a peripatetic. Although his Bluegrass readers could applaud his "Lay Sermon" because they could identify and empathize with the piece's sentiments, as soon as he dared to write something frank about his lack of religious beliefs the popular tide turned and Duncan felt compelled to bow to community pressure and fire him. But hard on the heels of this seeming setback, the editor of the *Daily Press's* closest competitor, the *Lexington Transcript,* took him on staff, and then something of a vicious, or at least a bitterly humorous, cycle started up. Within a brief while Moore came to carry a certain clientele of irreverent and satire-loving readers

---

[332] Ibid., 149. Among other occasions, "Looking for the Pantry Key," outlining Moore's exhaustive, unsuccessful search throughout his house for the said key only to give up and prepare to remove the pantry door from its hinges and then finding the key in the lock it was intended to open, was reprinted in the *Blue Grass Blade,* I, 28, October 25, 1890.

[333] Moore, *Dog Fennel,* 303. The passage in question strictly upbraids Christians for showing "respect of persons" between rich and poor.

[334] Ibid., *Behind the Bars,* 148-149.

[335] Ibid., 59.

along with him, and as soon as he got fired by one of the two papers for complaints about some piece that smacked of freethinking, the other inevitably hired him back. As he observed, it seemed that neither newspaper quite wanted him around for too long, but at the same time neither of the rival editors wanted the other periodical to have him.[336] At least it could be said that Moore's career as a journalist during this period was probably never boring, and he committed himself to it so thoroughly that he actually taught himself to write shorthand from a textbook, perhaps even too well. For the rest of his life he complained of a nervous quirk that compelled him to make the motions of writing shorthand with his right thumb and index finger, requiring a conscious effort on his part to keep his fingers still.[337]

In a Southern city such as Lexington it was no surprise that Moore's editors should feel compelled to satisfy the aesthetic sensibilities of a conventionally religious majority, but how did it happen that, in this Bible Belt heartland, as it were, an irreligious minority had grown so sizable—and so vocal—that the town's newspapermen found that they had to throw at least a sop to it as well? The main reason was that, in the years between the Reconstruction Era and World War I, infidels, atheists, and freethinkers of every stamp found as welcome a home in the United States as they had ever known or would ever enjoy. This is not to say that either skeptics or their sensibilities were ever accepted by a majority of Americans. They most certainly were not. But the proliferation of freethought periodicals in the United States, starting with the establishment of the *Truth Seeker* of Peoria, Illinois in 1873, began to give American atheists and freethinkers throughout the nation a sense both of their numerical strengths and ideological kinships, from the established freethinking communities of large cities through the movement's growth in Southern towns like Lexington to the solitary, lonely, and frequently ostracized "village atheists" in small Southern and Midwestern hamlets. Susan Jacoby classifies this period of history, with good reason, as the Golden Age of Freethought in America.[338]

---

[336] Ibid., 149.
[337] Ibid., 158-159.
[338] Jacoby, 149-157.

The editors of the various freethought periodicals, both including, and following along in the wake of, the *Truth Seeker*—and for that matter, even the editorial boards of individual magazines and newspapers—ran the ideological gamut all the way from total atheism to Walt Whitman-style pantheism and quasi-religious asceticism to classical Epicureanism, but all held in common the dual emphases of the validity of reason over the claims of any so-called revealed religion and the complete separation of Church and State as guaranteed by the Deistic framing of the Constitution and the Bill of Rights. Virtually all regarded argument and debate as not only acceptable but healthy. In less than fifty years most American citizens would come to associate any type of non-theism with one or more forms of Anarchism or Socialism, thereby pretty much demonizing the entire Socialist concept, but in these early days Socialist ideologues were just as open to criticism from freethought editors as the disciples of one more quasi-religious movement, as were apologists of orthodox Christianity for their stress on revelation over reason.[339] Even so, all freethought periodicals had their causes. Far from being mere hedonists or simply believing in *nothing,* common accusations thrown at freethinkers by religionists, both the periodical editors and most of the nonbelievers who kept the magazines in business were more often than not passionately committed to the advancement of science and science-based humanitarian goals for the betterment of society. Of course, this didn't mean that individuals in the movement couldn't be mere vulgar and hypocritical caricatures of progressivism just like the fictional druggist Homais in Flaubert's *Madam Bovary,* but these were in fact the exception rather than the rule; in the same defense Christians claimed for themselves, if freethinkers weren't perfect, and they certainly weren't any more than Christians could have been, at least the hearts of most of the outspoken ones were in the right place.

Among the more forthright of Moore's so-called "certain clientele" that he noted in his writings were the Lexington businessman, city council member, and liberal Jew Moses Kaufman, Moore's contemporary in age W. W. Goddard of Harrodsburg, and Louis or Lewis Pilcher of Nicholasville, about seventeen years younger than Moore and perhaps qualifying as the "village atheist" in his own community. But of

[339] Ibid., 231.

course Moore had to have enjoyed support from a good many other newspaper readers besides, and certainly one of the most intriguing, and endearing, of these "village atheists" was an individual whom Charles Chilton Moore knew well both before and during her career as a freethought activist: Josephine Williamson, the petite young teacher who had worked under Elizabeth Jameson at Woodford College in Versailles. As an instructor at the Disciples' girls' school she had to have been closely acquainted with the scandal Moore had caused when he left the Versailles Christian Church pulpit, and though she never wrote about this circumstance, we might hope that she stood up in support of Charles's poor sister Alicia in the terrible days when the clacking teeth and wagging tongues of Bluegrass society gossip would have appeared to the teenager to be devouring the family's reputation completely. But at any rate, she had married the Confederate veteran Captain William Henry in 1868, they founded their own school in Versailles, and not too many years elapsed before Josephine Henry became one of the most vocal, and perhaps indeed the most passionate, defender of women's rights that the state of Kentucky has ever known. Her delicate frame concealed a backbone like railroad steel and ribs more resilient than crossties, and she deserves a great deal more credit than she has been given for her tireless lobbying for the repeal of the restrictive nineteenth-century Kentucky property laws that made women no more than the chattel of their husbands and fathers.[340] In the years of her prime she was actually known as "The Woman Henry Clay of Kentucky."[341]

Josephine Williamson Henry
(1844-1928)

Photo courtesy Woodford County Historical Society, Versailles, Ky.

[340] Henry, "Married Women and Property Rights," 2-16. Also see Klotter,

Sadly, the principal reason Mrs. Henry was never recognized fully for her accomplishments, either within Kentucky or outside it, was her eventual complete repudiation of the traditional concepts of Christianity. Most other Kentucky feminists and suffragists such as Laura Clay were strongly religious albeit from a liberal standpoint, and like good liberal Christians they emphasized those Scriptures that presented Jesus and Christianity as loving, inclusive, and pro-women's rights while carefully ignoring or downplaying those Bible writings that didn't. As with the more so-called radical feminists Susan B. Anthony and Elizabeth Cady Stanton, though, for Josephine Henry this wasn't good enough. The New Testament advised that women were to be held in subjection because Adam was formed first, then Eve, and that the woman was more at fault because she was the first to transgress but that she could be saved in childbearing if she continued in faith and charity and holiness and sobriety,[342] while the Old Testament gave any insecure Israelite husband who suspected his wife of infidelity the right to bring her to a priest for a primitive trial by ordeal involving the drinking of contaminated water and called a "jealousy offering."[343] To Josephine Henry, when it came down to brass tacks, one of these Scripture passages was just as valid, and as dangerous, as the other. More moderate Kentucky feminists ultimately broke ranks with Mrs. Henry because of her mid-1890s participation in the editing of Elizabeth Cady Stanton's *Woman's Bible,* a volume that thoroughly dissected—nay, vivisected—women's roles and rights in Scripture from Genesis to Revelation.[344]

Kentucky Justice, 24, and Dew, "Women in Reform: Josephine Henry," http://www.womeninkentucky.com/site/reform/j_henry.html, http://www.womeninkentucky.com/site/reform/j_henry_prop_act.html, and http://www.womeninkentucky.com/site/reform/J_Henry_prop_act2.html

[341] Moore, *Behind the Bars,* 237-238, quoting an 1895 article from the *Freethought Magazine.*

[342] I Timothy 2:11-15.

[343] Numbers 5:11-31.

[344] Insofar as can be ascertained, Josephine Henry wrote no actual commentaries on any particular portions or texts of Scripture in *The Woman's Bible,* but she was a part of the book's editorial committee along with several other prominent United States feminists. However, *The Woman's Bible* did include two very outspoken essays by her on the various mistreatments of women that the Bible as a whole had caused. See Stanton, *The Woman's Bible,* 193-198 and 203-208.

We have already taken note of the tale that the Versailles community started when Charles Moore left the pulpit of the Christian Church: no young man in his right mind could think or act as Charles had, so he simply must have gone mad from heartbreak over Dessie Campbell. When Josephine Henry's change in beliefs became common knowledge she fared even worse at the hands of the town gossips. The more charitable of her neighbors appear to have theorized that she never completely abandoned belief in a benevolent God until her only son, Frederick, was killed in a railway accident, and that her pure wild grief and fury at the Deity caused her to become an atheist.[345] Though twenty-two year-old Frederick Henry did in fact lose his life in a freak and tragic railroad mishap near Chicago in October 1891, Charles Moore stated that Mrs. Henry supported his literary efforts from their very earliest[346] and of course he began writing freethought journalism several years before Frederick's death. Thus it is possible that Moore himself could have played a small role in Mrs. Henry's change of beliefs as early as 1865, when he left the fellowship of the Disciples; the only note taken of the issue in the relevant records of Versailles' St. John's Episcopal Church indicate that, at some unknown date after June of that year, Mrs. Henry was cited for being "absent from communion over three years without any excuse."[347]

Other Versailles gossips concocted a tale that conceivably could have had some miniscule actual basis in fact, but which, in a characteristically Southern small-town way, was designed specifically to present

---

[345] Many thanks to Danna Estridge of the Woodford County (Kentucky) Historical Society, Versailles, Kentucky, for this local anecdote about Josephine Henry.

[346] Moore, *Behind the Bars,* 79.

[347] St. John's Episcopal Church Records, Woodford County Historical Society, Versailles, Kentucky. We should also note here that, in the September 20, 1890 issue of the *Blue Grass Blade* (Vol. I, Issue 6) Charles Moore writes of a communication he has received from a certain lady, "who has done more for Prohibition and her sex than any woman in the State [of Kentucky]," that she used his *The Rational View* as "her hand-book." It's almost certain that he was speaking of Mrs. Henry here, and she is listed elsewhere in the same issue of the newspaper by name as a subscriber. If no other data can be used to try to ascertain the time of her change of beliefs, we may at least say definitively that she gave Moore this endorsement a good twelve months before Frederick Henry's death.

Mrs. Henry in the most undignified and humiliating light possible. An accomplished musician, Josephine Henry served for some years as the organist at St. John's. As the church's instrumentalist she was the lone woman in the congregation at that long-ago day and time entitled to wear any form of clerical garb during services, and so one Sunday morning as she stepped out of the church house to a nearby outbuilding to don vestments over her beautiful green silk dress in preparation for a service, an enormous hog got loose from a nearby pen and began to run wildly through the streets of the town. One variant of the story has the hog knocking Mrs. Henry down into a mud puddle just as she emerged from the church, the other has her being tripped up by it and actually riding on its back and screaming for help for some distance, but the tale ends the same in either case: she was too embarrassed ever to show her face at church again, the implication being that since she wouldn't come to St. John's and face the laughs of her neighbors she swelled up in her own selfish pride and became an atheist.[348]

Perhaps the recounting of such dull low-comedic yarns is to be no more than expected in small towns and rural hamlets both north and south of the Mason-Dixon Line even today, as community armor designed for protection against any individual who transgresses societal norms and whether the transgression is a matter of principle and conscience or not. However much Mrs. Henry's memory may have been tarnished locally by the complacent tongue-clucking and ridicule of her neighbors, though, her work in behalf of Kentucky women's property rights has withstood the test of time. Hopefully her one other great legal accomplishment will do so as well: until 1893, apparently it had never occurred to any Christian lawmaker in this most evangelical of states that there was something wrong or immoral about classifying a twelve-year-old girl as being mature enough to give legal consent to sexual activity. In short and to put it brutally bluntly, for most of the nineteenth century in Kentucky the word "jailbait" applied only to girls under twelve years old. And yet, despite whatever red faces and embarrassed sideways glances among the legislators that her blunt, no-

---

[348] Timothy Oliver, "The Pig." In *St. John's Episcopal Church, Versailles, Kentucky, One Hundred and Fifty Years,* 42. Again, thanks to Danna Estridge of the Woodford County Historical Society for further information about this tale.

nonsense words may have prompted, and though the tale of her taking a ride on the hog's back was already well ensconced in local legend, Josephine Henry managed to convince the members of the Kentucky State Legislature that they could, and should, do better.[349]

Of course, no "Golden Age" of any ideological movement would be quite complete without at least one high, mighty, bright star below which lesser lights could congregate, and so for the Golden Age of Freethought in post-Civil War America the star proved to be a rotund, jovial, stentorian attorney named Robert Green Ingersoll. A native of New York and the son of a poor Congregationalist minister, the largely self-educated Ingersoll had grown up along the east-to-midwest trail of his father's preaching career, and although he had a heart and a brain made for philosophy he could never see that his father's theology made any sense whatsoever. He had made a name for himself first as a central Illinois prairie lawyer not unlike Abraham Lincoln, then briefly as an officer in the Union Army, and after the end of the Civil War he might have enjoyed a long and successful career as a statesman if he had only been willing to remain silent about his skepticism of Christianity. This he refused to do, but since he possessed a voice, and a skill in using it, that any elected official would have envied, he soon found himself in great demand first in Illinois and then on a national level for the Republican Party as both a lecturer on political subjects and as campaign speechmaker for various Republican politicians. In the latter capacity he came to his finest hour at the 1876 Republican National Convention with an address nominating James G. Blaine as the party's candidate for the Presidency. Though Blaine lost out at the convention to Rutherford B. Hayes, Ingersoll's so-called "Plumed Knight" speech (he had dubbed Blaine "the Plumed Knight of the Republican Party") was widely considered, in the oratorical conventions of the time, to have been the ideal, even the perfect, political discourse. And though Ingersoll remained more or less active in the legal profession for the rest of his life, from the time of his "Plumed Knight" speech his career as a public lecturer was assured and he made a veritable fortune at it.

In the days before radio and television, lecturers were in great demand throughout the United States, like preachers, the more flamboy-

---

[349] Thompson, 23, 182.

ant the better. Men and women alike would travel miles to pay the scandalously exorbitant price of an entire dollar a head in order to hear a popular lecturer. Mark Twain established his national reputation as a humorist in this very milieu, and for his part Robert Ingersoll proved willing to visit and speak not only in large cities but midsized towns too, in his own day rapidly becoming every bit as well-known nationally as Twain. He could lecture not only on current political issues but literature and philosophy and even humor and whimsy as well; included among his favorite subjects for discourse were the life and works of Shakespeare, the poetry of Robert Burns and Walt Whitman, and the scientific accomplishments of Alexander Humboldt, but once he had firmly established his lecturing career he was willing to hold forth for hours on biblical criticism, the life and legacy of Thomas Paine, and his own personal reasons for being a freethinker too. As Jacoby observes, if he had attempted to start his career as a lecturer by dealing with freethought subjects he probably would have been a miserable failure, but since he first established his reputation lecturing on political questions and the humanities and only then graduated to Bible criticism and freethought philosophy he was able to carry the case for agnosticism and atheism to the American public as no one had since the days of Paine's *The Age of Reason*.[350] Though it is difficult nowadays to imagine any popular American speaker, much less a committed Republican, who would proudly bear the nicknames of The Great Agnostic and The Silver-tongued Infidel, this is exactly who Robert Green Ingersoll was and what he did. Many, if not most, of his auditors disagreed personally with his contentions, but they paradoxically admired him for the strength of his arguments and the courage of his convictions, and when he came to town to deliver a lecture it was always fun not only to watch him ruffle the feathers of local preachers but to observe their attempts to refute his reasoning.

Likewise paradoxical, though, was Ingersoll's relationship to an increasingly variegated American Protestant religious community. Certainly among Southern ministers and churches he was generally regarded not only as The Silver-tongued Infidel but a silver-tongued and cloven-hoofed devil, and not a few of the new, rising, and increasingly vocal breed of postwar Northern evangelical divines such as

---

[350] Jacoby, 157-167.

Dwight Lyman Moody and Thomas DeWitt Talmage shared this firm conviction as well. Others in the growing liberal Christian movement, like Rev. Alexander Clark of Washington D. C., the noted Episcopal priest Rev. R. Heber Newton of New York City, and the renowned brother of Harriet Beecher Stowe, the Congregationalist Henry Ward Beecher, in fact appreciated Ingersoll's take on the errors and cruelties of Scripture and actually voiced approval of his positions at least insofar as they could be used to advance the acceptance of their own liberal theological outlooks. Of course, the more puritanical or at least conservative of Ingersoll's ministerial critics made all the hay they could out of the celebrated alleged sexual scandal between Henry Ward Beecher and his parishioner, Elizabeth Tilton, in 1875, but they took a jaundiced view of the fact that they couldn't pin anything of the kind on Ingersoll himself.[351] Ingersoll's wife, incidentally, the former Eva Parker, was just as committed a skeptic as was her husband and she actually served along with Josephine Henry on the editorial committee of Elizabeth Cady Stanton's *Woman's Bible.*

Though Charles Moore had not been much interested in politics, or even particularly patriotic, ever since the days of his flawed, failed idealism in the Civil War,[352] the figure of Robert Green Ingersoll captivated him as thoroughly as his grandfather Stone and Alexander Campbell had once ensnared the hearts of the Kentucky pioneers of the faith tradition into which he had been born. To him, one of Ingersoll's most famous and oft-requested lectures, "Some Mistakes of Moses," was every bit as effective and convincing a piece of ammunition against biblical literalism and inerrancy as had been Bishop Colenso's *Pentateuch and Book of Joshua Critically Examined* a decade or so earlier, with the added bonus—certainly endearing to anyone who had grown up reading the *Millennial Harbinger* and other combatively-styled Stone-Campbell religious periodicals—of possessing a sense of whimsy and sarcasm and a peppery, if not quite vitriolic, rhetoric that Colenso completely lacked.[353] If Ingersoll happened to be visiting any city within two hundred miles of Lexington on one of his speaking tours, Moore would invariably be in eager attendance, and his press

---

[351] Ibid., 163-164.
[352] Moore, *Dog Fennel,* 320.
[353] Ibid., *Behind the Bars,* 72-73.

credentials gave him special access to private interviews with the famed lecturer. For many years he considered Ingersoll his fast friend while Ingersoll held Moore at least in sociable acquaintance, and at one time Moore even ventured to claim credit, possibly during the time of another journalistic interview, for encouraging Henry Ward Beecher to strike up his first dialogue with The Great Agnostic. Whether or not this was the case, at least until the early 1890s Moore considered Beecher and Ingersoll "two of the greatest minds in America, equally side by side together in the promotion of the great Christian work—strong oxen that pull against each other in the same yoke, but between whom there is a residuum of force to which they equally contribute, and which tends to draw the cart that contains the ark of America's hopes to its place of rest."[354]

So vocal was Moore's admiration of the Silver-tongued Infidel that he actually seems to have been accused more than once actually of being converted by Ingersoll himself to agnosticism or atheism, frequently enough anyway for him to stress in his own writings that he had come to his religious conclusions long before he had ever heard of Ingersoll or his reputation. Nonetheless, Moore did confess once—though certainly in a moment of angry, even furious, hyperbole that he might have had cause to regret later—that he had "bowed at the shrine of [Ingersoll's] mighty genius with an adoration and an idolatry far more genuine than that which the average Christian feels for his God."[355] One of his more memorable firings from the *Lexington Daily Press* occurred because he wrote a short article criticizing Thomas DeWitt Talmage for his outspoken condemnation of Ingersoll[356], and the one lone hint in Moore's memoirs of any marital discord between him and Lucy seems to have been connected not to his own skepticism or atheism but rather her concern over his infatuation with The Great Agnostic.[357]

Strangely, it does appear that Charles Chilton Moore and his old teacher Alexander Campbell's early partner in reform, the Kentucky

---

[354] Ibid., *The Rational View,* ix.

[355] Ibid, "Col. Ingersoll's Letter and My Answer To It," first published in *The Blue Grass Blade,* May 20, 1894; reprinted in *Behind the Bars,* iii-iv.

[356] Ibid., *Behind the Bars,* 149.

[357] Ibid, "Col. Ingersoll's Letter and My Answer To It," *Behind the Bars,* iii-iv.

Disciple pioneer Raccoon John Smith, had this much in common even though one had become as committed a freethinker as the other had been a Stone-Campbell Disciple: in a blunt statement unthinkable for any modern conservative evangelical or fundamentalist male to allow himself to utter, Smith once candidly admitted that the first time he ever met Alexander Campbell he wanted to sit and stare at the man for a full hour without anyone interrupting him or saying anything to him,[358] and Moore's admission noted above is convincing evidence that he was almost certainly equally captivated by Robert Green Ingersoll throughout the 1870s, 1880s and early 1890s. Too, both Smith and Moore ultimately became disappointed in their respective mentors, and for the same reason: both Campbell and Ingersoll were forced more or less to betray their two votaries slightly, in each case at a crucial moment and in both instances due to social and political considerations, though certainly Smith would never have admitted any disillusionment whatsoever with either Alexander Campbell or the Stone-Campbell Movement.[359]

Perhaps some individuals must have their savior figures even though they have abandoned belief in any divine salvation, and certainly this is how even Madalyn Murray O'Hair collected at least a portion of her following. But lest we lend it the impression that Moore should be condemned for an inconsistency or perhaps even a slight hypocrisy here, we must remember how genuinely and terribly lonely he must have felt, settled as he was deeply within the rural Kentucky folds of the Bible Belt, before the *Truth Seeker* ever came out as a national freethought magazine or Robert Ingersoll altered the primary topics of his lectures from literature and politics to Bible criticism. It was just as natural that an organized subculture should bloom from the "Letters to the Editor" column of the *Truth Seeker,* especially as that subculture fed on Ingersoll's latest pronouncements, as it was for so-called Science Fiction "fandom" to grow out of a similar journalistic milieu seventy-five or so years later. Charles Moore was, quite simply and naturally, an Ingersoll fan in the truest sense of the term.

Still, we must keep in consideration Moore's often complex and convoluted relationships with the exponents of the religion of his an-

---

[358] See Sparks, *Raccoon John Smith,* 26-27, 205.
[359] See Ibid., 329-375.

cestry and his childhood, especially those who, according to Moore's own exacting standards, lived up to the precepts of his favorite Book of James and were doers of the Word and not hearers only. We have already spoken of Richard Reid in this connection, and in the late 1870s or early 1880s Moore appears to have traveled to Mt. Sterling to visit with him on at least one occasion. Interestingly, by this time Reid had married to the woman who had almost become his sister-in-law back in the days of the Civil War: Elizabeth Jameson, whose own first husband had died rather suddenly after the couple had had one son. Reid, who was elected in 1879 to serve on Kentucky's Appellate Court and in 1882 on the newly-created Superior Court created to assist in adjudicating the Appellate Court's case backlog,[360] was as kind to his stepson as if he had been the boy's own natural father, but he never had any children of his own. It is actually possible that his physical handicap, which he still kept a strict secret to everyone except his spouse and his physician, had rendered him incapable of siring his own children. At any rate, both Richard and Elizabeth Reid welcomed Moore into their home, and if they didn't attempt to convert him back to Christianity he didn't try to convert them to infidelity either.[361]

Perhaps the oddest and certainly the most remarkable relationship that Charles Chilton Moore ever had with a Christian, or at least a preacher, though, was that of his friendship with George Owen Barnes, known in that day and time as the Mountain Evangelist. A decade or so older than Moore, Barnes hailed from Garrard County, Kentucky, and was the son of an English-born Presbyterian minister. Converted as a young man and trying to follow in his father's footsteps, Barnes attended the Presbyterians' Centre College at Danville, where like many a college student—perhaps, as we have seen, even Charles Moore briefly during sleigh rides with Kate Pendleton—he "backslid." After a brief stint as a soldier in the Mexican War Barnes was reconciled to the church, however, and his family even managed to save enough money to send him to Princeton Theological Seminary in New Jersey for his divinity training. Upon the completion of his studies he married Jane Cowan and began to raise a family, but he was interested in the foreign

360 Klotter, *Kentucky Justice,* 38-40.
361 Moore, *Behind the Bars,* 77.

mission field and so his first major preaching assignment was a seven-year stint as a missionary in India. His and Jane's two oldest children, Maria and William, were born there.[362]

Upon his return to Kentucky in 1861 he became the pastor of one of his father's old charges, the Stanford Presbyterian Church at the governmental seat of Lincoln County, and he built a house for his family about two miles from the town and the church and known locally as the "Pink Cottage." At Stanford he ministered capably throughout the Civil War years and even some time afterward, but perhaps his career as a settled pastor was not entirely without strife: though his biographer, W. T. Price, never makes Barnes's antebellum political sympathies quite clear, it is probable that he was pro-Union and not all of his neighbors would have been in harmony with him. After a period of contention between him and his congregants the Kentucky Presbyterian Synod finally brought him up on charges of preaching some sort of doctrinal irregularity, probably a modified Arminianism although his Civil War politics could have been a factor in his brother Presbyterians' accusations as well, and excluded him in 1872.[363] For all we know, this may have been one of the initial reasons Charles Moore became interested in him.[364] After all, the whole scenario was an experience that Barnes held largely in common with Moore's own grandfather, seventy-odd years apart in time. On one occasion Barnes even visited Barton Stone's grave—his body having been exhumed from its Missouri resting place by history-minded Disciples and transported back across the Mississippi to a newly-created memorial at the historic Cane

George Owen Barnes

Photo courtesy Johnson County Public Library, Paintsville, Ky.

---

[362] Price, 129.

[363] Ibid., 127-148.

[364] Moore, *Behind the Bars,* 154.

Ridge Meetinghouse in Kentucky—and he wrote of the pioneer preacher in the highest terms of praise.[365]

Unlike Stone at the turn of the century, though, George Owen Barnes had friends in higher places that were only too willing to help him out of his difficulties with the Presbyterians. John G. Owsley, a Stanford native who had moved north to Chicago and had become a successful businessman, outfitted Barnes with his own independent chapel on Harrison Street in that city and gave financial backing to both Barnes personally and the new church as a missionary endeavor. This was, of course, the period of Dwight Lyman Moody's rise to power and influence in Chicago as well, and with Owsley's encouragement Barnes fell in with both Moody and the Chicago minister's own primary spiritual and theological influence during this time: John Nelson Darby,[366] leader of the Exclusivist faction of the British-based Plymouth Brethren, and essentially the founder of so-called "dispensationalist" thought among American conservative Christians. This is to say that Darby believed that the history of the world must be properly divided into a certain number of separate covenants between God and humankind, or "dispensations of grace," according to one type of literalist and inerrantist take on the Bible, and that every historical event in each "dispensation" fit together in accordance with Darby's own version of Bible prophecy. Perhaps needless to add, the Darby definitions of the terms "prophecy" and "prophet" had little, if anything, to do with the ethical and social concerns of Isaiah, Jeremiah or even Jesus; prophecy was the God-appointed ability to foresee the future, and prophets were, in essence, merely inspired soothsayers.

Although the nineteenth century had already seen more than one claimed "prophecy expert" come and go before Darby—the ex-Baptist William Miller, who used the Book of Daniel to figure out that the world was ending in 1843 and thus wound up being responsible for the founding of the Seventh-Day Adventist denomination, comes to mind here, and even Alexander Campbell's Disciples of Christ once had their own prophetic exponent in no less a figure than Decima Campbell Barclay's father-in-law[367]—the Plymouth Brethren leader was the first

---

[365] Price, 347, quoting Barnes's journal.
[366] Ibid., 148-154.
[367] Brown, 440-441.

modern Protestant evangelist to try to cut and separate all the individual apocalyptic verses found in the Bible's Major and Minor Prophets, the Gospels, the Epistles to the Thessalonians, and the Book of Revelation as if each was a piece in a gigantic and mysterious jigsaw puzzle, shake them all up, and attempt to put the puzzle back together again in some kind of quasi-logical order that purported to resolve all the contradictions between the varying Scripture passages. Hence the introduction of such terms as "Rapture," "Great Tribulation," "Judgment Seat of Christ," "Great White Throne Judgment," and even the most recent commonly-held concepts of the "Man of Sin" and the "Mark of the Beast," into the vocabulary of American Christianity. It was Darby's version of biblical prophecy that informed the commentaries in the wildly popular English versions of Scripture known as the Scofield Reference and Ryrie Study Bibles, and so great has Darby's influence been on American fundamentalism and evangelicalism in general that to be regarded as an accomplished expositor of Scripture in many rural areas of the United States actually means to have mastered Darby's systems of thought and of prophecy, mixed in with whatever varied denominational traditions preceded them in different areas and served up all together to local listeners as old-time religion.

Ironically, though Moody and Barnes more or less broke with Darby before his death in 1881 (as early as 1876 Barnes came to disagree with the older minister on whether or not "unfaithful saints" would remain on earth after the "Rapture" to pass through the "Great Tribulation,"[368] whatever either man meant by this, and he seems to have regarded his change of heart from Darby's strict sectarianism as being "delivered from the reigning power of sin" and the beginning of his "growth in grace"),[369] both Barnes and Moody retained Darby's system of biblical interpretation as well as his technical theological terminology. Of course, D. L. Moody did more to popularize and perpetuate Darby's system of biblical analysis nationwide than any other exponent in the United States. Barnes was much the lesser light in this regard, but his chief significance lay in the fact that he was one of the first American evangelists to add a faith-healing feature, based on the ritual of anointing with oil as found in the fifth chapter of the Epistle of

[368] Price, 151-152.
[369] Ibid., 313, again quoting Barnes's journal.

James,[370] to his Darby-style preaching. In essence he proclaimed a ministry of salvation through Jesus Christ of both the soul and the body,[371] and in the process he became not only a pioneer preaching exponent of dispensational fundamentalism but one of the precursors of American Pentecostalism as well.

Thus as might be expected, the world of George Owen Barnes was as different from that of Charles Chilton Moore as daylight and dark. From what we can glean out of the preacher's own journal entries, the earth—at least during the final years of Barnes's ministry, a stationary flat earth at the center of the universe, circled by the sun and other stars and planets—was a stage of angels, devils, and phantasms wherein a simple head cold was the direct result of demonic mischief,[372] one where the Fallen Angel Lucifer himself was responsible for a child's getting its hand stuck between the slats of a church pew and thus causing a congregation to be distracted by its wailing from listening to the glorious message of King Jesus.[373] On the other hand, it was also in its own way a comforting place wherein the Bible harbored no inconsistencies whatsoever; to Barnes, "the only clue to *apparent* [emphasis added] contradiction in Scripture" was "the Great Tribulation."[374] Too, no matter how devilish that the devil might act, he could always be driven away smarting and cursing by eight or ten faithful, Spirit-filled alternating prayers and hymns during an altar call.[375] No one who is unfamiliar with Pentecostalism, especially American Southeastern country Pentecostalism, can even begin to comprehend this mindset, and although other fundamentalist groups might snub their noses at Pentecostalism their worldview is actually based upon the same type of medieval-style Scriptural literalism; the only difference is that, in non-Pentecostal fundamentalist traditions, the devil seems to act a bit more indirectly, subtly, maturely, and even gentlemanly. But to return, when Barnes came back home to Kentucky early in 1877 on a mission of conscience to convert the mountains of his native state to both John

---

[370] James 5:14-15.
[371] Price, 387-451, in a lengthy defense of Barnes's faith-healing practices.
[372] Ibid., 352, notation from Barnes's journal.
[373] Ibid., 212.
[374] Ibid., 229.
[375] Ibid., 223; the example noted in this instance took place in Pikeville, Kentucky in 1880.

Nelson Darby dispensational fundamentalism and his own new-found Holiness power of faith healing, he had the spiritual encouragement of no less a personage than Dwight Moody himself and all the financial backing he could possibly require from John G. Owsley to impress this version of the world upon the area's religious community at large.

For almost six years, between 1877 and 1883, Barnes kept his traveling hill-country crusade going, journeying with his retinue back and forth between the Big Sandy, upper Licking, and Kentucky River valleys and gaining converts by the houseful as eastern Kentucky's most notorious mountain feuds raged all around him. One of his earliest series of meetings occurred in Fayette County, whose citizens he seems to have remembered rather bitterly as a "cultured opposition" who made "a stubborn attempt to ignore" him.[376] What actually appears to have happened is that our own hero, Charles Chilton Moore, attended a few of Barnes's services in his capacity as a reporter, and decided to put the evangelist's faith-healing claims to the test. He returned and brought with him an aged blind man, possibly a tenant at Quakeracre or a resident of Maddoxtown and perhaps one of the Moore family's former slaves, and publicly and somewhat loudly asked the preacher to anoint and pray over him that his sight might be restored. Sadly, despite whatever salutary effects on his hearers' psychosomatic illnesses that Barnes's brand of therapy had accomplished thus far, nothing he said or did could give the old man back his sight.[377] In defending this inability it is likely that the preacher and his supporters fell back on two Scripture texts, one from St. Mark which stated that Jesus couldn't do any mighty works in his hometown of Nazareth because of his old neighbors' lack of belief in him,[378] certainly appealing as a direct stab against the infidel Moore. The other was a verse from the Gospel of John, from which the inference might be—or at least occasionally has been—made that no person had ever been miraculously healed from blindness without direct contact with Jesus himself in the flesh.[379] To either, the skeptic ex-minister Moore could have responded with another Bible quotation, likewise from John's Gospel and purported to be straight

---

[376] Ibid., 157.
[377] Moore, *Behind the Bars,* 154.
[378] Mark 6:1-5.
[379] John 9:32.

from the lips of the Lord: "Verily, verily I say unto you, he that believeth on me, the works that I do shall he do also; and greater works than these shall he do; because I go unto my Father."[380] But in any case, the whole scene was rather a tragedy all around. Few, if any, Fayette Countians disposed to believe in Barnes's powers were willing to change their minds after witnessing Moore's rationalist demonstration, and Moore himself appears to have made some extra enemies by "showing up" the evangelist.[381] And of course, the poor old blind man remained blind and disappointed, but presumably still faithful.

Undaunted by the bad publicity Moore's actions generated and, surprisingly, harboring no ill will against Moore whatsoever, Barnes preached and labored on and eventually gained 441 Fayette County converts from this initial revival series. As he and his entourage swung south and east his success snowballed, and in both Boyle County, the location of his old alma mater, and Bath County, a Disciples of Christ stronghold ever since the days of Raccoon John Smith, he numbered proselytes in the thousands rather than the mere hundreds.[382] At least two liberal Disciple ministers joined him to immerse any of his converts who requested baptism after that fashion, in complement to the sprinklings that he and a couple of willing Methodist divines administered,[383] and even Raccoon John's old home of Mt. Sterling was hardly any less prey to the enchantment of the Barnes message than it had been fifty-odd years earlier to Smith's own.

By this time the Barnes revival crusade had begun to attract all classes of citizens from the lowest to the very highest, and among the "anointings and prayers" that the Mountain Evangelist performed for Mt. Sterling citizens were ceremonies for both Elizabeth and Richard Reid, "Lizzie Reid" after a private consultation for some unknown malady and "the Judge (Reid)[*sic*]" during a public worship service the same day.[384] Thus if Barnes was willing to maintain a priest's degree of confidentiality, he may have been the sole individual besides Reid's

---

380 John 14:12.

381 Moore, *Behind the Bars,* 154.

382 Price, 155-156.

383 In his journal, Barnes noted the last names of these ministers, evidently preferring to call them "Brother" rather than use their first names: Glover, Bays, Williams, and Robinson. See Price, 195-216.

384 Ibid., 348.

physician and his wife who ever learned of the Judge's physical handicap during his lifetime. Sad to say, though, this "healing" worked about as well for Reid's bilateral hernias as it did for Charles Moore's neighbor's eyes, but Reid was too naturally shy and reticent to complain—or possibly he just considered himself to be too weak in the Spirit and lacking of the necessary faith for the Gospel to become a source of physical strength to him as well as spiritual sustenance. If the Judge made this supposition, it certainly had its own tragic consequences a few years down the road.

It's difficult to assess exactly what permanent effect the late 1870s and early 1880s ministry of George Owen Barnes had on eastern Kentucky as a whole. For a surprisingly long while the preacher's little Lincoln County "Pink Cottage" was regarded as something of a central Appalachian Lourdes or Oberammergau, a place where pilgrims could, and did, flock to be healed though his own prayers and impositions or those of his followers.[385] At first glance, at least, it would appear that several of the hill-country localities where he enjoyed his wildest and most joyous successes, such as Bath, Menifee, Morgan, Magoffin, Johnson, Pike, Harlan, Letcher, and Perry Counties in addition to Boyle and Lincoln, also became starting points for the establishment in eastern Kentucky of the Holiness denominations known as the Anderson, Indiana and Cleveland, Tennessee Churches of God, both titled for the cities in which they were first founded, the Indiana group in 1881 and the Tennessee church in 1903, and so called to differentiate one from the other.[386]

Well had it been for Barnes too if he had simply stayed on in the area and accepted a position as traveling evangelist, or even a settled pastor, with one or the other of these Churches of God, but as it was he made rather a laughingstock of himself before his ministry was over. Still under John G. Owsley's patronage and Dwight Moody's blessing, he followed up his mighty six-year eastern Kentucky crusade with missionary trips to Scotland and Australia. While in this latter country, and later in San Francisco, he heard the preaching of a fellow faith-healer, a Scotsman named John Alexander Dowie who proclaimed

[385] Moore, *Behind the Bars,* 155.

[386] For more information on this Church of God, see Sparks, *The Roots of Appalachian Christianity,* 279-289.

himself as the returning Prophet Elijah and forerunner of Christ's Second Coming. So convinced was Barnes of the imminence of the Apocalypse—in 1883 his biographer stated that Barnes believed at that time the "Rapture" must occur within five years[387]—he just knew that Dowie *had* to be right. Perhaps the Spirit he followed told him so, and he felt it was worth his very soul to resist. In any case, the doctrinal differences between Dowie and other rising stars of the dispensational fundamentalist movement simply made Barnes's new conversion another sad rehash of the story of Barton Stone and the Shakers, and as the Preacher in the Book of Ecclesiastes bitterly observed, there was no new thing under the sun.[388]

Thus, though he had been housed and feted like royalty throughout both eastern and central Kentucky in the peak years of his preaching there, George Owen Barnes spent the autumn of his life in relative poverty as an elder in Dowie's Christian Catholic (later Christian Catholic *Apostolic*) Church. He seems to have labored principally in Florida and Washington D. C., preaching Dowie's own special version of the Gospel complete with a flat-earth cosmogony and Anglo-Israelism (the dogma that the people of Great Britain and North America are descended from the Ten Lost Tribes of Israel), while the so-called Prophet lived in despotic splendor in Zion, Illinois, the supposedly utopian community he had founded for his faithful. Among Barnes's last known activities was the publication of a series of lectures on Anglo-Israelism in October 1906, when he was seventy-nine years old,[389] and so we must infer that he had to have known of both the ludicrous "prayer duel" that John Alexander Dowie staged between himself and the eccentric Chicago Muslim cleric Mirza Ghulam Ahmad in 1905, and of Dowie's condemnation as a despot, embezzler, and drunkard and his ouster by his second-in-command, Wilbur Glenn Voliva, in the year Barnes's Anglo-Israelism lectures were published. (Because of this latter unfortunate turn of events, by the way, Mirza Ghulam Ahmad claimed that he won the prayer duel and that God had lowered the boom of judgment on Dowie.) It is certain, at least, that

387 Price, 382-383.
388 Ecclesiastes 1:9.
389 Barnes, "A Lost People and a Vanished Sceptre," originally published 1906; World Wide Web, http://www.truthinhistory.org .

Barnes didn't live to see Voliva's own disgrace over similar accusations in 1942, or the Christian Catholic Apostolic Church's subsequent slow metamorphosis after Voliva's death into a run-of-the-mill and relatively harmless evangelical Protestant body[390] somewhat on the order of the World Wide Church of God a few years after the decease of Herbert W. Armstrong. One wonders what Barnes must have thought, at eighty and beyond, of all the twists and turns through which his impressions of the Spirit had led him across the span of his life. But regardless, although he has been completely forgotten in virtually all other areas where he once labored, at least in eastern Kentucky the work of the Mountain Evangelist is still remembered by a few, and with more than a small touch of fondness.

For his own part, Charles Chilton Moore never quite forgave the Kentucky newspaper industry for letting Barnes enjoy such an easy ride through the state's newsprint during his most controversial activities. If his own recollections were accurate it was almost as if some Bluegrass antecedent of William Randolph Hearst and Henry Luce had told every reporter in the commonwealth to "puff Barnes" much as Hearst and Luce themselves, two generations later, gave Billy Graham their editorial blessing.[391] Moore later claimed that he alone, of all newspapermen in the Bluegrass State, was willing to grill Barnes with the tough questions that his faith-healing claims demanded, and that even if he did succeed in putting Barnes through a rigorous cross-examination he still couldn't get his findings and conclusions printed. And for all that, surprisingly, he was genuinely kindly disposed and even affectionate toward the Mountain Evangelist, for one principal reason: though as a skeptic ex-preacher he had developed a set of fine-tuned antennae to sense sham and corruption, he perceived that Barnes was essentially honest and upright, and for Charles Moore those qualities in and of themselves went an extremely long way. He wrote of Barnes that "his errors were great[, it] is certain, but I have always hoped that they were of the head rather than of the heart. While it is true that in his palmy days he lived in luxury, and was feted and praised as is true of all very

---

[390] Zion City, Illinois, City Records 1888-1974. Newberry Library, Chicago, Illinois.

[391] Young, 12.

popular preachers, I never heard an intimation of any kind of immorality against him."[392]

Even after Barnes attached himself to John Alexander Dowie and the political and religious leaders of eastern Kentucky had distanced themselves and their region from association with him, Moore could still write of the Mountain Evangelist that

> I personally knew George O. Barnes. He was one of the most magnetic characters I ever knew. He was more like Jesus Christ than any other man that America ever produced. For years in religion he was the central figure of Kentucky, attracting more interest and more love of the people than all the other preachers in Kentucky combined. I watched him closely and never knew him in an instance of immorality. With all his vagaries I loved the man and was, and still am, proud of the fact that he loved me, and yet Barnes believed, or professed to believe, that he could work miracles and that he was miraculously cared for by God, and today he is a follower of Dowie, content to be to that arch impostor what John the Baptist was to Jesus—proud to decrease that the fame and honor of Dowie, the Elijah of God, may increase.[393]

Finally, perhaps the most bizarre aspect of this most singular friendship was that the unbeliever Moore actually claimed to obtain a successful "cure" of sorts at Barnes's Lincoln County Pink Cottage. Knowing full well that no Kentucky newspaper would print an unexpurgated article about what he really thought of Barnes's healing abilities, Moore visited Stanford once anyway, about a year after he had first met up with the preacher in Lexington and for the express purpose of writing a story on the Cottage and all the alleged healings occurring there. He didn't have to converse with many Stanford citizens before he found out that questioning the feats of either Barnes or the Pink Cottage locally would produce a good deal of righteous anger and a most unrighteous fight. So he rode out on horseback alone to the Cottage, like the bear who went over the mountain, just to see what he could see.

As he recounted the experience later, the Barnes family was gone somewhere on the sawdust trail, but he was met by a woman at the door who immediately asked him of what disease he had come to be healed.

---

[392] Moore, *Behind the Bars,* 154-155.
[393] Ibid., *Dog Fennel,* 79.

Upon his reply that he was not sick, but rather a newspaperman who had come to do a story on the Cottage, she snorted contemptuously and retorted that she knew he was sick in some way because she had never met anyone who was not. Upon his insistence that, no, he was as sound as a dollar in body, she then began to grill him about his attitudes and habits, and rather than let the cat out of the bag about being an infidel Moore finally admitted to his addiction to cigars and chewing tobacco. She then took him to the Cottage's back porch where they found "about a dozen lazy and ignorant looking people, about equally of the two sexes."[394] The woman informed the group of Moore's plight and his supposed request to be prayed for, and so they set him in a chair in their midst, knelt down all around him, and prayed for five or ten minutes, reminding God that he had promised in the Bible to cure people and now they claimed that promise and expected him to be as good as his word to rid Charles Moore of his tobacco addiction. Moore, meanwhile, apparently unfazed either by the prayers or the pray-ers, jotted notes vigorously in shorthand.

Still unaffected, that evening he proceeded to ride on to Crab Orchard Springs in the same county, where a small resort and hotel had been built near a local mineral spring. The next morning after breakfast he observed another man on the hotel's porch filling a pipe with tobacco and, with a gesture completely in character for him, he approached the smoker, introduced himself, and bluntly chided the man for coming to the Springs for his health yet continuing to ruin his constitution through the use of tobacco. Abashed, the man knocked out his pipe; then, in another completely characteristic gesture, Moore became ashamed that he had upbraided a stranger for a vice of which he himself was guilty, and before the morning was done, he, the stranger, and two other hotel visitors had gone into a group pact to forswear tobacco. Moore kept his vow for the rest of his life, too. As the writer of I Timothy stated, without controversy great is the mystery of godliness.[395]

Of course, none of the Lexington newspapers for whom Moore usually wrote would touch his Barnes story with a ten-foot pole, but he sold it to the Louisville *Courier-Journal* as a piece of humor—

---

[394] Ibid., *Behind the Bars,* 156.
[395] I Timothy 3:16.

the comic firsthand account of the only man who was ever cured of using tobacco at George Owen Barnes's Pink Cottage.[396] But the aftermath of Barnes's evangelistic journeys through the eastern half of Kentucky was not without its tragedies as well, and one of these comprised a series of events that culminated in a horror Moore would not have had occur for all the fame or riches in the world: the suicide of his good friend, the unhappy, crippled, but faithful Christian gentleman Richard Reid. In the spring of 1884, about a year after Barnes left Kentucky for a return to the foreign mission field, Reid stood as a candidate once again for a seat on the state's Appellate Court. He had retained his legal practice in Mt. Sterling, though, and in the capacity of a private attorney he had successfully argued a case for a fellow lawyer and brother in the Mt. Sterling Christian Church, John Jay Cornelison, who was also a son-in-law of Thomas Munnell, one of the most influential Bluegrass Disciple ministers of the day.

When Cornelison's opponent appealed the lower court's decision, the case had come up before the Superior Court; as Justice, Reid of course now had to recuse himself, and for some reason or other Cornelison's adversary won the appeal. Cornelison then got it into his head that the reversal had occurred because Reid had somehow turned traitor to him, decided he needed to avenge his honor after the horrible old Southern fashion, and so on the morning of April 16, 1884 he invited Reid into his office on a pretext and then proceeded to assault him with a heavy cane and a cowhide whip. He ran the disabled Reid out into the street, counting twenty-five blows with his cane and seventy-five to a hundred strokes of the whip upon the Judge's nonresistant form before a passerby pulled him away from the attack.

This public beating became a matter of statewide, and even national, news. By far most Kentucky newspaper editors were on Reid's side, although Thomas Munnell seems to have done his best to defend his son-in-law's conduct among the Kentucky Disciples and within the Disciple periodicals, even to the point of maligning Reid.[397] Nearly all the secular papers, though, called on Reid to respond to Cornelison eye for eye and tooth for tooth after the assailant's own method, that is, with the corrupt principles of the old Southern Code of Honor. Reid

---

[396] Moore, *Behind the Bars,* 153-158.
[397] Donaldson, 88-95.

refused to do this, ostensibly on account of his Christian pacifism, but of course his health—that terrible, secret condition for which he had made the leap of faith and been anointed by George Owen Barnes, but which had never gone away in spite of all his, and Barnes's, prayers—still precluded any kind of physical challenge to Cornelison anyway.

As Reid tried to continue his campaign for Appellate Court Justice and he was heckled for not exacting his revenge, editors and commentators both secular and religious batted around their opinions on his guilt or innocence of Cornelison's accusations as well as his obligation to avenge his honor (including more than one vigorous defense of both Reid's character and his pacifism written by an indignant Charles C. Moore).[398] Meanwhile, the Judge's home church at Mt. Sterling tried to make up its mind what to do and whether to listen to his own testimony or that of the influential Thomas Munnell, and Reid's spirits sank to an all-time low. He was caught between forces neither he nor anyone else could comprehend from the simple perspective of his faith, the orthodox, biblical Christianity that he and his entire community including both his attacker and the assailant's father-in-law claimed to profess; he could read "Vengeance is mine; I will repay, saith the Lord!"[399] in the Bible, yet continually heard "Vengeance must be yours; to be a man, *you* must repay, saith this Christian nation!" from the majority of his Barnes-saved eastern Kentucky voters. And so finally, on top of all else knowing that he would be a slave to his disability for the remainder of his life and lacking, in Evangelist Barnes's terms, the necessary mustard seed's worth of faith for his body to be saved as well as his soul, Reid lost all hope, scrawled a pencil note to his beloved Elizabeth ("Mad! Mad! Forgive me, dear wife, and love to the boy"),[400] lay down on a cot, and put a bullet through his cerebellum on May 15, 1884, twenty-nine days after the attack.[401]

Charles Chilton Moore could facetiously make a claim for a Barnes cure. Yet the joke must have turned bitter in his mouth to know that his beloved friend Richard Reid, whose case of all people's cried out for Divine intervention of some sort, if not actual physical healing, never

---

[398] Moore, *Behind the Bars*, 77.
[399] Romans 12:19.
[400] Klotter, *Kentucky Justice,* 89.
[401] See Ibid., also Donaldson, 88-95.

found his balm in Gilead. Without controversy, great was the mystery of godliness. And again, there was no new thing under the sun.

Almost immediately after Richard Reid's suicide his grieving widow, perhaps partially in a gesture of repentance since she, too, had questioned why he had never attempted to avenge his (and her) honor, began writing the story of his life and a vindication of his pacifist conduct. Her *Judge Richard Reid: A Biography* was published in early 1886, and included within its pages was a testimonial written by Charles Chilton Moore at her personal request, dated November 27, 1884 and recounting Moore's memories of rooming with Reid in Versailles as well as a tender expression of respect and affection for the memory of his fallen friend.[402]

Likewise in this very wake of Reid's disgrace and death a brand-new weekly newspaper appeared for sale on the streets of Lexington. It was entitled the *Blue Grass Blade*, and its offices, the "Blade Publishing Company," were at 155 West Short Street in the city. Though Charles Chilton Moore was also its editor, publisher, and principal contributor, its news articles contained little or nothing of the respect and tenderness with which he had memorialized Richard Reid. By the time of the Reid-Cornelison scandal Moore seems to have figured that times were ripe in the Bluegrass State for the establishment of his own freethought periodical as a complement to the *Truth Seeker* and to Robert Green Ingersoll's spoken and printed lectures: one that would not only question the accuracy and inerrancy of the Bible and the claims of Christianity, but which could, and would, take the kind of shallow, conventional, majority-rule, sham piety that had ultimately killed Richard Reid, and throw it right back into Kentucky's face.

---

[402] Reid, 41-44, quoting Moore's November 27, 1884 letter; see also Moore, *Behind the Bars,* 77.

One of C.C. Moore's favorite portraits of himself—

a sketch done by Missouri infidel cartoonist Watson Heston portraying Moore at work with his Bluegrass Blade attacking a brush patch of Pulpit Lies, Priestcraft, Popery, and Redeemer Rubbish while threatened by the poisonous snakes of Hypocrisy, Superstition, and Persecution. —*Courtesy of Young Library, University of Kentucky, Lexington, Kentucky.*

Chapter 6

The *Blade* and the Book

Up to an intermediate level of fear, the more fear the message arouses, the more persuasive it will be.... Death is the only thing that makes religion.

—Rev. Samuel Porter Jones, in a statement with which Charles Chilton Moore agreed completely—for an entirely different reason than Jones intended

In truth, the Reid affair was only one of several reasons Charles Chilton Moore felt compelled to start his own newspaper. Though Richard Reid's suicide very well may have been the proverbial straw that broke the camel's back for him as far as being a hired reporter was concerned, Moore's resentment against the senior editors for whom he worked alternately at the *Transcript* and the *Observer* had been growing for some time even before the Mt. Sterling scandal exploded throughout Kentucky's mass media and so many complacent newspapermen saw fit to call the Judge's manhood into question. By the summer of 1884 Moore had been a journalist for at least eight years, off and on, and there is no doubt that in the process he had learned a good many unholy things about Lexington as a city, Kentucky as a state, and Christianity as an organized religion that had nothing whatsoever to do with agnosticism or atheism.[403] Still, first impressions go a long way in

[403] Though the work does not mention Moore by name, an excellent study of Lexington corruption during this period can be found in James Duane

the formation of anyone's personality, and it's a likely bet that at least some vestigial ideal of periodical editors as prophets and agents of positive change had remained within his psyche ever since his childhood. Thus, when he weighed the editors for whom he now worked, in the balance with the editors he had known as a boy and a young man—the brave, defiant Cassius Marcellus Clay, whose abolitionist convictions had nearly gotten him killed only a short distance from the youthful Charles's own back yard, and Alexander Campbell and even his own grandfather Stone, who steadfastly and combatively held forth in their journals about the Bible and Christianity against all doubters and debaters and whose memory Moore still respected and honored, even after he had lost faith in the religion they upheld—he found the Lexington editors altogether too craftily political, too quick to respond to both bribes and threats from the rich and the powerful, and thus, in his estimation, worse than spineless. From their high-backed desks they could hurl accusations of cowardice at an upright Christian like Richard Reid for not only proclaiming "Turn the other cheek!" but for living his testimony, yet they themselves were like cats picking through cactus patches of special interest, both religious and secular.

We noted in the previous chapter that Moore based his journalistic career more or less on his reputation as both a humorist and a freethinking curmudgeon. His employment had seesawed back and forth between the *Observer* and the *Transcript* because the owners of both papers felt compelled to fire him from time to time due to public protests over one or another tart or outspoken observation he had made in his news articles and editorials. Moore could take this good-naturedly and even as a joke, because almost as soon as one paper fired him the owner of the other would hire him on again. Within this milieu, though, he absolutely couldn't abide having his news or editorial copy bowdlerized by a superior. He much preferred saying exactly what he thought, being fired for it, and then being rehired by the other paper, in the comic cycle that the two competitors maintained.

As time went on, however, he became more and more outraged to discover that, rather than fire him, his editors often either emasculated his prose or simply refused to run the news reports he brought them.

Bolin's *Bossism and Reform in a Southern City: Lexington, Kentucky, 1880-1940* (University Press of Kentucky, 2000).

True, they were willing to print his vigorous defenses of Richard Reid's Christian pacifism right alongside their own concurring, or opposing, pontifications; but he felt that when he brought either paper a report of, say, a barroom brawl somewhere in Lexington, the editors were likely to cover up the news either as a courtesy to the owner of the saloon where the trouble occurred, or to the numerous prominent Kentucky distillers and liquor dealers that sold their products to the even more numerous bars. In a sort of obverse similarity, virtually all of the city's editors guaranteed the most vocal and popular Lexington preachers "puffs" in the papers, regardless of whether, in Moore's estimation, their sermons were actually well-crafted or the complete opposite. And added to the mix of the thin veneer of respectability covering the faults and foibles of Fayette County and Kentucky society, he felt, was the habit of the wealthy distillers to make hefty contributions to the state's colleges and the Bluegrass region's churches in order to try to mollify their respective presidents, pastors, and other leaders, and thereby to keep them from pulling pranks like starting Prohibition crusades or Prohibition periodicals or otherwise giving too much aid and comfort to the growing Prohibition Movement. In short, Moore believed his editors could be, and were often, bought off just like church pastors and revivalists who accepted donations from questionable sources such as distillers. He trusted his own conscience; he knew that he couldn't be bribed, no matter what the size of the offer or the influence of its source. And so as he rode home from Lexington one Friday evening in the summer of 1884, ruminating over his too-heavily-edited articles, the perfidy of his superiors, and his lost friend Reid whom the gentle Christian churches as institutions had now condemned to eternal fire and agony in death after most of their members as individuals had branded him as a coward and a milksop in life, meditation transformed itself into action and *The Blue Grass Blade* was born.[404] It joined Kan-

[404] Moore, *Behind the Bars,* 167-168. We should take note here, however, of something of an inconsistency in Moore's writings about the history of the *Blue Grass Blade.* Most of the time he gave its founding year as 1884 and all of the later editions of the paper, up to its final issue in 1910, list that date for the paper's establishment; however, in at least two instances Moore gave 1886 as the *Blade's* starting date, once for an 1899 article printed in the Columbus, Ohio *Press-Post* and quoted in *Behind the Bars,* 5, and again in the *Blade,* XIV, 42, January 6, 1906. At least in this latter

sas' *Free-Thought Ideal, Free-Thought Vindicator,* and *Lucifer, the Light-Bearer;* Texas' *Iconoclast;* and of course the *Truth Seeker,* which by this date had relocated from Illinois to New York City, as a regional mouthpiece for America's small but growing freethought movement. Even so, and despite the subsequent, highly-publicized controversies in which Moore found himself embroiled with the *Blue Grass Blade,* the *Truth Seeker* remained the only nineteenth-century infidel periodical ever to achieve true nationwide circulation and notoriety.[405]

Though it immediately became the most controversial (and most thoroughly read) paper in central Kentucky, the *Blade* in its standard-issue form was pretty much a one-man, low-technology operation and surprisingly brief. Initially, subscriptions cost only a dollar per year, which incidentally had been the exact same cost of a twelve-month's worth of issues of Alexander Campbell's old *Christian Baptist* periodical some sixty years before. Moore confined himself mostly to writing, subcontracting virtually all the journal's press and design work out to local printer J. M. Byrnes[406], and like the Italian newspaper John Prine described in his introduction to the memorable song "Dear Abby," a *Blade* was usually only four 3' by 2' broadside sheets long and its columns were crammed chock-full of reports that just seemed to leap right out at its readers. Margins were adorned with the generous quantity of advertisements Moore always managed to sell to Lexington and Fayette County merchants, since the evangelical-fundamentalist idea of taking individuals and companies to task for their sponsorships wouldn't be born for almost another century, and somehow he made room as well for the spate of birth, wedding, and death notices that were commensurate with the paper's circulation. Moore gave the utmost courtesy and consideration to these advertisements and personal notices as well as to the businesses and families that purchased them, but he was a genuine and uncontrollable live wire when it came to the reporting of local affairs. As many conservative Stone-Campbell Christian preachers made it a habit to imitate the newspaper writing of a

---

instance, though, we might attribute the inconsistency of dates to the fact that Moore was in extremely poor physical health at that time and his mind may have not been at it sharpest.

[405] Jacoby, 155.

[406] Moore, *Behind the Bars,* 169.

young, brash Alexander Campbell and mock all other religious beliefs and traditions besides their own, so now did this ex-"Campbellite" divine use his paper to make fun of and disparage all religions and biblical traditions, period.

Unfortunately, no copy of the *Blade* from 1884 has survived, but in an 1890 issue and again in an 1899 memoir Moore recapitulated a partial record of the paper's initial content.[407] Originally he never intended his new journal to espouse any one particular cause such as Temperance or its outgrowth, Prohibition, and from the very first he flouted Southern newspaper conventions, abandoning the editor's customary first-person plural address to write all his essays and other editorial observations in first-person singular form.[408] Oddly enough, he seems not to have dealt with the Reid-Cornelison scandal in the *Blade's* initial pages, perhaps figuring that he had said all he could or should have about that subject in previous editorials and essays for his former employers. By now, however, Lexington was deeply involved in the hosting and entertainment of a brand-new religious interest: a quasi-George Barnes-style traveling evangelist from Georgia named Samuel Porter Jones, then only beginning to build his status in the South as a revivalist preacher. Jones actually appears not to have been a bad sort, at least as revivalists go, and although his biographer presents convincing evidence that he and virtually his entire family suffered from bipolar disorder[409] he didn't keep his head stuck in the clouds theologically quite so far as George Barnes did. The manner in which Moore reported and editorialized on his Lexington crusade, though, was a bolt of lightning right out of a clear blue sky to the unsuspecting city.

The incident was not without its own irony, since Sam Jones, as he was popularly called, was in his own way every bit as much a maverick as Charles Moore was. A hard drinker in his youth, he had been converted to Christianity at his father's death in 1872 in the genuine old-time shouting Southern Methodist born-again way and had become as strong a Temperance advocate as he had once been a thorough alcoholic. Though Jones claimed to be a through-and-through Scriptural

---

[407] Moore, *The Blue Grass Blade,* I, 26, September 20, 1890; *Behind the Bars,* 168.

[408] Ibid., *Behind the Bars,* 168.

[409] Minnix, 67-68, 77, 217-223.

literalist and inerrantist, he bluntly and casually dismissed as speculative rubbish the John Nelson Darby-style dispensationalism that had so captivated Dwight Lyman Moody and George Owen Barnes in the late 1870s, and while he retained the old-time Wesleyan Methodist belief in sanctification as a "second" work of grace[410] he never claimed to be any sort of physical faith healer. In fact, Jones's message was as simple as Darby, Moody, and Barnes could make theirs convoluted and terrifying: to him repentance and conversion were nothing more than a decision to "Quit your meanness," and a Christian man was merely one "who is known as a religious man in the community; it is a man who is at peace with God and all mankind; a man who, by the light of his conscience and the innocence of his soul, knows that he has done right, and that the declaration of his heart and mouth has been right."[411] In evangelical Christian preaching this was about as close one could get to the sentiments of the nonbeliever Moore's own favorite Epistle of James, and Jones turned his "quit your meanness" message upon church members as cheerfully and vigorously as he related it to sinners. He actually carried the principle to an even further extreme, one which would likely make a good many of the ministers and churches hosting his preaching crusades wince and might possibly bring a chuckle to the lips of even the most hardened infidel. Jones had little or no faith in deathbed repentance, especially that of old and long-established, sanctimonious, Pharisaical church members, and once he had actually advised an ailing but well-to-do and parsimonious penitent that "I don't see any good reason for asking the Lord to heal you. I can ask him to forgive and save you, and take you to heaven, but there is no reason I should ask him to preserve your life, as you are absolutely

Sam Jones

410 Ibid., 134-162.
411 Ibid., 81.

worthless to the cause."[412] With such down-home observations and exhortations Sam Jones quickly achieved the reputation, albeit more often than not egged on by wishful thinkers, of being able to empty the saloons and fill up the churches of any town or city he visited.

All things considered, then, one might expect the brand-new infidel editor Moore to have given Jones's views on Scriptural literalism and inerrancy a good-natured teasing in the pages of the *Blade,* but yet to have expressed at least a degree of admiration and appreciation for the preacher's country-style forthrightness, his seemingly rock-solid pro-Temperance stance, his simple "quit your meanness" message that Moore's own later editorials so often echoed (minus, of course, the Christian doctrinal principle), and his pithy advice to eleventh-hour penitents. After all, Moore had always allowed for the basic personal honesty of George Barnes. Not a bit of quarter would he allow for Sam Jones, though. We must repeat here that we have no direct contemporary record of this affair, only Moore's 1890 synopsis of his own words from six years earlier, but even in this abridged form the torrent of invective he let loose upon the Georgia visitor and his supporters fairly seethed with his fury and contempt. Sam Jones was nothing more than a snare and a deadbeat and a body snatcher, Moore raged, a hypocrite and pious fraud who had no more actual religion than a hearse horse. Jones was merely a mercenary, out for "the boodle," as the saying went in those days, while Moore, a complete and honest nonbeliever, claimed more real "Simon-pure" religion in his heart and his brain than an entire regiment of "such cattle." In fact, Moore continued with hardly a pause to catch his breath, he himself had, both orally and in writing, more openly professed his fealty to Jesus of Nazareth than had any man in the city of Lexington who did not get paid for doing so.[413]

What makes the issue problematic is that, though Moore preserved a fair record of all the names he had called Sam Jones in 1884, he never made it quite clear what had prompted him to speak of the traveling preacher after such an openly hostile fashion in the first place. He concluded his 1890 diatribe against Jones with the observation that, by that time, he could "blast [Sam Jones] and old [Thomas DeWitt] Talmage too, and make friends by it, though both of them are outspoken

---

[412] Ibid., 45.

[413] Moore, *Blue Grass Blade,* I, 26, September 20, 1890.

Prohibitionists."[414] We have seen already, by Moore's treatment of George Owen Barnes, that he didn't regard an individual's simply being a Christian, even a very vocal one, as any special cause for scorn or outrage; personal honesty was his main concern.

Between the above Prohibitionist comment, Jones's personal proclivities, and Moore's known pet peeves, we can most likely narrow the causes of Charles Moore's degree of antipathy toward Sam Jones down to two. For one, Jones loathed Robert Green Ingersoll with an obsessive, pathological hatred only exacerbated by the Great Agnostic's genial dismissal of him as a theological and ministerial lightweight, and he would often "throw off on" Ingersoll from the pulpit while on his evangelistic crusades.[415] Since Moore was such an unabashed fan of Ingersoll at this point he may have taken one of Jones's tirades against the Silver-tongued Infidel as personally as his erstwhile religious cohorts, the Disciples of Christ, had received criticisms from Baptists against Alexander Campbell fifty-odd years before. The other cause very well may have been, quite simply, Jones's sponsors for his trip to Lexington. All traveling evangelists had to have underwriters; the nature of their profession precluded their charging admission to their sermons, though they could and did take up free will offerings in their meetings, and even the idealistic George Barnes had had his industrialist friend John G. Owsley to foot the bills for all his religious enterprises. But Jones's biographer, Kathleen Minnix, herself admits that the outspoken Prohibitionist preacher was entirely capable of "crass compromise" on occasion,[416] and she quotes a popular evangelists' maxim from the late nineteenth century thusly: "The only tainted money I know is, 'tain't enough."[417] (Perhaps Juvenal put it better in ancient times: "Money has no smell.") But if it had happened that the owners of a few of the local Bluegrass distilleries had gotten together to help pay for Sam Jones's expenses either in Lexington in 1884, his previous year's excursion to and crusade in Louisville, or both, and Jones and his entourage had accepted their money, Moore would have felt that he had all the validation he needed to brand the preacher as the basest of

---

[414] Ibid.
[415] Minnix, 120-121.
[416] Ibid., x.
[417] Ibid., 117.

hypocrites. The fact that Jones, who usually made it a point to answer his critics back insult for insult as if his very honor and manhood depended on it, is not known ever to have had anything at all to say to or about Charles Moore, may lend credence to this latter supposition—though as we shall see, the evangelist could have had another excellent strategic reason to bridle his tongue in this case. But we can never really know for sure; though Moore almost certainly would have felt compelled to outline his reasons for blasting Jones in 1884, in his 1890 recounting he let his hot rhetoric completely drown out his justifications.

In any case, to the upright citizens of Lexington only one thing could have been worse than an infidel newspaperman hurling false accusations at a distinguished ministerial guest—that being, an infidel newspaperman hurling *true* accusations at a distinguished ministerial guest (it would have been different if Moore was still an active preacher, since in Kentucky prominent preachers were always hurling accusations both true and false at one another and everybody more or less had had to get used to it during the state's ninety-two years of existence). But for comparative purposes, we might take just a moment and evaluate the *Blade's* vitriolic reporting of the Lexington Sam Jones crusade alongside a more timely and greatly larger-scale, but nonetheless similar, news "scoop" that an investigative reporter pulled off a century or so later—Christopher Hitchens' 1995 exposé of some of the more curious fundraising and medical policies and practices of Mother Teresa and her Missionaries of Charity in Calcutta, outlined and discussed in a work entitled, of all things, *The Missionary Position.*

When all was said and done it didn't really matter how much detailed documentation Hitchens was able to supply for his accounts of Mother Teresa's relationships with, endorsements of, and indulgent attitudes toward the Marxist Albanian dictator Enver Hoxha, "Baby Doc" and Michele Duvalier of Haiti, John-Roger, Princess Diana, Robert Maxwell, and Charles Keating while she simultaneously preached extreme Catholic conservatism and the glorious sweetness and holiness of suffering to her Calcutta poor, or her habit of traveling abroad to obtain the best medical care for her own personal illnesses while her patients in Calcutta had to make do with procedures more septic than antiseptic and equipment substandard even by Indian state hospital regulations. The bottom line was that the investigator had attacked a beloved world icon and that was all the reason most people needed to turn on him in fury whether his claims merited further objective consideration or not. Thus with Moore and Jones: though of course Sam Jones would never attain the worldwide status of Mother Teresa, he nonetheless represented a figure even then recognized as iconic in the American South, the down-home self-taught country preacher who, seemingly, could cut through the theological haze of seminary sermonizing and present the simple Gospel of Jesus in all its power and purity to the people. The image was born with the pre-Revolutionary ministry of Shubal Stearns and Daniel Marshall in North Carolina, it had been perpetuated throughout Kentucky's and the South's histories by such luminaries as Barton Stone, Jeremiah Vardeman, Lorenzo Dow, Raccoon John Smith, and even George Owen Barnes, and it is yet maintained, perhaps even on a global scale, by Billy and Franklin Graham. And so the end result was that neither Mother Teresa nor Sam Jones ever had to answer the accusations that their respective Devil's Advocates had raked up. All they had to do was remain silent, or worse, openly "forgive" their accusers (which Mother Teresa did for Hitchens even before *The Missionary Position* was published), to make both Christopher Hitchens and Charles Moore appear all that much more egregiously sinful and immoral in the eyes of most of the public. In and of itself this would have been cause enough for Jones to allow Moore to earn the dubious distinction of being the first (and perhaps last) of his critics that he let off the hook without a single waspish retort, and of course neither Moore's saucy, provocative writing style nor Hitchens' double-entendre book title gave their respective cases much validation in the public's mind either.

Nonetheless, the first three *Blue Grass Blades* made for an interesting three weeks both for Sam Jones's and Charles Moore's respective ministries of the word and for the Bluegrass Region as a whole, and it went a long way in establishing the permanent degree of antipathy in Kentucky under which Moore labored for the rest of his professional career, if not his entire life. Moore compared the public's reaction to his rhetoric with the swarming of enraged bumblebees in a hayfield.[418] After the first *Blade* hit the Lexington streets, such a crowd of people would gather around J. M. Byrnes' print shop on its scheduled publica-

---

[418] *Blade,* I, 26, September 20, 1890.

tion days (Saturdays mostly, it would appear, although Moore was not unknown later to issue his paper under a Sunday publication date just for the sake of chafing Christian Sabbath traditionalists) that Byrnes was compelled to lock the street door from the outside and then stand in front of his windows to guard them from breakage. We have noted already that the journal's first subscription price was a mere dollar a year, yet Moore could make a great deal more money by hiring newsboys and selling the paper on the street corners. When weekly print runs got low the boys quickly and deftly started scalping, selling individual four-page issues for a quarter, a half-dollar, or even as high as a dollar apiece depending on the suspected juiciness of the contents. A "prominent Christian circuit judge" called a public meeting at the Fayette County Courthouse to formulate a strategy for combating Moore and the *Blade*, and as Moore recalled it the gathering's two leading speakers against the new paper were Lexington's most influential preacher and its richest saloon keeper, standing united for once in mutual opposition to Moore-style infidelity. One wonders if these two citizens might have been among the Sam Jones crusade's primary sources of financial support in the town, and were more outraged than most for that reason. Still, though Moore never specifically linked any acts of direct violence against him to the Jones affair, it would appear that so many other Lexington gentlemen got the idea that someone needed to avenge the honor of the Lord Jesus Christ and Sam Jones both that even Moore came to realize that he ran a risk of being injured or killed. He recalled that Lucy Moore often had to keep the lamps at Quakeracre muffled at night for fear that her husband, or even one of her sons, would be shot through one of the windows.[419]

Yet whenever the first actual attacks on Moore's person, as opposed to the hot Southern and Christian rhetoric, finally started coming, they would seem to have been on the whole more comic and ironic than tragic. Moore never recounted the name of his first physical assailant in the aftermath of his publishing the *Blade,* merely identifying him as an upright Lexington citizen. We do know, however, that although he was apparently not very much taller than the biblical Zacchaeus he was a veritable Samson when it came to righteous indignation. He rushed Moore on the street, but neither the mayhem on his mind, the honor of

---

[419] Moore, *Behind the Bars,* 169-170.

his intentions, nor the uprightness of his cause prevented the infidel editor from, as Moore put it, catching him and holding him.[420] We can fairly imagine Moore warding him off literally at arm's length, a well-placed and farm-callused palm to his forehead as he twisted his body and flailed with his fists in a futile effort to reach Moore's midsection, and he probably gave up the fight less from physical weariness than because of the public laughter that his behavior must have prompted.

The second attack was more serious, but it too had its moment of dark humor. This assailant, a man much younger than Moore, crept to his side on the street and without warning delivered a blow to his face, breaking Moore's spectacles, cutting his forehead, and endangering his eyes with broken glass. Perhaps the juvenile dandy thought that, since Moore had endorsed Richard Reid's Christian pacifism so thoroughly, he could likewise be counted on not to resist violence—but Charles Moore didn't claim to be the Christian that Reid was, and the youthful knight-errant got an extremely rude awakening. He pulled a pistol on the editor, but for some reason proved himself honorable enough to holster it when he saw Moore didn't have one of his own. In spite of the sight of the firearm, however, to say nothing of the blood running down his face and into his eyes, Moore turned on his attacker with the full strength of his fists. All his post-Civil War experience with the axe, saw, and hoe now did him yeoman's service—even the editor of a rival paper once observed that Moore had cut so many ironweeds and built up so many strong water gaps at Quakeracre that he had muscles like prizefighter John L. Sullivan,[421] and if the infidel cartoonist Watson Heston's sketch of Moore at work in a brush field (see page 186) was made to scale, this estimate of his physical strength would appear to have been very near the truth—and before long he had the young gallant running for his own safety. Both Moore and his assailant were arrested and remanded to the city jail for disturbing the peace. The irate editor stubbornly refused either to give bail or have any of his friends go his bond, but in the end he was acquitted of starting the fight and his youthful assailant was found guilty and fined by the police judge.[422]

---

420 Ibid., 169.

421 *Blade,* II, 22, November 28, 1891, quoting an earlier article published in the *Lexington Transcript.*

422 Moore, *Behind the Bars,* 169.

Charles Moore was not yet a nationally known infidel. Ironically enough, it would take at least eight more years for him to earn that degree of notoriety, from his denunciation of a large and influential Bluegrass Disciples church that responded by prosecuting him for malicious libel and a stroke of luck that alerted a canny reporter from the *New York World* to a titillating little case of Kentucky cloak-and-dagger ecclesiastical and journalistic espionage.[423] But in the summer of 1884, three weeks of stress and strain simply wore Moore, his family, and his printer all down nearly completely. And so it was with a rueful heart, yet to the unabashed relief of Lucy Moore, that the new infidel editor ended the *Blade's* initial run after its third issue and remitted the balance of his subscribers' money *pro rata.*

Though he hated the fact that his paper had come to such an ignominious end, Moore remained defiant. His credit was still good, he averred, and he gave his outraged Fayette County neighbors the Parthian shot of reminding them that in 1868 they had similarly castigated and mistreated his old Dog Fennel chum W.C.P. Breckinridge for daring to support blacks' rights to testify as witnesses in Kentucky courts as equals to whites. Despite the loss of the Fayette County Commonwealth's Attorney's position that his progressive advocacy had cost him, at the very time of the *Blade's* first closure Breckinridge's reputation had rebounded to the point that he was running for a seat in Congress, and that fall he was elected to the office.[424] Moore felt that history would similarly vindicate both him and the *Blade,* and in one small measure at least he was correct. Sam Jones's carnival-style showmanship and his manic-depressive tendencies (which ran a great deal more to the manic than they ever did to the depressive) ultimately made him a worse enemy to himself than either Robert Green Ingersoll or a little four-page Southern infidel newspaper and its editor could ever hope to be, and so sure enough, by 1890—truth be told, 1886, even—Lexington believers had gotten a few of the stars out of their eyes and were ready both to laugh with Moore at Jones's crudities and idiosyncrasies and to criticize his mannerisms and practices.[425]

---

[423] Ibid., 170-171.

[424] *Blade,* I, 26, September 20, 1890; see also Klotter, *The Breckinridges,* 148-152.

[425] *Blade,* I, 26, September 20, 1890; Moore, *Behind the Bars,* 168.

Yet for all that, the legacy of Sam Jones still lives on in a mighty way in the South, and after a most unusual manner. Not quite a year after the Lexington escapade, Jones preached a hugely successful revival in Nashville, and one of his converts, a profane old riverboat captain named Thomas Green Ryman, was so grateful to the bombastic little earthly instrument of his salvation that he decided to build Jones his very own church right in the city's downtown area.[426] Between crusades hither and yon, Sam Jones preached more or less regularly at the Union Gospel Tabernacle, as its builder fondly named it, until his sudden, unexpected death a day short of his fifty-ninth birthday in 1906. Ryman had gone to his own reward a couple of years earlier, and so the building passed from owner to owner and purpose to purpose until the 1930s, when it began to be used regularly to host a live, radio-broadcast musical program known first as the Station WSM Barn Dance and later as the Grand Ole Opry; and thus, the Ryman Auditorium became popularly, and accurately, known as the Mother Church of Country Music. We might wonder if Sam Jones's feisty, bellicose little spirit somehow yet lives on in the place, with the dichotomy of all the cheating and drinking songs and Southern hymns and spirituals sung back-to-back in the old building throughout the long years as a sardonic continuity of the two choices he had once given so many listeners squirming uncomfortably in those very pews: either quit your meanness or get a stiff upper lip and face hell like men.

Unquestionably one of the harshest, most outspoken and consistent critics Charles Chilton Moore ever gained after he began publishing the *Blue Grass Blade* was a Cincinnati, Ohio physician named John Byers Wilson. For the most part, Wilson cut Moore hardly any more slack than the editor had ever given Sam Jones. Though he acknowledged that at times Moore could be the most tolerant, liberal, and consistent of men, Wilson charged that Moore was as often, or even more so, the epitome of the exact opposite of each of those qualities. Similarly, though Wilson knew Moore actually to be very sensitive and tenderhearted underneath his gruff exterior—it was he to whom Moore had confided the unrelenting sharpness and intensity of his grief over his daughter Eliza's death, and which we noted in the previous chap-

[426] Minnix, 1-15.

ter—the physician also considered the editor to be extremely self-opinionated, leading him frequently to be unkind, dictatorial, and unsparing of others' feelings. Broad, comprehensive, and farsighted on some of the great questions and principles of life, Moore was narrow and lacking vision on others just as important. Topping the whole portrait off were Wilson's observation that he intensely disliked Moore's slangy style of writing, and his accusation that Moore had never really outgrown his gentry-class upbringing: he was improvident and impractical, often not even thinking of the consequences of his actions, under that tough infidel carapace still every inch the spoiled rich planter's son both socially and emotionally. The main trouble with Moore, though, Wilson concluded, was that he had been a preacher once and had never quite gotten out of the preacher's rut.[427]

To these blistering barbs Moore is known only to have replied with a pout: "[Wilson] says things that are unnecessarily hard on me, and almost unjust to me."[428] Had Wilson himself ever been an evangelical preacher or writer, the editor might have had a great deal more vitriol to hurl back at him, but he took the physician's caustic analyses to heart perhaps for the same reason that we should. J.B. Wilson was, like Moore, a committed freethinker. In addition, he was a regular subscriber to the *Blade* and was Moore's true friend through thick and thin, and one of the few Bible verses that the two might perhaps have endorsed mutually was the proverb that "Faithful are the wounds of a friend; but the kisses of an enemy are deceitful."[429] But in any case, sadly, at hardly any point in Moore's writing career did Wilson's criticisms hit home more accurately than with his second attempt at publishing the *Blue Grass Blade.* We have already discussed the reasons why Moore was angry and frustrated with the shallow lip service that passed for true religion and honest piety in the world around him, but anger and rationality have never been known to mix well and, true to form, the editor's temper ultimately overreached itself once again.

---

[427] Most of Wilson's criticisms of Moore can be found in an essay in the *Blade,* VIII, 3, February 19, 1899 and repeated in *Behind the Bars,* 174-183; and *In Memoriam,* 7-11.

[428] Moore, *Behind the Bars,* 174.

[429] Proverbs 27:6.

Charles Moore had a newsman's good memory for events, but as he got older neither the recollection of proper names nor exact chronology was among his strong suits. To try to put the events of his life into some semblance of accurate linear order is to engage in a game of virtual hopscotch all the way around and across the three books he published during his lifetime, his newspaper articles and essays, and the meager secondary sources from his college and journalistic years. Thus in 1899, when he recalled running the *Blade* for three months in 1884, terminating its publication and remitting his subscribers' money, and then restarting the paper after another three-month period, his memory shows a touch of Doppler-style distortion. If one assumes that Moore began the *Blade* in 1884 using the customary sequential volume and issue numbers, only three issues appeared in that entire year, and "Volume I, Number 4"—the first *Blade* of which we have an entire copy—was not published until Saturday, February 6, 1886. We cannot be sure of the exact catalyst that prompted Moore to make his second publishing endeavor at this juncture, but it is tempting to think that memories of Richard Reid had once again exercised some influence on him, perhaps revived by certain contemporary local events. Elizabeth Jameson Reid's biography of her husband, including Moore's own contribution to the volume, had just been printed and among the first advertisements the brand-new version of the *Blade* carried was a call for agents to help market the book on consignment.[430]

At least the initial focus of the *Blue Grass Blade,* Version Two, was slightly more refined than Moore's furious, scattershooting tirades against the hypocrisy of Sam Jones a little less than two years before. In his 1890 recapitulation of his publishing career Moore stated that in 1886, although he had not yet attempted or even intended to give the *Blade* any particular editorial slant, he now intended its main purpose and thrust to be for "good morals… with Prohibition as a basal principle [ellipse added]."[431] Nonetheless, like his old mentor Alexander Campbell he seemed hardly able to restrain his pen where his personal values were involved, and of course, with him personal values almost always *were* involved.

---

[430] *Blade,* I, 4, February 6, 1886; I, 5, February 13, 1886.
[431] Ibid., I, 26, September 20, 1890.

With the first 1886 *Blade* we can perhaps form a clearer picture of what Moore had initially hoped to accomplish editorially. Besides the usual public announcements and paid advertisements, his principal reports included an article about the death of Congressman Joseph Rankin of Wisconsin, who had passed away in Washington D. C. on January 24, certainly not the most pressing or even relevant news for Kentuckians, though Rankin was fairly well known and admired for his time, but it allowed Moore the opportunity to write a detailed essay exploring his thoughts on death in general and to make his readers think about the subject without relying on platitudes about angels and harps and golden streets. In a way Moore's essay on death partially mirrored the observations found in Hamlet's soliloquy: death was the ultimate mystery, no one could be sure about what, if any, existence followed it, and so humans, even the most avowedly religious ones, would rather remain in this life with the evils with which they are familiar than to go into the cold, dark unknown—whether of soundless eternal sleep or unending good dreams or nightmares—with only a profession of faith to accompany them. Since it was a fate that humanity had to share, it might as well be accepted and faced stoically and with common sense. Fear of death had led not only to the human race's most outlandish religious superstitions, but the consequent construction of entire houses of cards built on those same superstitions and known as orthodoxies, over which religionists had warred and killed one another through the ages. If Congressman Rankin had lived a life useful to his fellow men and women it was all that could have been asked of him, and in so doing he had already squared up his accounts with death. So, then, must Charles Chilton Moore and every one of his readers do likewise, no matter what mythologies in which they might try to wrap themselves for fear of the unknown.

The Rankin story was followed up by at least two others of a similar slant, though since both involved local affairs Moore may have elected to refrain from further personal meditations: the recent suicide of a fellow Fayette County farmer named Clarendon Young, and the shooting of a city policeman by an unnamed and possibly still uncaught criminal. The officer in question had survived the attack against him, but his recovery looked doubtful. In spite of the tragic local news, though, Moore was still able to inject just a touch of whimsy into the remainder of the paper, surprisingly enough in fairly good taste to boot.

One of his other lead articles debated a question of contemporary fashion, specifically the propriety of men being clean-shaven versus their wearing of mustaches or beards, and since the personal appearance of both men and women had been a recurring dogmatic controversy since the days when the Old Testament was new Moore was able to use it for another springboard to discuss the finer points—and fallacies—of conservative Christianity. The full-bearded editor pointed out that his own preferences jibed more or less with the Mosaic Law, although he had his beard cut every year at sheep-shearing time in violation of the Pentateuch's precept that "Ye shall not round the corners of your heads, neither shalt thou mar the corners of thy beard."[432] Still the loyal pupil of Bishop Colenso, however, he warmed to his subject by outlining the contradiction to the Law found in the Apostle Paul's question to the Corinthians: "Doth not even nature itself teach you that, if a man have long hair, it is a shame unto him?"[433] This, of course, immediately begged the question as to whether Jesus, as God's Son and sinless, would have had long flowing locks and a beard as per most artists' depictions of him, or whether he would have been Paul's prime example of short-haired clean-shaven masculine faithfulness to the precepts of the First Epistle to the Corinthians. And finally, Moore described how one and another of the Early Church Fathers such as Origen and Tertullian had come down on either side of the dispute, be it the position of Moses or of Paul, to the conclusion that the whole controversy was one of absurd hairsplitting (pun probably intended) that wasn't really worth wasting time debating, no matter what verse or passage of Scripture that scholars or preachers might declare to be timeless truth.

It would have perhaps been too much to expect, even by this time, that Moore had had his last word on Sam Jones or would not have his say about at least one church scandal. And so sure enough, in this issue he also printed a letter from a writer calling himself (or perhaps herself) "Stylus" and who more or less endorsed the editor's 1884 vigorous anti-Jones stance, as well as a juicy account, borrowed from another newspaper, of "a church racket"—though fortunately for him, this particular imbroglio occurred in Wabash, Indiana[434], a good safe dis-

---

[432] Leviticus 19:27.
[433] I Corinthians 11:14.
[434] *Blade,* I, 4, February 6, 1886.

tance away from Lexington. Thus when all was said and done with the four pages of the *Blue Grass Blade,* Volume I, Issue 4, they may have constituted Moore's only effort in the newspaper line that didn't bring the open wrath of at least some portion of the Lexington and Bluegrass citizenry down on his head. All that was to change within a week, though, in classic Moore fashion, and thus perhaps we had best simply let the good editor introduce his next controversy on his own terms:

> I bought a new weed scythe last summer. It was a daisy cutter, and death on weeds. When I got through the weeds I tackled some elm sprouts in a fence row. They had been cut down several times with an ax and were as hard and knotty as the dickens. I went for them vigorously, and never thought anything but downing those sprouts until I had cleaned out the whole capoodle. Then I dropped the little end of the scythe upon the ground and started to put my arm over back of the bright new blade to rest on it, and saw it was gapped from point to heel. Maybe you think I didn't moralize over that some. If you do you think a mistake. Dollars were mighty scarce, I was eight miles from town and had more weeds to cut, and honor bright, I like to have cried. But I had a boss grindstone, a regular hummer. I unrigged that blade and put it on that grindstone, and with a nice pedal I made it buzz. When I got through it was as good as new and when I swung it over my shoulder again, and walked out into the woods, it seemed to me that the weeds, like Davy Crockett's coon, just tumbled over before I got there.
>
> Now I am going to stick the *Blade* into another knotty subject. It may be that when it gets through it will be worse hacked than a jig saw that has run against a nail, but it is going in all the same. The racket may be a little rough, but Time is a regular #7 DeLong grindstone that will smooth the hacks. If I say anything that is not true, and anybody knows it is not, let him print my words in any newspaper in town, and right below it say "That's a lie," and sign his name like a little man.[435]

The "knotty problem" that required such an involved parable for a preamble was a public vendetta between two prominent Lexington citizens, a well-known musician and composer named Rudolf de Roode and a city businessman and one of Moore's fellow newspaper editors from the *Lexington Gazette,* Henry Howard Gratz, the son of the late

---

[435] Ibid., I, 5, February 13, 1886.

patriarch of Lexington's Jewish community, Benjamin Gratz. Though both de Roode, a Netherlands native and a Roman Catholic, and the cultivated and well-educated Gratz could have been expected to be more urbane than to allow themselves to descend mutually into a dirty Kentucky-style honor feud, apparently this is exactly what had happened, and Charles Moore had an axe—and evidently, a *Blade* as well—to grind with both of them.

Apparently the entire rhubarb started with an accusation to which Moore would have been particularly sensitive even as an uninvolved third party: Gratz called de Roode, who was in fact a subscriber to the *Blue Grass Blade*[436] in spite of his Catholic faith tradition, an infidel. Since de Roode earned a great deal of his income from playing the organ at worship services, christenings, weddings, and funerals not only for Lexington's Catholic churchgoers but in many of the city's major Protestant churches as well, plus serving as music teacher to the crème of Lexington female society (including both Lucy Moore and Mary Brent, interestingly), he seems to have felt that he could not leave Gratz's accusation unanswered—especially since he had settled among a people that put such a high, quasi-medieval premium on personal honor and vengeance. And so he attacked Gratz physically with what must have been the most readily available weapon to him: he came up behind the editor and beaned him on the back of the head with a piano tuning hammer. After Gratz regained his feet (assuming that de Roode had even come close to knocking him out with the anemic hammer to start with), he prosecuted the musician in court, adding seasoning to the scandal not only with the renewal of his charge of infidelity but by hurling at the physically delicate, severely myopic de Roode the patently ridiculous supplemental accusations of cheating at cards and setting a fire that had destroyed Gratz's downtown jewelry store. Ballyhooing his infidelity charge against de Roode, Gratz won his case—and here the angry editor Charles Moore entered the picture, swinging his *Blade* both ways and not really caring whom he might nick with it.

What right had Gratz to call de Roode an infidel to start with, Moore wanted to know, especially since Gratz himself knew so little of Scripture either from the New Testament or the Old, and cared less,

---

[436] de Roode's name is found in Moore's September 20, 1890 public list of subscribers.

that he perfectly exemplified the proverbial stone thrower living in a glass house? What justification did he assume to accuse de Roode of arson when his insurance policy on the burned-down jewelry store had already paid off, as if it were a mere accident—or *was* it really an accident, and did Gratz know more than he said? And as for the cheating allegation, Gratz owned at least one other Lexington building, this one on Cheapside, wherein a sporting man might find a nice little illicit game of chance in progress nearly any time he wished to look; Gratz had plenty more dangerous Lexington cardsharps to deal with than de Roode, so maybe that particular charge came from some unhappy player who "had got [*sic*] scooped and squealed." Furthermore, what business had Gratz of prosecuting de Roode as if the musician were a common criminal, when Gratz himself *just might have been* [emphasis added here] involved in his own affairs of honor before, with weapons somewhat more lethal than tuning hammers to boot, yet had been exonerated because of his good old father's wealth and family connections? All in all, Moore concluded, though the venerable Benjamin Gratz had indeed been, in a paraphrase of the words of Jesus found in the first chapter of John's Gospel, "An Israelite in whom there was no guile," his son Henry certainly didn't deserve the title of "a chip off the old block." And Henry and his well-compensated attorneys had ganged up on Rudolf de Roode "as remorselessly as Mr. Gratz's Jew forefathers would have done the woman 'taken in the act,' except they (the Jews) had enough of conscience to be restrained by the words, 'Let him that is without fault among you [first cast a stone at her].'"[437]

We must further address the issue of Charles Moore's added post-Civil War ethnic prejudices and their possible origins subsequently. Sad to say, few Protestant readers in that day would have found fault with his choice of words for the above declaration even if they disagreed with his opinions about either Gratz or de Roode. But as if his anathemas against Henry Howard Gratz were not strong enough language for a newspaper editorial, he now waded into his analysis of the defendant. Though de Roode might be the smartest man in the Bluegrass region, and Moore figured he came near to meriting the title—he had once heard de Roode defend his Catholic faith against a gang of

[437] *Blade,* I, 5, February 13, 1886. Scriptural references used by Moore found in John 1:47 and 8:1-11.

three Lexington Protestant ministers who had joined forces to convert him, and had handled his case so adroitly that Moore confessed that the scene reminded him of the boy Jesus reasoning with the doctors in the Temple[438]—his attack on Gratz had been "the biggest fool thing" he had ever done since coming to America. If "the only Amsterdamned Dutchman in Lexington and Fayette County" (yes, Moore called de Roode exactly that, and got it past Lexington's squeamish postal censors too) had felt obliged to fight Gratz for casting aspersions about his spirituality, the absurd little tuning hammer was the only means in the world left to him because he was so nearsighted he couldn't possibly hit a barn door fifteen feet off even with a shotgun. Still, his life as compared to that of Henry Howard Gratz was as a beautiful piece of music to the neighing of a herd of rampant stallions, and Gratz's idea that de Roode had desecrated any of Lexington's churches with his presence at their organs was the height of the ridiculous. Moore knew from the inside, he argued, what it was like to be an infidel complete with all the opprobrium attached to the title, and if de Roode was any kind of infidel he had yet to prove it to the editor, even though—or perhaps even because—he had taken vengeance Kentucky-style into his own hands. Even if de Roode was "not as orthodox as he might be," Moore grumbled, "I may be slightly, sorter, kinder in the same boat with him; and it would look a little hard to me, if under the circumstances of my case, I could not have as fair a show before a civil court as the solid Brother Gratz."[439]

Moore thus finally revealed the real purpose of the long, satirical, waspish piece not far from the end of it, coupled with a challenge to the churches of Lexington to join with him in the Temperance/Prohibitionist crusade and for the furtherance of other good and moral civic causes:

> Everybody admits the right of the church to send a man to the devil because he don't [*sic*] believe in something, and I am not going to raise any row about that because I want to go into a pool with the ministers, if they will give me a square deal, in their work against the liquor traffic and about a half dozen more things as soon as we get that fixed up all right. But if it is going to be the case that a man un-

---

[438] The Scriptural reference is in Luke 2:41-52.

[439] *Blade,* I, 5, February 13, 1886.

> der trial in a Fayette County court is going to have his case damaged because he is not religiously orthodox, we all ought to know whether we are going to be examined out of the Catechism or the Bible. Business is business. We will want an examining board and certificates that we have passed muster. When it all gets fixed I will rub up in some of the hardest questions, and see if I cannot pass, in case I should ever get into the hands of the court. If I pass, I will run the *Blade* right here; if I don't, I will move with my family...[440]

Here, then, was Moore's point: when an individual's religious beliefs, or the lack thereof, were made a test of his or her citizenship as had seemingly occurred in the de Roode matter because of Gratz's agitation, *everyone's* constitutional liberties were at risk. It was a good, solid, and defensible purpose, but perhaps simply because the entire sad, weird Gratz-de Roode scandal reminded him so much of his dead friend Richard Reid and the twists of fate in which he had found himself caught after the attack by John Jay Cornelison, Moore made his editorial take on this brand-new honor feud resemble nothing so much as Shakespeare's Mercutio's scorn of the Montague and Capulet families alike, a plague on both their houses, as it were. And of course, since Moore had pronounced a plague on both houses, both houses— and not a few readers— responded in kind with the warmest wishes for a plague upon him.

We do not know exactly how long this second run of the *Blade* lasted. Since Moore started the third printed version of the paper with "Volume 1, Number 26" in September 1890, it is possible that he could have continued printing this second version for approximately five more months, that is, until about the middle of July 1886. Or for all we know, the February 13 Gratz-deRoode issue might have provoked such a furious backlash against him that he discontinued the *Blade* then and there, and that the issue labeled "Number 26" in 1890 represented a printer's typographical error that he took in stride and decided to live with. In any case, it is certain that there are no extant copies of the second version of the *Blade* after the infamous February 13 issue. And whether in February or July 1886, Moore once again remitted the balance of his subscribers' money, this time with the Parthian shot to his critics that he had actually been conservative and kept back many

[440] Ibid.

things that he wanted to say; but out of a thousand people who would help a man to gain distinction nine hundred would turn against him and help to drag him down once he has attained it. And this, declared Moore acidly, had been exactly his experience, not once but twice.[441]

In the four-year interim between Versions Two and Three of the *Blue Grass Blade,* Charles Chilton Moore involved himself in two noteworthy projects. One was the petition drive to get the brothels off Upper Street in Lexington that we discussed in the previous chapter. The other was the preparation and publication of his first book, a plea for the principles of freethought entitled *The Rational View*. Like many a good and enterprising nineteenth-century author including both Mark Twain and Walt Whitman, he financed his writing venture by advertising the book's prospectus in various other local newspapers and magazines and then by selling subscriptions to it; once he had his money in hand, he self-published using the Louisville *Courier-Journal's* job office as his printer, and sold the finished product through both agents and further newspaper and periodical advertisements. We have already drawn extensively on the supplemental family and autobiographical data Moore provided in this work, and John Crump, the American Atheists member who assisted Madalyn Murray O'Hair in readying it for reprint in 1984, rightly characterized the remainder of the volume's contents as "a serious attack on supernaturalism within the christian [*sic*] religion" and "a good companion to Thomas Paine's *Age of Reason.*"[442]

When we make a detailed comparison of Moore's work with Paine's, though, we must concede that *The Rational View* essentially exemplifies the philosopher Martin Gardener's observation that any fundamental view one can take toward any significant metaphysical question has been so well expressed and so expertly defended by great thinkers of the past that it is almost impossible to say anything new on the topic or to improve old arguments. Even at its best *The Rational View* represented no real advancement from the thought of *The Age of Reason* or, for that matter, from any of Robert Green Ingersoll's lec-

---

[441] Moore, *Behind the Bars,* 168.

[442] See John Crump's introductory notes to Moore's *Dog Fennel in the Orient,* ix.

tures or published essays on similar subjects, and it was in some crucial aspects clearly inferior to the works of both Paine and Ingersoll. Even so, it represents Moore's honest articulation of his own beliefs and disbeliefs, and in its day it was a relatively popular book within the freethought community at large, especially in the Bluegrass State. For our purposes, however, it serves more as a barometer for Moore's personal thought processes than as any sort of freethinker's creed or manifesto even for infidels in that day and time.

At least we can say truthfully that Moore came to the task of writing *The Rational View* largely without the Texas-sized chip on his shoulder that characterized so much of his newspaper work. Throughout his career as a writer he defended the principles of freethought and the primacy of human reason using three basic arguments: first, that both the Old and New Testaments of the Bible were full of contradictions and inconsistencies that no thinking individual could accept while maintaining his or her intellectual integrity; second, that modern science was in the process of formulating a much more trustworthy worldview of creation and humanity's place within it than blind acceptance of the precepts of some supposedly sacred book could ever hope to produce; and third, that in general the behavior of most professedly religious folk, whether their conduct was examined from an individual or a collective standpoint, belied the contention that they were under the guidance of any sort of supernatural, spiritual, or divine power.

The latter of these three postulates, which for lack of a better term we might label as Moore's Hypocrisy Principle, governed a great deal of the content of the *Blue Grass Blade,* and so within that context Moore perhaps felt he needed the consistent moral support of his shoulder chip—although Lord knows his Stone-Campbell religious heritage by itself could have made him think that a newspaper's text had to be both sarcastic and combative in order to do its job, and as we have seen in his writings about Richard Reid and George Owen Barnes he was apt to bestow almost too much praise on believing individuals whom he considered as exceptions to his hypocrisy rule. With *The Rational View,* however, he attempted to concentrate on his two former arguments and, albeit with the glaring exception of one particular subject, he now proved himself to be able to write and present his case with the courtesy of a refined and progressive Southern gentleman. The trail of the serpent is over the purest of human purpose, he pontificated in the book's introduction (he was never able to get away from the use of biblical and religious imagery in his writing, but then again, in his day Scriptural metaphor was almost the only kind that any of his readers would have either recognized or appreciated), but insofar as human beings were ordinarily unselfish in such matters his purpose was to do good to his fellow pilgrims on life's highway.[443]

After a personal introduction in the book's first chapter, outlining his lifelong engagement with the questions he hoped to address, Moore took up his parable in Chapter 2 with an exploration of the most fundamental question of all: who, or what, was God, and what could humankind's purpose be in light of such an entity? Moore didn't believe that it was possible either to prove or disprove the idea of a god, or a creator, as an abstract principle; to him, the word "god" was, to any intelligent mind, so indefinite and vague that no one could be warranted in making a dogmatic affirmation or denial of his, or its, existence. After all, myriads of years before a human being ever existed, before a line had been drawn or an angle measured, it was nonetheless eternally true that the number of degrees of the three angles of a triangle were equivalent to those of two right angles, and that parallel lines never meet—so which was older, the supposed creator god, or the fundamental mathematical and geometric truths of the mechanics of creation? That being the case, could those basic physical laws of nature themselves properly be classified as "god"? Considering Moore's professed dislike for mathematics, it is remarkable that he would have made this sort of comparison—though by this point in his life he probably entertained the same degree of distaste for theological speculation as he had for higher mathematics back in the good old days at Transylvania College. Then again, he may simply have equated higher mathematics and the concept of a Creator God in his own mind as two separate yet interrelated mysteries, both beyond his comprehension.

Of one view of the nature of God, though, Moore spoke with great confidence: God was *not* what he, or it, was represented to be in Christian Scripture. Moore allowed for Jesus' supposed description of God in the fourth chapter of John's Gospel as "a spirit," with the qualification in the last chapter of Luke's Gospel that "a spirit hath not flesh and

[443] Moore, *The Rational View,* vii.

[bones],"[444] insofar as one could equate the word "spirit" with a philosophical abstraction. The remainder of the characterizations of God in the Bible, however, be they technical or poetic, could virtually all be shown more to reflect and represent the character of the people who entertained them than to depict any sort of objective description of a superhuman creator. In other words, the God of the Bible could be demonstrated, by and large, simply to be an extension of the minds of the ancient Hebrews who first pondered their place in the world, even as the gods of the Greeks, Romans, Indians, Chinese, and Native Americans served for their own people.

The proof of this proposition now became Moore's task, and thus he continued to Chapter 3 in a fairly organized, though sometimes digressive, fashion. In this section of the book he offers his own version of comparison and contrast between the traditional biblical creationist, and emerging Darwinian, views of the beginnings of life on earth. Straightaway he states that he himself believed Charles Darwin's theories to be fundamentally sound; the origin of the human race as given in the Pentateuch, he observes, had so little of plausibility about it that apologists for biblical inerrancy generally admitted its incredibility except upon the supposition of the inspiration of Moses—*then* they turned around and claimed that the accuracy of the Pentateuch was proof positive of its inspiration. Such circular reasoning always irritated Moore, possibly because he had been guilty of it himself in the days when he was a believer and a preacher. One fact being admitted, he writes here, makes possible a logical deduction of another fact, but a logical conclusion absolutely cannot be made from a proposition which itself needs to be proven. Hence his approval of Darwin's *Origin of Species* and *The Descent of Man:* though there were gaps in Darwin's theories, Darwin, Thomas Huxley, and their fellow scientists cheerfully subjected them to the rigors of scientific examination, and on that basis Darwinism could be depended upon far more than any supposedly orthodox tradition or claimed revelation.

As a continuation of Moore's discussion of creationism versus Darwinism, Chapters 4, 5, and 6 of *The Rational View* represent something very deeply personal if not quite altogether original. Here Moore begins a slow, still digressive deconstruction of the dogma he had

[444] John 4:24; Luke 24:40.

imbibed as a child and had been taught as a young man at Bethany College, a scathing critique of Alexander Campbell's doctrine of Christian faith as nothing more or less than the visual and auricular reception of the written and spoken testimony of Scripture. To Campbell, the existence of spoken language had been one sure proof of the existence of God, since he was certain that the only way our primal forefathers ever could have framed a language was by hearing God talk[445]; yet even the basic linguistics that Moore had learned along with his Greek, Latin, and English literature at Bethany had led him to suspect, at least in hindsight, that Campbell's claim for the divine origin of language was a gross oversimplification. In these chapters Moore proposes an alternate theory of the development of languages based more or less on the principles of Darwinian evolution, and although he was certainly no trained linguist, his hypotheses are well thought-out, well-stated—and remarkably modern, considering that the field of evolutionary linguistics gained credibility only in the late twentieth century, with most qualified nineteenth-century scholars in the discipline insisting that inquiries into the origins of language were futile.[446] "Whosoever shall call upon the name of the Lord shall be saved," wrote Paul in the Epistle to the Romans. "How then shall they call on him in whom they have not believed? And how shall they believe in him in whom they have not heard? And how shall they hear without a preacher?"[447]

On the basis of these declarations Alexander Campbell had constructed an elaborate system of logic that, according to his own youthful boasts and, soon enough afterward, the confident pronouncements of many of his followers, had definitively trumped all other methods both of biblical thinking and of Gospel preaching. Moore's discussion of the evolution of languages called everything Alexander Campbell had ever said or written about speaking, hearing, and preaching, into question. Though Moore admitted that evangelical churches outside the Stone-Campbell Movement had more philosophical justification in proclaiming that human conscience, rather than Campbell's concept of the spoken word and the written New Testament, would be the most

---

445 Moore, *The Rational View,* 27.

446 A good contemporary treatment of evolutionary linguistics can be found in Christine Kenneally's *The First Word* (Viking Press, 2007).

447 Romans 10:13-14.

likely means of communication between Creator and creation, he believed conscience itself to be such a subjective entity full of humankind's own hopes, fears, and self-projections that not even the existence of conscience, let alone the existence of language, could be taken as definitive proof of the existence of the God of traditional theism. And as we have noted more than once already, the best argument he could have made for such a conclusion came from his own family history: his grandfather Stone's bitter experiences with the Shakers.

Moore's discussion of language, as well as conscience, serves as a prelude to the remainder of the major arguments in *The Rational View:* nine chapters expounding upon the manifold contradictions, inconsistencies, and errors in Old and New Testaments alike. If God could, or would, communicate with humankind by the means of a book, Moore reasoned, it was only to be expected that such a divinely-inspired book would be inerrant, consistent both internally between its own component portions and externally with the physical and biological laws of nature, veritably perfect. And yet anyone who had gone through the two Testaments of the Bible with a fine-toothed comb as he had, starting with his 1863 reading of Bishop Colenso's *Pentateuch and Book of Joshua Critically Examined* and continuing through his own personal researches even before Robert Green Ingersoll had given the infidel cause a modicum of chic, must needs be compelled to admit that the so-called Holy Bible was anything but inerrant or consistent. Of course, it did not directly follow that the existence of contradictions and errors in the Bible proved the *non*-existence of a god, or gods, and Moore knew this. In fact, his own "Hypocrisy Principle" made a more compelling case at least for the notion that, if God existed, he or it did not involve himself or itself in the affairs of humankind, and without Moore's own bitter experience of Northern and Southern preachers and believers demonizing one another during the Civil War we might wonder if he ever would have abandoned conventional religion completely. Even so, the great majority of his Bluegrass readership clung so persistently to the notion of the inerrancy of Scripture that to them, admitting the possibility that Scripture harbored errors or contradicted itself was tantamount to confessing a complete disbelief in God. Moore himself had believed as much at one time.

Thus the proof of biblical error and inconsistency naturally became one of the primary weapons in Moore's debating arsenal, and now he wielded it well—very possibly too well, since nine full chapters outlining, to the fullest nitpicking extent, all the contradictions and inconsistencies one meticulous researcher intent on proving a point could glean from the sixty-six books of the Bible is nothing if not overkill. In partial excuse for Moore's literary and scholarly shortcomings in this section of *The Rational View,* we might point out that at least he has come to enjoy a fair amount of company: a great many modern apologists of atheism and agnosticism, particularly young and inexperienced ones writing on Internet websites, still fall prey to this same picky, lily-gilding tendency just as surely as equally-green evangelical Christian apologists of the same caliber alternately endanger their own throats with Occam's Razor and mouth loud but maddeningly vague proclamations that good orthodox evangelical Protestant research carried out by good orthodox evangelical Protestant scholars has somehow managed to resolve perfectly all of those same Scriptural contradictions and inconsistencies.[448]

And yet Moore's reasoning embraces a much more dangerous fallacy than this pesky carping over the details of Scriptural inconsistencies, one which, to my knowledge, has not been commented upon so much as once either in his own day or in ours. Like so many other aspects of his story too, it is fraught with irony, since it concerns the one single and unique theme of the New Testament that for some reason Moore never saw fit to call into question or doubt. Throughout the four Gospels and the Book of Acts the Jews as a people are presented in a consistently bad light, and many modern Bible scholars have hypothesized that this negative characterization of the Jewish race was written into the Jesus story between 65 and 135 C.E. in a deliberate

[448] We should take note of one remarkable exception to the "Internet-greenness rule": J. F. Till, former editor and publisher of *The Skeptical Review* magazine and at present the operator of the Internet website of the same name (http://www.theskepticalreview.com). Interestingly, Till was at one time a preacher on the conservative side of the same faith tradition once espoused by Charles Chilton Moore, and came to abandon his religious beliefs for strikingly similar reasons. Though Till's essays on Scriptural errors and inconsistencies can be so minutely detailed as to be complex and convoluted, he brings the skills of a Scripture scholar, Scottish Common Sense Realism logician, and ex-minister to his work and is a force to be reckoned with at any theism-versus-atheism debate in which he participates.

effort to distance the fledgling Christian movement from Judaism in the eyes of the rulers of the Roman Empire. As such, Church diplomats with the object of ingratiating the Christian faith with the Roman government, the temporal power in Palestine both during and after Jesus' lifetime and who represented the only entity that could, or would, have executed him by crucifixion, could use this new angle to blame his murder not on the Romans, but on the Jews instead. There is scant, but enough, internal evidence in Flavius Josephus' *The Jewish War* and his *Antiquities of the Jews,* Paul's letters (especially the first three chapters of Galatians and the ninth chapter of I Corinthians), Moore's own favorite Epistle of James, and even the Book of Acts, at least in the twelfth, the twenty-fourth, and the text between the fifteenth and nineteenth chapters, to give at least some credibility to the notion that in its earliest years, the Jesus movement was merely one more recognized and quasi-legitimate expression of Judaism in Jerusalem and its surrounding territories, and that it was led during this period not by the Apostle Peter but rather by James, the Brother of the Lord.

The relationship between Christianity (or "the sect of the Nazarenes," as Acts refers to the movement at one point[449]) and other expressions of Judaism is said to have deteriorated not so much after the death of Jesus as it did after the murder of James the Lord's Brother in 62 C.E. and its repercussions that ultimately led the Roman general Vespasian and his son Titus to raze Jerusalem to its foundations eight years afterward. The "Jacobite" form of Jewish Christianity once led by James in Jerusalem thus pretty much faded into oblivion between 70 CE and the suppression of the Bar-Kochba Rebellion in 135 CE, while the more anti-Semitic Pauline or Gentile form, articulated and led by a self-proclaimed apostle who openly admitted that he had never met the historical Jesus in the flesh, endured and prevailed.[450]

---

[449] Acts 24:5.

[450] Paul gave James "the Less" this appellation in Galatians 1:19. For further information on the topic of the early Jesus movement, the reader is referred to the writings of Flavius Josephus and, in more modern times, to Robert Eisenman's *James the Brother of Jesus* (Viking Penguin, 1997), John Shelby Spong's *Liberating the Gospels: Reading the Bible With Jewish Eyes* (1996), *The Sins of Scripture* (Harper SanFrancisco, 2005) and *Jesus For the Non-religious* (Harper SanFrancisco, 2006), and *The Brother of Jesus: James the Just and His Mission,* Bruce Chilton and Jacob Neusner, eds. (Westminster John Knox, 2001).

This is essentially the view of the historical development and subsequent breakdown of Jewish-Christian relations that is taken at present by many liberal Christian expositors. As might be expected, it is largely scorned by fundamentalist and evangelical apologists as spineless wishful thinking rather than true Bible doctrine, although these conservative elements of the Christian faith are not often disposed to evaluate their own current take on the Jews—that is, largely as actors in the dramatic bloodbath that is supposed to play across earth's stage during the expected John Nelson Darby-flavored fulfillment of the Book of Revelation—with any of the same historical or textual criteria they use to condemn the liberal belief. But of course, whether or not the modern liberal Christians' theorized scenario actually envisions accurate historical events in turbulent first-century Palestine, it is certain that all too many Christians, both individually and collectively and from ancient times all the way up to the mid-twentieth century and beyond, have seized upon the Four Gospels' consistent and virulent anti-Semitism—*"his blood be on us, and on our children!"*[451]—as all the excuse they have ever needed to practice every conceivable form of persecution upon the race into which their peace-loving, enemy-forgiving Lord and Savior had been born. *How odd of God to choose the Jews,* wrote the nineteenth-century British journalist William Norman Ewer. And this same wit received a reply to his short poem from his colleague Harold Wilmington, one which hopefully gave him at least a second's pause for reflection:

And odder still for men to choose
The Jewish God, yet hate the Jews.

Charles Chilton Moore was familiar enough with the basic concepts of the so-called Documentary Hypothesis, brand-new in his day and which explained the contradictions in the Pentateuch by postulating that it was assembled from the works of as many as four separate ancient authors redacted together, to have made at least one comment upon it in *The Rational View.*[452] In addition, he had inherited a fine leather-bound copy of the works of Flavius Josephus from his father's

---

[451] Matthew 27:25.
[452] Moore, *The Rational View,* 20.

library,[453] and thus we know that from his youth he had enjoyed access to this alternative take on the history and the character of the Jewish people. Although of freethought icons Voltaire, at least, is known to have been a virulent anti-Semite,[454] Moore's mentor Robert Green Ingersoll was himself as critical of conventional anti-Semitic stereotypes as he was of traditional Judaic and Christian orthodoxies[455] and in fact his printed lectures and essays were among the most popular English-to-Yiddish translations made in the nineteenth century.[456] By both his experience and his temperament, then, we might reasonably assume that Charles Moore should have been every bit as skeptical of the Gospels' negatively-biased depiction of the Jews as he was of the claims that Moses had split the Red Sea or that Jesus had calmed a storm, driven a herd of pesky devils into a herd of pesky hogs, or fed five thousand people with five loaves and two fishes. And yet, sadly, to Moore the Jews were, at least historically, without question every inch the melodramatic one-piece two-dimensional villains that both the Four Gospels and Mel Gibson's *Passion of the Christ* have made them out to be, twenty centuries apart though the characterizations were made. Witness this acerbic observation from *The Rational View:*

> In giving the history of the Jews, as it appears in their account of themselves in the Bible, it will be found that they give themselves a very bad character. This admission of their own imperfections has been urged by many apologists as an argument in favor of the truth of the entire Bible because it shows their candor. It is true that a man's claiming he is truthful and honest is no evidence that it is so; but it certainly must be equally true that his admission that he is not truthful and not honest is not a proof that he is truthful and honest. The Old [Testament] states that God made use of lying prophets, and the New Testament states that Peter, when put to a test, stated with oaths, and to a woman at that, that he did not even know Jesus. These admissions, as told in the Old [Testament], that the most prominent apostle in the New Testament and prophets sent out by God lied

---

[453] Ibid., *Behind the Bars,* 24-25.

[454] See *Letters of Certain Jews to Monsieur Voltaire,* special collections, Kentucky Historical Society.

[455] See Ingersoll, "The Jews," from his Collected Works on the World Wide Web, http://www.infidels.org/library/historical/robert_ingersoll.jews.html.

[456] Jacoby, 152.

> [*sic*], may be given as an instance of candor in these particular cases; but certainly no just reasoner would use these particular cases to prove that the people who wrote the Bible are truthful. Not only this, but…if the Jews show themselves to be depraved in other matters, it is reasonable to suppose that they would be lacking in veracity….If it be claimed that God is the author of the Bible from his having selected men to write it, it must occur to us that the character of the men alleged thus to have been selected must have much to do with the probability of their having been really thus selected [ellipses added].[457]

And this gem, only two pages further on in Moore's analysis of Scriptural origins; while it is neither as hate-filled as Martin Luther's or Voltaire's anti-Jewish polemics, nor as psychotic as Buckner Harrison Payne's attempt to prove by Scripture and Scottish Common Sense Realism that the Negroid race wasn't human,[458] Moore's evaluation of Jewish history is still shockingly bad enough:

> In alluding to the character of the Jews, I have reference to simply that which they have given of themselves in the Bible. I have no reason to discriminate against the character of the modern Jews. I believe the records of our courts show them to be fully the peers, in morals, of the Gentiles. They are generally intelligent, and my acquaintance with them has indicated that as a general thing they do not believe the supernatural part of their own Bible. *They are, perhaps, mercenary beyond the average, and their disposition to segregate themselves is probably not abreast of the most advanced thought of the age; but it is a* natural *disposition, and certainly not a criminal or immoral one* (italics added for emphasis).
>
> But the Jews, as they were when they wrote the Bible, and especially the old part of it, were perhaps the last people on earth to be trusted for intelligence or integrity. They stand (sic), in respect to moral and intellectual quality, markedly inferior to any race of people of whose history I know anything. Their statement[s] about themselves [in the Old Testament are] worse than any other nation has admitted of itself, and worse than anybody has charged against anybody else.[459]

---

[457] Moore, *The Rational View,* 52.

[458] See Payne (pseud. "Ariel,") *The Negro: What is His Ethnological Status?*

[459] Moore, *The Rational View*, 54.

Although we could present a great deal more evidence of Moore's predisposition in this regard, we should perhaps try to make do with only one more example to fill out his simplistic portrait of the Jewish race—and his equally simplistic portrait of the nineteenth-century freethinker's Jesus of Nazareth:

> There was, doubtless, in the very peculiar utterances and upon some occasions in the actions of Jesus something to justify the Roman officers in the supposition that Jesus was planning to seize the government of Judea and gain the independence of the Hebrews. But the Romans were broadminded, liberal, and generous people, and if the officers had at all noticed this suspicious conduct of Jesus, they had regarded his aims as so impracticable of accomplishment that they had paid no attention to him, and probably would not have done so had the Jews allowed them to ignore the language and conduct of Jesus. He was engaged in teaching the people a most beautiful code of morals which said that the way for men to be happy was to be kind and good and generous and forgiving to each other. ...But the Jews' idea of moral dignity was an eye for an eye and a tooth for a tooth. They believed in retaliation, and had the idea that is known at this day of "defending one's honor." All of their heroes had slain their enemies...so that when Jesus began teaching his ideas that were just the reverse of all that they had ever believed, they considered that it was intended as personal insult and rebuke, and they were indignant that one of their number should thus repudiate the special pride and boast of their race... and so they forced upon the unwilling attentions of the Romans the suspicion that the young Nazarene was plotting against the throne of Caesar.
>
> It was the policy of the Roman government in the management of its provinces not to interfere in the domestic arrangements further than was necessary to establish the Roman authority. Therefore, when the Roman government saw that the Jews killed heretics, they considered the moral effect of the popular rumor that Jesus was plotting against Caesar, and evidently against their consciences and inclinations allowed the Jews broad sway, and in this way Jesus was condemned by a combination of civil and ecclesiastic courts that seems very strange when it is remembered that the Romans are the authors of the best laws that obtain among us until this day. But the persistence in which the Jews labored to accomplish the ruin of this beautiful character, and the exultation they manifested when they had accomplished their purposes, show them to be unequaled in brutality in the annals of men.

> A large part of the Bible is devoted to the development of the fact that the Jews were a nation of thieves, liars, and murderers.[460]

Perhaps by this point we should take a moment to remind ourselves that Charles Chilton Moore was *not,* in fact, a Christian, be it Catholic, Protestant, liberal, moderate, conservative, or otherwise, when he penned *The Rational View.* He didn't believe in the virgin birth of Jesus, the vicarious atonement of the cross, angels, devils, prophets, heaven, hell, or God in any conceivable theistic form. Let us also recall that, in addition, he had never shared his neighbors' view of the biblical justification of slavery even when he had been a Christian, let alone afterward. All these fundamental articles of antebellum *and* postwar traditionalist Christian dogma Moore was willing to question, criticize, even lampoon and ridicule, and we have already demonstrated his fondness for lampooning and how it could, and did, get him into trouble. However, insofar as Jesus could be classified as a peaceful and wise humanitarian and teacher like Confucius, Zarathrustra, or the Buddha, as opposed to some sort of god, demigod, prophet, or miracle worker, Moore, just like Pontius Pilate is claimed by John's Gospel to have uttered, could and would "find no fault in him."[461] In the concluding chapter of *The Rational View* Moore even used the teachings of Jesus on nonresistance and nonviolence to argue eloquently and persuasively for the formation of a "congress of nations" as an international alternative to individual countries' maintaining standing armies and more or less continually fighting wars among one another[462]—an idea that the majority of Americans, even many freethinkers, regarded as simply too radical until the Atomic Age all of a sudden made it seem sensible and even necessary. And yet, alas, all of Moore's progressive and in retrospect, quite good ideas about both international politics and evolutionary linguistics in *The Rational View* are as overshadowed by his casual and unthinking anti-Semitism as an eclipse hides the face of the sun, with only a penumbra of light shining around its periphery. He carelessly branded the entire Jewish people, in good dogmatic wholesale form to boot, not as Christ-killers but as Enlightened Teacher-killers, in essence taking the Gospels' story of the Jews at complete

---

[460] Ibid., 61-62.
[461] Ibid., 181. Scriptural reference from John 18:38, 19:4, and 19:6.
[462] Ibid., 186-187.

face value minus the Christian argument for Jesus' divinity, virgin birth, and resurrection. Thus whether his anti-Semitism simply echoed that of Voltaire, Barton Stone, Alexander Campbell, or most infidels and Christians alike in that day and age, his use of the woman-taken-in-adultery story in the eighth chapter of John's Gospel for his 1886 criticism of Henry Howard Gratz all of a sudden appears to assume an entirely new, and sinister, meaning: like the good Dr. Wilson so aptly stated, *The trouble with Moore is that he was a preacher once and has never gotten out of the rut.*[463]

But perhaps the bitterest irony in the entire story of *The Rational View* is that not one of Moore's contemporaries, not a single Christian minister or even the broadminded Dr. Wilson, appears ever to have stated publicly that there was *anything* amiss about his characterization of the Jews, let alone to have attempted to take the editor to task for it. The only nineteenth-century infidel newspaperman who is known to have been stigmatized either in or out of the freethought community as any sort of racist was William Cowper Brann, the virulently pro-Aryan publisher of the Texas *Iconoclast* who was shot in the back and killed by an irate Baptist intent on defending the honor of his Lord and Savior (and that of his daughter as well, since she attended Baylor University in Texas and Brann had publicly made the claim that no pretty young coed on good terms with any of Baylor's sanctimonious, Pharisaical male professors was likely to remain a virgin any too long).[464] Though near the end of his life Charles Moore himself remarked that he had endured so many close calls that he could gaze back at the one-eyed stare of a big pistol with the same *sangfroid* that he could look through an opera glass at a circus,[465] back in the Bluegrass, ministers denounced him for his personal refusal to accept Jesus as the biblical Messiah and for making fun of the Virgin Birth, not for saying anything negative about the race from whence Jesus came—a people who likewise rejected the possibility of virgin birth. The Lexington merchant Moses Kaufman, whom we met in the previous chapter and who had sup-

---

[463] Ibid., *Behind the Bars,* 183. quoting J. B. Wilson.

[464] Jacoby, 155. Thanks to Jon Musgrave, fellow historian and the operator of the website http://www.illinoishistory.com for the anecdote about Brann, who was an Illinois native, and his denunciation of Baylor University's professors.

[465] Moore, *Dog Fennel,* 16-17.

ported Moore both before and during the publication of the first two versions of the *Blue Grass Blade,* remained unswerving in his loyalty to the editor after *The Rational View* was published; throughout all Moore's subsequent legal troubles Kaufman gave him unstinting allegiance, even standing for him as bail bondsman when he was arrested in Lexington on the archaic, anachronistic charge of blasphemy and years afterward contributing a touching eulogy at the crusty old infidel's funeral service.[466] Were Kaufman and other Lexington and Bluegrass Jews simply afraid of raising their voices in protest against *The Rational View*—or had they been forced for so long to accustom themselves to doing business with people who scorned their heritage with the same casual disdain Charles Chilton Moore evidenced in his book, that they felt that they had to let his, and their other Kentucky neighbors', cool, careless anti-Semitism roll right off them like water off ducks' backs?

Tragically, both hypotheses are logical—and complementary. It's unsettling to think that the only remarkable thing about Charles Chilton Moore's anti-Semitism was that, for his own day and time, it was completely unremarkable, whether the sentiments were shared by believers or nonbelievers. But from all evidence this was precisely the case, and it very well may have remained so for another generation or two until Adolf Hitler, Joseph Goebbels, the Nazi Party, and six million starved, tortured, and cremated European Jews shocked and horrified Kentucky along with the rest of America out of its comfortable and comforting complacency of thought. For all that, though, one wonders if the late twentieth and early twenty-first century melodrama envisioned for the Jews by so many American and Kentucky Christians informed and inspired by John Nelson Darby, George Owen Barnes, and their latter-day counterparts Tim LaHaye and Jerry Jenkins, is really any better than the late nineteenth-century play scripted for them by Charles Chilton Moore. Or again, for that matter, the similar Oberammergau-style *passionspiel* set loose upon the public by Mel Gibson.

Moore's career as a writer of books was far from over, and we would like to think that at least one passage in his third published volume might partially atone for the gross racial injustice that he perpe-

---

[466] See one of Kaufman's letters to Lucy Moore in *Behind the Bars,* 32, and the eulogy in *In Memoriam,* 13.

trated in his first—especially since he had his moment of anti-Semitism, at least against American Jewry, in that work as well. Too, a few thoughtful and repentant newspaper editorials he penned after the turn of the century speak in favor of something of a change of heart on his part about some of his earlier hasty words. But these are all part of another story, more than a decade yet into the future, and as we leave discussing *The Rational View* we must take one more backward glance in an attempt to envision the plethora of Moses Kaufman's facial expressions as he first combed through the crisp new pages of the initial edition of the book. Could one discern rage, indignation, grief, sardonic amusement, a succession of each, or an amalgam of all? Perhaps Kaufman just quietly muttered to himself, with the words of the Kentucky gentleman he had become in spite of his neighbors' casual prejudices against his race and his heritage: *Charley Moore's done the best he's known how, bless his heart. The trail of the serpent over the purest of human purpose, indeed. Bless his heart. Bless. His. Heart.*

The third and longest-running manifestation of the *Blue Grass Blade* hit the streets of Lexington seven months after *The Rational View* first came out, with Volume I, issue 26 on September 20, 1890. With the release of *The Rational View* Moore felt (for at least a brief time, anyway) that he had succeeded in saying all he would ever need to say about religion, and so now he proposed to make his newspaper a through-and-through hard-line Prohibition and anti-vice periodical and form alliances when and where he could with infidels and Christians alike in the furtherance of the Temperance/Prohibition anti-liquor cause.[467] As might be expected, though, Moore wasn't quite accurate when he claimed that he was done with talking about religious matters in the *Blade*. Although one of the strongest aspects of his success with the third version of the paper was his "outing" of rich urban church members and leaders with connections to the liquor industry, when the prominent physician C. C. P. Clark claimed he could prove that Jesus' alleged resurrection had actually entailed his survival of the crucifixion, and sent his written conclusions round to several American freethought periodicals for evaluation and publication, Moore picked the essay right up and ran it, perhaps unable to resist ruffling just a few more Ken-

[467] *Blade,* I, 26, September 20, 1890.

tucky Christian feathers.[468] Criticisms of religion aside, neither was the *Blade* ever an exclusively one-cause mouthpiece. With such provocatively-titled articles as "Why I Am a Woman Suffragist"[469] and "Mr. George Handy of Harrodsburg Talks Like a Man for Women"[470] Moore likewise espoused Josephine Henry's Kentucky women's rights movement, and perhaps his own most vivid personal expression of this profeminist sentiment can be found in an 1892 article about the divorce of the brother and sister-in-law of his old southeastern Kentucky preaching partner, Overton Asbell. Moore recalled baptizing the brother, whose name was Whitefield Asbell, back in his Civil War missionary days, and he observed that "If I ever get him in the water again, with his back down [and] while I have him with both hands, I'll bet he will never fuss with his wife any more."[471]

And so this time, between such pro-suffrage articles and vociferous Prohibition exhortations mixed with old comedic favorites like "Looking for the Pantry Key"[472] and poems and essays contributed regularly by Josephine Henry, Moore's paper survived and became accepted within the Lexington community in a way almost parallel to the later journalistic career of H. L. Mencken and those of the modern nationally-syndicated radio programs of Rush Limbaugh, G. Gordon Liddy, Oliver North, Don Imus—and even Howard Stern. In other words, one could either love the medium of news or hate it, but regardless, the personality behind the venture was the one who laughed all the way to the bank. All in all, in spite of Moore's newly adopted hard-line stance against liquor we should perhaps classify this third version of the *Blue Grass Blade* as a Progressive periodical rather than a strictly Prohibition or anti-vice newspaper, since, as we have observed earlier, at that time Prohibition was regarded largely as a Progressive rather than a conservative cause. Yet even so, no one could disagree that, Prohibition or no, the *Blade* was *aggressive* even more than Progressive most of the time. Subsequently Moore even adopted a then-current fashion among American infidels and freethinkers by dating the *Blade* according to the

---

[468] Ibid., I, 37, January 19, 1891.
[469] Ibid., I, 28, October 25, 1890.
[470] Ibid., I, 29, November 1, 1890.
[471] Ibid., II, 29, January 16, 1892.
[472] Ibid., I, 28, October 25, 1890.

anniversary of the execution of the scientist and philosopher Giordano Bruno by the Holy Inquisition in 1600 for advocating the principles of Galileo, and other so-called heresies; thus "1890 A. D." became "290 E. M.," and so forth, with "E. M." as an abbreviation for "the Era of Man."[473]

Thus despite Moore's battles throughout the 1880s over Richard Reid, John Jay Cornelison, Sam Jones, Rudolf de Roode, and Henry Howard Gratz, and his sad, sick take on the Semitic race that no one ever considered worthy of dispute, by late 1891 it appeared that the third time was the charm for him. After more than a year the *Blade,* Version Three, still survived, and it looked like the fifty-four year-old publisher was finally going to make a successful career simultaneously as a Prohibition crusader and a freethought writer and editor. Still, the paper continually—and often precariously—teetered between a coherent program of freethought-based philosophy and morality and Moore's own furious scatter-shooting against those aspects of his world that chafed at him personally, and as cartoonist Richard Stevens recently had one of his creations observe, a constant struggle against a hated foe cures existentialism every time. The 1890s caught both Charles Chilton Moore and his orthodox Christian antagonists right up in the very vortex of this latter maxim, and a couple or three more bizarre twists of fate and dribbles of newspaper ink now known in the annals of Bluegrass history as the Issue That Ventilated Paris, the Breckinridge-Pollard Hyphenation, and the Law of Population brought him what amounted to nearly a decade of State and Federal legal woes. To beat it all, the Commonwealth of Kentucky prosecuted him pretty much for writing as a raging extremist, and the Federal government for writing and speaking, in his own mind at least, as a thoughtful progressive. As we have seen already, in some ways Moore was ahead of his time and in others, he was simply too hasty, period.

There is no question that Charles Chilton Moore left behind a positive legacy for both the Freethought Movement and for Kentucky at large. Yet in many if not most ways, in order to see its good points his work must be viewed from retrospect, through the lens of the twentieth and twenty-first centuries. For the time being, though, we must make do with Moore in Moore's own element, the turbulent 1890s Bluegrass,

---

473 Winn, "Current Comment II," from *Winn's Firebrand,* II, 1, January 1903.

and as such, the reader should take warning that our examination of his actions during this final decade of the nineteenth century neither can nor will present any of the characters involved as outright, through-and-through heroes or villains any more than would a Kurt Vonnegut novel. Real life, it appears, must always somehow manage rather with a great number of plain, simple human beings plainly and simply doing that which human beings plainly and simply seem to do best—acting in haste, repenting at leisure, and gleaning what lessons they can learn from the entire mess only after most of the action is over, often while trying to avoid admitting that any mistakes have ever been made. Life is, after all, lived forwards but remembered backwards. Therefore, we should perhaps approach the following chapter with one more nod to Moore's literary idol, Mark Twain, and his 1884 disclaimer for *The Adventures of Huckleberry Finn:* persons attempting to find a motive in this narrative will be prosecuted; persons attempting to find a moral in it will be banished; persons attempting to find a plot in it will be shot. By order of the Author, per G. G., Chief of Ordnance, whoever *that* may have been.

And so with Twain's warning in mind, let us proceed onward to Paris and thence to the successive storms of Ventilation, Hyphenation, and Population that Charles Chilton Moore conjured up: Paris, Kentucky, that is, and a haunt that Moore compared unfavorably to Belle Brezing's Lexington whorehouse but which most Bourbon County citizens knew as the First Christian Church.

Chapter 7

The Wall of Separation

It sometimes seems to me that the grayer we get,
the less sense we have.
—William Campbell Preston Breckinridge

Strangely enough, in the late fall of 1891 Charles Moore himself would have had at least one good reason to have been reminded entirely on his own of Mark Twain and *The Adventures of Huckleberry Finn*—specifically, that portion of the novel that described the King and the Duke's performance, for a small Arkansas river town, of an impromptu, risqué show entitled "The King's Cameleopard; or, the Royal Nonesuch." When the Duke prepared the posters for the performance he made sure to write the words "Ladies and Children Not Admitted" in the largest possible letters across the bottoms, advising the youthful Huck that "If that line don't fetch them, I don't know Arkansaw [*sic*]!" Similarly, one of the signal events in real-life central Kentucky as the 1891 Christmas season approached was a sermon delivered on November 29 by the eminent Disciples of Christ minister and Bible college president John W. McGarvey at Lexington's Broadway Christian Church, entitled "Horse Racing, the Liquor Traffic, Whoredom, and Corruption in the City of Lexington" and every bit as closely restricted to "men only" as the fictional "Nonesuch." In his discourse McGarvey regaled his jam-packed audience of approximately two thousand curious males with both reaffirmations of the traditional evangelical Christian condemnations of drunkenness, gambling, and fornication, and with indignant and hair-raising tales of how these sins and depravities were, at that very moment, holding high carnival in the fair and holy city of Lexington—in spite of the fact that, from all appearances, the town's anti-Sabbath breaking ordinance was then being enforced as stringently as the Commonwealth's statutes against homicide.[474] McGarvey's own testimony seems to indicate that he got in such a rabid dither over Lexington's vice problems when he received the shocking news (to him anyway) that "procuresses" in the city were attempting to influence young country girls, put out of their houses by their parents or for other reasons freshly come to town and on their own, to take up lives of prostitution. At his sermon's end McGarvey held up a copy of his primary source of information: none other than a particularly hot, humid, and spicy issue of Charles Chilton Moore's, and Lexington's own, *Blue Grass Blade* from a week or two beforehand. As a sort of benediction to the entire proceeding as well as to Moore's now-successful career as a modern Bluegrass mass-media muckraker, McGarvey then intoned, "Charley Moore has said some hard things, but I have never caught him in a lie." When he uttered this final pronouncement he was actually applauded, and Moore later observed that this was the only time he had ever heard of a sermon being applauded in Lexington.[475]

Moore had managed a remarkable feat with his third attempt at publishing the *Blue Grass Blade:* as a brand-new hard-line Prohibition and anti-vice mouthpiece, the newspaper had united at least a portion of Kentucky's freethought community with a surprisingly large number of rural, moralistic, impressionable, and extremely conservative Christians in the Bluegrass State in battle not only against the liquor industry but in combat against what they perceived as immorality in general. He had

---

474 In searching through Fayette County's Circuit Court records from the early to mid-1890s for records of Charles Moore's legal problems, at the Kentucky Department of Libraries and Archives at Frankfort, I found more true bills for the "crime" of breaking the Sabbath than any other charge handed down to the commonwealth's attorney by Lexington grand juries.

475 *Blade,* II, 28, January 9, 1892; Moore, *Behind the Bars,* 173. McGarvey's written comments about his motivations for preaching the sermon appeared in the *Blade,* and apparently other city papers, a week later—in the *Blade's* case II, 29, January 16, 1892.

somewhere between 2500 and 4500 subscribers at least as far away as Frenchburg and West Liberty on the east and Middlesboro to the south,[476] mostly Baptists, Methodists, Stone-Campbell Christians, and members of the newly-organized Anderson, Indiana Church of God, all on crusade to stamp out the sale of liquor across America and their enthusiasm so fanatical that they were willing to put up cheerfully with a few infidel pronouncements so long as Moore kept his rhetoric against saloons, distilleries, race tracks, and bawdy houses up to a boil.

And yet from all appearances Moore's zeal was so blindingly hot that we must wonder if he actually believed some of the things he allowed himself to say. Did he really think that a vote for any Presidential candidate in the 1892 elections besides that of the fledgling post-Civil War Prohibition Party was a vote in favor of liquor, and that any such implied tolerance of strong drink was also a vote for whoredom and gambling? (If he did, and had lived a century later, he probably could have made a fortune as a Republican strategist, provided he could have been talked into joining the GOP.) Did he, who subsequently confessed to drinking small amounts of beer as medicine for nausea and who once admitted to bringing a bottle of wine home to Lucy Moore at Quakeracre as a gift,[477] genuinely accept the idea that a professing Christian who happened to drink one small glass of wine or brandy with his or her dinner, or one mug of cool beer after a long and hot day's farm labor, was a hypocrite fit only for the lowest circle of a fiery hell in which he himself didn't even believe?[478] Did he honestly evaluate a preacher's absolute worth as a human being entirely on the question of whether or not the cleric in question advocated complete Prohibition, and were churches who held to the nearly nineteen hundred year-old tradition of using wine as an element of Holy Communion rather than the good Dr. Welch's new pasteurized, vacuum-canned grape juice, all to be justifiably tarred with his same vitriol-saturated brush? And if, as John W. McGarvey claimed, he could not catch Moore in a lie, was it then Gospel truth that the editor's former employer, the *Lexington Transcript,* was nothing more than an "organ of

---

[476] The *Blade,* II, 21, November 21, 1891 contained letters from subscribers living in both locations.

[477] Moore, *Dog Fennel,* 12-13.

[478] *Blade,* II, 32, February 6, 1892.

Presbyterianism, Catholicism, whiskey, and Democracy" whose owner accepted a hefty bribe from a saloonkeeper to boost his candidacy for mayor of Lexington?[479] Between 1890 and 1894 Charles Moore asseverated all this and more besides through the pages of the *Blade,* mystifying his more thoughtful readers (both with and without religious beliefs) who couldn't comprehend the moral connection he made by rejecting *both* the fundamental, literalist doctrinal claims of Christianity *and* any professed expositor of Christianity who didn't live up to his own personal interpretation of the faith's highest doctrinal ideals. Even so, it was this very inconsistency that enabled him to make friends by the hundreds among Christian Prohibition zealots from the Ohio River to the Tennessee border. The infidel editor cultivated these partners and supporters to his work exactly as Sam Jones and other fire-eating American fundamentalist evangelists made and influenced theirs, by the use of cheer and smear rather than any balanced, thoughtful emphasis on Temperance, much less Prohibition, in his speech and writing, and if the success of the Prohibition cause in local-option city, ward, and precinct elections throughout rural and small-town central and eastern Kentucky in the 1890s was any indication of the end justifying the means he had all the affirmation he could ever have required to continue his journalistic efforts.

Was Charles Chilton Moore truly this contradictory, even hypocritical, in his beliefs and disbeliefs and his method of presenting them, to the point of resorting to the rabble-rousing techniques of a Great Revival camp-meeting evangelist to further the cause of Prohibition? His motives are a bit difficult to gauge. On one hand, it's easy for us to appreciate Moore's golden opportunity here to laugh up his sleeve at his detractors. After two failed attempts at maintaining a freethought periodical he had finally become a journalistic success by employing the same methods that religious conservatives had so often used against him as both a reporter and the editor of his own paper: the skillful incitement of a rather simple-minded mob with only one cause on its collective mind and one bit between its collective teeth. If he did manage to create and facilitate this entire state of affairs as some sort of clever, mocking intrigue, though, Moore proved himself to be not only an accomplished puppeteer but an excellent actor as well. He was never

[479] Ibid.

known, either before or afterward, to have exercised subtlety of this sort in any other aspect of his life, be it public or private, and for all his consistent bitterness he never otherwise stooped to this level of cynicism. Josephine Henry, who ought to have known, once declared in an essay that he simply didn't have any such guile in him.[480] Thus we must keep in mind that his early religious training and doctrinal heritage had made him anything *but* immune to writing out extremist statements and then attempting to prove them to be plain old common horse sense and logic, and so it is just as likely that he either simply got caught up just a little too far in his own rhetoric against liquor in the early 1890s, as Alexander Campbell did with his so-called Ancient Gospel and Ancient Order in the late 1820s—or unthinkingly allowed one or more of his new Prohibition allies of either Christian or infidel persuasion to put him in such a position. The reader may judge from the available evidence.

In any case, it is both ironic and wryly amusing that, in spite of Moore's dating of the *Blue Grass Blade's* issues according to the so-called Era of Man, counted from the 1600 death of Giordano Bruno, his very first formal and official "martyrdom" at the hands of Church and State in 1892 (or E. M. 292, in Moore's preferred accounting of time) couldn't be compared any more aptly to Bruno's horrible fate than it could to the persecutions of Galileo, Michael Servetus, or Ann Hutchinson. It rather conjured up shades of Savonarola raging through the streets of Florence against the pretensions of Lorenzo the Magnificent, with Moore himself in the role of Savonarola, and although no one ever got quite completely incinerated in the resultant Bluegrass Bonfire of the Vanities that he managed to kindle, the light from the blaze certainly made for easy, and intriguing, newspaper reading. Truth be told, Moore would have done well to borrow a page or two from another of Mark Twain's books. That being the 1889 work *A Connecticut Yankee in King Arthur's Court,* specifically, the Yankee's silent worries over the damage that the crass, sophomoric, and inflammatory rhetoric in his newspaper, the *Camelot Weekly Hosannah and Literary Volcano,* might ultimately cause—even though the rhetoric was entirely his own creation.

---

480 *Behind the Bars,* 234, quoting an article Mrs. Henry wrote for *Freethought Magazine* in April 1895.

We must now shift our attentions northeast of Lexington and Dog Fennel to Bourbon County and its governmental seat of Paris, by the last years of the nineteenth century caught right in the middle of its own ironic and intriguing juxtaposition. The Prohibition movement had been so successful within Bourbon's territories that, for better or worse, the area now actually belied its own name: each and every county voting precinct but one had by this period voted to "go dry," the sole exception to the populist tide being the city of Paris itself.[481] Added to this, Bourbon and virtually every other county in the Bluegrass, not to mention the whole of Kentucky and all other states across the South, were in the midst of another sort of turmoil as well. These were the years in which the Stone-Campbell Movement was slowly but inexorably splitting into moderate/liberal and conservative factions, ostensibly over disagreements about the propriety of musical instruments in church and organized missionary societies but with a good many more unspoken, even inarticulate, root causes also. During this period the conservatives mostly abandoned the title of Disciples to the moderates and liberals and styled themselves rather as Churches of Christ, or perhaps less often as independent Christian Churches.[482] In a good many instances this feud took the form of modest rural congregations versus well-to-do town churches as well, and so Bourbon County, Paris, and its First Christian Church were all thus caught in the crossfire of no less than four separate tensions all tangled together by chance: the "wets" versus the "drys" in county precinct elections, the Disciples of Christ versus the Churches of Christ among the historic old county congregations of the Stone-Campbell Movement, city streets versus rural farms, and the common folk versus those whom they perceived as rich and haughty "high hats." If a single one of these vari-

[481] *Blade,* II, 32, February 6, 1892, quoting a letter to Moore from an unnamed individual identified as "A Member in Paris."

[482] Two of the better historical chronicles of the nationwide and regional Disciple/a cappella Church of Christ splits are Leroy Garrett's *Stone-Campbell Movement* and Richard T. Hughes' *Reviving the Ancient Faith: the Story of Churches of Christ in America,* listed in this work's bibliography. The split more often associated with those congregations calling themselves "independent Christian Churches" actually occurred twenty to thirty years after the original Stone-Campbell division.

ables had somehow been spared the scrutiny of the court of public opinion in Bourbon County of the 1890s Charles Chilton Moore might never have gotten himself caught up at least in this one particular fiasco, and a church might have avoided being compared to a brothel.

On January 9, 1892 Moore announced that the *Blade* was now being produced by a new printing company, a little jobbing shop at the Bourbon County hamlet of Centerville and operated by a conservative Disciple, or Church of Christ, preacher named Robert Burns Neal.[483] In addition to his prejudices against instrumental church music and organized missionary societies Neal happened to nurse something of an obsession against the doctrines of the Church of Jesus Christ of Latter-Day Saints as well, and just like Alexander Campbell, Moore's grandfather Stone, and so many other of the Stone-Campbell Movement's less significant but more ambitious nineteenth-century exponents, he aspired to the status of an editor as well. With printing the *Blue Grass Blade,* then, Moore generously gave Neal the opportunity not only to turn a little extra profit with his press but to indulge in a bit of his own editorializing, and if the letters the preacher printed in the pages of the *Blade* denouncing churches that used musical instruments looked odd alongside Charles Moore's own infidel observations and pronouncements, well, Neal was, after all, a keen expositor at least of Mormon errors and inconsistencies, if not those of his own and other denominations. Besides, he was a good true-blue Prohibitionist, and although Moore couldn't have cared less about the musical-instrument or missionary-society controversies he would defend any preacher on the basis of the individual's commitment to the Prohibition cause. Even with Neal's safe anti-Mormon orthodoxy, though, once he mixed two separate printer's inks, as it were, that of Prohibition and that of the Stone-Campbell conservative-moderate controversy into Moore's personal third ingredient of infidel-

R.B. Neal (1847-1925)

[483] *Blade,* II, 28, January 9, 1892.

ity, one might venture a reasonable speculation that it was only a matter of time before an explosion occurred—Mormons, anti-Mormons, or no Mormons.

The final element of the batch of editorial nitroglycerin that Moore and Neal thus cooked up took the form of an aged member of the Paris First Christian Church, one W. T. Ficklin. As far as we can ascertain, Ficklin had no specific axes to grind against Mormons, musical instruments, or missionary societies; rather, he appears to have come to regard most hairsplitting biblical and dogmatic controversies with extreme impatience and contempt. He was, however, a strict, nearly pietistic moralist at least so far as the Prohibition cause was concerned, and after subscribing to the *Blade* as a Prohibition periodical he had quickly developed a keen appreciation both of Charles Moore's stalwart anti-liquor stance and his contemptuous yet practical and commonsense dismissal of obscure and insoluble religious questions. It galled him to the very soul that his pastor at Paris First Christian, J. S. Sweeney, and what seemed to him to be the majority of the congregation were moderates or perhaps even liberals on the liquor issue, very possibly opposed altogether to State- or Federally-enforced Prohibition, and worse, that one of the church's elders was actually a wholesale dealer in whiskey and other alcoholic beverages.[484] He began to supply Moore and Neal with inside information on those elements of the life of his church and pastor that he perceived as hypocritical—and within two weeks of Moore's announcement about Neal, fire touched gunpowder. The January 23 *Blue Grass Blade* was long remembered as the Issue that Ventilated Paris, a veritable Sam Jones *redux* in classic Charles Chilton Moore foaming-mad style too, and Moore himself later declared that it was "but a patching" of what he could say about the congregation.[485]

Moore specifically recalled falling foul of the Bourbon County ecclesiastical and judicial authorities for making one specific statement in the *Blue Grass Blade*: that "If I had a contract to bore for hell fire, I would pick the place where the earth's crust is thinnest and rig my derrick right in front of that Christian Church in Paris." He further related that a local barkeep added insult to injury by replying to this

[484] Moore, *Behind the Bars,* 171-172.
[485] *Blade,* II, 32, February 6, 1892.

suggestion with an offer to build a new saloon, to be called "The Derrick", right in front of the church, and to supply Moore with drinks on the house for the rest of his life.[486] While the "derrick" declaration was completely in character for him, though, the two indictments for malicious libel issued against Moore by the Bourbon County Circuit Court in March 1892 quoted passages from the January 23 issue of the *Blade* that were actually a good deal hotter—and in one case, racier. The court clerk's clarifying interpolations are in parentheses, the author's explanatory additions in brackets:

> That shebang calling itself the Christian Church of Paris (meaning thereby the certain congregation or religious society known as the Christian Church of Paris, Ky.) is run by a Republican preacher (meaning thereby... J. S. Sweeney), in cahoots with a lot of whiskey makers, sellers, and drinkers, that never would have been heard of in the world except for the riches they have accumulated from money more illy [*sic*] gotten than that of Judas Iscariot or Dives in hell [the "rich man" of the parable found in Luke 16:19-31].
>
> ...The Megowan Street house of Madam Belle Breezing [*sic*] (meaning thereby a certain bawdy house in the city of Lexington, Ky., known by that name), who was lately a member of the Broadway Christian Church Sunday School and whose loss of $1500.00 worth of diamonds has lately been published in the Lexington papers[—]probably as a paid local [advertisement] or possibly to be taken out in trade[—]or the toughest saloon in Lexington, is no engine for evil at all compared with that Paris Christian Church.[487]

For what it's worth, we cannot ascertain the truth of Moore's claim that Belle Brezing was a member of Lexington's Broadway Christian Church's Sunday School. From the data supplied by her biographer, Madam Brezing's religious leanings appear to have tended towards Roman Catholicism rather than Protestantism, though there can be no doubt that a great many of her girls came from good conservative Protestant—*and* Catholic—households with appropriately Pharisaical and unforgiving fathers and mothers. She once even made the comment that

---

[486] Ibid., 238. Quoting an 1899 Columbus, Ohio newspaper article on page 6 of the same work, Moore relates a slightly different variant of the words.

[487] *Commonwealth of Kentucky vs. C. C. Moore,* cases 3612 & 3613, 1892, Bourbon County, Kentucky Circuit Court records; Kentucky Department of Libraries and Archives.

as long as there were cruel fathers, she would have little trouble getting girls,[488] a thought that gives J. W. McGarvey's spluttering ire about the existence of Lexington "procuresses" an entirely new dimension. But the upshot of this entire mess—and that's exactly what it was, too, a loud, boisterous, confusing mess resembling nothing so much as the Book of Acts' description of the infamous riot at Ephesus, an entire city filled with confusion, some calling one thing, some another, and the greater part of the witnesses not even understanding truly what was going on[489]—was that almost the whole of Bourbon County's citizenry split into factions over the accusations Moore made against the church, from the standpoints of both Prohibition versus tolerance of liquor and liberal versus traditionalist Stone-Campbell Christianity. Even the most God-fearing conservatives in both disputes gloried over the town congregation's discomfiture. The only conceivable way Charles Moore could have advanced the cause of freethought in this instance was that he managed to get most or all of the Christians in one locale hating and fighting one another over the various tensions he had stirred up, but then again that wasn't really such a difficult task at any time with evangelicals. At any rate, Paris First Christian's members and supporters responded with predictable furious outrage and so Moore and W. T. Ficklin both wound up being arrested, tried, found guilty, paying fines, and spending time in the Bourbon County jail, in both cases for malicious libel against pastor Sweeney and the church's other leaders although Ficklin's fine and sentence were a good deal less harsh than Moore's. Robert Burns Neal appears to have gotten off without so much as a scratch, let alone an indictment, but Moore later recounted being taken into custody as the result of a four-man citizens' arrest at the Centerville train station after paying a visit to his new partner. One wonders what this strict, conservative Church of Christ divine thought about setting up the type for a report that speculated as to Belle Brezing settling up her classified-ad debts with "trade," but then again, his rural Bourbon County compatriots in faith and the Prohibition cause were probably so happy over the humiliation of the "big fancy town" church that Neal may even have justified the act within his own conscience as some sort of necessary evil for the greater advancement of the King-

[488] Thompson, 96-98.
[489] Acts 19:29-32.

dom of God. Be that as it may, in common with yet another riot described in the Book of Acts, the four vigilantes who arrested Moore appear to have bound themselves under something of a curse as well: to practice fisticuffs upon him until he revealed his journalistic source, at which time they would leave off personal violence of Moore to engage in a similar assault upon the source. The four were all professed Christians and members of the denounced church,[490] but evidently when they learned Ficklin's identity they withdrew their physical threats and satisfied themselves with committing both him and Moore to the custody of the jailer.

Moore paid his hundred-dollar fine, the bulk of it donated to him by fellow Prohibitionists mostly of Methodist persuasion, and he spent two months in jail at Paris. He described his reaction to his imprisonment differently at different times. In one instance he spoke of being treated with such courtesy and liberality by the jailer and his family that it was as if he were a political prisoner rather than a criminal.[491] Considering the division of opinion over both Prohibition and proper church customs within the various congregations of Bourbon County, it is quite likely that Moore *was* more or less a political prisoner too, and the jailer had to handle him with kid gloves simply in order to keep a sizable contingent of his voters happy. Yet in another instance Moore spoke of his two-month confinement as exercising an extreme adverse effect upon his nerves; to put in the long hours he scribbled out an early draft of the autobiography that he would later entitle *Behind the Bars,* yet by the time he had completed it he was so overwhelmed with despondency that he tore up the entire manuscript and cast it into the fire.[492] In still one more account, a letter to Robert Green Ingersoll in fact, he wrote of the unqualified horrors of being locked "in a stone and steel cell for two months with Negro thieves and murderers, for saying in the defence [*sic*] of good morals what every intelligent man in the Blue Grass region knows was true" and the grief and worry he endured from not being allowed so much as one day's respite from incarceration to visit Lucy, even under guard, when she was seized with a sudden

---

[490] Moore, *Behind the Bars,* 170-171. Scriptural reference is to Acts 23:12-14.
[491] Ibid., 171-172.
[492] Ibid., 6, quoting the Columbus, Ohio article referenced above.

illness.[493] No doubt the truth of the matter can be ascertained somewhere between the extremes of the three accounts, but it's difficult to determine exactly where.

Nonetheless, Moore's Paris jail time proved to be absolute gold for him. Whether through pure chance or with the direct involvement either of Moore himself or one of his infidel friends, some reporter from the pioneer American mouthpiece of "yellow" journalism, Joseph Pulitzer's sensationalistic *New York World,* got hold of the story. We cannot now determine the identity of the journalist in question, but we must wonder if it could have been the famous Nellie Bly, who was working for Pulitzer and traveling throughout the country in search of attention-grabbing headlines at that period. Regardless, though, when the story of Charles Moore and the Paris First Christian Church thus hit the Associated Press and made national news, all the controversies over Prohibition, Stone-Campbell worship practices, and Moore's shockingly coarse language pretty much went by the board and the issue was presented simply as that of a professing infidel newspaper editor whose interpretation of the First Amendment hung in the balance against that of a Kentucky Circuit Court intent on breaching the wall of separation guaranteed by the Constitution between Church and State in the United States of America and muzzling anyone who dared question its authority. Moore was able to work this fresh angle on the affair for all it was worth,[494] and suddenly, the *Blue Grass Blade* grew from a mere Kentucky Infidel-Prohibition paper to a multi-state, if never quite a national, mouthpiece for freethought. It actually earned him as many subscribers in Massachusetts and Nebraska as he had ever maintained in Kentucky,[495] and all because he had chosen once again to become an evangelist—or perhaps, an anti-evangelist.

Robert Burns Neal quietly dissolved his partnership with Moore at some time in the mid-1890s, and Moore replaced him with the printing firm of Veach and Walker of Lexington. Neal moved east, serving as pastor to Christian Churches and Churches of Christ in Carter, Lawrence, and Pike Counties in Kentucky and from 1902 until his death in

---

[493] Moore to Robert Green Ingersoll, May 14, 1894; quoted in the preface of *Behind the Bars,* iv.
[494] Moore, *Behind the Bars,* 170.
[495] Ibid., 6.

1925 publishing his own little anti-Mormon, pro-Campbell newspaper entitled *The Helper* and managing to place a few of his essays with at least one better-known Stone-Campbell journal, *The Christian Standard.* Even so, and though he was a founding member and an office-holder of the so-called National Anti-Mormon Missionary Association of the Churches of Christ, he seems never to have become the dreaded scourge of the Latter-Day Saints that he had aspired to be throughout his ministry.[496] The elderly W. T. Ficklin became one of Moore's few bona-fide converts to infidelity (if that isn't a contradiction in terms), serving as Moore's literary and journalistic agent for both the *Blue Grass Blade* and *The Rational View* in Bourbon County and its surrounding area[497] and outliving Moore by a few years. And northward in Cincinnati, Dr. J. B. Wilson must once again have rolled his eyes upward towards the heaven in which he did not believe, and sighed deeply. Having made lemonade out of a lemon and with a flourish at that, Charles Chilton Moore was happy and loquacious once again in his preacher's rut; rural Southern Christians had Sam Jones', Gipsy Smith's, and George Owen Barnes' bombastic speechifying and evangelistic crusades, while agnostics and atheists across Kentucky, Ohio, and the Midwest enjoyed the mirror-image comforts of the *Blue Grass Blade* and the eloquence and moral uprightness of Barton Stone's grandson. As Moore himself had observed when he had begun the *Blade's* second publication, it was a funny old world for a fact.[498]

Moore's skewering of Sam Jones, and perhaps Henry Howard Gratz as well, had gone a long way towards making him the most hated man in Lexington, at least for a while. Similarly, his pillorying of J. S. Sweeney and the Paris First Christian Church may have earned him a promotion to the most hated man in the Bluegrass Region.

---

[496] Further information on Robert Burns Neal as an eastern Kentucky anti-Mormon activist can be found on the website of Dale Broadhurst, *Joseph Smith's History Vault: Robert B. Neal Newspapers, Kentucky, Early 1900s.* World Wide Web, http://olivercowdery.com/smithhome/1900s/1895Neal.htm. See also Broadhurst's *Readings in Early Mormon History,* http://www.sidneyrigdon.com/wht/WhitRevl.htm.

[497] Moore, *Behind the Bars,* 172.

[498] *Blade,* I, 5, February 13, 1886.

For all that, though, even those who disagreed with his opinions on both Prohibition and Christianity kept buying his paper, if for nothing else the sheer entertainment value of the fiery periodical; even at its absolute tamest and driest it was never boring. But the statement that likely went the furthest to make Charles Chilton Moore the most hated man throughout Kentucky appeared in the *Blue Grass Blade* in March 1894, and in this case it is improbable that very many conservative believers in his home town, his region, or his state ever entirely forgave him for it. It certainly lost him a great deal, if not virtually all, of the moral support he had garnered from Christian Prohibitionists before and during the Paris controversy, and the argument could be made that every one of his subsequent arrests and trials was in some manner linked, either directly or indirectly, to the furor that this new outrage caused. Even so, just like the Paris fracas it had a back story, and a sordid one, at that. Perhaps most amazing of the case's aspects was the degree of Moore's personality it revealed, the mixture of erudition and coarseness, cunning and naïveté that J. B. Wilson so astutely discerned and which make so many of the editor's escapades, most particularly the Paris fight, difficult for us to fathom now.

We have had occasion already to speak of the political career of Moore's old boyhood friend W. C. P. Breckinridge. From the 1868 "rough spot" caused by his more or less progressive views on race, Breckinridge had rebounded sufficiently by 1884 to be elected to the United States House of Representatives from the Bluegrass district encompassing Fayette and its surrounding counties, and for a decade his constituents kept him ensconced comfortably in Congress as the kind of politician we would hear described today (by his backers at least) as a traditionalist, "family values-oriented" statesman. In keeping with Breckinridge family custom he remained a good, ostensibly strait-laced Presbyterian, and among his better-known public addresses were one to the Bourbon County Female College in 1872 in which he proclaimed "chastity" as "the foundation [and] corner-stone of human society" and another to the Sayre Institute, a similar school in Lexington, wherein he advised the young lady students to avoid "rumpled hair", rubbing their cheeks with flannel rags in order to give themselves a blush, "useless hand-shaking, promiscuous kissing, needless touches, and all exposures." They must make themselves able, he urged the girls, "to look every living being in the eyes, and yourself also, without conscious guilt." [499]

And all this might have been well and good if only Breckinridge hadn't secretly kept a mistress throughout his entire decade-long tenure in Congress. Her name was Madeline Valeria Pollard, and he had met and initiated a sexual relationship with her in connection with a trip to yet one more girls' college in the spring of his initial candidacy for Congress, when she was seventeen and he, forty-seven. (It will be remembered that, in the days before Josephine Henry's crusades for feminist legal reforms, the age of consent for a female in Kentucky was twelve.) Through ten years and trips back and forth from the Bluegrass to Washington D. C. Madeline Pollard had remained a quiet, more or less cloistered presence in Breckinridge's life, and within that time she had even borne him three children, at least one of whom survived when her story became public. The facts finally emerged after Breckinridge's wife, the former Issa Desha, died in 1892 and he remarried to a cousin, Louise Wing, ostensibly so that his new wife would thereby gain the affections of his legitimate children more easily. Pollard filed suit against him in Washington in late 1893 for breach of promise, claiming that he had pledged to marry her instead of Louise Wing, and that he had affirmed this intention to her in the presence, no less, of Julia Churchill Blackburn, widow of former Governor Luke P. Blackburn (whom we have already met both as chief state executive during James Cantrill's tenure as Lieutenant Governor, and as Belle Brezing's pardoner).

The Breckinridge-Pollard lawsuit was, for its time, the Kentucky equivalent of the modern exposure of the seemingly puritanical New York Governor Eliot Spitzer as a patron of high-priced call girls: in other words, the worst combined sexual-political scandal in the history of the Bluegrass Region. After a fall and winter rife with depositions, motions, allegations, and rulings, the trial began in Washington on March 8, 1894 and continued until April 14. Breckinridge prepared an aggressive defense including claims, some backed up with affidavits, that Pollard had had the reputation of a whore when he met her, and that in any case he certainly hadn't been her first sexual partner; that they were both people of "passion," and that she had been as much at

---

[499] Klotter, *The Breckinridges,* 160-161.

fault as he; and that after he had arrived in Washington and had secured her a job in the United States Department of Agriculture (where, incidentally, Moore's own son Charles III had begun a career as a chemist around this very period, very likely with assistance from the same political source) she had clung to Breckinridge like a parasite, threatening alternately to ruin him completely, kill him, or kill herself if he wouldn't marry her. Among the attorneys on his legal team were his Lexington law partner, John Todd Shelby, and even one of his own grown sons by Issa Desha. But for all Breckinridge's self-righteous posturing, Pollard's lawyers successfully presented him to Court and jury as evil, lecherous "Grandpa Breckinridge" taking advantage of a girl less than half his age and then trying to claim her as his "daughter" to Washington society. The jury found him at fault, and awarded Pollard a judgment of $15,000, less than a third of the amount she had asked for but in that day the equivalent of three years' salary for a Congressman.[500]

Breckinridge was expelled from his family's Presbyterian congregation for four months for his sin (he might consider himself lucky that he didn't have to sit in the church's "creepie chair" like Robert Burns had in Scotland, more than a century before and for the same offense; one of the accusations levied against the Congressman was that he had once gone to see Pollard right after teaching a Sunday School class)[501], but for the better part of a year after the trial no Bluegrass newspaper editor could go wrong, in the eyes of Lexington readers, by condemning the transgressor with the most vitriolic and descriptive rhetoric imaginable. The Congressman was vilified in turn as a self-confessed libertine, an insult to every pure woman and a menace to every virgin, a rapist, and a wild beast of prey, and one Lexington paper even observed that he had come under attack by literally everyone in the city from preacher to prostitute.[502] That he attempted to campaign that same year for yet one more term in the House of Representatives is a testament to the brass in at least one portion (or two) of his anatomy, and the very fact that he lost his seat in Congress that fall by only 255 votes out of a

---

[500] Ibid., 161-164; Pollard, 17-37.
[501] Klotter, *The Breckinridges,* 165.
[502] Ibid., 164-165.

19,000-vote canvass[503] very well may go to prove the philosopher and semiotician Umberto Eco's claims about the existence of the process he calls ostension: it's hard for us to understand how the era's males, who alone in nineteenth-century Kentucky were permitted to vote, could have communicated any support for Breckinridge whatsoever between one another, and gotten away with it, except through winks and nudges.

Thus to return to our story: it was only to be expected that Charles Chilton Moore and the *Blue Grass Blade* would have a heyday with the whole affair, especially since this was the very sort of hypocrisy on which Moore loved to pounce. As luck would have it, though, Moore actually succeeded in drawing at least some of the furor away from Breckinridge and onto himself and his paper, right in the middle of the trial to boot—and leaving us scratching our heads, wondering if he possessed some uncanny gift to choose the very worst possible words at the very worst possible time. Witness a mere two lines' worth of Moore's editorial in the *Blade* of March 18, 1894, when the Breckinridge trial had been in progress for only ten of its thirty-seven days and Lexington newspapers were reporting new testimony and developments as soon as they came in by telegraph from Washington: "When I say that Jesus Christ was a man just like I am, and had a human father and mother exactly like I had, some of the pious call it blasphemy. When they say that Jesus Christ was born as the result of a sort of Breckinridge-Pollard hyphenation between God and a Jew woman, I call it blasphemy; so you can see, there is a standoff."[504]

Again we must repeat: considering the news, the times, and the seasons, Moore couldn't have put together a poorer combination of words in this instance if he had searched meticulously through the *Oxford English Dictionary* from A to Z in order to find and assemble them. It wasn't enough for him to say that he disbelieved the story of the Virgin Birth of Christ, or even that he considered it to be a myth on the level of ancient Egypt's Most Blessed Isis and her child Horus, any

---

[503] Ibid., 169.

[504] *Commonwealth of Kentucky versus C. C. Moore,* Fayette County Circuit Court case # 154, April 1, 1894; Kentucky Department of Libraries and Archives. The offensive quote is also recounted in Moore, *Behind the Bars,* 229, but unfortunately, as with several other of the quotes that subsequently got Moore in trouble, the relevant *Blade* issues have not survived in any existing collections.

of the rest of Kersey Graves' claimed sixteen crucified saviors throughout the history of the world, or for that matter, the ancient Greeks' Leda and the swan. That much restraint might have saved him a great deal of trouble. Even if he had repeated Thomas Paine's eighteenth-century Deists' jibe about the Virgin Mary being "debauched by a ghost"[505] he might have fared better at the hands of his readers, so long as he had noted *The Age of Reason* as his source. But no, nothing else would do for Moore but to try out this brand-spanking-new Kentucky metaphor and put God in the position of lecherous old "Grandpa Breckinridge," the Virgin Mary in the role of the possibly opportunistic and more than likely highly passionate Madeline Pollard, and the baby Jesus as the illegitimate result of their illicit sexual relationship, and then set the comparison out upon a reading public already so humiliated and outraged by their Congressman and his paramour's antics that they were spoiling for a flight with any and all who dared pick one with them. We have noted earlier that Moore recalled staring up the wrong end of so many big pistols that he had learned to remain as calm in that predicament as when looking through opera glasses at a circus, and there can be little doubt that he got much of his practice at this feat over the remainder of the month of March. It is certain that he received death threats again, at least.[506]

From all outward appearances, Moore simply thought he was being very witty and that his novel turn of phrase had merely gotten off a good joke at the expense of Kentucky religionists. It seems never to have occurred to him that his "hyphenation" observation could be at any way at all inflammatory, even as daily telegraph reports from Washington rubbed more salt into the wounds that the Breckinridge scandal—and now his own comment—had opened in the Bluegrass. Thus when he was finally arrested on April 9, a few days away from the windup of the Breckinridge trial, on a so-called nuisance warrant for blasphemy with the charge having been presented to the Fayette County Grand Jury by Edward Lush Southgate Jr., a leading Methodist minister in Lexington,[507] it was Moore's own turn to be outraged. In his mind there were no mitigating circumstances whatsoever on either his

---

[505] Paine, 156.

[506] Moore to Ingersoll, May 14, 1894; from *Behind the Bars,* vi.

[507] *Commonwealth vs. Moore,* 154, April 1, 1894, KDLA.

side of the question or Southgate's. He was being persecuted once more by a corrupt judicial system and a local government bound and determined to do away not only with the wall of separation between Church and State but with the First Amendment altogether, simply for exercising his right to say that he believed that Jesus had a father and mother just like any human being had. He refused to give bond for himself although he could have avoided incarceration completely if he had done so, and thus spent three more months in jail, as he put it, "to show plainly to the world that the Church [would still] imprison a man for his religious opinions...just as it once did when it had unrestricted power [ellipse added]."[508] Insofar as this went, he was largely correct in his basic analysis of the situation, but again, he seems never to have made the connection, much less given any allowances for it, that his accusers' better judgment might have been clouded by sheer shock at his remark's utter tastelessness.

Even so, Moore himself was opportunistic at least to this degree: he or, more likely, one of his friends in his behalf, somehow contacted the Associated Press with this new story, and so once again he and his *Blue Grass Blade* became an item of national interest for the *New York World* and more responsible papers alike. Now Lexington and the Bluegrass State again owned not only the fastest horses and the prettiest women in the country, but a randy old billygoat for a Congressman to boot—with the whole portrayal topped off by the tale of a freethinking newspaper editor determined to have his say about the Congressman and gambling and immorality and the cause of separation of Church and State all, despite religious persecution. Too, now that he had been arrested formally on the rather nebulous and abstract charge of blasphemy rather than the more specific malicious libel of the Paris affair, Moore felt that in beating (or for that matter, even losing) this case he had a genuine opportunity to set an important precedent in both State and Federal Constitutional law. And so some time around the last week of April, while he was still cooling his heels in jail, he eagerly wrote to his old acquaintance Robert Green Ingersoll in New York, asking him to come to Kentucky and represent him at his anticipated blasphemy trial. After all, Ingersoll had already defended *pro bono* the only man brought to trial on the charge of blasphemy thus far in the history of the

[508] Moore, *Behind the Bars,* 172.

United States under the Constitution, the ex-preacher Charles B. Reynolds of New Jersey, and had even paid Reynolds' fine himself when the trial judge instructed the jurymen that they could not rule on the question of the constitutionality of New Jersey's archaic pre-Revolutionary blasphemy law but only as to whether or not the law as it stood had been violated.[509] There can be little doubt that Moore hoped for the same, or at least a similar, result in Kentucky, and with the Great Agnostic's help a great deal of positive publicity for the free-thought cause.

He got the shock and hurt of his life when Ingersoll flatly turned down his request. In retrospect it is not difficult for us to see why the Silver-tongued Infidel would have done so. For one thing, the 1886 Chicago Haymarket Riots had put the cause of infidelity into an extremely bad light in the urban North, equating freethought with Anarchism in the minds of many Northerners and which prejudice Ingersoll had been unwilling to risk exacerbating by his presence as a celebrity attorney at the Haymarket defendants' trial. Another factor was the number of technical differences between the Reynolds and Moore blasphemy cases. The Reynolds blasphemy case, which had been tried in New Jersey that same year, had involved an idealistic ex-minister, admittedly not entirely unlike Moore, who had attempted to hold a Freethinkers' Conference in rural New Jersey much as Methodists and other, newer denominations conducted outdoor camp meetings. Reynolds' tent had been vandalized and he himself pelted with rotten eggs, and he had finally been jailed and charged with New Jersey's "blue" anti-blasphemy statute at the insistence of a mob. It is probable that the Great Agnostic would have been every bit as willing to defend Charles Moore in similar circumstances, or for that matter if he had written only that which he, and even so thoughtful an infidel writer as Josephine Henry, attempted to claim that he had: Jesus was merely a man with an earthly father and mother.[510] But, although Ingersoll himself appreciated wit as much as any man and perhaps more than some, he had to have seen, or at least sensed, that Moore's Breckinridge-Pollard remark was a powder keg that could blow up right in his face if he attempted to

---

[509] See Ingersoll, "Trial of C. B. Reynolds for Blasphemy." From the Collected Writings, World Wide Web, http://www.infidels.org/library/historical/robert_ingersoll/.

[510] April 1895 *Freethought Magazine* article quoted in *Behind the Bars,* 235.

journey to Kentucky and defend the editor for having made it. To most people both then and later it was obvious that Moore's jibe was as much shockingly egregious bad taste as it was religious heresy, and while bad taste was no more a felony than was blasphemy under the Constitution, and Ingersoll remained a committed crusader for the First Amendment in spite of his hesitance in the days of the Haymarket tragedy, he realized that the privileges of the Amendment carried with them the necessity for a modicum of common sense and responsibility. Any defense he made for Moore would thus be an attempted justification for careless, even frivolous, journalism more than for free speech or separation of Church and State, and so he would have felt it incumbent to stay aloof from the entire controversy. Even so, he seems to have tried to put a better face on the matter, and his own opinions of it, than perhaps he should have. He gave Moore the same essential excuse that he had given the Haymarket rioters' defense team eight years before for his private, rather than public, support for their cause, the possibility that his very presence at the Chicago trials as a freethought spokesman might be prejudicial against the defense's case[511]:

> New York City
> 400 Fifth Ave.
>
> May 8, 1894
>
> My dear Mr. Moore:
>
> I am sorry that you are in trouble—sorry that you may have touched the feelings of your neighbors—but I do not think you have violated any law—though you may have lacked courtesy.
>
> It is impossible for me to take your case. My time is already mortgaged. Besides, if I should appear it might injure you by fanning into flames all the bigotry of your section. I guess you will not need much help.
>
> Yours always,
> R. G. Ingersoll [512]

[511] Jacoby, 180-184.

[512] Ingersoll to Moore, May 8, 1894; quoted in the preface of *Behind the Bars,* iii.

Moore was still supervising the publication of the *Blade* though he was behind bars, and on May 14 he gave vent to possibly the bitterest rhetoric of his life in his open reply to Ingersoll's rejection of his case. To quote the entire missive would amount to an overkill of proof, but we might make the observation that the letter's defining thoughts centered principally around the fact that Moore simply could not comprehend Ingersoll's suggestion that he "lacked courtesy":

> Where did you get the idea that I had "lacked courtesy"? You are the first man that has ever suggested it. Certainly no Kentucky infidel has said it, and if Christians may have said it, are you absolutely certain that the whole Christian world has concurred in the sentiment that you were absolutely courteous?
>
> Though I am a gentleman to the manor—and manner—born, I have lately worked with Negroes, and I have been imprisoned and treated as if I were an outlaw; and if, under these circumstances, I may not have lived up to my Chesterfield so punctiliously as you who have lived on grand stages and "Fifth Avenue" may have done, is a little lack of courtesy a thing for which I ought to be imprisoned?
>
> I hope that your time is all of you that is "mortgaged," and that your soul is not in the same fix, with the devil as mortgagee. It was so considerate in you to suggest that your presence might injure me by fanning into flame all the bigotry in this section.[513]

Again, though Moore was likely entirely correct in his interpretation of United States Constitutional law, in terms of discretion—and we must employ a very tired cliché here for lack of a better one—he absolutely did *not* get it. In his economy, influenced as it was by traditional Stone-Campbell journalism, "courtesy" meant hospitality to visitors and the proper practice of manners in face-to-face discussions and similar encounters; the printed page, and what was and was not acceptable to put on it, was an entirely different arena altogether. Hence seems to have occurred his apparent confusion, and resultant rage, over Ingersoll's observation. But at any rate, although he broke with Ingersoll completely over the Great Agnostic's response to him, he actually found a friend in the one place he did not anticipate, the Kentucky judicial system itself. There was only one statute on Kentucky's books that could be classified as anything resembling an anti-blasphemy law,

[513] Moore to Ingersoll, May 14, 1894; Ibid., iii-vi.

and that specifically involved a misdemeanor: profane swearing, or in the vernacular, "cussing," in public.[514] And so finally, as the summer 1894 term of Circuit Court in Fayette County approached, Moore agreed to be released from custody on the security of bondsmen, among them the patient, longsuffering Moses Kaufman; then Circuit Judge Watts Parker ruled that, strictly speaking, Moore's Breckinridge-Pollard comment hadn't broken any extant Kentucky law, and summarily threw out the entire case against him. The decision didn't make Rev. Southgate or his supporters any too happy, and some evidence suggests that the preacher or at least his lawyers made an attempt to get it overturned by the State Court of Appeals, but for all practical purposes Judge Parker's ruling set the precedent on blasphemy that Kentucky State law has followed ever since.[515]

Charles Moore was a free man once again and as full of vituperation as ever, now directed as much against both Robert Ingersoll and W.C.P. Breckinridge as it had ever been aimed at John Jay Cornelison, Sam Jones, Henry Howard Gratz, the Paris First Christian Church, Belle Brezing's Upper and Megowan Street bordellos, or the most disreputable saloons in Lexington. In the blush of his judicial victory he even made a public proposal to Madeline Pollard to accompany him on a lecture tour, proclaiming that "she knew more than all Breckinridge's lawyers put together, and that she did not lie once like all of them did."[516] In the simplistic, black-and-white fashion in which he viewed both his own actions and the causes to which he subscribed, though, he probably never realized the precariousness of his position at this point any more than he could comprehend his neighbors' fury over his Breckinridge-Pollard quip. In good Alexander Campbell media-tradition fashion, he seems honestly to have believed he had written in his *Blade* editorials only that which was plain common sense to all intelligent readers, and yet like Dr. Wilson, any of those same intelligent readers familiar with his circumstances and those of his opponents could see that he had brought at least a portion of his troubles on him-

---

514 Lexington, Kentucky, attorney Bob Treadway to the author, August 29 & 30, 2007. The law in question has subsequently been limited to entail the specific offense of personal harassment.

515 Ibid.; also *Commonwealth vs. Moore,* case 154 Fayette County. A complete copy of Judge Parker's ruling can be found in *Behind the Bars,* 229-232.

516 *InterOcean,* January 4, 1895.

self in both instances. He had unnecessarily alienated friends and multiplied enemies, and with his judicial victory in the Lexington blasphemy case his detractors gained all the more impetus to keep their eyes peeled for just one more of the *Blade's* literary excesses. And if state charges of libel or blasphemy couldn't shut Moore up, there were always the Federal obscenity statutes, called the Comstock Laws after the obsessively single-minded little grocery clerk and small-time politician, Anthony Comstock, who had gotten them pushed through Congress in 1873 and wrangled for himself a veritable lifetime government appointment as special postal inspector to boot—if only an obliging Federal judge or a government postal censor would classify one of Moore's peppery, off-the-cuff editorial volleys as obscene. Of course, Charles Moore being Charles Moore, they didn't have long to wait for the perfect chance to arraign him once again.

It is possible that, in some sense, Josephine Henry may have felt partially responsible for Moore's first actual brush with Federal, as opposed to State, justice, though it was an escapade that neither he nor she ever made part of their personal memoirs. The issue at stake in this case was women's rights, however, and men's too, for that matter; and in spite of Moore's more or less open disagreement with her over the style of language appropriate for a freethinkers' newspaper (she once chided him for his "profligate use of the letter D," meaning that he said "damn" and "damned" a little too often for her sensibilities, and he replied—completely in character—that what other people thought about what he said didn't amount to a tinker's damn to him[517]) his personal loyalty to her, and in turn her cause, was unquestioned.

The fact is that, whether his activism for this issue was the result of his private convictions or merely a favor to a longtime personal friend whom he wished to shield, like some chivalric Southern knight, from the kind of legal difficulties that he had already experienced, in 1895 Charles Chilton Moore agreed to serve as the retail agent in central Kentucky for an extremely controversial British pamphlet: *The Law of Population, Its Consequences, and Its Bearing Upon Human Conduct and Morals,* written by the English Theosophist and social reform crusader Annie Besant. This pioneer work, roundly condemned by

[517] *Blade,* VI, 52, October 3, 1897.

conventional moralists in Besant's home country as well as in the United States, was among the first to explore the ramifications of the problems experienced by single families, nations, and an entire world with too many children to care for adequately. Among the solutions Besant suggested and described were such methods of birth control as existed in that day and age: the women's options of the insertion of small soaked sponges as pessaries before intercourse and douching with water and/or vinegar afterwards, and for males the employment of the *baudruche* (translated from the French variously as "rubber skin," "goldbeater's skin," or "bubble," of course meaning a condom).[518] Under United States statutes as they stood in this era (and indeed, the wording of our Federal obscenity laws has changed surprisingly little from that day to this; rather, the terms "obscene" and "obscenity" are interpreted much more narrowly by the courts than they were years ago[519]), anything that could be considered even tangentially to advocate birth control was equated with abortion and was strictly off limits for the mails, and so *The Law of Population* had been classified by the postal service as nonmailable matter ever since its first publication in 1877. It is therefore impossible for us to determine how and where Charles Moore obtained his cache of Besant pamphlets in 1895. The notoriety that his 1892 and 1894 arrests and trials had given him had enabled him to establish correspondence and generally engage in what we would now call networking with other infidel newspaper editors across the country, but it's likewise difficult for us to believe that Josephine Henry wasn't also involved in this particular case at least to some degree.

Whether or not Mrs. Henry was his silent partner in the Besant venture, though, in Charles Moore's mind the entire question of birth control seems to have been, in a large sense, one and the same with his condemnation of liquor: drunken fathers and mothers, and parents in extreme poverty without adequate means of family planning, both made for housefuls of starving, neglected children. Although he exhibited as much naïveté as most Prohibitionists of that day in his belief that governmental regulation somehow had the power to stop the sale

[518] Besant, 32-37; quoted in *U.S. vs. Moore,* case # 5349, 1895, National Archives.

[519] Ernst and Schwartz, 31.

and use of alcohol altogether, he knew that neither he, nor the pious platitudes mouthed in the "marriage manuals" of the day, nor anyone or anything else could prevent husbands and wives—or indeed any willing male and female—from having sex just because of the biological consequences of their actions. Thus, the sensible exercise of birth control was a matter of plain logic to him and, characteristically, he could not understand why everyone else could not grasp the idea as readily as he did—even Anthony Comstock and his nationwide network of postal inspectors. And so with the June 30, 1895 issue of the *Blue Grass Blade* he began to run this announcement, accompanied by selected readers' endorsements:

> I am the agent for Mrs. Annie Besant's book "Law of Population [*sic*]," which tells married women how not to have children when they don't want them—or any other woman, for that matter—under such circumstances as you would suppose they would have them. Though this book was suppressed in England, where it was first published, and where Mrs. Besant lives, 35,000 of them have been sold, and I will send it to any address that will send me 25 cents, with all possible privacy. It will not come from Lexington, or from anywhere near here, and without having anything about it that will attract the attention of anybody; [but] like Buck's bedbug, it will get there just the same.
>
> I have read the book, and as evidence that I think that I am assisting in the circulation of a good and proper book, I am ready to show it to any authorized officer of this state or city.... [but] I will use every precaution to keep secret the names of parties who order the book, not that there is any crime in their buying it or my selling it, but simply because it is a delicate matter
>
> Charles C. Moore,
> Agent for "Law of Population [*sic*]" [520]

Of course, there wasn't a thing about birth control in *The Law of Population* that Belle Brezing, Lettie Powell, or any other madam in Lexington didn't know about already. The welfare of the girls that a substantial number of upright men both within and outside the city kept in business, and whose existence J. W. McGarvey had so deplored from the pulpit in November 1891, depended upon that fact. Yet it horrified

---

[520] Matter from the June 30, 1895 issue of the *Blade* taken from affidavits in *U.S. versus Moore,* case # 5349, National Archives, Southeastern Division.

many of these same upstanding male citizens to think that, with twenty-five cents and Charles Moore's help, their wives and daughters could now be privy to such physiological secrets themselves, and even the traditionalist Christian Prohibitionists who remained as subscribers to the *Blade* after Moore's Breckinridge-Pollard comment were once again bewildered and outraged by what seemed to them another complete moral inconsistency on Moore's part. Even if he had made fun of W. C. P. Breckinridge, Madeline Pollard, Jesus Christ, and the Virgin Mary all, how could such an intrepid crusader against hypocrisy, or for that matter any individual who claimed to be a moralist, advocate something as sordid as *birth control?* Thus as Bluegrass citizens once again started to complain and Moore's already-established enemies began to lick their chops, Lexington's nervous postmaster, William McChesney, brought postal inspector W. J. Vickery in on the case to suppress Moore's Besant ad, as well as, apparently, another related article in the July 28 issue of the *Blade* entitled "Shall We Or Shall We Not? That's the Question." Yet in spite of this setback, and though he had to have known he was skating on the thinnest possible legal ice, Moore persisted in running this final *Blade* advertisement on September 29, accompanied by a brief note advising readers that they could obtain relevant information on actual birth control techniques in the third chapter of the offending pamphlet:

Besant's "Law of Population"

> Our "Uncle Samuel," who lives at Washington D.C., having suppressed my other advertisement for Mrs. Besant's book, "The Law of Population," for which I am agent—price 25 cents to any address—I insert this advertisement in its place. From time to time I will print some of the endorsements of the book that are written to me by good and intelligent people. — Charles C. Moore[521]

And so the erstwhile Savonarola was arrested again in October, this time by Federal authorities, and for one reason alone: no obscenity as we would define the term in modern times, not even so much as he had expressed with his 1892 comparison of the Paris Christian Church to Belle Brezing's whorehouse, but simply because he had attempted a

[521] *U.S. versus Moore,* case # 5349, National Archives, Southeastern Division.

frank discussion of birth control, and had advertised a small manual for it, in the *Blue Grass Blade.* Though his stance and persistence, and more so those of Margaret Sanger and H. L. Mencken a generation later, were the very reasons the courts ultimately eased and narrowed the interpretation of obscenity laws, it is actually no wonder that Moore's autobiographical writings never mention this particular arrest. If he had ever attempted to give any coherent description of its causes and circumstances he knew he would probably fall foul of Anthony Comstock and United States justice yet once more. Calling on postmaster McChesney, postal inspector Vickery, Lexington mail clerk G. R. Warren and mailman Andrew Scott, private complainants E. H. Warren, M. N. Bass, and George Denny, and even the printer E. B. Veach, as witnesses, the United States Attorney for the Western District of Kentucky levied against the editor no less than ten counts of sending obscene matter through the mails, each specifying either the Besant pamphlet, one or both of Moore's advertisements, or one or another of the *Blade* articles supporting Besant's work. A jury promptly found him guilty of all counts at the Federal Court in Louisville in October; the wording of the Comstock statutes, equating the prevention of conception with abortion and strictly interpreting the advocacy of both as obscenity,[522] made any other verdict virtually impossible. Judge John Watson Barr imposed a fine of one thousand dollars but promptly (and considering the times and legal climate, extremely generously) suspended it on the condition that Moore would promise not to advertise *The Law of Population* any more. Furthermore, the Judge even agreed to dismiss the case entirely in twelve months' time for the editor's "good" behavior. Whether for himself, or in a gallant effort to maintain a lady's honor, Moore appears to have acquiesced meekly, and his career as a birth control advocate was over.[523] Though he still regarded the idea of calm and peaceful submission with every bit as much contempt as did Shakespeare's Mercutio, in this case there was nothing else he could do.

---

[522] Ernst and Schwartz, 31-33.

[523] *U.S. versus Moore,* case # 5349, National Archives, Southeastern Division.; see also *In Memoriam,* 19.

As soon as Judge Barr's sentence was pronounced, Veach and Walker dissolved their printing contract with Moore and absolutely refused to work with him or the *Blade* any further. For the briefest instance he was at a complete loss as to how to keep the newspaper alive, but at this crucial juncture one of his younger supporters, a Mt. Sterling, Kentucky printer about the same age as Moore's sons Leland and Brent and named James Edward Hughes, offered to become both his typesetter and his partner. After making an initial effort to establish a jobbing office in Lexington Hughes moved his printing operations northward to Cincinnati for a time, and in mailing the *Blade* from across the Ohio River rather than from a Kentucky address within Judge Barr's jurisdiction he and Moore seem to have believed that they had established a modicum of safety for themselves and their newspaper.[524] As it turned out, this wasn't exactly so, but then again Moore had never yet softened his editorial style either. Now all his rhetorical shortcomings, and the legal problems he had heretofore experienced because of them, seemed to come together against him. The resultant conglomeration of cause and effect earned him a five-month term in prison and the leisure finally to write his autobiography.

As with so many other of Moore's adventures and misadventures, we have a back story here as well, beginning with his September 1890 establishment of the third version of the *Blade* as a hard-line Prohibition mouthpiece and a curious, almost schizophrenic love-hate relationship he maintained until perhaps 1896 or 1897 with a professor and dean at Georgetown College named James Jefferson Rucker. Like Charles Moore, Rucker claimed to be a strict Prohibitionist, and on that sole basis he subscribed to and otherwise supported the *Blade;* unlike the editor, Rucker was a (supposedly) devout Christian, a Baptist of the old-fashioned type that had first founded the college at Georgetown back in 1829, and his letters to Moore published in the *Blade* during the early 1890s are a bizarre mix of Temperance/Prohibition advocacy and support and the hottest imaginable righteous indignation against Moore's expressed scorn for the idea of Scriptural inerrancy. Along with a Lexington Disciple leader named James W. Zackary, Rucker

[524] Taken from James Hughes' recollections of his partnership with Moore, published in the *Blade,* XVII, 7, June 7, 1908.

seemed literally to want use the *Blade's* "Letters to the Editor" section as a soapbox to argue with Moore over the Bible, and yet Moore was a great deal more patient with and courteous to the Professor than he was either to Zackary or to most other *Blade* correspondents of the same ilk.[525] Rucker taught all three of Charles and Lucy Moore's sons at Georgetown,[526] and as we have already noted, Charles III had proven so adept at his scientific studies that he had qualified for a position as a chemist with the United States Department of Agriculture at Washington (though state and national politics being what they were, he had probably had to depend on the now-disgraced Congressman Breckinridge's help in securing it). Even Lucille Moore, youngest of the family, had attended a girls' preparatory school that Rucker and his wife had operated in Scott County,[527] and by her late teens she was well on her way to a career as a musician and music teacher. Thus, even though Moore and Rucker appeared to be at a word and a blow all the time, up to this point they seem to have nourished a genuine respect for one another.

Perhaps the first souring of the Moore-Rucker relationship occurred when Rucker got the idea that, if an infidel newspaper could represent the Prohibition cause with as much fanfare as did the *Blade,* a Christian paper ought to be able to do the job better. Accordingly he began publishing his own periodical, the *Temperance Star,* in Georgetown, but the new paper cut such a shabby figure in comparison to the flamboyance of the *Blade* that, according to one contemporary observer, no one who lived more than ten miles outside the city ever even heard of it, much less subscribed to it. The *Temperance Star's* failure gave Moore the occasion to bestow a fair quantity of mostly good-natured but characteristically rough-edged ribbing upon the head of its Christian editor, but no real breach between the two men seems to have occurred until a rich Bluegrass distiller, John M. Atherton, gave charitable donations amounting to $7000 to both Georgetown College and Rucker's home church—and Rucker, as representative of both, cheerfully and gratefully accepted the money. We have already seen the effects that such acts of apparent hypocrisy on the part of either a professed Christian or

---

[525] E.g. *Blade,* II, 21-22, November 21 & 28, 1891.
[526] Moore, *Behind the Bars,* 177, quoting an article by Dr. J. B. Wilson.
[527] See Moore's replies to letters, *Blade,* II, 32, February 6, 1892.

an avowed Prohibitionist had on Moore's good nature, and so now he bestowed upon Rucker as thorough a blasting within the pages of the *Blade* as he had ever given Sam Jones, J. S. Sweeney, or the Paris First Christian Church. Even the objective Dr. J. B. Wilson, the severity of whose criticisms against Moore was matched only by the closeness of his personal friendship to the editor, conceded these basic facts, observing that, if Moore had made any false or libelous claims about Rucker's character, the professor had enjoyed every opportunity to obtain legal redress.[528]

Finally, though, having had a high old time reporting and editorializing about the Rucker-Atherton-Georgetown controversy but still smarting from the suspended fine and the promise of "good" behavior coerced from him by Judge Barr, in the summer and fall of 1897—approximately a year after Barr had honored his own pledge and dismissed the 1895 obscenity case altogether[529]—Moore let slip within the pages of the *Blade* some honest but, for the times, dangerously unguarded opinions and observations about the failures of conventional morality as a final solution for humanity's sexual problems. Unfortunately, only one issue of the *Blade* from this period survives, Volume VI, Number 52 from October 3, 1897, and in it we find Moore in the midst of this new hullabaloo rather than at its inception. Unlike Moore's 1895 Louisville court writs, most nineteenth- and early twentieth-century Federal obscenity indictments were maddeningly evasive about specifics, and so we cannot ascertain in this case exactly what Moore said that touched off a brand-new round of scandal. The most culpable surviving statement, though, is from a Moore essay in the July 18 issue of the newspaper, which an Anderson County, Kentucky, lawyer and jurist named Farris R. Feland repeated thusly in a letter to the editor that Moore published on October 3: "If the sexes may enjoy the heart and brain qualities of each other, and do it with genuine pleasure and profit to themselves, there is no reason why they may not, and with the same pleasure and profit, enjoy each other sexually, and so far from having any priestly mummery to sanction such enjoyment, have it with no more civil sanction than is now necessary for a mere

---

[528] Moore, *Behind the Bars,* 177, quoting Wilson's article in the *Blade,* February 16, 1899.

[529] *U.S. versus Moore,* case # 5349, National Archives, Southeastern Division.

social and intellectual friendship between congenial men and women."[530]

It's hard to say whether we should infer any old, longstanding regrets on Moore's part here. Could he have been thinking of the charming Kate Pendleton, now as gray-haired as he, and perhaps a temptation that both he and she piously but regretfully resisted for the sake of God, W. K. Pendleton, Alexander Campbell, and conventional morality back in the days before a terrible war had destroyed both Moore's theism and his idealism? Whether or not this was the case, if Moore truly espoused such sentiments we must once again wonder over his condemnation of the "immorality" of James Lane Allen's *The Choir Invisible,* which appeared in print this same year, and even many of his *Blade* readers at the time must have been mystified once again by his simultaneous strict denunciation of prostitutes and brothels along with liquor and his apparent approval, at least in the abstract, of this supposedly "higher" form of sexual relationship. Feland, who was in fact a faithful supporter of Moore through thick and thin, couldn't help indulging in a bit of pointed wit to illustrate the droll irony of the situation even while attempting to warn Moore of the risks he was taking with his pen:

> I wish you would look over, in the clear afterglow that follows that sort of surging "hot stuff" from the brain of a genius and a reformer, the...extract from your comment...in the *Blue Grass Blade* dated July 18.... Now, do you not think that the theory there stated is a little broad, if taken without qualification, and is, if not stated with such clearness and circumstantiality (sic) that it hardly merits any saving qualification, unless we wring the meaning from the plainest kind of phrasing? Understand, I am not complaining for myself, nor indeed, complaining at all.... But will you not remember, do you refuse to consider, that while it is true you are "not running a Sunday-school paper," yet women and children read it, and some of them at least need the milk of the word and not such strong meat? Some of your readers will not understand... they will not like it; some will understand fully and they are certain not to like it. Of course, you can say to all such, "Go to hell," but then, they won't go, and the whole transaction does not decrease the chances of the *Blade* to take that

530 *Blade,* VI, 52, October 3, 1897.

> route. Now, I take it, we want the *Blade* to continue. As Speaker Reed says, "We want to do business."
>
> Can one not be a little practicable without going against that unspeakable hobby, the resolution never to be politic? You never said anything better (though to me all you say is well said) than that Liberals must show by correct living that their theories tend to the general good. Nothing can be truer, for a blameless life will answer almost any sort of an argument. Is it best then to announce and contend for a theory that many well-meaning people will understand to strike directly at the only kind of living considered moral?... [531]

As full of caustic wit as ever in spite of his brush with Federal justice at Louisville, Moore responded in kind. Observing tartly that while the editor of the Kansas infidel paper *Lucifer, the Light-Bearer,* often chided him for condemning "free love," now both "Judge" Feland and Josephine Henry "vilified" him because he seemed to support it, putting him in the unenviable position of the prey of a hawk on one side and a buzzard on the other, he shot back that

> For your qualities of heart and head, Brother, I have the highest consideration. You have been a true and tried friend to the *Blade,* in money and in sympathy, for a long time, and from your being a lawyer I think the matter under consideration is in the line of your specialty.... I have read carefully, several times, the extract...that you quote. I am willing to stand by what I said, it being understood, of course, that I do not speak *ex cathedra,* but simply give my best judgment and am not merely open to conviction but want to be influenced by argument, and that alone....
>
> This small newspaper has but one policy, and that is to have no policy. If I was satisfied that every reader of the *Blade* would drop it like a hot horseshoe for what I say, I would say it just as sure as you are a foot high. I glory in just that kind of pluck.
>
> I want the *Blade* to continue because it is the only newspaper in the world that says just what its editor thinks when the editor has any sense and any morals and thinks what he pleases. But I do not want the *Blade* to continue one day longer than I am willing to say just what I think if my mug and catawhampus signature are to stick up in that Northwest corner [of the front page]. If I had not been built that way there never would have been any *Blue Grass Blade.*

---

[531] Ibid., quoting Feland's letter.

> On one point I radically differ from you. I believe that under the head of sexual relation we ought to print the very things that all of us are thinking. [532]

Now, it probably didn't help matters all that much for Moore, in a tangentially-related article in the same *Blade* issue, both to praise the biblical character Shimei for once cursing and throwing rocks at King David,[533] and then take the personal liberty of informing his readers that King Solomon was "a damned old son of a bitch."[534] He may have been trying to see how far he could goad certain correspondents like Rucker and Zackary anxious to see him arrested for blasphemy again, but he was never indicted either for his endorsement of Shimei, whom the pious David later ordered Solomon to have assassinated,[535] or for the slur against Queen Bathsheba, for whom David likewise had a cuckolded first husband murdered.[536] As it turned out, in the Comstock era Moore's mere expression of his opinions about honest and proper sexual relations—even if the only words classifiable as "dirty" that he used in the relevant issues of his paper were a few gratuitous "damns" and "hells" and one lone "son of a bitch"—seems to have given the embittered James J. Rucker all the ammunition that the Georgetown professor needed to swear out yet another warrant against him for Federal obscenity charges. According to J. B. Wilson, who was an eyewitness to

MOORE IN CHURCH

The Heathen Editor Attends Services at Christ's Cathedral at the Dean's Invitation.

FIRST TIME IN YEARS

Heathen Charles C. Moore attended Church at Christ Church Cathedral Sunday morning, as announced in the daily papers. There was no notable increase in the attendance, but on the contrary the pews did not appear to be as well filled as usual, all of which goes to show that the desire to see how a heathen would behave in church was not so tumultuous as one might expect.

From the *Lexington Morning Herald*, July 24, 1899

---

[532] Ibid.
[533] II Samuel 16:5-13.
[534] *Blade,* VI, 52, October 3, 1897.
[535] I Kings 2:8-10.
[536] II Samuel 11:14-15.

Moore's second Federal trial and most of the events surrounding it, the teacher came to the task in full Pharisaical form and splendor, "as perfect a case of splenetic and debilitated piety as ever trod the halls of justice."[537]

Anticipation of this second Moore trial even managed to give the Spanish-American War, for which Moore's son Brent had decided to live up to his honored name and enlist in the army, a run for its money as an item of news in the Bluegrass. Though Moore and Hughes had moved publication of the *Blade* back to Lexington in April 1898,[538] their offensive remarks had been issued from Cincinnati and so this new case was finally tried in that city at the February 1899 term of the United States Court, District of Southern Ohio, with Judge Albert Clifton Thompson presiding. For this case Hughes was indicted right along with Moore, and F. R. Feland, who may have felt partially responsible for their plight (the indictments against the two men specifically mentioned the October 1897 issues of the *Blade* wherein Moore and Feland had argued about the ramifications of the idea that the editor had voiced originally in July,[539] which, ironically, could have made Feland an unintentional and unsuspecting whistle-blower for Rucker) offered to come up from Kentucky and represent both men *pro bono.* Hughes accepted the offer gratefully, but Moore, whether from some stubborn idealism about the rightness of his cause or simply because he was irked at Feland for having challenged his thought and, in his own mind at least, gotten him into this mess, insisted on acting as his own lawyer. It was probably the worst tactical error he ever made either in a courtroom or newsroom. Feland moved successfully to sever the cases against Moore and Hughes and then got Hughes off with only a twenty-five dollar fine plus court costs,[540] while Moore's attempt at self-representation merely irritated a judge and jury already openly prejudiced against him. Moore couldn't even take Rucker, his principal accuser, through a proper cross-examination without both Judge Thompson and the United States attorney, William Bundy, calling him down on every small technical violation of court procedure, and the judge and at least one of the jurymen nodded their heads and appeared

[537] Moore, *Behind the Bars,* 178-179, quoting Wilson.

[538] *Blade,* XVII, 7, June 7, 1908.

[539] *United States versus Charles C. Moore,* case # 1993, February 1899. United States District Court, Southern Ohio District. National Archives, Great Lakes Branch, Chicago, Ill.

[540] Moore, *Behind the Bars,* 186.

to go to sleep during Moore's rambling and digressive summation. In the end, the jury brought back a verdict of guilty after only a token deliberation, and although Moore had expected to receive a stiff fine such as Judge Barr had imposed upon him and then suspended in Louisville back in 1895, Judge Thompson summarily sentenced him to two years in the State Penitentiary at Columbus, Ohio,[541] which since the days of the Civil War the United States Government had contracted also to house Federal prisoners. Moore's past thus may have come to an ironic sort of full circle here: the most famous Kentuckian ever incarcerated at the place had been General John Hunt Morgan, jailed there briefly as a prisoner of war after the Battle of Tebbs' Bend and then having daringly and romantically escaped through a tunnel to ride and fight for the Confederacy once again at Kellar's Bridge.[542]

The level-headed Dr. John Wilson was shocked by the severity of Moore's sentence. Moore had been rebuked both by postal inspectors and a great many of his own friends and subscribers, including Josephine Henry, F. R. Feland, and Wilson himself, for using language neither dignified nor refined. For that, Wilson believed he certainly deserved some form of censure, though Moore was actually more bull-headed than profane. However, in a strict sense Wilson considered Moore's language in the actual articles for which he had been indicted neither lewd, obscene, nor lascivious, and even if he had speculated on the propriety and acceptability of sexual relations outside marriage it was highly debatable whether an open discussion of this question was "of an indecent character." After all, the English novelist Thomas Hardy was only one of several literary figures whose writings had lately attempted to address various aspects of this very same question, and his *Jude the Obscure* had stirred up more ire and controversy both national and international than Moore's little infidel paper could ever hope to agitate.[543] Wilson thus considered Moore to be not a martyr but at least a scapegoat in the "free love" debate, and as soon as Judge

---

[541] Ibid., 184-186.

[542] Ibid., 6, quoting the 1899 *Columbus Press-Post* article.

[543] Hardy's *Jude the Obscure* had been published in England only a year before Moore's fateful newspaper contributions to the dispute. We cannot say for sure if, or how much, the battle of words engendered by Hardy's novel contributed to Moore's thought. Considering his low estimation of Allen's *The Choir Invisible,* it's hard to say even if he would have approved of *Jude the Obscure;* one hopes that the old saw about consistency being the bugbear of small minds holds true.

Thompson had imposed the sentence the physician busied himself trying to procure a competent lawyer and arrange bail money for Moore pending an appeal.

As it turned out, gaining sympathy, to say nothing of a bail bond, for Moore in Cincinnati was no easy matter. The city's infidel/freethought community actually held a surprisingly (or perhaps unsurprisingly) low opinion of the Kentucky editor; he had alienated many of their number with criticisms and accusations as harsh as any he had ever heaped upon Professor Rucker or any of his earlier Prohibition targets, and they had come to view both him and his paper as outside the mainstream of freethought philosophy. Nonetheless Wilson managed to talk a majority of the members of the Ohio Liberal Society into submitting an appeal for Moore simply for the sake of principle, but by the time he had returned to court with collected funds for bail he found, to his dismay, that Moore had been packed up and hustled off to the penitentiary at Columbus only half an hour after Wilson had signified his intent to Federal Prosecutor Bundy to see the appeal filed. Whether or not his conversation with Bundy had any effect on the speed with which Moore had been transferred from the court house to the prison, Wilson could not say, but it did look suspicious to him. Still, he felt that Bundy could be accused of doing nothing more than his duty under the law, even though Wilson believed the law in this matter to be grossly unfair.[544]

And yet for all this, Moore did have one fine and eloquent moment in court, as he was being handcuffed and led away to a holding cell after the judge had rapped his gavel concluding the case. "You are not shackling me," he roared to Judge Thompson, Attorney Bundy, and the jury. "You are shackling American liberty!"[545]

Thus was Charles Chilton Moore, now Prisoner #31498, once again forced behind the wall of separation in its true, rather than metaphorical, sense at the Ohio State Penitentiary. Still, his period of incarceration at Columbus proved to be a blessing in disguise in many ways,

[544] Moore, *Behind the Bars,* 186-188.
[545] Recalled by Wilson at Moore's funeral. See *In Memoriam,* 11.

and he later admitted as much.[546] His son Leland, whom Moore had been compelled to persuade not to do physical harm to Professor Rucker at the end of the trial, managed Quakeracre for him, taking most actual hard farm labor off Moore's hands not only for his prison term but, as it turned out, for the rest of his life. The prison's warden, E. G. Coffin, was known (and on occasion vilified) as a liberal and progressive administrator,[547] and his treatment of Moore was even more in keeping with that of a political prisoner than the editor could have enjoyed at the jails either in Paris or Lexington in Kentucky. Coffin housed Moore on "Banker's Row," the most comfortable and spacious wing of the prison and generally reserved for extremely well-heeled inmates (though if the photograph of the "Row" is any true indication of its appearance, we might wince at the thought of the place's *worst* cell blocks), and put him to work on the prison's own newspaper. In addition, Moore was allowed a near-complete liberty for all the written correspondence he wished to maintain, and so with James Hughes' outside assistance he kept right on editing and publishing the *Blue Grass Blade* as if nothing at all had ever happened to him, happily praising Warden Coffin and excoriating Professor Rucker, the Bible-thumpers, and Kentucky whiskey distillers with equal vigor.[548] And as we have noted, he finally penned his autobiography, which he titled *Behind the Bars: 31498.* It was and is without question the most scattered, disorganized, and rambling work he ever published, in more than one instance emphasizing minutiae over larger questions and giving almost every point he managed to make a mile-wide perimeter of incidental information. Still, some Kentucky writers do tend to ramble (so it is said, anyway), and many of the autobiography's deficiencies in construction can be attributed to Moore's lack of access to written records in Kentucky while he was in prison and his haste to get the book on the market—as well as the sheer number of other irons he had in the fire when he wrote it.

---

[546] Moore, *Behind the Bars,* 225.

[547] Lore, "The Ohio Penitentiary: Inside the Pen." *Columbus Dispatch,* October 28, 1984.

[548] Moore, *Behind the Bars,* 193-197.

"Bankers' Row" in the old Ohio State Penitentiary, Columbus, Ohio. Moore spent five months incarcerated here for alleged "free love" articles in the *Blue Grass Blade.*

Photo courtesy Beth Santore, Columbus, Ohio

And so all things considered, it would appear to be rather a shame that Moore seems never to have made a connection with the one other literary man inside the Ohio State Penitentiary at the same time, a trusty serving a five-year sentence for embezzling funds from a Texas bank and paying his debt to society as the prison's night-duty pharmacist. Prisoner #30664, otherwise known as William Sidney Porter, was a North Carolina native who had packed a lot of jobs into his short, checkered life including bank teller and newspaper reporter in addition to being a licensed druggist, and it so happened that at this time he was beginning to smuggle short stories out of the penitentiary to a friend, or friends, who got them published for him under a pen name so that none of the magazine editors who accepted them would discover that they had been written by a convicted felon. One legend even has it that Porter picked the name of a prison guard, Orrin Henry, to use as his pseudonym. Whether or not this is true, though, if Charles Moore had only gotten acquainted with Porter, and if Porter himself hadn't been so profoundly ashamed of being a convict, the *Blue Grass Blade* just might have made the literary scoop of the clove of the nineteenth and twentieth centuries: publishing the very first short stories of O. Henry.[549]

As Moore languished at Columbus, his friends' efforts to get him released continued unabated. The Ohio Liberal Society, goaded to its duty by the steadfast and patient Dr. Wilson, hired the Cincinnati attorneys Charles Phares and D. C. Keller to appeal the case on the grounds that Judge Thompson and one or more of the jurymen had appeared to go to sleep during part of the trial,[550] but nothing seems ever to have come of the endeavor. A more fruitful attempt was spear-headed in Lexington by R. C. O. Benjamin, the leading newspaper editor of the Bluegrass Region's African-American community. At the time of the February 1899 trial Benjamin's *Lexington Standard* gave an account of Moore's case that seemed to the infidel editor to be too flippant and derogatory, and though perhaps Moore should have considered the Scriptural maxim "Physician, heal thyself,"[551] he responded in the *Blue Grass Blade* with his customary vitriol. Benjamin openly apologized, declaring that anyone who could have denounced slavery as wrong back in antebellum days had to be a true friend to blacks, and he wrote, circulated, and sent in a petition to President William McKinley, deploring Moore's treatment at the hands of the Cincinnati Federal Court and asking for his pardon. Though the President himself was a religious man he was inclined to be tolerant, and although he chose not to pardon Moore he did commute the stubborn old editor's sentence to six months, with one month's time off for good behavior. Moore was released from Warden Coffin's custody on July 7, 1899, two weeks before Robert G. Ingersoll died in New York, and so at the banquets and parties given in his honor by Moses Kaufman, Josephine Henry, and his other friends at Lexington upon his return to the city he was able to take the high moral ground with Professor Rucker, Judge

---

[549] Gall, "Death of a Legend," *Motive,* November-December 1971; Smith, 146-152.

[550] *U. S. vs. Moore,* case # 1993, February 1899.

[551] Luke 4:23.

Thompson, United States Attorney Bundy, and Ingersoll alike and issue a blanket declaration of forgiveness to them all for their crimes and injustices against him.[552] It will be admitted that at least in Ingersoll's case, his "forgiveness" had just a bit too much unction, but then again Moore had the temerity to compare his case to that of Alfred Dreyfus on Devil's Island as well.[553] Perhaps he was simply overjoyed to be home, and appropriately verbose and hyperbolic.

No one could say, though, that Moore had been "rehabilitated" to conventional mores in any sense of the term. Almost as soon as the welcoming feasts were over he and Hughes were stirring up the fretful complacency of the Bluegrass saints once again, most particularly with an essay in the November 26 *Blade* written by one M. Grier Kidder and entitled "The Virgin Mary." Subsequently published in pamphlet form, Kidder's article ridiculed and repudiated the idea of the Virgin Birth and speculated as to whether Jesus had actually been Joseph's son or simply illegitimate, perhaps the base-born son of a Roman soldier. In essence, we might classify it as something of a lengthened and refined articulation of Moore's own Breckinridge-Pollard quip of 1894, minus the political volatility that the mention of the Breckinridge and Pollard names had brought to the issue then.[554]

Too, by January 1900 Moore appeared ready to take on the Federal Court system again, at least from what he considered a safe distance to do so. Judge Barr, who had imposed the thousand-dollar fine on him back in 1895 and had then suspended it on condition of a year's good behavior, had now retired from the bench and his place had been filled by Judge Walter Evans. Moore wrote both Evans and the United States attorney for the Western Kentucky District, R. D. Hill, with the news that he proposed to compile yet another book, to be titled *Extracts From the Bible: King James' Version* and with "no other word" in it "except on the title page." He wanted to know if he would be allowed to market such a volume through the mails, a notion to make any Bible student well enough acquainted with both the Comstock Laws and the

---

[552] Moore, *Behind the Bars,* 191-192, 198-216.

[553] Ibid., 205; Jacoby, 212.

[554] *Blade,* XVII, 7, June 7, 1908; see particulars in *U. S. vs. Moore,* case #6523, February-October 1900, United States Court, Western Kentucky District.

salty erotica and Rabelaisian humor of the Old Testament weep and gnash his teeth, and Moore knew it.

Judge Evans tried to extricate himself from the pregnant question by advising Moore simply and vaguely to "consult counsel." Attorney Hill, though, perhaps already a little more painfully familiar with such Scripture passages as Onan's death from *coitus interruptus* and Judah's sexual relationship with his daughter-in-law as a prostitute in Genesis chapter 38, the traveler's giving up his concubine to gang-rape and murder in Judges 19:22-30, the seduction of Bathsheba by King David in II Samuel 11:2-27, the incestuous rape of Tamar by her half-brother Amnon in II Samuel 13:1-20, and the full-blooded words of the Assyrian military commander Rabshakeh to the Israelites in II Kings 18:27 and Isaiah 36:12, than he wished to be, treated the letter with what an article in the *Louisville Evening Post* of January 22, 1900 called "dignified silence." Except, as Moore noted sourly in the *Blue Grass Blade,* to the Louisville news media, who couldn't have had any other source but Hill for the January 22 report, which gratuitously noted that there was "a touch of sacrilegious sarcasm in [Moore's] epistle" with "veiled irony arising from the fact that Moore has had a taste of the penalties for sending obscene matter through the mails already."

For his part, Moore, to whom the Louisville paper had referred as "the rampant editor of the *Blue Grass Blade,"* replied scathingly in the February 11 issue of his newspaper that

> Not only does the pious idiot who wrote that thus admit that the Bible is "obscene literature," but he says that even the suggestion to print parts of it in a newspaper is "sacrilegious." ...Hill not only declines to give me any answer but races off to a newspaper reporter whose bigotry and narrow-mindedness are manifest, to exploit to the world his animus against the "rampant editor" who asked him a fair question, which it was his duty as an officer, to say nothing of his obligation as a civil gentleman, to answer. Let this question come before the courts, and the *Louisville Post* is already committed to doing all it can to get me sent to the penitentiary again.
>
> When this is printed I will send marked copies of it to the President and to Attorney [General] Griggs at Washington, with a letter to each asking instruction in the matter. I want to know if it be true that

a Christian has rights to the use of the United States mail that an infidel has not.[555]

As it happened, Moore dropped his *Extracts* project soon afterward, if indeed he had ever been serious about completing it at all—mostly, it seems, because he got hailed right back into Federal court at Louisville within two weeks of his article about Hill. On February 22 Judge Evans issued a warrant for Moore's arrest on a complaint from the Lexington Disciple leader James W. Zackary, who claimed that he and fellow victims C. L. Braxton of Indiana and James Griffith and J. O. Sehorn of Lexington had received obscene matter in the mail from Moore on February 16—specifically, copies of the November 26, 1899 issue of the *Blue Grass Blade* with its offending article about the Virgin Mary.[556] From all evidence it would appear that Zackary and his cohorts had actually been so brazen as to request back copies of the fateful *Blade* issue from the unsuspecting Moore specifically for the purpose of swearing out the complaint against him. While the editor probably should have known better than to send such a controversial back issue out to known enemies, his naïveté still cannot be held as an excuse for his accusers: their entrapment of him in this instance was as underhanded an action as had ever been employed against him by any opponent, professedly Christian or not. In a write-up from the *Blade's* rival *Lexington Morning Herald* dated, oddly, two days *before* the aggrieved plaintiffs claimed they had received Moore's offensive paper, Zackary huffed self-righteously that he "may have said something about the piece that helped to lead to this investigation, but my mind is so entirely filled with my extensive work that I cannot remember whether I did or not. If I did, it has escaped me."[557]

This new case came to trial in October 1900, prosecuted by a United States Attorney and presided over by a Federal Judge both already so aggrieved by Moore's discomfiting letters that it looked as if the old infidel hardly stood a chance of overcoming their prejudices. Some witnesses to the proceeding even recalled that Judge Evans ap-

---

555 *Blade,* IX, 1, February 11, 1900, quoting an article from the *Louisville Evening Post* of January 22.

556 *U. S. vs. Moore,* case #6523, February-October 1900, United States Court, Western Kentucky District.

557 *Lexington Morning Herald,* February 14, 1900.

peared determined to invoke the retired Judge Barr's thousand-dollar fine against Moore in addition to any other penalties that a guilty verdict might entail, on no other grounds than that Moore had somehow violated Judge Barr's conditions of suspension by the very fact that he had been hailed back into court. There was one notable difference between Moore at Cincinnati in February 1899 and Moore at Louisville in October 1900, however: this time around the old editor was grateful for any legal help offered to him, and so he had submitted the preparation of his defense to a committee of prominent Lexington and Cincinnati liberals and freethinkers including, evidently, not only J. B. Wilson but Moses Kaufman as well. This committee in turn had arranged for the services of the eminent John Graham Simrall of Louisville, and John Rollings Charlesworth, an English freethinking attorney who was practicing at the time in Texas, to act as Moore's lawyers.

Simrall and Charlesworth opened their defense by presenting Judge Evans with a closely-argued motion for dismissal of the entire case on the grounds that, under the law, blasphemy and obscenity were two completely different entities; prosecution of the former was prevented by the First Constitutional Amendment, and the charges against Moore for the latter were unsustainable in this case. The two even got Judge Barr to testify, either in private deposition or orally in Judge Evans' chambers, that Moore had faithfully met the legal obligations he had imposed in 1895 and thus took away any legal grounds Evans may have claimed for reinstating the fine.[558] And surprisingly enough, despite whatever grudges he may have held against Moore, Evans felt compelled to agree and grant the motion. His decision reads, in part, that

> I would not have found it difficult, and indeed it might have been pleasant, to hold that the paper mailed in this case was, at least, "obscene." ...However, mere obscenity in a publication is not sufficient to make the mailing of it an offense. In addition to being obscene, the paper mailed must also be lewd and lascivious, the court holding that all these words were used in the statute to describe one and the same offense....
>
> The matter mailed in this case questions the chastity of Mary, the wife of Joseph and mother of Jesus, and ridicules, in coarse fash-

[558] See *In Memoriam,* 19.

> ion, the idea of the supernatural origin of the Son. This, indeed, is the chief idea of the article, but unless infidelity and atheism are to be proscribed as beyond the bounds of the rule of the freedom of religious thought and speech which prevails under Constitutional protection in this country, it cannot be justly said that the man who believes that the child Jesus came in the ordinary way of humanity may not advocate that belief and thus attempt to establish his contention that the Christian religion is not the true one, or indeed that there is no true religion at all. The manner of the advocacy of such views will doubtless depend upon the vulgar coarseness upon the one hand or upon the refinement upon the other of the mind and taste of the person advocating the doctrine, but the right to advocate it cannot be made to depend upon such a test. Nor can the right to advocate such views depend upon their unpopularity. The language in this publication respecting God, in which the writer insists that Mary was unchaste or else that Jesus was the son of Joseph, may be blasphemous, but the statute does not forbid the mailing of merely blasphemous writings. What was mailed in this instance might be libelous of Mary if she were now living, but libels even as disgusting to every refined, even if unbelieving, person as this must be, is not unmailable under the statute....
>
> In this case it seems to the court that the paper complained of was not obscene, lewd, or lascivious in the sense of the statute as construed by the Supreme Court, because, while it may tend to change, corrupt, or destroy the religious views of those who read it, it does not invite any obscene, lewd, or lascivious conduct upon their part. And this seems to suggest the test by which the matter is to be determined, for otherwise the process of the court might be perverted into protecting the advocacy of one set of religious notions as against another. ... If the Christian religion is divine it can withstand all attacks, but whether divine or not, the Constitution of the United States gives to all the right to discuss it from whatever standpoint they please, and unless obscene, lewd, or lascivious these discussions are not, under the statute, excluded from the mails.[559]

In his sixty-third year of life and the sixteenth of his career as a newspaper editor Charles Chilton Moore thus finally returned to Lexington in triumph, bringing, just like the last verse of Psalm 127 said, his sheaves with him. He was victorious now not only over James W.

---

[559] *U. S. vs. Moore,* case #6523, February-October 1900, United States Court, Western Kentucky District.

Zackary but even J. J. Rucker and Anthony Comstock himself, earning a landmark Federal judicial decision both for freedom of religion and for freedom of the press as well. He was never prosecuted again. It had been a long, hard decade.

No villains, no heroes. Charles Chilton Moore could be the soul of Southern chivalry in person, and was frequently so rude, crude, and obnoxious in print that he offended even those who agreed with him personally on matters of freethought. He was as anti-Semitic as any nineteenth- or early twentieth-century Christian, and yet he could inspire loyalty and generosity in Moses Kaufman. He took his Prohibition crusading past the point of all reason, even to employing camp meeting-style evangelistic bombast and hyperbole in order to maintain it and goading not only unbelieving readers but Christians to excess. For his publicized comparison of a living private citizen to Judas Iscariot and Dives in hell, and his printed summary condemnation of an organized religious society as worse than a whorehouse, he was convicted of malicious libel and spent two months in jail. He insisted on voicing a disbelief in the Virgin Birth of Christ, which was his Constitutional right, yet he chose the most inflammatory words possible for the time and place in which he uttered them and in so doing lost even the support of his mentor, Robert Green Ingersoll. And yet, he was progressive—and brave—enough to advocate rational, sensible birth control in an era that would have made a martyr of him simply for stating his convictions, and his two principal Christian accusers in his Federal trials stooped to the exercise of blatantly unfair tactics in order to see him prosecuted, bringing their own cause into disrepute, even among their fellow believers, for so doing. Josephine Henry, John Byers Wilson, and Farris R. Feland alike, committed liberals and freethinkers if not atheists themselves all, despised Moore's slang, his coarseness, and his bullheadedness, and criticized his faults to his face as well as in print—and yet any of the three would defend him and his right to speak his mind, apparently, to the very death. Why should it be so?

Because, quite simply, though a land without either heroes or villains is the purview of the philosopher, philosophers generally just aren't all that competent at writing news or selling newspapers. Were it not for George Whitefield, Shubal Stearns, and a few dozen other lesser-known rustic and gaunt prophets pointing skyward in the days before and immediately after the American Revolution, the Unitarian Church might have become the faith of the South and Thomas Paine's *The Age of Reason* its Gospel. Had it not been for saucy, obnoxious young Alexander Campbell and his aggressive black-and-white Scottish Common Sense Rationalistic editorials in the *Christian Baptist,* to say nothing of his equally brash and insufferable lieutenants such as Raccoon John Smith, Charles Moore's cultured and gentlemanly grandfather Stone might have lived and died as a mere footnote in Kentucky religious history. By the same token (and perhaps even to bring the idea full circle), even if the *Blue Grass Blade* regularly aired each and every one of its editor's most disagreeable qualities, Charles Chilton Moore put his very soul into the paper, using its journalistic pulpit wholeheartedly to state his case for unbelief and defend it by hook or crook against all comers—exactly like the hardball evangelism of his believing ancestors. Whether right or wrong (and all too often in the gray area between the two), he would *not* let an opponent defeat him; if, like Archilochos' hedgehog, he knew only one trick, to burrow in and fight, he knew that one trick in a big way and sooner or later it usually wound up working for him. The *Blade* was often the only platform that more cultured freethinkers such as Wilson, Feland, and Mrs. Henry could find for the expression of their own philosophical efforts to engage both religious believers and other infidels in dialogue, and no matter how often they became irked at Moore either individually or collectively, any of them would have gladly paraphrased the sentiments of the poet William Ernest Henley to thank whatever gods may be for Moore's friendship, his bloody but unbowed head, and his unconquerable soul.

Kentucky has always had a reputation for honoring bravery, even when it is accompanied (and overshadowed) by foolhardiness. With Charles Moore's final judicial victory it seemed almost as if he had achieved some measure of this Bluegrass hero status: if he was still Kentucky's most hated man, he was now also the man that Kentuckians most *loved* to hate, and this quirky difference allowed him to spend his declining years, in and around Dog Fennel and Lexington, in relative peace and contentment—and of course, argument. He had graduated from being a mere Lexington infidel newspaper editor to become the village atheist of the State of Kentucky, a veritable Bluegrass institution, and he would have asked for nothing better. Or worse.

Chapter 8

Tamám: Beyond the Hyphenation

If you would not be forgotten
as soon as you are dead and rotten,
either write things worth the reading,
or do things worth the writing.
—Benjamin Franklin

In the summer of 1908, the Neale Publishing Company of New York and Washington, then well known both for its catalogue of Southern and Civil War historical fiction and nonfiction titles and its patronage of Kentucky authors, released a remarkable volume entitled *Tamám.* Part local-color historical fiction, part gothic romance, and part philosophical discourse, the book told the story of a strange, tragic, unfulfilled love affair between the unnamed "posthumous daughter" of a Southern Civil War hero not unlike Thomas and Mary Brent's younger offspring, and her faithful, steadfast, but proud and likewise unnamed suitor. Although different parts of the novel were set in places as far apart as Arlington National Cemetery and the pyramids of Egypt, the author spun a considerable amount of its plot around the plantation graveyard of an old central Kentucky estate called Forest Retreat. In *Tamám,* the suitor remains faithful to the posthumous daughter through good times and bad, travels across the United States and over the seas, and takes his own life finally after a last proud, headstrong rejection by his beloved, who has devoted her life to charity. In turn the posthumous daughter dies of grief upon learning of the suicide, yet all seems to be made right in the afterlife: the posthumous daughter is reunited not only with her lover but with the father whom she had never seen in life, and the three are happy together in a land where time is no more until they meet the Supreme Ruler of the place. Neither God nor devil but portrayed as something of a mixture of the classical Judeo-Christian concepts of both, this entity calls itself Oblivion and informs the three that the sole reason for their existence after death is the fact that they are still remembered among the living. Sooner or later, they are told, all are forgotten and then Oblivion claims them for a cold, dark, silent eternity as his own. *Tamám* concludes with a somber plea from the departed to their loved ones still living, taken from Shakespeare's Ophelia: "There's rosemary, that's for remembrance: pray, love, remember." The concluding thought of the melancholy novel is thus something of a precursor for at least one of Edgar Lee Masters' poetic "epitaphs" in his 1915 *Spoon River Anthology,* that of the Village Atheist: immortality is not a gift but an achievement, and only those who strive mightily shall possess it. One wonders if Masters ever happened to read *Tamám.*

The book's title was said to have been taken from an enigmatic Persian word written by the poet Omar Khayyam at the end of his famous quatrain verses, translated variously as "the end," "completion," or "fulfillment," and its author was listed as Charles Chilton Moore. Publisher Walter Neale was gratified to receive positive reviews of *Tamám* from the *New York Times,* the *New York Journal,* the *Louisville Courier-Journal,* and the *Philadelphia Book News* alike[560] (although accompanied by at least one very bad one packed full of Texas sarcasm in the *Dallas Morning News*)[561], but it would appear that the only periodical that emphasized the fact that the book was actually written by Charles Chilton Moore III rather than his father, the irrepressible old infidel editor who had made the Moore name both famous and infamous, was Lexington, Kentucky's own *Blue Grass Blade.*[562] The elder Moore had died two and a half years previously, and the still-iconoclastic newspaper was now being published by James E. Hughes with assistance from John R. Charlesworth, John B. Wilson, and Jose-

---

560 A compendium of the reviews of *Tamám* was published in the bookseller's and bibliophile's periodical *The Dial,* XLVII, 553, on July 1, 1909.

561 *Dallas Morning News,* January 4, 1909.

562 *Blade,* XVII, 11, July 5, 1908.

phine Henry. Even with the *Blade* and its editors' publicity of *Tamám* as the quality work of a chip off the old freethought-literary block, however, Bluegrass tradition has largely associated *Tamám* with the father rather than the son, and even the modern *Kentucky Encyclopedia* attributes the novel to the elder Charles Chilton Moore.[563]

Though Charles Chilton Moore III is not known to have written another book besides *Tamám,* that is unless one counts his published contributions to scientific research as an agricultural chemist,[564] it does seem somewhat odd that he never made much of an attempt to differentiate himself from his father as an author in his own right. After all, the entire misconception about the authorship of *Tamám* might have been avoided by the mere inclusion of a numeral on the book's cover and title page. One reason for the misapprehension, though, simply may have been that the older Charles Moore was indisputably the source of a considerable amount of the novel's anecdotal material, not only the tales of the old antebellum Forest Retreat plantation and of the heroic young Confederate officer who sired the posthumous daughter but stories about well-known neighbors such as the Breckinridges of Cabell's Dale and Major Nicholson too. Added to this fatherly influence could have been the simple possibility that Charles III himself never really cared to be known as a literary figure anyway: his young and beautiful wife, Helen, had died only two months after the passing of his father in 1906, leaving him with a little boy named Charles IV, and on this basis we can perhaps understand *Tamám* more than anything else as the effort of a young scientifically- and philosophically-inclined man, reared in a home where the ideas of a personal, anthropomorphic God and an afterlife had been viewed with equal skepticism, to come to terms with his grief over the loss of both his wife and his father. Charles Chilton Moore III died in 1940 in San Francisco, California,[565] and we will probably never know the entire truth about his motives as a novelist.

Yet there is one more reason why Bluegrass readers may have chosen to insist on viewing *Tamám* as the product of fiery old Editor

---

563 "Charles Chilton Moore," *Kentucky Encyclopedia,* 647.

564 Included among these was at least one treatise on the chemical composition and potential toxicity of cassava. See Bibliography.

565 Lexington Cemetery, Lexington, Ky.; burial records, 1851-2007.

Moore's pen rather than that of his son. Fantastic stories of the deathbed and gallows represent one of the fundamental motifs of Christian, and indeed general rural American, folklore, from the touching tales of "feather crowns" found within the pillows of the pious departed (they really do occur sometimes in old-fashioned feather ticks and pillows, incidentally; the reason for their formation and existence is the matter in dispute) to the hair-raising accounts so often associated with the evil, unbelieving, and unrepentant, the dying sinner screaming in horror on seeing black cats crawling up and down the walls and smelling meat frying in hell and what not. As folktales they probably evolve naturally, exactly as did the Josephine Henry hog story and the rumor that the young Disciple preacher Charles Moore had lost his faith only because he had gone crazy for the love of Alexander Campbell's daughter, and by the same means they allow largely religious and otherwise conservative rural cultures one of several means to define and reinforce their moral boundaries—again, just as had the hog-and-lunatic yarns in post-Civil War Versailles, Kentucky. Of course, deathbed scenes of atheists and agnostics seeing the light, as it were, at the very last moment, have always been among the most powerful of such folktales, and although the older Charles Moore's terminal illness and passing were so closely scrutinized by the Kentucky news media that any word-of-mouth anecdotes about the death would have immediately come up for comparison against contemporary newspaper reports, many of his kinfolk, neighbors, acquaintances, and even opponents and enemies would have been gratified to hear, or at least think, that he had "gotten right" according to conventional Christian mores before dying.

If *Tamám,* whether written by Moore the elder or Moore the younger, wasn't assumed to contain a bit of circumstantial evidence that this may have occurred, the novel—whoever wrote it—was in general more respectful of at least some religious concepts than had been either the three books the old editor had self-published during his lifetime or most of the content of twenty-odd years of the *Blue Grass Blade.* It was therefore perhaps only natural that well-wishers and wishful thinkers in and around Lexington would have preferred to view *Tamám* as the creation of an old infidel reassessing his thoughts and positions, rather than that of the son of an old infidel who had died hard-hearted and unrepentant—and for all we know, some members of the extended Moore family could even have been complicit in the misunderstanding simply for the sake of the patriarch's reputation.

The ambiguity thus surrounding the authorship of *Tamám* is only heightened by the pathos and poignancy of its story and its narrator's observations about life, death, love, loss, grief, eternity—and God. Though this deity is spoken of with considerable respect if not outright reverence, in the author's conception he, she, or it is neither an anthropomorphic Super-Being hurling lightning bolts down to earth from a Great White Throne in Heaven nor even the aloof and serene Divine Engineer of Aristotelian philosophy and the Deistic thinkers of the Enlightenment. Rather, in the narrator's mind God seems to be a mere nebulous idea, perhaps only an aspiration *of* the human race rather than the source of any inspiration *to* the human race—but an entity, whoever or whatever it is, that by fits and starts does somehow manage to improve upon a very, very earthy humanity simply through the race's never-ending search for ultimate meaning. Similarly, though it is obvious that *Tamám's* narrator is no Scriptural literalist or inerrantist, he quotes several poetical Bible passages, hymns, and other traditional religious sayings with a sense of esteem almost completely lacking in the books and essays definitively known to have come from the senior Moore's pen. And even if the author, whether Moore *`pere* or Moore *fils,* couldn't conceive of any life beyond the grave apart from the memories of loved ones left behind, perhaps the most touching mystery of all is the question of *Tamám's* observations on prayer, as in the following excerpt:

> When we train the little child to kneel and pray in his innocence of our ignorance, we do so in the spirit of arming him against the day when he will have arrived at the milestone in life from which the figures have been erased, and some vandal has inscribed the word "doubt."
>
> Prayer is the sublime of conditions attainable by the mind. It is the introspective review we make of our secret motives as they file by, in the solemnity of isolation, for judgment at the hands of the good instincts that lie within us. It is primarily a confession; the recognition of our inferiority; an acknowledgment of ignorance; the confiding of hope. The postures of upturned face, bowed head, or kneeling are the admissions of helplessness, and serve to augment the attitude of the mind. That prayer is wholesome, helpful, and natural, is the testimony of the Christian era. So we should teach the child to pray, to kneel and pray, and in so doing we instill into his life the value of communing with his own conceptions. And all this will be

to him the slow unfolding of the existence of a mystery hopelessly unfathomable.[566]

Now, regardless of whether the older Moore wrote or simply contributed anecdotal material to *Tamám,* all this might still appear to be pretty fragile, shallow evidence for any eleventh-hour reconciliation with God and classical theism. Yet before we dismiss outright the suggestion that some readers couldn't have interpreted *Tamám* after this very fashion, we must remember the disagreement that surrounded, and still seemingly lingers over, British philosopher Antony Flew's much-publicized shifts of belief between 2004 and 2008. After he grew old, Flew seems to have jettisoned his longstanding strict atheism, initially for a sort of bare-bones Deism with no more of a personal, anthropomorphic God and even less hope of an afterlife than *Tamám* offers. Apparently, though, within a few years he came to accept Anglican Bishop N. T. Wright's argument for the logic and historicity of the Resurrection of Jesus even while he still disavowed a personal belief in the miracles of the Bible. Flew's conversion, if it could be called that, set the evangelical Christian apologetic world completely atwitter with joy, and of course it provoked every bit as much corresponding outrage among advocates of atheism. At this writing partisans on both sides of the belief-unbelief question still appear to be wrangling over the state of Flew's soul—to say nothing of his mental status—while the aging scholar looks bemusedly (and perhaps confusedly) on, accepts awards and honoraria offered to him by evangelical and fundamentalist Christian colleges, and travels around with Bishop Wright as the cleric proclaims and explains the Resurrection as a definite, logical and provable event.[567] *Tamám* easily could have inspired a similar reaction among Kentucky Christian apologists a century before, especially with Editor Moore no longer around to clarify his positions.

---

566 Moore III, *Tamám,* 252-253.

567 Among several readily-available articles addressing both sides of this question are Beverly, "Thinking Straighter: Why the World's Most Famous Atheist Now Believes in God," *Christianity Today,* April 2005, http://www.christianitytoday.com/ct/2005/april/29.80.html; Carrier, "Antony Flew Considers God…Sort Of." The Secular Web, http://www.secweb.org/index.aspx?action=viewAsset&id=369; and Oppenheimer, "The Turning of an Atheist," *The New York Times Magazine,* November 4, 2007; World Wide Web, http://www.nytimes.com/2007/11/04/magazine/04Flew-t.html.

Did Charles and Lucy Moore raise their children to think, act, and pray after the fashion addressed in the above passage of *Tamám,* or did Charles III, perhaps reacting to some sensed spiritual or philosophical deficiency in his own upbringing and even though he himself was no traditional believer, resolve to make good the perceived lack in the life of his little Charles IV? Or, were father, son, and grandson alike all instead simple lay contemplatives, as it were, in the same sense that the modern advocate of atheism, Sam Harris, practices Buddhist meditative techniques?[568] We may never know for sure, and that just might have been the way a good many faithful Kentuckians of yesteryear wished to keep it. But it now becomes our task to tell of the final illness and death of Kentucky's most hated man, and although the *Tamám* controversy makes it obvious that the events entailed a degree of dispute not entirely unlike that between theists and atheists over Antony Flew's mind and soul, Archangel Michael and Satan over Moses' body, the seven cities of ancient Greece over the nativity of Homer, or even the towns and villages of La Mancha over the ownership of Don Quixote—well, at the very least we can endeavor to recount the diverging stories, and hope that final truth lies somewhere in the midst.

The five years after Charles Moore's final criminal prosecution were more or less kind to the old editor. He discreetly toned down his newspaper rhetoric just enough to avoid any more legal trouble, but still managed to keep it sharp enough to irritate his erstwhile Scripture-inerrancy enemies such as Professor Rucker, James Zackary, and B. N. Grahan, the latter of whom he engaged in a lengthy and vigorous written debate over the merits and demerits of Christianity that was published in both the Lexington *Leader* and the *Blue Grass Blade* in 1902.[569] Even so, Moore finally found one more degree of empathy with the memory of the politically savvy Robert Green Ingersoll and yet another belief system against which to crusade after the assassination of his pardoner, President McKinley, in 1901: Anarchism, which ideology had produced the McKinley assassin Leon Csolgosz. Moore's

---

[568] See Saltman, "The Temple of Reason: Sam Harris on How Religion Puts the World at Risk," *The Sun,* 369, September 2006, 7-11.

[569] See John R. Charlesworth's biographical sketch of Moore in *In Memoriam,* 19.

enraged pronouncements against Anarchists of all types, who were by definition freethinkers themselves albeit of a much more left-wing cast even than Socialists, not to mention old-style American infidels such as Moore and Ingersoll, got so intense that at least one American Anarchist periodical editor, Ross Winn of Tennessee, started paying the *Blue Grass Blade* back in its own flippant and hyperbolic coin and much to Moore's personal amusement:

> Charles C. Moore is the publisher of an Infidel paper at Lexington, Ky., called the *Blue Grass Blade.* Both Charley and his paper are perfectly harmless, however, otherwise we might take their existence as proof positive that the fool-killer was neglecting his job. Moore has a habit, which has become habitual, of saying foolishly funny things about himself and Jehovah and others, but he really doesn't mean anything by it. Moore is never so excruciatingly funny as when he is being solemn and serious. It is his attempts at humor that impel one to uncork the tear jugs of grief, and to shed the scalding brine of pathetic sorrow. The mission of the *Blade* is to demolish the Christian religion, and Moore goes about it conscientiously and with considerable vim. All of which is very commendable, I cheerfully grant. But Editor Moore's journalistic assaults upon the battlements of heaven are often as heroically comical as Don Quixote's tilts with the windmills, and about as barren of practical results. The chief trouble with Moore is that he doesn't know anything, and lacks sufficient astuteness to conceal the fact. Even in his chosen field of Bible criticism he allows himself to be tripped up by Christian critics; and upon all occasions, when he undertakes to discuss serious matters, he flounders around in illogical circles, like a rudderless ship, or a bashful suitor trying to corral a coy maiden. By which I do not mean that Charleyboy is bashful—oh, lord, no! Bashfulness and modesty are two weaknesses that do not appertain to the character and mental make-up of the *Blade's* editor.
>
> But however little Moore knows in general, his knowledge of political and economic questions amounts to still less. This is illustrated in his furious and foolish diatribes against Anarchism and Anarchists. His ignorance of well-known historical facts is absolutely appalling. His reference to "seven men executed in Chicago for Anarchy [the 1886 Haymarket Riot agitators]" is on par with his assertion that there are no Infidels in Italy. Possibly he never even heard of Giordano Bruno, who in 1600 was burned in the plaza at Rome for his Infidel opinions. Yet Moore dates his paper "E. M. 303," which means the Era of Man, dating from the martyrdom of this Italian

> Freethinker. He further asserts that all Anarchists are orthodox Christians... Moore, however, is a gay old rooster who cares no more for facts than an orthodox divine. And if he knows anything on any subject, he manages to keep it carefully concealed. C. C. Moore is a ripe, rosy peach [ellipse in original].[570]

Winn, who was young enough to be Moore's son, died of a combination of tuberculosis and malnutrition less than a decade after he penned the above diatribe. Needless to say, Anarchism never caught on anywhere in the world, much less the United States of America, and there is a modicum of irony in the fact that Winn never lived to see the ideology pretty much swallowed up in terms of practicality by Bolshevism on one hand and Fascism on the other—and that all three philosophies have now come to be more associated in America's consciousness with atheism than the older home-grown infidelity of Ingersoll and Moore. And since Winn always lived in abject poverty, even spending his last sixty dollars not on food and medicine for himself and his wife and son but on a new printing setup to try to continue his Anarchist journalism,[571] it's sad too that he had never asked Moore for a friendly hand when he had had the chance, because he undoubtedly would have gotten one despite the older editor's personal disagreements with him. Though Moore's political thought, like that of Ingersoll, never strayed far from the Deism-influenced Founding Fathers, he did believe that deeply in the freedom of speech. And besides, he despised McKinley's successor in office, Theodore Roosevelt, quite as intensely as Winn must have.[572]

More enjoyable for the aging *Blade* editor even than trading verbal and rhetorical barbs with Christians, Anarchists, and Roosevelt supporters, though, were the fulfillment of a long-cherished dream and the writing of a memoir to document it. Charles Moore's children had all grown up hearing him speak fondly of his 1865 tour of the British Isles and France, and how he had foregone journeying to Italy and the Holy Land and had returned to America after visiting Paris due to a premoni-

---

570 *Winn's Firebrand,* II, 1, January 1903.

571 Goldman, "Obituary of Ross Winn, 1871-1912." http://libcom.org/library/obituary-for-ross-winn-1871-1912-emma-goldman

572 Besides numerous negative references to Roosevelt in the *Blue Grass Blade* between 1901 and 1905, see Moore, *Dog Fennel,* 291.

tion that all was not well at home. In late 1902 or early 1903, then, perhaps partially as a reward from a proud son to a resilient father who had weathered so much during the last decade of the nineteenth century, Charles Chilton Moore III offered to pay a part of the old man's passage on a ten-week luxury cruise offered by the British and American travel agency of Thomas Cook and Sons—literally a Cook's tour, as the origins of the proverbial expression were associated with the firm—of the Mediterranean and Black Seas and the Nile River, with stops at points of interest all along the coasts of both seas as well as a junket through Palestine. Not to be outdone by her oldest son, Lucy Moore sold a flock of Quakeracre's sheep for $261 to contribute to her husband's vacation; James Hughes gladly agreed to take care of the *Blue Grass Blade* while its his senior partner was on sabbatical; and so Charles Moore merrily departed Lexington around the latter part of January 1903, journeying by rail to New York City from whence he sailed on the German twin screw steamer *S. S. Moltke* on February 5.[573] He came back two and a half months later, hale, hearty, suntanned, and carrying the manuscript for a brand-new book, a travelogue which he had entitled *Dog Fennel in the Orient.* As Madalyn Murray O'Hair noted in 1984, the title was entirely appropriate: the earth of the Dog Fennel Precinct was verily the dust from whence he had come, and no matter how far or how high he had happened to go in the world, he was still the same plain, outspoken, freethinking Charles Moore wherever one encountered him.[574]

Dog Fennel in the Orient is by far the most humorous, optimistic, and readable of Moore's books, and he obviously prepared it for publication with his *Blade* subscribers in mind. He signed his name to it as "Charles C. Moore, X.D.D.", meaning, undoubtedly, "ex-Doctor of Divinity," and within its pages he mixed matter-of-fact narrative with engaging, sometimes funny and sometimes touching comparisons of the Middle East and the characters he met with individuals and sites in Kentucky that many of his readers would recognize, overlaying the whole with his own trademark attitude of genial skepticism. Even if the work is derivative of Mark Twain's *The Innocents Abroad* and *Roughing It, Dog Fennel* is still entirely recognizable as the dyed-in-the-wool

[573] Moore, *Dog Fennel,* 1-2; 137.
[574] See Murray O'Hair's introductory comments for *Dog Fennel,* v.

product of Moore's own pen. For example, in writing of some large, gaudy hearses he saw in Algiers Moore was reminded of a friend thousands of miles away, the longtime Lexington undertaker W. R. "Colonel Will" Milward, and he pondered with wry amusement on how much Milward might profit by renting out such big carriages for Irish Catholic funerals back home.[575] In a similar vein, on having his tour guides point out to him the so-called "House of Dives" in Jerusalem, that is, the claimed residence of the legendary rich man in the Lucan parable,[576] he recalled not the Paris Christian Church pastor he had once compared to Dives but rather the deceased (and unnamed) "wealthiest man in Lexington," a good straitlaced Presbyterian who had kept sharp nails driven upside down into the seat on the back of his buggy to prevent poor boys from catching a ride on it. Moore figured that if there was a hell, Dives and that Kentucky Presbyterian mogul were both in it, and very well ought to be.[577]

We have already spoken at length of Moore's conventional and almost religiously residual anti-Semitism, and unfortunately, it appears in at least one passage of *Dog Fennel* too. On his travel group's stop at Petrea, some miles from Jerusalem, the tour guides took note of an historical claim that Herod the Great had once killed 800,000 Jews there within one day's time. Moore, who expressed doubt over the tally of the dead, nonetheless observed that "A little matter of a million or two in giving an account of the number of people killed as the result of a difference of opinion upon a religious issue, in any one of these Oriental countries, does not cut much ice, anyway, and can easily be adjusted to current demands in statistics.... [Another man in the group], upon hearing this statement from the guide [about the number of Jews killed] said, 'Good for Herod!' That ... man had probably gone up against some Jew in a business transaction at some time and had gotten the hot end of it."[578] Though such a casual dismissal of the story of the ancient tragedy was bad enough in the day in which Moore and his companion first uttered their hasty words, their responses seem absolutely blood-chilling when considered a century after the fact, in the

575 Moore, *Dog Fennel,* 59.
576 Luke 16:19-31.
577 Moore, *Dog Fennel,* 161-162.
578 Ibid., 115.

light of the Holocaust. From such cavalier views of history and man's inhumanity to man has been born the entire depraved ideology of Holocaust Denial; yet for all that, we might still hope that the horror of Hitler's Final Solution ripped away many more superficial prejudices from Americans than it ever engendered, and that Moore and his traveling companion both might have been ashamed of their hasty words if only they had been allowed to live a generation later.

Still, during and after his Holy Land excursion, Moore adopted his old mentor Robert Ingersoll's policy and now mostly reserved his greatest scorn and ridicule not for either Jews, Christians, or Muslims in an ethnic sense but rather for the statements of orthodoxy of the three faiths themselves and most especially of the way the bishops, priests, chief rabbis, and imams of the respective religions lorded it over the common people in Palestine like so many petty feudal baronets. He was shocked to see beggars such as he had never observed at home, closer in appearance to the boil-covered Lazarus of the Bible than he had ever thought really possible, and he developed an appreciation for the Gospels' negative characterizations of rich men, priests, and Levites that he had never enjoyed even during his long-ago days as a believer and preacher. Witness his description of the Church of the Holy Sepulcher in Jerusalem:

> The Church of the Holy Sepulcher is, of all the holy humbugs around Jerusalem, the one that takes the cake—in fact, [it] walks off with the entire bakery. The whole plant and the scoundrels that run it would have made me laugh if they had not made me so mad. I suppose the Mohammedan [*sic*] soldiers in it would not have let me do what I felt like doing in there, and if those fellows had had charge of Jerusalem when Jesus cleaned out the Temple by kicking out the money changers, and kicking over their tables, the Mohammedans would have run him in and, before the police court, would have made him answer to a charge of "drunk and disorderly." But I tell you, I burned with the ambition of gaining worldwide fame by rushing in through the crowd and kicking the rear elevation of the anatomy of the Patriarch of Jerusalem when I saw the rascal tramping around there in his Christian flubdubbery of gold and jewels, when old blind and leprous women sat out in the rain with their bare feet in the streams of cold water, shivering like cold wet dogs in rags and dirt and ignorance, when those priests inside did not have half the sympathy for one of those old women that a Constantinople Mohammedan has for the meanest

> of the 200,000 dogs in Constantinople. ...If Jesus Christ was the sissy that the picture books represent him to be, or if he was the vagabond doing no work but getting cooking school pies and handouts from anybody that would give them to him, or inviting himself to dinner with bankers, as all of which the New Testament represents him, I don't want any of him in mine; but if he was a big horny-handed carpenter with a number ten foot on him, and he once did kick out of the Temple such a gang as they have there now in the Church of the Holy Sepulcher, I am for him, by a large majority, myth or no myth.[579]

Considering that this particular Greek Orthodox Patriarch of Jerusalem had styled himself as Damianus I, it's a nine-day wonder Moore never attempted a play on words with his name—especially considering where he wanted to plant his right foot. Ever the idealist at heart, though, Moore did envision how better times might be made to come to Palestine than could be effected through the unhealthy fruits of the anemic, hypocritical quasi-industry of religious tourism. Though he felt even at the time he penned the proposal within *Dog Fennel's* pages, he would never live to see such a change occur, he called for massive, American- and European-aided rebuilding of the Holy Land (led by "Carnegie the Infidel, Rockefeller the Christian, and Rothschild the Jew," as he put it), complete with railroads, new construction, and the introduction of modern healthcare. In this magnificent vision no one's religious privileges would be curtailed, yet no religion would be allowed to extort money from anyone, and superstition would be exposed exactly for what it was. The sick, down to the most severe case of leprosy (and here Moore paused a moment from his visualization to express wonder why John Alexander Dowie, Mary Baker Eddy, and all the rest of the tribe of American faith healers seemed never to feel behooved to come to Jerusalem to exercise their gifts, as it were, among people who obviously needed physical healing so badly) would receive adequate care in hospitals and asylums, and the poor could find homes and employment on collective farms. When he expounded his proposal to some of his shipmates aboard the *Moltke* they immediately objected that Jerusalem and all Palestine was the property of the Ottoman Empire, and as such, no other nation could interfere with Turkish

---

[579] Ibid., 135-136.

rule to that degree without violating international law. Moore, with a twinkle in his eye, reminded the lot—almost all American Northerners—that their fathers hadn't seemed to feel just exactly that same way when Lincoln had asked Congress to declare war against the South in 1861, and yet forty-odd years later it was accepted even within some sections of the South that Lincoln had done the right thing.[580]

Perhaps needless to say, Moore had in fact here envisioned and proposed a program that entailed every bit as egregious an oversimplification of the tasks and issues involved as had been his grandfather Stone and his old mentor Alexander Campbell's concept of a completely restored "Ancient Gospel" and "Ancient Order." And yet portions, perhaps even a great deal, of the content of this grandiose Moore vision have in fact been brought to pass, and not altogether by the efforts of any Carnegies, Rockefellers, or Rothschilds either. Rather, what change has come began slowly, in small increments and with fighting both without and within all along the way through and beyond World War I and the British Mandate, starting around 1907 with small groups of none-too-observant Jews establishing collective farms in Palestine of a not-dissimilar type to those Charles Moore had proposed to his shipmates and readers four years before in *Dog Fennel in the Orient*. From these *kibbutzim* came many, if not the great majority, of the first leaders of the modern State of Israel, and if the old infidel Moore had lived to see what they ultimately accomplished we might hope that he would have been as proud of their pluck and as repentant of his prejudices as he would have been alternately irked and amused by the quarrels of the more religiously orthodox against them. Thus we are left to wonder if Moore's Lexington friend Moses Kaufman may have had a touch of the visionary about him, too, an ability to see through all of his editor friend's anti-Semitic blather to admire and embrace a contradictory, prejudiced, and infuriating but basically honest and altruistic man.

Moore spent the better part of two years in the pleasant, roseate glow of his travel memories, and among his follow-up activities to the trip was one last good old-fashioned Stone-Campbell Movement-style debate, with a young preacher named Ulysses Grant Wilkinson,

---

[580] Ibid., 202-205.

over the empirical evidences of Christianity and Scriptural inerrancy[581]—no doubt, with both sides of the discussion claiming victory as was usual in such occurrences. On the occasion of New Year's Day 1905 the editor greeted his *Blade* readers with a flourish, with the publication of two comic strips from the pen of the famed (or maybe infamous) Missouri infidel cartoonist Watson Heston. One illustrated the story of the creation of Eve from Adam's rib in Genesis 2:18-25, complete with Scripture captions and even a little extra human interest subplot: Heston showed Adam's dog stealing the rib and running away with it while God was sewing the sleeping Adam's midsection back up, and in subsequent panels an enraged Deity chased the mutt all over the Garden of Eden ("And the anger of the LORD was kindled") and finally kicked it clear into the Land of Nod ("Vengeance is mine, saith the LORD") after retrieving the bone. The other, more in the style of a political cartoon, was a sketch of Moore himself in the high-topped boots, suspenders, and everyday work clothes of a Bluegrass farmer. Evidently inspired by the old editor's February 1886 "weed scythe" editorial about the quarrel between Rudolf de Roode and Henry Howard Gratz, Heston showed a silver-haired but still muscular Farmer Moore ready to pit the strength of his arms and his "Blue Grass Blade" against a high brush patch full of "Superstition," "Priestcraft," "Pulpit Lies," "Popery," and "Redeemer Rubbish," while trying to keep an eye out for the dangerous snakes of "Superstition," "Hypocrisy," "Persecution," and "Comstockery."[582] Indeed, Heston's rough wit allowed Moore to begin the year 1905 with a bang, and it was obvious that he was still immensely enjoying himself and his jousts with his disputants.

Still, though Moore was as defiant as ever toward his former legal adversaries and other detractors, there were some things about which he was never flippant. One of these was his attitude toward death, specifically his own, which from all appearances he had never altered since the days of his essay nineteen years before about the decease of Congressman Rankin. In other words, in spite of his rough jest in 1894 about the hyphenation between the names of Breckinridge and Pollard, the similar mark between the birth and death dates on an individual's

---

[581] From Charlesworth's biographical sketch of Moore in *In Memoriam,* 19.

[582] *Blade,* XIII, 44, January 1, 1905. The Heston sketch of Moore and his "Blue Grass Blade" can be found on page 186 of this work.

tombstone, so ironically and poetically metaphoric of an entire life lived in a mere instant between two eternities, was a completely serious matter. In the February 5, 1905 issue of the *Blade* he speculated that, although so far as he knew he remained in fine health for a man of his years, he would probably die before his seventieth birthday.[583] Neither the Stone nor Moore families could be considered a long-lived people even in that day and age: his grandfather Stone had died in his seventy-second year, his grandmother had been cut off in the bloom of her youth, his mother had passed away at only sixty-seven, and his father had died at seventy-one. Even if Charles Moore overcame the law of averages and wound up as the longest-living of his family, he still knew he would have to face death one day all too soon. And yet he could still be philosophical and matter-of-fact about the eventuality: according to his personal creed, everyone should try to live in such a way as he or she should be ready to die any day, but death, even to those best prepared for it, was still too serious a thing to be spoken of lightly or flippantly.[584] Even with his mortality in mind, though, he remained constant in his unbelief, and at some point during this year he composed and published a concise statement of his mature convictions about religion. By this time he appears to have embraced, at least for the moment, what would be classified nowadays as a "strong" or a "hard" atheism:

> While now sound in mind and body, I make these declarations of faith. I do not believe in any God, or in the existence of the Christian heaven or hell. If such a being as Jesus Christ existed, he was human like ourselves. I make these declarations now, knowing that when a man gets old his body gets feeble and his mind is impaired in the same ratio, and at such times he should not be held accountable for anything he may say, or any retraction of his faith that he may make. I want it understood that these declarations stand as my final expression of faith.[585]

March found him and his son Leland at Quakeracre, engaged in the Southern farmer's yearly ritual of planting seed potatoes, and Moore used the occasion to write an encomium in the *Blade* for the freethink-

---

[583] Ibid., XIII, 49, February 5, 1905.
[584] Ibid., XIV, 42, January 6, 1906.
[585] Quoted by J. B. Wilson in *In Memoriam,* 12; see also *Dog Fennel,* vii.

ing California horticulturist Luther Burbank. Though Burbank had been vilified for years by reactionary elements of the American religious community for interfering with some supposed Divine natural order of things, not to mention being criticized by the academic scientific community as well for not keeping meticulous notes of his experiments with plant breeding, neither the Church nor the Academy had been able to prevent the Burbank Russet potato, and other fruit and vegetable strains that the freethinking agriculturist had developed, from revolutionizing American farming. Moore noted happily that, because of Burbank's supposedly sinful questioning of some poorly-imagined superhuman god's unquestionable ways, he and his fellow farmers in Dog Fennel and throughout Kentucky were able to produce potato crops twice to three times as large as, and individual potatoes even bigger than, their fathers and grandfathers had grown on the same lands—and this though continuous planting had leached so many nutrients out of central Kentucky's soil that most Bluegrass farmers now had to use extra fertilizer to grow any crops at all, and they now had to contend with a voracious "potato bug" that had not even existed in Kentucky before the days of the Civil War. Let the pious pray, stay in the dim little corner where they felt safe, and not interfere with progress, Moore reasoned; he and Luther Burbank would plant their potatoes and continue their questioning of nature's order, and the human race as a whole would be the beneficiary.[586]

Still, Moore was Moore, and he was still every bit as willing to criticize other freethought/atheist activists as he was to mock traditionalist Christians whose vocal professions of faith didn't match their actions. Ever the advocate of the ideology of the Epistle of James and its emphasis on works over faith, in the May 28, 1905 issue of the *Blade* he observed moodily that

> I am daily getting to care less and less what a man believes or disbelieves, and to care more about what he does. I am about as tired of reading about what Infidels do not believe as I am of reading about what Christians do believe, and I have found that Infidels are just as dogmatic and overbearing as Christians are and that they will persecute you just as quick [*sic*] for not agreeing with them as the Christians will. A man's belief, or disbelief, has nothing whatever to do

---

[586] *Blade,* XIV, 2, March 19, 1905.

> with his life, and we all believe or disbelieve just according to heredity and surroundings that are purely accidental and over which we have no control and for which therefore we deserve neither commendation nor blame. The average preacher preaches for money and the average Infidel editor edits his paper for money or other purpose of self-aggrandizement, and if we say we do this unselfishly we lie just as the preachers do.[587]

Sad to say, a good many aspects of Moore's analyses of both Christian evangelism and freethought—of course, now more commonly known as atheist—activism still ring true today. Ideologues of both fundamentalist religion and atheism neither were, nor are, often patient, nor open-minded, nor even polite, and Moore's criticisms, though directed as much against himself as anyone else, and repeated countless times since by both believers and nonbelievers of a more thoughtful cast as they witness the antics of their more "faithful" (or at least committed) compatriots, have fallen on ears equally deaf on both sides of the theism-atheism controversy. The phenomenon of Madalyn Murray O'Hair and her former fundamentalist evangelist crusading partner splitting the take after every night's staged argument between them is apt to occur again and again through time; as we have observed already, there is no new thing under the sun.

And so it went through one more spring and summer. *The Kentucky Encyclopedia* notes the articles within the July 2, 1905 issue of the *Blade* as pretty much characteristic of the entire spectrum of Moore writings: "He Assails Bible for the Young," an editorial arguing that Sunday Schools were dull, weak, farcical, and cheap; "Sunny Side," an exploration of the question of the existence of a benevolent God when viewed in light of the problems faced by the human race; "Sunday Baseball and Prohibition," the subjects touted tongue-in-cheek as equal ways to waste time; and the self-explanatory "Bible Stories are Myths."[588] Thus apparently did Moore intend to keep up his peppery rhetoric through the remainder of yet another Bluegrass farming cycle, but this year gathering time was different. Though apparently he and James Hughes had written and saved back enough editorials and news

---

[587] Ibid., XIV, 12, May 28, 2005.

[588] Ibid., XIV, 17, July 2, 1905, as quoted in *The Kentucky Encyclopedia,* 90.

pieces to last at least a month, by October 22 Hughes was compelled to print an announcement in the *Blade,* the *Cincinnati Enquirer,* and the Louisville *Courier-Journal* all: Charles Chilton Moore was seriously ill, from what Hughes described as "a joint attack of heart disease and asthma." The old man had suffered the first onslaught of this debilitating combination of symptoms four weeks before, right around the first day of autumn, but he had been unwilling to admit to a serious illness and seems to have believed that a few days of rest would set him right again. However, Moore had grown progressively weaker, and since the middle of October he had been compelled to sleep in a rocking chair every night because he could no longer catch his breath when in a reclining position. The report concluded with the information that he remained home at Quakeracre, and was attended by a Dr. Coffman of Georgetown.[589]

It is risky to try to analyze an illness more than a century after the fact and in light of succeeding medical research. For example, it is fairly certain that George Washington died of suffocation due to a swelled throat, but even in his own time his three physicians could never quite agree on a diagnosis and at this distance it is impossible to ascertain whether the primary cause of his upper respiratory inflammation was diphtheria, a particularly virulent Streptococcal infection, or some form of influenza virus. Nonetheless the combination of ailments noted by Hughes and, apparently, Moore's physician as well, heart disease accompanied by asthma, is suggestive. One wonders if the old editor might have suffered a light-to-moderate heart attack, perhaps while working a little too hard while harvesting crops on his farm; a heart muscle so weakened by an infarction was an extremely likely catalyst for congestive heart failure and pulmonary edema, and the combination of these two conditions in turn would have shared many characteristics of a severe and incapacitating case of asthma as well. Regardless, though, to anyone who has seen such a malevolent blend of symptoms in action it becomes obvious that Moore was completely miserable: if he was so short-winded he couldn't even lie down without feeling as if he were suffocating, and had to try to catch what sleep he could while sitting up, even walking through his own house must have seemed like a major chore to him. With intermittent to constant chest

---

[589] Ibid., XIV, 30, October 22, 1905.

pains added to the mix his nights had to have been a veritable hell. Too, almost the only drugs available to treat cardiopulmonary conditions at that time were digitalis and morphine, one therapeutic under certain conditions and the other a mere palliative, and in the days before pressurized oxygen tanks and breathing masks there was simply not much that Dr. Coffman or any other physician could have done except to medicate him, wait, and hope that the old patient's own strong constitution would somehow cause him to rally.

Yet even in his weakness Moore contributed two essays for the October 28 *Blade.* One was an announcement that he expected Dr. J. B. Wilson shortly to come down from Cincinnati and assist James Hughes in operating the newspaper for the course of his illness, and evidently to serve as a consultant in his medical care as well. Though Moore admitted that he and Wilson certainly hadn't agreed on everything during the course of their acquaintance, the physician was an intelligent, articulate, honest, and trustworthy man, altogether deserving of the complete confidence of the *Blade's* most discriminating readers. The second piece might well have been intended to serve as the older editor's swan song as a journalist. Poignantly titled as "An Appeal to Christians and Infidels to Work Together to Do Good," Moore had managed to complete it while sitting on his front porch on a warm and beautiful fall afternoon. He had begun to have some second thoughts about his editorial excesses of days gone by and now for the first time in decades took an apologetic tone, asking forgiveness from any individual whom his hasty words had injured, and although the piece wasn't frantic by any means it did carry with it a note and undercurrent of urgency. Moore knew his days were numbered, that his time of balancing precariously upon the narrow hyphenation between his own birth and death dates was almost at an end; he really did long to see believers and nonbelievers unite to promote moral causes for the betterment of humankind, and in such a light he hoped to leave this kind of legacy behind him, rather than one of mere bitterness and accusation. James Hughes added a grim postscript. He had spoken to his partner by telephone out at Quakeracre, and although Moore had been able to walk to his old-style wall-mounted, party line receiver and converse a few minutes he now admitted he was growing steadily weaker. Still, Hughes concluded, the old man's robust Kentucky farmer's constitution was "enabling him to make a gallant fight for life."[590]

At this time Moore was being attended by at least three, and sometimes four, family members in addition to Dr. Coffman and Quakeracre's domestic servants: his wife Lucy and son Leland at home; his sister Mary Brent, who still lived on the neighboring farm; and intermittently by his daughter Lucille, who was a music teacher in Louisville and came back to Quakeracre by rail as frequently as she could. After Dr. Wilson arrived on the scene in November he relieved Dr. Coffman and engaged the additional assistance of a trained nurse from Tennessee, a Miss Gibson.[591] Though it is not recorded that either Brent or Charles III were able to visit their father during this fall or winter (upon coming back from the Spanish-American War, Brent had matriculated and attended graduate lectures at Oxford University in England and was now engaged in similar work at Columbia University in New York, while Charles III was now in Miami, Florida, engaged in government research on the cassava plant in its natural habitat[592]), with Dr. Wilson's arrival it seemed, ironically, that Kentucky's most hated man suddenly metamorphosed into one of the Bluegrass Region's most beloved native sons. Visitors poured into Quakeracre from Lexington and all its outlying districts, mostly Christians, many belonging to the old man's former faith tradition, and not a few of them eager to seize upon the contrite tone of Moore's October 28 editorial as a topic not only of conversation but of conversion.

And so was born the rumor, apparently first given public voice at the Broadway Christian Church in Lexington about the middle of November 1905 by a Disciple evangelist named Small who didn't even know Moore personally, that the infidel editor's sickness had finally made him see the light and the error of his unbelief and flee back to the bosom of the Church. In a certain sense, such assumptions on the part of Moore's neighbors, and even Rev. Small, were almost understand-

---

[590] Ibid., XIV, 31, October 28, 1905.

[591] Ibid., XIV, 34, November 12, 1905.

[592] Ibid., XIV, 46, February 11, 1906; for Charles III's published research on cassava, see *Cassava: Its Content of Hydrocyanic Acid and Starch and Other Properties* (Washington, DC, 1907). One might wish Charles III had used just a tiny bit more of his poetic inclinations for titling his other works besides *Tamám.*

able. By this stage of Moore's illness Dr. Wilson and Miss Gibson were administering injections of morphine to the sufferer every five to six hours round the clock, so of course neither his mind nor his emotions could possibly be at their most controlled and composed. Moreover, he was known always to have been extremely tenderhearted towards anyone who showed him even the smallest kindness, and thus it is probable that Moore shed a few tears and on occasion even threw his arms round a few necks when his visitors expressed concern for his health and his comfort and asked if they could kneel down and pray for him. Moore had already issued a public request for forgiveness from any individual who felt himself or herself wronged by his words or actions; to many, it was simply a matter of course that such an open evidence of repentance could conclude only with the return of the old man's Christian faith.

Dr. Wilson thus found himself caught in a most awkward dilemma. On one hand, he knew that Moore's frequent and numerous visitors were wearing his patient down both physically and emotionally. On the other, although he could discern something of a mercenary, as well as a missionary, glint in the eyes of several of the more ostensibly pious, he knew that most of the callers really did want to do his ailing friend a kindness. If he attempted to forbid visitors to his patient he ran the risk of being cast in the role of Satan himself, shutting up the doors of mercy against those who would point an old sinner in the proper direction towards heaven, and this though the number—and enthusiasm—of the guests were pretty much ensuring that Moore would leave this life sooner than later. And so finally for the November 19 issue of the *Blade* the physician gave James Hughes a brief written notice appealing to the reason and good judgment of Moore's neighbors: people were coming out to Quakeracre every day to see Moore, and the sick man most definitely appreciated their kindness. However, Dr. Wilson suspected that at least a few of them were taking advantage of his physical and emotional weakness to try to *force* a profession of Christian faith out of him rather than letting him make his own decisions, and so he urged the Lexington and Dog Fennel communities to adopt a course of moderation. Let the old man regain his strength at least to the point where he might be able to get a night's sleep in bed rather than a rocking chair, be reasonable about paying calls, remember that Moore had been a preacher once and already knew all the proselytizing arguments they were using from the inside out, and let him request their prayers if he wanted them.

Finally, however, the bubble of hope around the possibility of Moore's repudiation of freethought pretty much burst when a local journalist helped the family put two and two together about what was going on. A reporter from one of the other Lexington newspapers telephoned Lucy Moore and asked her if the claim that Rev. Small had made at the Broadway Christian Church was true. Lucy replied that her husband wasn't feeling well enough that day to come to the phone, but she assured him that the report was completely unfounded and she asked that a correction be published immediately.[593] No, even if Moore had experienced a change of heart about some of the more acerbic portions of his writings, he had gone through no change of mind, and it was not for any unfounded concern that he had published his final statement of unbelief before this illness had seized him.

Now, though, disaster fell upon disaster, and as the Christmas season approached, Dr. Wilson had to rush home to Cincinnati to be with his only daughter, Marjorie, who was suffering from scarlet fever. Josephine Henry began to assist James Hughes in the day-to-day operations of the *Blade* during Wilson's absence, and many of the articles appearing in the paper during this time were written by her. Even so, Charles Moore himself tapped into some reservoir of his own stubborn resilience to pen a few final brief pieces, most of which, ironically, allowed him to serve one final time in a capacity usually reserved for the clergy: ten year-old Marjorie Wilson died on January 10, 1906, and it was in the meditations on the untimely deaths of beloved children written by a stubborn, confirmed old unbeliever that the distraught physician and his wife found a tiny modicum of comfort. Praising young Marjorie's spirit, her fund of knowledge, and her intellectual and artistic accomplishments, Moore compared her to his own "curly-headed little girl" Eliza, dead now this quarter of a century, and for whom he still grieved as intensely as he had on the day he had buried her in late 1879.[594] And if Moore himself could take comfort in nothing

---

[593] The entire story of Moore's dealings with his visitors, Dr. Wilson's concerned response, and the reporter's call is given in the November 19, 1905 issue of the *Blade,* XIV, 35.

[594] E.g. *Blade,* XIV, 45, February 4, 1906; the pieces in question may have

else, he knew that his own feelings of grief and loss over Eliza could not last much longer. As it was, he merely tried to give a grieving family the friendly aid of another father who had walked that same painful road.

Moore's health continued to decline through January 1906, and in his lucid moments he affirmed his wishes for his funeral arrangements: the undertaking firm of his old friend Colonel Will Milward was to prepare his body for burial, he wanted to be interred next to little Eliza in the Lexington Cemetery, and his memorial service should be held in the historic burying ground's chapel house with Moses Kaufman, Josephine Henry, and John B. Wilson delivering the eulogies. By January's end he had not been able to sleep in a bed for nearly two and a half months, and yet he somehow found physical strength enough to hang on even though his periods of hypoxic disorientation became more and more frequent. But as it happened, on the day after his final *Blade* eulogies of young Marjorie Wilson came out, it became obvious that Charles Chilton Moore's time was at hand.

Though global warming may soon render the old maxim moot, it's long been observed in rural Kentucky that, no matter how inclement a particular winter season has been, the month of February always brings with it a few beautiful and spring-like days. Another time-honored proverb is that the health of a moribund individual can often be observed to improve ever so slightly immediately before death; in the words of the ancient saw, one "gets better to die." And so did nature appear to take its course at Quakeracre on the fateful afternoon of February 5, 1906. Though he had been physically weaker than ever, Charles Moore had felt well enough on this day to sit by the window in his rocking chair and savor the mild weather and bright sunlight, and Mary Brent recalled that among his final coherent remarks to her, Lucy, Leland, and Lucille was the following: "What a beautiful day. I want to thank you all for what you have done for me. I want to thank God, if there be a God, for this beautiful day and all that he has done for me."[595] Not long afterward his head sagged; he appeared to lapse into a coma, and Lucy and the children and servants finally transferred him to

---

been written by Moore as much as two to three weeks earlier.

595 In slightly different wordings, this quote was taken down by two separate reporters and both variants were published in the *Blue Grass Blade* on February 11, 1906 (XIV, 46).

the bed in which he had never been able to gain ease since his heart had begun to falter. Though he appeared to experience fleeting moments of recognition of individual family members up until the evening of February 6, he never entirely gained consciousness again, and at two o'clock in the afternoon of February 7, 1906 Lucy noticed that he had ceased to breathe. The old infidel had passed away so peacefully that his loved ones had not even been aware of the precise moment of his death.[596]

Lucy telegraphed Charles III in Florida and Brent in New York with the sad news, and in accordance with the customs of the time and place called for Colonel Will Milward and his assistants to bring a coffin out to Quakeracre and to prepare and dress her husband's body for burial. Hundreds from all over Fayette County and the Bluegrass came to Dog Fennel to call at the home as he lay in state, and when Milward's hearse (undoubtedly not as gaudy as the ones the old editor had observed in Algiers, but perhaps fancy enough to have prompted a rough joke from him had he only been able to speak) left Quakeracre for the Lexington Cemetery chapel on the afternoon of February 9 the funeral cortege was attended by many of the leading men—and even the leading ministers—of the city. The only one of Moore's children who had not yet arrived at home was Brent, who had been forced to take a late train from New York and consequently had to meet the funeral procession at the cemetery. He caught up with his mother, brothers, and sister in front of the chapel just as the pallbearers were removing the coffin from the hearse, and James Hughes and other Lexington and Cincinnati reporters covering the solemn event all remarked that his grief was heart-wrenching to behold.[597]

---

[596] Ibid., XIV, 46, February 11, 1906. At this point perhaps we should take note, however reluctantly, of one local Fayette County anecdote about Moore's death that somehow seems to have survived the scrutiny of comparison with newspaper accounts. Collected by Louisville researcher Michael Adcock, it holds that Charles Chilton Moore lost his temper and cursed at one of Quakeracre's African American domestics and then immediately fell dead. Both Mr. Adcock and I believe that the tale was concocted out of whole cloth simply to discredit the old infidel editor's reputation.

[597] Ibid., quoting accounts from the Lexington *Herald-Leader,* the Louisville *Courier-Journal,* and the Cincinnati *Enquirer.*

The funeral, if such Moore would have wished it called, began at 2 pm. Reporters estimated that the chapel was packed with perhaps as many as two thousand attendees, and all of the orators the deceased had requested were present and in their most eloquent form. Josephine Henry spoke first, about death as an incomprehensible mystery—but yet a mystery that gave a frame of comprehension and meaning to life itself. In that brief frame, that hyphenation, of the barely knowable sandwiched between the unknowable, Charles Chilton Moore had endeavored to live his own life and to come to the assistance of his fellow creatures to the utmost of his own ability:

> How little do we know of this wondrous thing called death? It makes no noise, occupies no space; it speaks no word. One moment life is here, the next moment death has taken its place, but so gently, so quietly, that one seems only the shadow of the other. This invincible presence sanctifies whatever it touches. What can we say of this wonderful mystery of death? What it is no one knows; what lies beyond it no one can tell. All that we know is that it is nature's way of ending life. It is natural, therefore, nothing to fear. …Whatever is universal we must, somehow, regard as best….
>
> Charles C. Moore was a thinker, a student, a reasoner, a humanitarian. He loved his fellows, and for this reason he rebelled against the wrongs that are visited upon the ignorant and defenseless. He rose above the superstitions of revealed religion, which lay the sins of the whole world upon an innocent victim and sacrifice, to give a small portion of the human race eternal happiness in a city somewhere beyond the clouds, but which no telescope has ever yet discovered, and consigns millions to everlasting punishment. Our beloved friend, in his love and sympathy for humanity, rejected the monstrous doctrine of eternal punishment for the deeds done in the body; a doctrine that has blanched the cheeks of millions and filled the human heart with fear. In his strong manhood, Charles C. Moore faced life and its responsibilities with splendid courage and absolute mental integrity. He felt the mysterious power of the ego within him, and the majesty of nature in the glory of the morning and the stillness of the night… And now we must reverentially bear our loved and honored dead to its couch of unending rest. Let us not weep for him, for he lived a long and useful life. In nature's course, his time had come. The seasons were almost complete in him. He had almost taken life's seven steps. The measure of his years was full. Words are but ashes to this mourning family in this hour of their deep bereave-

> ment. Time alone can assuage their grief. Their comfort will be in the remembrance of how his love blessed their lives, how his service and sympathy comforted them, and the priceless heritage of his noble, useful life, whose deeds will blossom into new life in coming generations .[598]

John B. Wilson, himself still grief-ravaged from the loss of his beloved Marjorie, reminisced at length about his and Moore's battles, both against one another and side by side in mutual defense against common adversaries, and when all was said and done he had to praise this stubborn, iconoclastic "Daniel Boone on the frontier of Freethought" not only for his bravery and resilience but his successes in making Lexington and Bluegrass ministers consider the implications of historical and form biblical criticism and to rethink some of the more barbaric implications of the doctrines they preached. He, too, spoke of death and life after death as the ultimate mysteries, yet mysteries to be explored boldly and rationally rather than fearfully:

> If there is a future place of happiness it was made for such as C. C. Moore, and he is there. If there is a future of any kind he is there. He had no fears. His family have no fears. His friends have no fears. It will be as it will be, and that is all that honest people know. I have lately lost my little girl, my only child. Rather than that any human being, however mean and unworthy, aye, rather than that a dog should go to the Christian hell to be tortured, either mentally or physically, forever and ever, I will forego all chances and hopes of her existing ever again. Aye, I will agree myself to sink into endless oblivion. ...
>
> Let us all hope to live again, to meet again, and to be happy again. That which should most command our attention right now is the duties and obligations involving upon us and this life. Let us all strive to be better men and women. Let us, like Mr. Moore, be courageous in standing up for that which is rational and right—for truth, for justice, for liberty of thought and speech. Let us be more loving, kind, considerate, and charitable in our attitudes toward the faults of others. Misery, misfortune, sickness, sorrow, hunger, and despair are all around us. Let us try daily to mitigate as much of the distresses of life as we can. If there be another existence, where we will bring anew where we leave off here, then our reward will be in the intellec-

---

[598] *In Memoriam,* 3-5.

> tual and moral advancement we established here. This is the kind of future I pray for, and the only kind. …His fight is finished, and well has Charles Chilton Moore earned the peace that has come to him.[599]

Perhaps the most poignant of the memorial discourses, though, came from the third speaker, Moses Kaufman, especially in light of Moore's ostensibly benign but casual and unthinking anti-Semitism. Kaufman was the sole orator at the funeral whose remarks entailed anything approaching a religious cast:

> Here lies my friend of forty years. He was dear to me as a brother. I admired him for his splendid manhood. I loved him for his rugged honesty, and I respected him for doing that which he thought was right and for maintaining it and doing battle for it at the risk of life and liberty. It was [Alexander] Pope who said, "An honest man is the noblest work of God." My friends, here lies an honest man!
>
> Hillel, the great Jewish rabbi who lived just before the Christian era, being asked one day to give the summary of the [Mosaic] Law in its most concise terms, said, "What is hateful to thee, do not unto thy fellowman. This is the whole Law; the rest is mere commentary." Later, Jesus taught the love of one's neighbor to be the second great commandment beside the love of God.
>
> C. C. Moore adopted Tom Paine's motto: "The world is my country, [and] to do good is my religion." This was his decalogue, and who shall say it is not the purest, the divinest, the most exalted religion? "It is the whole Law; the rest is mere commentary." He who loves his fellowman, he who holds holy the Golden Rule, "Do unto others as you would have them do unto you," cannot lie, or steal, or kill, or bear false witness, or covet his neighbor's goods. It comprises all of the Ten Commandments in one grand-all comprehensive moral code—and Charles C. Moore worshiped at that shrine.
>
> There was more of the true faith in Charles C. Moore, following that one great precept, than in all of those who opposed him, who persecuted him, who threatened him with his life, who tore him from his beloved family to be imprisoned like Galileo and Bruno, and had he lived in Bruno's time would have brought him to the stake. Charles C. Moore was a martyr to his convictions. In all ages it has taken men like Moore, brave, unflinching, with a courage which is an inspiration and a tragedy, to come to the front and bear the brunt of the battle so that civilization may advance, that truth may prevail,

---

[599] *In Memoriam,* 6-11.

> and [that] humanity be benefited. ...He was the fearless champion of free speech and free thought, and since the days of Thomas Paine America has seen no greater. And we shall never look upon his like again [ellipse added].[600]

Friends and loved ones passed by the coffin for a final gaze upon the pale, lifeless form; the pallbearers carried the casket to a beautiful tree-lined avenue a short distance behind the chapel, where the oldest Moore daughter Eliza had lain since November 1879; and there, in the midst of the desolate places left to the kings and counselors of the Bluegrass in the historic cemetery, Charles Chilton Moore was buried under the epitaph "Remember me as one who loved his fellow man." We have noted already that his daughter-in-law Helen, the wife of Charles III, was the next family member to be interred in the Moore plot, in April; following in succession were Lucille in 1918, Brent in 1924, the mother Lucy in 1928, and finally Charles III in 1940, he having been cremated in San Francisco and his ashes shipped back to Lexington for burial.[601] Leland Moore seems to have disappeared from the public eye, and any further knowledge of him or any other family he might have had appears not to have been retained in the Lexington community. For her part, Mary Brent became the last person ever to be buried in the old Forest Retreat plantation cemetery on her property, near her parents and beside her husband, in 1915.[602]

---

[600] Ibid., 13.

[601] Lexington Cemetery, Lexington, Ky.; burial records, 1851-2007.

[602] Bevins, "Monuments Falling in Cemetery...," *Lexington Herald-Leader,* 7/5/64, 18. Bethany College collection.

From the Lexington *Morning Herald*, February 8, 1906

DEATH CLAIMS NOTED INFIDEL

Charles Chilton Moore, the noted infidel author and editor of the Blue Grass Blade, died yesterday afternoon at 3 o'clock, at his country home, Quakeracre, which is near this city, aged seventy-eight years. [illegible] disease was the cause of death, which was not unexpected, as Mr. Moore had been practically unconscious for twenty-four hours before the end came. The end was peaceful and without a struggle. Mr. Moore [illegible] [illegible] remarked that he was a very unusual man and a good one, but a politician rather than a preacher. During the war I was an abolitionist and a union man and I did a great deal of good work for both sides.

"Shortly after the close of the war I made up my mind to walk to Palestine, starting on my walk [illegible] [illegible]

From the Lexington *Morning Herald*, February 10, 1906

LOVING TRIBUTES OVER THE GRAVE

Charles C. Moore Lowered to Final Resting Place Without Rites of Clergy

ADDRESSES MADE BY THOSE WHO BELIEVE IN THE PRINCIPLES WHICH WERE ADVOCATED BY FAMOUS INFIDEL EDITOR AND WRITER.

All that is mortal of Charles Chilton Moore, Kentucky's most noted free-thought writer and editor, was laid to rest yesterday afternoon in the Lexington cemetery. The funeral services, consisting of orations over the body, were held at the cemetery chapel and the grave. Mrs. Josephine K. Henry, of Versailles; Dr. J. B. Wilson, of Cincinnati, and Moses Kaufman, of this city, delivered the orations. The last tribute paid to Mr. Moore was an occasion at which hundreds of his friends and admirers assembled. The chapel was too small to accommodate the number of persons who had assembled, and although there were no songs, no prayers—nothing but addresses—many of the crowd disregarded the severity of the weather and remained on the outside of the chapel until the services were completed.

Brent Moore, of New York, son of the deceased, was delayed in reaching Lexington until after the funeral cortege had left "Quakeracre" for the cemetery. The meeting between Mrs. Moore and her son was touching and noted sympathetically by all who saw the mother and the son stand weeping beside the casket containing the husband and father.

Dr. Wilson was also delayed in reaching Lexington, not being in time to be present when the cortege left "Quakeracre" for the cemetery. The services began at 2 o'clock and were concluded at 4 o'clock. Mr. Kaufman, who sat with Mrs. Henry and Dr. Wilson near the bier, which was covered with floral designs, arose at 2 o'clock and announced the order of the services. Mrs. Henry then made her oration, which is as follows:

Mrs. Henry's Address.

[illegible] religion, which lay the sins of the whole world upon an innocent victim and sacrifice, to give a small portion of the human race eternal happiness in a city somewhere beyond the clouds, but which no telescope has ever yet discovered, and consigns millions to everlasting punishment. Our beloved friend, in his love and sympathy for humanity, rejected the monstrous doctrine of eternal punishment for the deeds done in the body; a doctrine that has blanched the cheeks of millions and filled the human heart with fear. In his strong manhood, Charles C. Moore faced life and its responsibilities with splendid courage and absolute mental integrity. He felt the mysterious power of the ego within him and the majesty of nature in the glory of the morning and the stillness of the night. The universe, broad, deep and high, was to him a handful of dust that nature enchants with the mysterious magic which possesses the world. Universal mental liberty was his hope, to do good and promote happiness was his religion. Justice was his motto and truth his aim. He believed in the brotherhood of man and the equal rights of woman. He believed in, and practiced, that morality that makes good citizens, pure and good wives and husbands and affectionate children. He exemplified in his life the sentiment of Pope's immortal lines:

"'Teach me to feel another's woes
To hide the fault I see,
That mercy I to others show,
That mercy show to me.'

"He warmed himself by the fireside of human affection. He did not keep the alabaster boxes of love and kindness sealed until his friends were dead, but he broke them and scattered the fragrant perfume of affection and sympathy in the path of the living.

"Pure and undefiled religion consists in the endeavor to fill human lives with brightness, in speaking kind words to the living while their ears can hear them and their hearts can be encouraged by them.

"Now that death has claimed our beloved friend, Charles C. Moore, his character is rounded out in all its grandeur and majesty. It is given to few human beings to be a positive and elevating force in shaping the destiny of the human race. Charles C. Moore belongs to this small class of immortals and the influence of his stern convictions, deeds and words will appear and reappear in the lives, thoughts, legislation and destiny of future generations. This man with his giant intellect, lofty ideals, peerless courage and mental and moral integrity, rose like a superman among his fellows. He can be compared to a great mental and moral leviathan on the tempestuous ocean of life, flying from its mast-head the flags of reason and justice, while surrounding it were millions of struggling, frail barks on the sea of mystery with no guide but the jack o lanterns swung by priestly hands who have no knowledge whatever of life's mysteries and the destiny of humanity. The clergy do not know, we do not know, we are all but mystified mariners on life's unsounded sea.

"No man had been more persecuted or made to suffer more for his honest convictions. Pursued and hunted in every earth, let his family, his neighbors and friends extend their charity in word and deed in memory of Charles C. Moore, whose religion was love for humanity. All this is better than storied urn or marble shaft.

"And now we must reverentially bear our loved and honored dead to his couch of unending rest. Let us not weep for him, but rather for the living. He lived a long and useful life. In nature's course, his time had come. The seasons were almost complete in him. He had almost taken life's seven steps. The measure of his years was full. Words are but ashes to his mourning family in this hour of their deep bereavement. Time alone can assuage their grief. Their comfort will be in the remembrance of how his love blessed their lives, how his service and sympathy comforted them, and the priceless heritage of his noble, useful life, whose deeds will blossom into new life in coming generations.

"Farewell, deather brother! Sleep on! We would not call you back into life's conflict. Your name will be placed high in the Pantheon of fame. Because through sacrifice and suffering you heralded the spirit of the on-coming civilization. May the present age catch the echoes of thy wisdom and philosophy.

"'And if record of genius like thine,
Or eloquence fiery and deep,
Shall remain to the centuries regnant
From centuries lulled into sleep;
Then thy memory as music shall float,
Amid actions and aims yet to be,
And thine influence cling to life's good,
As the sea vapors cling to the seas.'

"And now into the bosom of nature, our universal mother, we consign our departed friend and brother. He is forever past the trials of life and free from sorrow and pain. Rest, dear friend, under the blue canopy of the sky, in the moonlight, starlight and sunlight, in summer's golden dawn and autumn's chilling frost. Sleep, sweet sleep. Rest, eternal rest. A last, long and forever, farewell."

Dr. Wilson followed Mrs. Henry with his address. He is the President of the American Free Thought Society and has labored for years with Mr Moore in an effort to sow the seeds of free thought. He will become the editor of the Blue Grass Blade.

Dr. Wilson opened his remarks by pointing out the eccentricities of Mr. Moore, and then he spoke of his virtues. He dwelt on the fact that no one could question the honesty of the deceased. He spoke of him as being one of Kentucky's greatest men. He said that the two men of Kentucky who stood out prominently as her greatest sons were Cassius M. Clay and Charles Chilton Moore. "They," he said, "had done something, and in advocating the principles they believed had done so in communities where the sentiment was hostile to the principles they had advocated."

At the conclusion of Dr. Wilson's address the body was moved to the

The *Blue Grass Blade* lasted until the summer of 1910, apparently failing finally due to lack of financial support, the increasing identification by Americans of freethought with Socialism and Anarchism, and the still-enduring popularity of similar but better-known national periodicals such as the *Truth Seeker*. Shortly after its founder died, James Hughes converted the newspaper to magazine format, lengthened it, dropped its original editor's emphasis on Prohibition, and even briefly pondered changing its name to the *Age of Reason* in honor of Thomas Paine's famous work. Still, sadly, it became glaringly obvious that the fiery, almost mirror-image Alexander Campbell-esque writing style of the *Blade's* creator had been the basis of much of its popularity both within and without Kentucky, and in the mighty shadow of Moore's legacy young James Hughes simply could not make the periodical thrive, even with the help of John B. Wilson, John R. Charlesworth, and Josephine Henry all.

Not that Hughes didn't make a noble effort, though, to address controversies in his best imitation of his editorial mentor. Among his lead articles in the week following Moore's funeral was an account of the open anger and indignation expressed at the memorial service by various members of the Lexington ministerial community over the facts that while Moore's 1905 confession of unfaith, as it were, had been read at the service with the approval of Lucy Moore and her children,[603] nothing had been mentioned of Moore's final words as Mary Brent had recalled them, and that Josephine Henry had dared to suggest to the congregation—mostly *their* own Sunday listeners!—that they did not and could not know what followed them beyond death. Mrs. Henry made a poised and lengthy response,[604] and although she elected not to engage in any of the bellicose sophistry her old journalist friend had loved so much, she very well could have quoted one Bible verse, from the ninth chapter of Ecclesiastes, that even her detractors would have had to admit that Charles Chilton Moore had followed to the letter and beyond: *Whatsoever thy hand findeth to do, do it with thy might; for there is no work, nor device, nor knowledge, nor wisdom, in the grave, whither thou goest.*[605]

---

[603] *In Memoriam,* 11-12.
[604] *Blade,* XIV, 46 & 47, February 18 & 25, 1906.
[605] Ecclesiastes 9:10.

Our story of the life of Charles Chilton Moore and his *Blue Grass Blade* is now at its end, so in conclusion, what in fact *should* we say about that one controversial dying utterance apparently heard so distinctly by Mary Brent but never commented upon by any other of Moore's family members or friends? Was Mrs. Brent, who herself had never left the Disciples of Christ, simply engaged in wishful thinking for the benefit of a beloved brother who had always been there for her and who had tried to fill Thomas Brent's shoes as a father figure to her daughters? If Moore did make such a statement, should we dismiss it, in light of his 1905 declaration of unfaith, as merely the confused and disoriented musings of an aged, senile brain deprived of the oxygen required to nourish it, and wearied past the point of all reason by constant sickness and pain? Or, as a third and final possibility, did Charles Chilton Moore in fact "get better to die" mentally as well as physically? Was he in a rational frame of mind when he made his expressions of gratitude both to his family members and to "God, if there be a God," and could he have truly meant what he said?

As with the question of *Tamám's* advocacy of some form of prayer, we can never hope to know the absolute truth, and so the question must remain unsolved and insoluble. Yet when it comes down to brass tacks the human race has *always* loved mysteries, even—and perhaps most especially—when they involve notorious, controversial personalities. It is almost certain that the reading public in and around Moore's hometown latched onto the remark as some sign of hope for him, or perhaps more of a hope for themselves and their own religious beliefs, and in and of itself the quoted statement could have been all that was necessary to establish the longstanding misconception that the old man, rather than his son, had penned the novel *Tamám.* In whatever frame of mind Moore had been on his last afternoon of consciousness, though, I think that we can be fairly certain that he tried his best to face that fateful day exactly as he had always hoped to: like his father's old War of 1812 adversary Tecumseh, he simply wished to sing his death song and then pass from life like a hero going home. Even if he wasn't at his sharpest mentally, whatever expressions of thanks he made were heartfelt and honest—not based on some last-minute disoriented and craven fear of possibly losing the fallacy-ridden wager of belief proposed in the seventeenth century by Blaise Pascal.

Earlier in this work we made a comparison of Lexington's response to the *Blue Grass Blade's* very first editorial topic, Moore's blasting of the Sam Jones evangelistic crusade, to the negative reactions generated worldwide by Christopher Hitchens with his criticisms of Mother Teresa and her Missionaries of Charity—and strangely enough, a little of the subsequent controversy surrounding the venerated nun might serve as an apt comparison and contrast of how Charles Chilton Moore may have viewed both life and death as he stood ready to pass from one to the other. Not until roughly a decade after Mother Teresa died was it revealed by Father Brian Kolodiejchuk, a priest of her same religious order and her Postulator of the Cause of Beatification and Canonization (her official sponsor for sainthood, as it were) that for a great deal of her life as a nun in Calcutta she languished spiritually in a cold, silent, horrifying "dark night of the soul" that caused her more than once to express terrified doubt about the existence of God to her confessors and superiors. Prior to being given permission by the Catholic Church to found the Missionaries of Charity in India, Mother Teresa had experienced "interior locutions" and visions so dramatic and flamboyant as to match those of Joan of Arc, Anne Catherine Emmerich, Mother Ann Lee, A. J. Tomlinson, and Joseph Smith: Christ himself speaking to her, sometimes in auditory messages and others in full-blown visible glory and hanging from the cross in her awed presence, bidding her to go to India to her duty and inspiring her to "love Him as He had never been loved" and to wish "to drink only from His chalice of pain." On one occasion she even wrote—whatever she might have meant by it—that "Jesus gave Himself to me."[606] Yet no sooner than Teresa had settled in Calcutta it seems that the messages and visions dried up completely, and she could no longer sense any presence of God whatsoever either within the private witness of her conscience or in the Holy Eucharist at Mass. At least one could not accuse her of mincing words in her letters to her confessor:

> They say people in hell suffer eternal pain because of the loss of God—they would go through all that suffering if they just had a little hope of possessing God.—In my soul I feel just that terrible pain of loss—of God not wanting me—of God not being God—of God not really existing (Jesus, please forgive my blasphemies—I have been

[606] Kolodiejchuk, ed., 13-103.

> told to write everything). That darkness that surrounds me on all sides—I can't lift my soul to God—no light or inspiration enters my soul.—I speak of love for souls—of tender love for God—words pass through my words (lips)—and I long with a deep longing to believe in them.—What do I labor for? If there be no God—there can be no soul.—If there is no soul then Jesus—You also are not true.—Heaven, what emptiness—not a single thought of Heaven enters my mind—for there is no hope.—I am afraid to write all those terrible things that pass in my soul.—They must hurt You.[607]

In the end, between the patient if not unbiased advice and instruction of her confessors and superiors, plus her own dogged determination to maintain her Catholic faith and her Catholic traditions in the face of all conceivable temptations, inclinations, and evidences to the contrary, Mother Teresa finally felt she understood the tumult occurring daily within her mind and conscience. As Father Kolodiejchuk phrased it, her "darkness" was nothing more and nothing less than an overwhelming empathy and identification with those she served. She was drawn mystically into the deep pain of Calcutta's poor, the unwanted, the rejected and, above all, those living without any true faith in God as she would have interpreted such. Thus, paradoxically, it had to be that the more remote she felt *from* God and the *less* that she could sense a Divine presence within her life and soul, the *closer* she actually was to Jesus and the chalice of his pain for which she had once thirsted so greedily.[608] Of course, such a discovery on either her part or that of her superiors could not, and cannot, be quantified objectively. According to Mark's Gospel, Jesus once said that "If thou canst believe, all things are possible to him that believeth,"[609] and, if nowhere else, the precept is certainly true within the boundless elasticity of the human mind. At the very least it can be said that Mother Teresa's rationalizations ultimately gave her the strength and impetus to continue her work in Calcutta under the auspices of the Catholic Church, and there can be no doubt that she carried out her duties to the best of what she saw as her ability.

---

[607] Ibid., 192-193.
[608] Ibid., 215-216.
[609] Mark 9:23.

Which brings us back to the questions raised so saucily and provocatively by Christopher Hitchens in *The Missionary Position.* Had Mother Teresa allowed her mind to wander away from its Church-, tradition-, and fear-circumscribed limits, might she have worried a little less about her personal problems with faith and put some of the fortune in donations that she collected over the years from such world luminaries as Jean-Claude and Michele Duvalier, John-Roger, and Charles Keating, to bolder use in biomedical research or other worthy causes to help her Calcutta poor? Would she have opposed artificial birth control as tenaciously as she did, not only in India but before the occasions of crucial elections in the Republic of Ireland and on her visits to the United States as well? And might she have treated her dying Hindu and Muslim patients with perhaps a little more understanding, a modicum of concern for their lives rather than for their deaths, and a little less zeal for her nuns to baptize them discreetly while pretending merely to wash and cool their faces and foreheads with water?

Although her organization lives on, Mother Teresa is gone, so again, we will never know the answers. All that is left to us is an odd and ironic juxtaposition of the beloved nun's memoirs, Father Kolodiejchuk's commentaries, and Christopher Hitchens' skeptical condemnations in the story she once told of an indigent at her Calcutta hospice, in the final agonies of inoperable cancer and writhing on his cot in indescribable pain. For some reason Mother Teresa never advocated administering large doses of palliatives to the dying patients under her care and so, doubtless drawing upon the philosophical paradox by which she had reassured herself of the existence and benevolence of the Christian God, the nun informed the moribund man that since he was suffering like Christ on the cross, it must mean that Jesus was kissing him at that very moment. With an indulgent smile she recounted to a television interviewer the patient's sharp reply: "Then please tell him to stop kissing me!"[610] Within the details of the anecdote one can almost hear the surly voice of Paul Newman's character Lucas Jackson to the prison camp warden in the movie *Cool Hand Luke,* "I wish you'd stop bein' so *good* to me, Captain," and the official's sanctimonious reply—after having knocked Luke down for making the statement. After all, even

---

[610] Hitchens, 41-42.

Mother Teresa herself would have been compelled to acknowledge that what they had here was failure to communicate.

We have noted that the young and impressionable Disciple missionary Charles Chilton Moore very probably had a nervous breakdown, or something close to it, back in 1863 right after he finished reading Bishop Colenso's *Pentateuch and Book of Joshua Critically Examined,* but ultimately he could not have responded more differently to his own personal crisis of faith. Despite his hesitations and misgivings, even to the point of attempting to get himself impressed into service by General John Hunt Morgan so he could run away from his faith and family problems altogether, he eventually turned around and faced his demon fearlessly and squarely and finally came to view it as a mere figment of his own imagination. There were no new and colorful visions and revelations in his faith tradition, only God speaking through Scripture in the logical system of Scottish Common Sense Realism that Alexander Campbell thought he had uncovered therein; and so when Moore could see, and know, that supposedly Holy and Divine Writ was full of contradictions and inconsistencies and therefore in terms of that same Scottish Common Sense logic, outright errors, he wasn't willing to lie to himself or anyone else to pretend otherwise. If he had never had to watch and listen to his brother preachers of all Protestant denominations express hatred towards each other over the political stances of their respective congregations back during the dark days of the Civil War, things might have turned out differently for him; but his life was as it was, and with the shattering of his illusions of Scriptural inerrancy and infallibility also perished any further use he might have entertained for religious faith. The concept of an anthropomorphic God became nothing to him, an idea as dark and desolate as Mother Teresa had ever entertained in her most disconsolate musings, and yet, bereft of all he had cherished spiritually except the power of his own reason, he found—to borrow one more final bit of classic cinematic imagery from writer Donn Pearce and actor Paul Newman—that this "nothing" could be, and was, "one real cool hand."

And so with this stark hand of cards dealt to him he lived his life joyfully, married the woman he loved, reared his children and mourned the little curly-headed girl that preceded him to the grave, worked to put bread on his family's table and clothing upon their backs, gave of the fruits of his farm, field, and publishing office to those he saw in need, and always said exactly what he wanted to utter in behalf of the moral causes he espoused every time he published a brand-new issue of the *Blue Grass Blade*. Whether right or wrong, at times overly enthusiastic in either case, his convictions were nonetheless entirely his own and through the course of his life he stood up firmly for every one no matter how unpopular any of them made him. Thus he became not only an outspoken freethinker but Kentucky's own State infidel, as it were, engendering controversy in his death even as he had in life and leaving in his wake a mixture of contempt and admiration from those he left behind.

Our comparisons and contrasts of Charles Chilton Moore to others who were subjected to influences similar to those that shaped him could go on and on. Richard Marius, the talented, tortured writer, historian, and ex-Baptist minister from Tennessee, whose fiction and nonfiction alike reads like funeral dirges to be sung by heartbroken mourners around God's grave, might be a good candidate for such a study—or on the other side of the coin, Kurt Vonnegut, fourth generation of a German-American freethinking family who was, in his own words, a Christ-worshiping agnostic. Robert Funk, himself a child of the Stone-Campbell Movement and who left his preaching ministry to devote his life to researching the historical Jesus, might make a good comparison case as well. A half-decent theological brief might even be made from the tale of that cocky young fool I once knew who was powerfully and dramatically converted to Christianity in his sixteenth year, powerfully and dramatically "called to preach" a little less than two years afterward, got to reading and experienced an equally powerful and dramatic yet unconfessed gut feeling that Gottfried Wilhelm Liebniz's *The Best of All Possible Worlds* made complete nonsense out of any rational notion of a benevolent God, and then spent twenty-odd years preaching, working in hospitals watching people live and die, and writing religious history, all in the hope that he could one day reconcile the dichotomy between a fundamentalist view of Christianity and plain logic. Yet as the old Preacher once said, of making many books there is no end, and much study is a weariness of the flesh;[611] and so perhaps the important thing to remember about Charles Chilton Moore was that, in the end, as he felt his consciousness and his life slipping away from

[611] Ecclesiastes 12:12.

him on February 5, 1906, he had nothing to say about either angels coming down from the sky to plait a feather crown within his pillow or the black cats of hell crawling up and down his walls. I think he was simply aware that he was enjoying one last beautiful late winter afternoon, pregnant with the promise of the coming spring in the endless cycle of the earth's seasons of hot and cold, winter and summer, seed time and harvest, life and death—and he could look upon those he loved, and back over the life he had lived, and be grateful for all the blessings he had ever experienced. Could it have been even remotely possible, then, that even as the old man felt his faltering heart ebbing and fluttering to its inevitable standstill he found himself ready to express honest and passionate thanks not only to his family but to a tiny, brief, fleeting glimpse of some super-transcendent yet immanent God-beyond-God, One Whom he had unknowingly served all his life simply by his honest search for knowledge and truth and his promotion of the Golden Rule and the public good, One Who didn't mind being either questioned or cursed and Who now invited him to one of two equally appealing options: a sweet, dreamless, eternal sleep, or entry into a reality altogether beyond earthly life and the comprehension of humankind with its tawdry, bloody, anthropomorphic imaginings and projections that make a mockery of all that which is truly Divine?

"We cry aloud," observed Robert Green Ingersoll on the occasion of the burial of a beloved brother, and all we can hear in answer "is the echo of our wailing cry." And yet, even to the mourning Ingersoll "in the night of death hope sees a star and listening love can hear the rustle of a wing."[612] Balancing ourselves as best we can upon the narrowness and brevity of our own Breckinridge-Pollard hyphenations—between knowledge and ignorance, faith and doubt, love and loss, hope and despair, life and death—we ponder the great, terrible, wonderful mystery.

---

[612] A Tribute to Ebon C. Ingersoll, http://www.infidels.org/library/historical/robert_ingersoll/tribute-e_c_ingersoll.html

BIBLIOGRAPHY

Allen, Ethan. *Reason: the Only Oracle of Man.* Reprint, Boston: J. P. Mendum, 1854.

Allen, James Lane. *The Choir Invisible.* New York: MacMillan, 1897.

————. *The Reign of Law.* New York: MacMillan, 1900.

The American Heritage Dictionary of the English Language. Fourth Edition. Boston: Houghton-Mifflin, 2000.

Ault, James M., Jr. *Spirit and Flesh: Life in a Fundamentalist Baptist Church.* New York: Knopf, 2004.

Baker, Catherine. *The Evolution Dialogues.* James B. Miller, ed. Washington, D. C.: American Association for the Advancement of Science, 2006.

Barnes, George Owen. "A Lost People and a Vanished Sceptre." Intro. by Charles A. Jennings. Originally published October 1906; World Wide Web, http://www.truthinhistory.org. Accessed June 27, 2007.

Baum, Henry Mason. "Philosophy and the Knowledge of God." *The American Quarterly Church Review,* XIII, I, 1860.

Berger, Peter L. *Questions of Faith: a Skeptical Affirmation of Christianity.* Malden, Mass.: Blackwell, 2004.

Berry, Mattie L. *A Sketch of the Christian Church of Versailles, Kentucky.* Versailles, Ky.: privately published, 1930.

Besant, Annie. *The Law of Population, Its Consequences, and Its Bearing Upon Human Conduct and Morals.* Originally published 1877; reprint, Whitefish, Montana: Kessinger Publishing, 2005.

Beverly, James A. "Thinking Straighter: Why the World's Most Famous Atheist Now Believes in God." *Christianity Today,* April 2005. World Wide Web, http://www.christianitytoday.com/ct/2005/april/29.80.html; accessed February 5, 2008.

Bevins, Anne. "Monuments Falling in Cemetery That Was Inspiration for *Tamám.*" *Lexington Herald-Leader,* July 5, 1964, 18. Bethany College collection.

The Blue Grass Blade, 1886-1910 (microfilm, partial collection with several issues missing). Young Library, University of Kentucky,

Lexington, Kentucky. Copies, Kentucky Department of Libraries and Archives, Frankfort, Kentucky, and Lexington Theological Seminary, Lexington, Kentucky.

The Blue Grass Blade, II, 33, February 13, 1892. Original copy. Kentucky Department of Libraries and Archives, Frankfort, Kentucky.

Bojaxhiu, Gonxha Agnes (Mother Teresa). *Come Be My Light: the Private Writings of The Saint of Calcutta.* Fr. Brian Kolodiejchuk, ed. New York: Doubleday, 2007.

Boles, John B. *The Great Revival: Beginnings of the Bible Belt.* Lexington, Ky.: University Press of Kentucky, 1972.

Bolin, James Duane. *Bossism and Reform in a Southern City: Lexington, Kentucky, 1880-1940.* Lexington, Ky.: University Press of Kentucky, 2000.

Breckinridge, Helen Congleton. *Cabell's Dale: The Story of a Family.* Frankfort, KY.: Privately published, 1983. Kentucky Historical Society.

————. *Descendants of John and Mary Cabell Breckinridge.* Frankfort. Ky.: Privately published, 1980. Kentucky Historical Society.

Broadhurst, Dale. *Joseph Smith's History Vault: Robert B. Neal Newspapers, Kentucky, Early 1900s.* World Wide Web, http://olivercowdery.com/smithhome/1900s/1895Neal.htm; Accessed November 16-17. 2007.

————. *Readings in Early Mormon History.* World Wide Web, http://www.sidneyrigdon.com/dbroadhu/OH/miscoh06.htm; Accessed November 16-17, 2007.

Brodie, Fawn M. *No Man Knows My History: the Life of Joseph Smith.* New York: Knopf, 1945; reprint, New York: Vintage Books, 1995.

Brown, John T. *Churches of Christ in the United States, Australasia, England, and Canada.* Louisville, Ky.: John P. Morton & Co., 1904.

Butler, Joseph. *Works: Containing the Analogy of Religion, and Sixteen Celebrated Sermons.* London: William Tegg, 1867. Reprint, Boston: Adamant Media, 2000.

Campbell, Alexander. "Obituary of A. W. Doniphan Jr." *The Millennial Harbinger,* Series V, I, 6, June 1858. Bethany College

Archives.

————. "Tribute of Respect to A. W. Doniphan Jr." *The Millennial Harbinger,* Series V, I, 9, November 1858. Bethany College Archives.

Carrier, Richard. "Antony Flew Considers God…Sort Of." The Secular Web, http://www.secweb.org/index.aspx?action=viewAsset&id=369; accessed February 5, 2008.

Chatterjee, Aroup. *Mother Teresa: the Final Verdict.* Calcutta: Meteor Books, 2002.

Chilton, Bruce, and Jacob Neusner, eds. *The Brother of Jesus: James the Just and His Mission.* Louisville, Ky.: Westminster John Knox, 2001.

Clay County, Kentucky, Federal Census, 1860. Timothy Spence, compiler. http://www.rootsweb.com~kyclay2-census-1860-index.pdf.url . World Wide Web, accessed June 13, 2007.

Cobb, Jeanne, Archivist and Research Librarian at Bethany College, Bethany, W. Va., Letters to the author dated June 11, 2006, May 24, 2007, and May 30, 2007.

Colenso, John William, Rev. *The Pentateuch and Book of Joshua Critically Examined.* Originally published London, 1862; reprint, New York: D. Appleton & Co., 1863.

Commonwealth of Kentucky vs. C. C. Moore, cases 3612 & 3613, 1892, Bourbon County, Kentucky, Circuit Court records; Kentucky Department of Libraries and Archives.

Commonwealth of Kentucky vs. C. C. Moore, case 154, 1894, Fayette County, Kentucky, Circuit Court Records; Kentucky Department of Libraries and Archives.

Compiler not listed, "Eastern State Hospital, Lexington, Kentucky: Deaths Reported in Newspapers, 1826-1890." World Wide Web. http://www.rootsweb.com/~kyfayett/esh_newspapers.htm. Accessed June 12, 2007.

Dallas Morning News, January 4, 1909. Courtesy Charlie G. Hughes, Wind Publications, Nicholasville, Ky.

The Dial: A Semi-Monthly Journal of Literary Criticism, Discussion, and Information. XLVII, 553, July 1, 1909. Chicago: Dial Company, 1909.

Dawkins, Richard. *The Blind Watchmaker.* New York: Norton, 1986.

———. *The God Delusion.* New York: Houghton Mifflin, 2006.

Dew, Aloma. "Women in Reform: Josephine Henry." World Wide Web, http://www.womeninkentucky.com/site/reform/j_henry.html, http://www.womeninkentucky.com/site/reform/j_henry_prop_act.html, and http://www.womeninkentucky.com/site/reform/J_Henry_prop_act2.html. Accessed July 17, 2007.

Donaldson, Everett. *The Legacy of Raccoon John Smith.* Mt. Sterling, Ky.: North Ridge Publishing, 1995.

Eisenman, Robert. *James the Brother of Jesus.* New York: Viking Penguin, 1997.

Ernst, Morris L. and Alan U. Schwartz. *Censorship: The Search for the Obscene.* New York: MacMillan, 1964.

Fortune, Alonzo Willard. *The Disciples in Kentucky.* Lexington, Ky.: Convention of the Christian Churches in Kentucky, 1932.

Fort Worth Star-Telegram, February 18, 1906; courtesy of Charlie G. Hughes, Wind Publications, Nicholasville, Ky.

Friedman, Richard Elliott. *Who Wrote the Bible?* New York: Harper-SanFrancisco, 1987; reprint 1997.

Fuller, Robert. *Naming the Antichrist: The History of an American Obsession.* New York: Oxford University Press, 1995.

Gall, Joe. "Death of a Legend: Book Closing Another Chapter in Ohio History." From *Motive,* November-December 1971. World Wide Web, http://www.drc.state.oh.us/web/historyop.htm. Accessed January 2, 2008.

Gardener, Martin. *The Whys of a Philosophical Scrivener.* New York: St. Martin's Griffin, 1983.

Garrett, Leroy. *The Stone-Campbell Movement.* Joplin, Mo.: College Press, 1983; reprint, 1995.

Garry, Patrick. *An American Paradox: Censorship in a Nation of Free Speech.* Westport, Conn.: Praeger, 1993.

Gerhart, E. B. "Mansel's Limits of Religious Thought," *The Mercersburg Review,* XII, I, 1860.

Goldman, Emma. "Obituary of Ross Winn, 1871-1912." First published in *The Anarchist,* September 27, 1912; World Wide Web, http://libcom.org/library/obituary-for-ross-winn-1871-1912-emma-goldman. Accessed January 24, 2008.

Gooch, B. J., Special Collections Librarian and University Archivist, Transylvania University, Lexington, Ky., Letter to the author dated July 13, 2006.

Goodnight, Cloyd, and Dwight E. Stevenson, *Home to Bethphage: A Biography of Robert Richardson.* St. Louis, Mo.: Christian Board of Education, 1949.

Graham, Billy. *Just As I Am.* San Francisco: HarperSanFrancisco, 1997.

Harp, Scott. "Charles Chilton Moore, 1837-1906."

http://www.therestorationmovement.com/cc_moore.htm. World Wide Web, accessed July 11, 2006.

Haught, John F. "Amateur Atheists: Why the New Atheism Isn't Serious." *The Christian Century,* 125, 4, February 26, 2008.

Hawkins, Anthony. *Of Savage Fury: the Battle of Richmond, Kentucky.* Prestonsburg, Ky.: Reformation Publishers, 2004.

Heck, Frank H. *John C. Breckinridge: Proud Kentuckian.* Lexington, Ky.: University Press of Kentucky, 1976.

Henry, Josephine. *Marriage and Divorce.* Lexington, Ky.: James E. Hughes, 1905.

————. "Married Women's Property Rights under Kentucky Laws: An Appeal for Justice." Kentucky Equal Rights Association, 1889.

————. *Musings in Life's Evening.* Lexington, Ky.: James Byrnes, n.d.

Hill, Sam E. *Report of the Adjutant General of the State of Kentucky: Soldiers of the War of 1812.* Frankfort, Ky.: E. Polk Johnson, 1891.

Hitchens, Christopher. *The Missionary Position: Mother Teresa in Theory and in Practice.* New York: Verso, 1995.

Hofstadter, Richard. *The American Political Tradition and the Men Who Made It.* New York: Knopf, 1948.

Holloway, Clinton. "Archives Receives Campbell Communion Chalice." *The Envoy,* V, 4, November 1999, Emmanuel School of Religion, Johnson City, Tenn.

The Holy Bible, Authorized King James and Revised Standard Versions.

Huber, Leslie Nash. *The History of Old Union Christian Church.* Lexington, Ky.: Privately published, 1998.

Hughes, James E., ed., *In Memoriam: Dedicated to the Memory of the Late Charles Chilton Moore, Founder of the Blue Grass Blade.* Lexington, Ky.: Editor, 1906.

Hughes, Richard T. *Reviving the Ancient Faith: The Story of Churches of Christ in America.* Grand Rapids, Mich.: Eerdmans, 1996.

Ingersoll, Robert Green. Collected Writings, 1867-1899. Emmitt F. Fields, compiler. World Wide Web: http://www.infidels.org/library/historical/robert_ingersoll/ Accessed July 2006-December 2007.

InterOcean, January 4, 1895. Courtesy Charlie G. Hughes, Wind Publications, Nicholasville, Ky.

Jackson, John Glover. "The Black Atheists of the Harlem Renaissance." Presented at the American Atheists' Convention, 1984. World Wide Web, accessed July 13, 2006. http://www.africawithin.com/jgjackson/black_atheists.htm .

Jacoby, Susan. *Freethinkers: A History of American Secularism.* New York: Henry Holt, 2004.

Jennings, Charles A. "Life & Ministry of John Alexander Dowie." World Wide Web, http://www.truthinhistory.org. Accessed June 27, 2007.

Jones, Kathleen. "Domino." World Wide Web, http://www.thoroughbredchampions.com/biographies/domino.htm Accessed October 26, 2006.

The Kentucky Encyclopedia. John E. Kleber, chief ed.; Thomas D. Clark, Lowell H. Harrison, James C. Klotter, eds. Lexington, Ky.: University Press of Kentucky, 1992.

Kenneally, Christine. *The First Word.* New York: Viking Press, 2007.

Kerr, Mary. *Family Tree.* http://worldconnect.rootsweb.com, accessed June 22, 2007.

Klotter, James C. *The Breckinridges of Kentucky.* Lexington, Ky.: University Press of Kentucky, 1986.

———. *Kentucky Justice, Southern Honor, and American Manhood: Understanding the Life and Death of Richard Reid.* Baton Rouge: LSU Press, 2003.

Letters of Certain Jews to Monsieur Voltaire, Containing an Apology for Their Own People and for the Old Testament. Rev. Philip Le-Fanu, trans. Paris/Covington, Ky.: G. C. Moore and J. L. Newby, 1845. Special Collections, Kentucky Historical Society.

Lexington Cemetery, Lexington, Ky.; burial records, 1851-2007.

Lexington, Ky. Morning Herald, miscellaneous articles between January 12, 1897 and February 10, 1906; courtesy of Charlie G. Hughes, Wind Publications, Nicholasville, Ky.

Lore, David. "The Ohio Penitentiary: Inside the Pen." *Columbus Dispatch,* October 28, 1984. World Wide Web, http://www.mrps.org/ohiopen2.htm; accessed January 1, 2008.

McDougall, Ian. "William Paley's Wonderful Watch." World Wide Web, http://www.butterfliesandwheels.com/articleprint.php?num=232. Accessed March 13, 2007.

Mackie, John Leslie. *The Miracle of Theism: Arguments For and Against the Existence of God.* Oxford, UK: Clarendon Press, 1982.

Mansel, Henry Longueville. *The Limits of Religious Knowledge Examined, in Eight Lectures Delivered Before the University of Oxford in the Year 1858.* Originally published 1858; reprint, Boston: Gould and Lincoln, 1860.

Mead, Andy. "Atheists Laud Founder of 'Heathen' Paper." *Lexington (Ky.) Herald- Leader,* April 23, 1984.

————. "Strong Feelings Accompany Opening of Atheists' Convention." *Lexington (Ky.) Herald-Leader,* April 21, 1984.

Merton, Thomas. *The Seven Storey Mountain.* New York: Harcourt, Brace, and World, 1948.

Miller, James B. "God's Nature and Nature's God: From Natural Theology to Theological Naturalism." From *Sci-Tech: Journal of the Presbyterian Association On Science, Technology, and the Christian Faith,* 15, 1, February 2006.

Minnix, Kathleen. *Laughter in the Amen Corner: the Life of Evangelist Sam Jones.* Athens, Ga.: University of Georgia Press, 1993.

Moore, Charles Chilton. *Behind the Bars: 31498.* Originally published Lexington, Ky., 1899; reprint Austin Tex.: American Atheist Press, 1984.

————. *Dog Fennel in the Orient.* Originally published Lexington,

Ky., 1903; reprint Austin, Tex.: American Atheist Press, 1984.

————. "Night of December 10, 1857." *The Neotrophian Magazine,* III, 5, April 1861. Bethany College Collection.

————. *The Rational View.* Louisville, Ky.: Courier-Journal, 1890; Reprint, Austin, Tex.: American Atheist Press, 1984.

————. letters to Richard Prewitt dated February 15, 1857 and January 28 and February 26, 1858; Bethany College Collection.

————. (pseud. "Chalybs") articles and letters to the editor in *The Wheeling* (Va.; now W. Va.) I*ntelligencer,* dated December 6, 10. 11, 12, 18, 21, and 22, 1857; Bethany College Collection.

Moore III, Charles Chilton. *Cassava: Its Content of Hydrocyanic Acid and Starch and Other Properties.* Washington, D.C.: Government Printing Office, 1907.

————. *Tamám.* New York: Neale Publishing, 1908.

Moore Family Papers, Special Collections & Digital Programs, University of Kentucky Libraries; Margaret I. King Library.

Moore, Charles C., Vertical File, Special Collections, Transylvania University, Lexington, Ky.

Murray, William J. *My Life Without God.* Nashville: Thomas Nelson, 1982.

Nelson, Larry L. "Dudley's Defeat and the Relief of Fort Meigs during the War of 1812." *The Register of the Kentucky Historical Society,* Winter 2006, Vol. 104, No. 1, 5-42.

Noll, Mark A. *The Civil War as a Theological Crisis.* Chapel Hill, N. C.: University of North Carolina Press, 2006.

Oakes, Stephen, and Leslie Nash Huber, *Old Union Christian Church Cemetery.*Lexington, Ky.: Privately published, 1998.

Old Union Christian Church Record Book, 1823-1892. Bosworth Library Special Collections, Lexington Theological Seminary, Lexington, Ky.

Oppenheimer, Mark T. "The Turning of an Atheist." *The New York Times Magazine,* November 4, 2007. World Wide Web, http://www.nytimes.com/2007/11/04/magazine/04Flew-t.html. Accessed February 5, 2008.

The Oxford Dictionary of Current English, 4th ed. Julia Elliott, Sara Hawker, and Catherine Soanes, eds. New York: Oxford University Press, 2006.

Paine, Thomas. *Writings,* IV: *The Age of Reason.* Moncure D. Conway, ed. This edition published 1896; reprint (ebook), Oxford, Miss.: Project Gutenberg Literary Archive Foundation, 2004.

Paley, William. *Evidences of Christianity.* Originally published 1794. Reprint, Teddington, UK: Echo Library, 2007.

————. *Natural Theology.* Originally published 1802. Reprint, New York: Oxford University Press, 2006.

Paley's Natural Theology, Revised to Harmonize with Modern Science. F. LeGros Clark, ed. London: Society for Promoting Christian Knowledge, 1890. Reprint, Boston: Adamant Media, 2001.

Payne, Buckner Harrison (pseud. "Ariel"). *The Negro: What Is His Ethnological Status?* Cincinnati: self-published, 1867. Disciples of Christ Historical Society.

Polkinghorne, John C. *Science and Theology: An Introduction.* Minneapolis, Mn.: Augsburg Fortress Press, 1998.

Pollard, Madeline Valeria. *The Celebrated Trial: Madeline Pollard vs. Breckinridge, the Most Noted Breach of Promise Suit in the History of Court Records.* New York: American Printing, 1894. Kentucky Historical Society.

Price, W. T. *Without Scrip or Purse; or, the Mountain Evangelist, George O. Barnes.* Louisville, Ky.: Author, 1883.

Reid, Elizabeth Jameson. *Judge Richard Reid: A Biography.* Cincinnati, O.: Standard Publishing, 1886.

Richardson, H. Edward. *Cassius Marcellus Clay: Firebrand of Freedom.* Lexington, Ky.: University Press of Kentucky, 1976.

Richardson, Robert. *Memoirs of Alexander Campbell.* 2 vols. Philadelphia: Lippincott, 1870.

Russell, Bertrand. *Why I Am Not a Christian; and Other Essays on Religion and Related Subjects.* New York: Simon and Schuster, 1957.

Saint John's Episcopal Church, Versailles, Kentucky. Records of Communicants, Baptisms, Marriages, and deaths, 1865-1893. Woodford County Historical Society, Versailles, Kentucky.

Saltman, Bethany. "The Temple of Reason: Sam Harris on How Religion Puts the World at Risk," *The Sun,* 369, September 2006.

Seaman, Ann Rowe. *America's Most Hated Woman: The Life and Gruesome Death of Madalyn Murray O'Hair.* New York: Continuum Press, 2005.

Smiley, David L. *Lion of White Hall: the Life of Cassius M. Clay.* Madison, WI: University of Wisconsin Press, 1962.

Smith, Charles Alphonso. *O. Henry Biography.* New York: Doubleday, 1916.

Sparks, John. *Raccoon John Smith: Frontier Kentucky's Most Famous Preacher.* Lexington, Ky.: University Press of Kentucky, 2005.

————. *The Roots of Appalachian Christianity: The Life and Legacy of Elder Shubal Stearns.* Lexington, Ky.: University Press of Kentucky, 2001.

Spong, John Shelby. *Jesus for the Non-Religious.* New York: HarperSanFrancisco, 2006.

————. *Liberating the Gospels: Reading the Bible With Jewish Eyes.* New York: HarperSanFrancisco, 1996.

————. *The Sins of Scripture.* New York: HarperSanFrancisco, 2005.

Stanton, Elizabeth Cady, et al., *The Woman's Bible.* Originally published New York: European Publishing, 1895; reprint Seattle, Wash.: Coalition on Women and Religion, 1974.

Stone, Barton Warren. *Autobiography.* Originally published 1847; reprint in *Voices From Cane Ridge,* Rhodes Thompson, ed., 31-134. St. Louis: Bethany Press, 1954. http://www.mun.ca/rels/restmov/texts/bstone/barton.html World Wide Web, accessed August 3, 2006.

Thompson, Elmer Ira. *Madam Belle Brezing.* Lexington, Ky.: Buggy Whip Press, 1983.

Treadway, Bob, J. D. Letters to the author, August 29 & 30, 2007.

United States versus C. C. Moore, case # 5349, October 6, 1895-February 28, 1900. United States District Court, Western Kentucky District. National Archives Southeastern Branch, Atlanta, Ga.

United States versus Charles C. Moore, case # 1993, February 1899. United States District Court, Southern Ohio District. National

Archives, Great Lakes Area Branch, Chicago, Ill.

United States versus C. C. Moore, case # 6523, February 22, 1900-October 2, 1900. United States District Court, Western Kentucky District. National Archives Southeastern Branch, Atlanta, Ga.

Van Biema, David. "Her Agony." *Time,* 170, 10, September 3, 2007.

Various authors, *Saint John's Episcopal Church, Versailles, Kentucky: 1847-1997, One Hundred and Fifty Years of Faithful Witness and Ministry in the Name of our Lord and Savior Jesus Christ.* Versailles, Ky.: Privately published, 1997.

Ward, William Smith. *A Literary History of Kentucky.* Knoxville, Tenn.: University of Tennessee Press, 1988.

Williams, D. Newell. *Barton Stone: A Spiritual Biography.* St. Louis: Chalice Press, 2000.

Winn, Ross. *Winn's Firebrand,* II, 1, January 1903.

Wolever, Terry. *The Life and Ministry of John Gano.* Springfield, Mo.: Particular Baptist Press, 1998.

Wrather, Eva Jean. *Alexander Campbell, Adventurer in Freedom: A Literary Biography.* D. Duane Cummins, ed. Vols. I & II. Fort Worth, Tex.: Texas Christian University Press, 2005 (I) & 2007 (II).

Young, Perry Deane. *God's Bullies: Power Politics and Religious Tyranny.* New York: Holt, Rinehart, and Winston, 1982.

Zion City, Illinois, City Records 1888-1974. Newberry Library, Chicago, Illinois.

INDEX

A

B

C

D

E

F

G

H

I

J

K

L

M

N

O

P

R

S

T

U

LaVergne, TN USA
02 June 2010
184481LV00005B/6/P